DESCRIPTION

CHRIST'S VENTRILOQUISTS is a work of investigative history. It documents and describes Christianity's creation-event, in the year 49 or 50, in Antioch (present-day Antakya, Turkey), 20 years after Jesus had been crucified in Jerusalem for sedition against Roman rule. On this occasion, Paul broke away from the Jewish sect that Jesus had begun, and he took with him the majority of this sect's members; he convinced these people that Jesus had been a god, and that the way to win eternal salvation in heaven is to worship him as such. Paul here explicitly introduced, for the first time anywhere, the duality of the previously unitary Jewish God, a duality consisting of the Father and the Son; and he implicitly introduced also the third element of the Trinity, the Holy Ghost.

This work also explains and documents the tortuous 14-year-long conflict Paul had had with this sect's leader, Jesus's brother James, a conflict that caused Paul, in about the year 50, to perpetrate his *coup d'état* against James, and to start his own new religion: Christianity.

Then, this historical probe documents that the four canonical Gospel accounts of the words and actions of "Jesus" were written decades after Jesus, by followers of Paul, not by followers of Jesus; and that these writings placed into the mouth of "Jesus" the agenda of Paul. Paul thus effectively became, via his followers, Christ's *ventriloquist*.

A work such as this can be documented and produced only now, after the development (during the past 70 years) of modern legal/forensic methodology. Previously, the only available methods, which scholars have used, simply *assumed* the honesty-of-intent of all classical documents, especially of canonical religious ones, such as Paul's epistles, and the Four Gospels. Only now is it finally possible to penetrate deeper than that, to reach the writer's intent, and not merely his assertions, and to identify when this intent is to deceive instead of to inform. Whereas scholars have been able to discuss only the *truth or falsity* of particular canonical statements, it is now possible to discuss also the *honesty or deceptiveness* of individual statements. This opens up an unprecedented new research tool for historians, and *CHRIST'S VENTRILOQUISTS* is the first work to use these new methods to reconstruct, on this legal/forensic basis, not just how *crimes* took place, but how and why *major historical events* (criminal or not), such as the start of Christianity, actually occurred.

The author explains: "What I am doing in this work is to reconstruct from the New Testament the crucial events that produced it, without assuming whether what the NT says in any given passage is necessarily true or even honest. Instead of treating the NT as a work that 'reports history,' the NT is treated as a work whose history is itself being investigated and reported. Its origin goes back to this *coup d'état* that Paul perpetrated in Antioch in the year 49 or 50 against Jesus's brother James in Jerusalem, whom Jesus in Jerusalem had appointed in the year 30 as his successor to lead the Jewish sect that Jesus had started. The Gospel accounts of 'Jesus' reflected Paul's *coup d'état* – not actually Jesus, who would be appalled at the Christian concept of 'Christ.' That concept was radically different from the Jewish concept of the messiah, and Paul knew this when he created it."

CHRIST'S VENTRILOQUISTS

The Event that Created Christianity

Eric Zuesse

Winner of the Mencken Award for investigative reporting,
and author of *IRAQ WAR: The Truth*, and of
WHY THE HOLOCAUST HAPPENED

Hyacinth Editions, NYC

Hyacinth Editions, New York, N.Y.

hyacintheditions@mail.com

ISBN-13: 978-0615573014
ISBN-10: 0615573010

*"News is what other people want to keep hidden.
All the rest is publicity."*

Bill Moyers (interview), *KD Viations*, Winter 2006

We cannot control the future,
unless we know the truth about the past.
History must be cleansed of myths,
in order to *control* the future.
There's no other way,
but catastrophe.
The choice
is ours,
now

.

NOTE ON STYLE

Whereas the norm is to italicize the titles of books, except for the titles of the books in the Bible, the titles of all books are italicized here. For example, *Mark* is italicized. This is done not only in order to be consistent, but in order to avoid confusing the reader between a book and the author of that book. The author of the book of *Mark* is referred to here as Mark (no italics), regardless of what that person's name actually was; no assumption is being made here that a person by the name of Mark wrote *Mark*.

Ampersands (&) are sometimes used here to abbreviate strings of references within the same chapter of a biblical book. For example, *Galatians* 1:1&11&12&15&16 is referring to 1:1, 1:11, 1:12, 1:15, and 1:16, in *Galatians*.

Footnotes are used here in order to amplify upon a point in the discussion, not to cite sources – which are identified within the discussion itself.

The References/Sources section at the end provides further information regarding the documentation conventions used here.

CONTENTS

The Evidence, Part Two: Christianity in Light of *Galatians*

Conclusion: How Scientists Think About History: 335

• • • • • • • •

BOXED ITEMS:

Why Read This: The Topic's Importance

This book is about our ethico/moral assumptions that are so widely shared they're not even questioned – but that nonetheless might be false. These assumptions are what make Western Civilization Western Civilization. To investigate them is not to prefer other civilizations, but is only to understand our own. And in order to understand Western Civilization, one must accurately know the event that caused it, that shaped it.

Western Civilization – the *shared* civilization of all Christian-majority countries – started when the religion that defines it did. The moral base in each of these nations is Christianity; and, though different Western nations may vary in their respective interpretations of Christianity's Scripture, that Scripture – the New Testament – is the *source* of the moral bases in *all* of these many countries. It's what we all share. So, understanding what created the New Testament, is understanding the real source of our common moral base. We cannot comprehend the civilization in which we live, unless we know how the New Testament came about – the event that caused it – because the New Testament is the moral foundation for Western Civilization itself.

Some people erroneously think that Christianity is
Jesus, not the New Testament. However, in reality, they know
Jesus *via* the New Testament, which is the only part of the
Bible that quotes him. Some *non*-biblical documents also
contain quotations attributed to Jesus, but those alleged Jesus-
statements are *not* part of Christianity, and therefore
explaining what caused them is of no concern. Even if a
person we think of as Jesus existed and uttered those
statements, our world hasn't been shaped by them, and so
there will be no inquiry here into what caused the writing of
those "words of Jesus."

"The words of Jesus" that are in the Bible were not
written by Jesus, but the Roman Catholic Church canonized
them as representing what he said. The present book
investigates to determine who actually wrote them, and why.
The "why" turns out to be every bit as important as the "who"
here, because this investigation finds that the people who
wrote those words were followers of Paul, not followers of
Jesus as they claimed. Of course, Paul himself claimed to be a
follower of Jesus; but this investigation finds also that, in the
later part of his career, when Paul wrote the letters by which
he subsequently became known to history, he had, in fact,
broken away from Jesus's followers, and was competing
against those people, no longer working for or with them.
Paul's followers were actually enemies of Jesus's followers,
and wrote the Gospels. They never met Jesus, and he would
have been shocked and appalled at many of the quotations
they attributed to him. These preachments being made in his
name would have outraged him.

That's a thumbnail sketch of my findings in this
investigation which had started as a search to discover the
event that created Christianity – the ultimate *beginning* of all
this history. Originally, the purpose of this book was, indeed,
to find and describe this singular event; but, in order to do
that, it was necessary at the very start to re-define this goal
concretely or operationally, as discovering the precise
sequence of circumstances that had caused the New

Testament to be written as it is. My process here was thus inevitably one of working backwards in time from the New Testament documents to their ultimate cause, which couldn't be *merely* an individual (either Jesus or anyone else) but which would instead necessarily have to be that individual (*whomever* it was) acting *within the context of the precise circumstances that had motivated him to do* this momentous act, an act which has since turned out to be the most important one in all of human history: namely, the creation of Christianity. Finding the event, that created the Christian faith, was, indeed, my aim at this investigation's start, and it remained my objective after the question was thus concretely defined. This question drove me because I'm an investigative historian, and because I thought that scientifically reconstructing, from the available evidence, the event that created Christianity, was the most important objective an investigative historian can possibly pursue. This is why I undertook to find: What happened at this event – *who did it, when, where, how, and why?*

For an investigative historian, this challenge is like Mount Everest. George Mallory, when asked why he tried to climb the world's highest peak, said famously, "Because it's there." The only way to do such a thing is step by step, and many people think that reaching a peak like this is impossible. So, I invite you to take this trip now along with me, step by step, to experience for yourself the scaling of *history's* peak.

This book will answer all of these questions (who, when, where, how, and why) in such detail, you'll become like a fly on the wall, present at the occasion when Western Civilization itself started. This event wasn't like anyone today would imagine. It will surprise everyone. New scientific methodology has made its discovery possible – at last, after 2,000 years, excavating from ancient documents the actual circumstances that caused these documents to be created as they are; so that, for the first time ever, they scientifically make sense. However, what these documents scientifically tell us, isn't what they *seem* to tell. The truth behind them is a lot

more interesting than the myth in front of them. And the path
to this truth doesn't pass through an assumption that that
myth is true. Nor through an assumption that it's false. This
path passes through no such assumptions, whatsoever. Where
other paths assume, this path instead *investigates*.

According to *Matthew* 16:18, Jesus said to Peter, "You,
Peter, are the rock upon which I will build my church."
However, scholars widely question the authenticity of this
alleged quotation;[1] and many scholars (even some who don't
question its authenticity) question the *meaning* of this
statement, since the Greek term, "ekklesia," which was used
there for "church," signified, in that time, *any* sort of an
assembly, even a political one; and a Jewish assembly (or – as
it was then called – "sunagoge" or else "synagoge") was also a
type of "ekklesia." Did Jesus start a Jewish sect – a synagogue,
or assembly of Jews? Christianity isn't that. Moreover, a few
chapters earlier in *Matthew*, 10:5-6 quotes Jesus as telling his
disciples, "Don't go to the Gentiles, ... but only to the lost
sheep of Israel," and then again in 15:24, Jesus is quoted as
saying, about himself, "I was sent [by God] to only the lost
sheep of Israel." Thus, this "ekklesia" – relating to those verses
at least – would have constituted Jesus's *synagogue*, unless

---

[1]   For an extensive overview on the matter, see Brittany C. Burnette, 2005,
"Additional Considerations on the Exegesis of Matt 16:18," at bible.org, which
opens by saying of the entire passage 16:17-19, that "many scholars deem the
verses to be questionable." Even this fine overview, however, leaves unmentioned
numerous commentaries that challenge 16:18, such as Jürgen Moltmann's 1993
The Church in the Power of the Spirit, which (p. 142) questions whether Jesus
founded a church at all, and Hans Küng's 1967 *The Church*, which (p. 73)
dismisses 16:18: "The saying at Matthew 16:18, of which authenticity and
interpretation have been much debated – and which in any case was not a public
utterance. ..." Perhaps Küng meant there: Would Jesus likely have been so casual
about starting Christianity? Would he not have produced a written record of the
event, if *he*, in fact, did it? Would he not have made such a momentous
announcement at a public forum in which Peter was consecrated? Of course, if
someone *else* founded Christianity, that would be entirely different: such a person
wouldn't *want* the public to know who did it, or when, or how, or where, or why.
Such an event would then have been private – but it *wouldn't* have been 16:18.

God subsequently changed his mind and his instructions to Jesus, to start a new religion. Furthermore, if the intent in 16:18 was to start a religion, the word for that would have been "threskeia," not "ekklesia." But this "Jesus" didn't start any "threskeia"; he didn't start a *religion*. Therefore, 16:18, even if it was authentic (which is in doubt), fails to answer the key question: *Who* started *Christianity* – and when, where, how, and why?

The only other Scriptural candidate for Jesus's having authorized Christianity is *Matthew* 28:18-20, in which the resurrected Jesus is quoted as reversing the command of the living Jesus (in 10:5-6), by commanding his disciples, "Go throughout the world to make all peoples my disciples by baptizing them in the name of [the Trinity] the Father, the Son, and the Holy Ghost." However, this command directly contradicts *Matthew* 5:17-20, which quotes Jesus as saying "Do not think I have come to do away with the Law of Moses, ... for it will be eternally binding." The first three of the "eternally binding" Ten Commandments (*Exodus* 20:3-7, and *Deuteronomy* 5:7-11), given from God to Moses and all of God's people, ban permanently any such thing as the Trinity, and demand worshipping *only* the Father, never to include any second object.[2] Even more emphatically, the Third of these

---

[2]   The original Hebrew of the First Commandment is translated literally as "Other ones of power and authority will not exist for you before my face." Jews always understood this as meaning "You shall not have other gods in my presence," or, more simply yet, as "Worship no god but me." More colloquially, Jews see the original as meaning "I will not tolerate your having other gods than me." However, some Christian bibles translate this Jewish commandment as "Worship no god *before* me" (as opposed to "Worship no God *but* me"). The focus there is on the "before my face" two-Hebrew-word phrase that closes the statement, rather than on the rest of the statement, its first five Hebrew words, the clear statement that those two closing words modified. The difference between the views is that Jews do not see the two-word "before my face" clause at the end as *narrowing and weakening* the commandment's meaning. Christians are inclined to narrow and weaken its meaning, because otherwise the Trinity (and thus Christianity itself) is outright banned by the First Commandment.

As to the question of which view is authentic to the intent of the Commandment's author: the law was allegedly received by Moses, coming from an Egyptian society in which the worship of Egyptian gods was obligatory. Tacking on these last two words enabled Jews to survive within a society that demanded the acceptance of other gods. The Second Commandment then adds "I tolerate no rivals." Jews thus could accept Egyptian gods, but only as *subordinate* gods to Judaism's God. This still gave Jews a chance. Yet, this phrase "before my face" was actually meaningless to them, because in *Genesis* and the rest of their Scriptures, their all-powerful creator God saw everywhere, and so it had no "face," and no unseeing side at all. It was portrayed as omniscient.

Furthermore, *Deuteronomy* 6:4 could hardly be clearer when it quotes God as saying (literally translated here): "Hear, Israel, the Lord is our God; the Lord is one alone." The plural "our" refers here to God and His people, not to the solitary God of Judaism. A freer translation of this would be: "Worship only me." Moreover, Moses is quoted in *Deuteronomy* 10:20 as saying "Worship only Him. ... Make promises only in His Name."

By contrast, the Christian interpretation of those final two Hebrew words in the First Commandment, having them mean "before me" instead of "but me," automatically assumed Judaism to be a polytheistic religion which ranks deities, rather than a monotheistic religion. The concept of the Trinity starts and derives from this *underlying* assumption about Judaism – a basic assumption that the vast majority of Jews reject.

Some Jews, however, accepted the concept of "before me" instead of "but me." Judaism's vestigial polytheism was even reflected in *Genesis* 1:26-27, which quotes God as saying, "Let us create man in our image." This confusing use of the plural "us" form is then followed there by the unequivocal use of the singular "his": "And God created man in his own image." Early Christians, and some Jews, interpreted the "us" form in 1:26 as referring to God and his angels, but later Christian theologians interpreted 1:26 as instead meaning that, because man was created in God's image, God wouldn't prohibit worshipping a man, in addition to worshipping God. This view was never accepted by Jews, who reject the idea that any "we" had *created* man, or that worshipping a man is ever acceptable. Jews see the plural form in 1:26 as being like a President signing a piece of legislation and saying "We now make this a law." Thus, the idea that creation was produced by the Father, the Son, and the Holy Ghost, is rejected by Jews, as being no truer than the idea that creation was produced by God and his angels. The Jewish God is solitary. Furthermore, *Deuteronomy* 10:17-20 opens with Moses saying "Your God The Lord is the God of gods," and closes with "Worship only Him," which means that worshipping any other god is prohibited. Even more emphatically, *Deuteronomy* 17:2-5 quotes God as demanding that if any Israelite is caught "worshipping other gods," his neighbors must "stone that person to death." Clearly, other gods than the Creator-God are not to be worshipped.

Christian theologians, however, built upon this vestigial polytheism, by alleging God to be actually three persons in one – as if the Father, the Son, and the Holy Ghost, could never contradict each other (such as the allegedly resurrected "Jesus" *did* contradict the "Father's" First Commandment, in *Matthew* 28:18-20). This assumption that the living Jesus, the resurrected Jesus, and the Father, could never contradict each other (much less contradict himself) is the foundation-stone upon which all of Christian theology rests. [continued]

Ten Commandments says "Do not take the name of God in vain." Thus, the alleged resurrectional baptismal command of 28:18-20 (in the *name* of the Trinity) would have been clearly in violation of those "eternally binding" commandments from God. In addition, *Matthew* quotes Jesus in 19:16-19 as saying "Obey the commandments if you want to win eternal life," and as specifically citing some of the Ten Commandments as examples of what one must do in order to go to heaven. Furthermore, the early Christian church didn't consider 28:18-20 to be itself binding, and as late as the 16th Century that statement was widely understood as having been directed only at Jesus's disciples in his own time, not at future generations, and the obligation was thought to have been fulfilled by them. In any case, this statement doesn't assert that a person who fails to comply with it will be viewed less favorably by God, or denied salvation. Moreover, only relatively recently did this alleged statement come to be called "The Great Commission," and considered as the start of Christianity. That change of belief occurred at the time critical scholarship on the Bible first emerged, The Enlightenment. It's not how Christianity had seen itself during the religion's first 1,600 years. On top of all this, the oldest of the four Gospels, *Mark*, had no equivalent passage. It ended at *Mark* 16:8. Later (after the two most ancient manuscripts of *Mark*, both of which date from the Fourth Century and both of which ended at 16:8), some anonymous person added the current ending (16:9-20), which copies and expands *Matthew* 28:18-20. Thus, "The Great Commission" was apparently concocted long after *Mark* was written. What's the likelihood the earliest-written

---

In order to achieve that unified multiplicity of God, Christian theologians, with scant support from the New Testament that they claim to revere, created the concept of "the Godhead," *replacing* the Trinity that's put forth in *Matthew* 28:18-20 and in Paul (who, as this book will show, created the Trinity, for reasons that this book will explain). Unlike the Trinity, the Godhead is a "Father," "Son," and "Holy Spirit" who are one-and-the-same: mere synonyms for each other. As this book will show (from Paul's letters), the "Father," "Son," and "Holy Spirit," are separate, *not* the same; theologians violate their Scripture.

Gospel would have omitted this statement (which *Matthew* alleged to be Jesus's *last*) if it was *authentic* – if Jesus had actually said this? Would Mark have *ignored* such a statement? And, in addition: This earliest-written of all the four canonical Gospel accounts of "Jesus," *Mark*, at its passage 12:29-30, quotes "Jesus" as saying outright, "The most important commandment of all is that the Lord God is one and must be loved with your entire being," which statement paraphrases the First Commandment, virtually identically to the way Moses did in *Deuteronomy* 10:12, and thus this "Jesus" prohibits belief in the Trinity; so, the reason why *Mark* included *no* "Great Commission" (until some anonymous person added it centuries later) is obvious: everyone in the time when *Mark* was written knew that Jesus would never have said such a thing.

Finally regarding *Matthew* 28:18-20, Moses is quoted in *Deuteronomy* 10:20 as saying that God told him to tell everyone, "Worship only Him. ... Make promises only in His Name." Contrast that with the statement alleged from Jesus at the end of *Matthew*, 28:19-20, "Go then to all peoples everywhere, and baptize them in the name of the Father, the Son, and the Holy Spirit, and teach them to obey all my commands." This supposed "Son" isn't merely telling his followers to violate the Father's command "Worship only Him," but to violate the Father's command "Make promises only in His Name." This "Jesus" is moreover telling his followers to obey the "commands" of the Son, even though those "commands" violate the first three of the Ten Commandments from the Father. And yet this "Son" *also* supposedly said (as was earlier noted) in *Matthew* 5:17-20, "Do not think I have come to do away with the Law of Moses, ... for it will be eternally binding." So, *yet again*, the author of the first-written Gospel, *Mark*, had good reason for *not* alleging that Jesus claimed to have overridden any of God's commandments: unlike the authors of *Matthew*, *Luke*, and *John*, the author of *Mark* wasn't writing late enough to be able to get away with so blatant a fabrication.

Thus, no evidence whatsoever exists that Jesus started Christianity.

If Jesus *didn't* create Christianity, if a different person created it, then would Jesus have approved of what that individual was doing? Might Christianity even have been created by an *enemy* of Jesus? But why would an enemy of Jesus have produced a myth that "Jesus" was a god, who should be worshipped? Wouldn't any enemy of Jesus be, to the exact contrary, extremely *dis*inclined to do such a thing?

All that's clear here, at the outset, is that the event that created Christianity – whoever did it, whatever it was, and wherever it occurred – was the most important event in all of human history, because the world 2,000 years later has been so profoundly affected by it. If Christianity had not been created, then the world today would be so different that it would be unrecognizable.

Try, if you can, to visualize the world without Christianity: you'll quickly realize that it would be a very different place, EVEN in Muslim lands.

Islam, after all, is based upon the Quran, and the Quran accepts both the Old Testament and the New. (See, for examples, Quran verses 2:31, 2:85, 2:136-7, 3:03, 4:47, 4:136-7, 10:37, 10:94, 21:7, 29:46, 35:31, and 41:9-12.) The New Testament is itself the DISTINCTIVE PRODUCT of Christianity's founding event, and so Islam would be very different if this event had not taken place.

Jews, too, have been immensely affected by it: for more than 1,500 years, they've been surrounded by Christian culture, and their lives have been largely shaped by it.

Thus, on a global basis, not just in the Christian realm, this event has emerged as our culture's very kernel, an essential reality, for virtually all of humanity.

In other words, by creating the world's largest religion, this event has shaped the lives of practically everyone today, all the way down to our cultural roots, so that humanity could be said to be virtually sleepwalking through our days and years with this occurrence constantly in the invisible

background, unheralded and unrecognized, not even
discussed, but still always present, guiding us unknowingly in
what we do and have done, throughout our entire wakeful,
conscious, lives.

Furthermore, for Christians, this event doesn't concern
just a person's ritual behaviors, such as going to mass, or
crossing one's heart. Even though we're ignorant of this
event's existence, every Christian's ethical-moral viewpoint is
ROOTED, ultimately, in this single historical occasion, which
was the conception of Christianity.

As will be made clear in the later part of this book, this
event also transformed, throughout the Christian-majority
areas of the world, the relationships between law and
morality, and between Church and State, and thus profoundly
shaped the *political* world that we live in today. Politics is the
very opposite of the ritual sphere; and yet, politics, just as
much as religious ritual *per se*, has been transformed by this
single event.

Though many people assume that if an event is
historically important, the event must be known to the public,
this assumption is sometimes false, because things that occur
in secret, or that are known to only a restricted number of
people, can occasionally have an enormous impact –
sometimes even bigger than the impact of any famous event.
The present book documents and describes one such private
event, which occurred 2,000 years ago, and which has never
even been publicly recognized until now: the event that
created Christianity.

Since the news of this event will be coming only now,
two millennia after the fact, this news might shock believing
Christians (people who believe the Bible). These readers'
concerns should be specifically addressed here, and now will
be. (Readers who don't find the following of interest might
prefer to skip ahead here, straight to the Introduction.)

A well-established central finding of psychological
research, concerning "confirmation bias" or "motivated
reasoning" (which are two phrases referring to people's

tendency to believe whatever they want to believe, *regardless* of any contrary facts), is that individuals evaluate whatever they read according to their *pre-existing* ideas about the given subject. Specifically, psychologists have found that people tend to pay attention to whatever *confirms* their existing ideas, and tend to ignore whatever *contradicts* those pre-established beliefs.[3] This tendency most people have (though the research studies make clear also that some *rare* individuals do not possess this unfortunate tendency), to reinforce their beliefs, even in the face of contrary evidence – even in the face of contrary evidence that *disproves* those beliefs – has been found to be *especially* strong if a person is conservative in his/her beliefs (such as the studies show that most people are who

---

[3]   For examples, the following studies are available online:

"Motivated Skepticism in the Evaluation of Political Beliefs," in the July 2006 *American Journal of Political Science*, reported: "We find a confirmation bias – the seeking out of confirmatory evidence – when [people] are free to self-select the source of arguments they read. Both the confirmation and disconfirmation biases lead to attitude polarization ... especially among those with the strongest priors [prior beliefs] and highest level of political sophistication [the highest degree of exposure to, and involvement in, the given subject-matter that the study was dealing with]." Prejudices were stronger among supposed experts than among non-"experts": The more indoctrinated a person was, the more prejudiced. "People actively denigrate the information with which they disagree, while accepting compatible information almost at face value." Moreover, "Those with weak and uninformed attitudes show less bias" (and this is actually one reason why the best jurors at trials are generally people who are not personally or professionally involved in any aspect of the given case – they are "*non*-experts").

Sharon Begley's article in the 25 August 2009 *Newsweek* titled "Lies of Mass Destruction: The same skewed thinking that supports a Saddam-9/11 link explains the power of health-care myths [such as that Obama's health plan had 'death panels']" summarized the study in the May 2009 *Sociological Inquiry*, "'There Must Be a Reason': Osama, Saddam, and Inferred Justification," which had surveyed, during October 2004, 49 conservative Republicans who admitted they believed that Saddam Hussein had caused the 9/11 attacks. This study found that 48 of these 49 extreme conservatives were utterly impervious to the overwhelming factual evidence which was provided to them by the presenters that contradicted this false belief they held. [continued]

think Jesus started Christianity).[4]

That research explains why most people interpret the Bible (or any other writing) in whatever way they want. A typical example of this phenomenon is the issue of rich and poor, in the Bible. Some people (usually conservatives) interpret the Bible as indicating that the rich are especially blessed by God, while others (usually liberals) interpret it as indicating that the poor are especially blessed by God. The Bible actually supports and contradicts *both* views, as the

---

A study concerning not political conservatism but merely resistance to new technologies is James N. Druckman's "Framing, Motivated Reasoning, and Opinions about Emergent Technologies," which was presented at a technological conference in 2009. He reported that, "factual information ... is perceived in biased ways ... (e.g., there is motivated reasoning)." "Facts have limited impact on initial opinions." Moreover, "Individuals do not privilege the facts. ... Individuals process new factual information in a biased manner. ... Specifically, they view information consistent with their prior opinions as relatively stronger, and they view neutral facts as consistent with their existing" views.

"Motivated Reasoning With Stereotypes," in the January 1999 *Psychological Inquiry*, found that, "When an applicable stereotype supports their desired impression of an individual, motivation can lead people to activate this stereotype, if they have not already activated it. ... People pick and choose among the many stereotypes applicable to an individual, activating those that support their desired impression of this individual and inhibiting those that interfere with it." Similarly, another research report, "The Undeserving Rich: 'Moral Values' and the White Working Class," in the June 2009 *Sociological Forum*, found that John Kerry had probably lost the 2004 U.S. Presidential election to George W. Bush at least partly because white working class voters overwhelmingly believed that Bush was like themselves because he behaved like themselves, and that Kerry was not like themselves because his manner seemed "snooty."

[4]   For examples online: "On Perceived Conflicts Between Religion and Science: The Role of Fundamentalism and Right-Wing Authoritarianism," in the April 2000 *Psychological Reports*, found that fundamentalism and right-wing authoritarianism were essentially the same group; this group was hostile toward science, and even hostile to technology. Also: "Political Conservatism as Motivated Social Cognition," in the May 2003 *Psychological Bulletin*, found that prejudices were even stronger among conservatives than among the general population.

following shows:

On the side of the rich, are these biblical passages:

In *Matthew* 10:24, "Jesus" says: "A student is never superior to the teacher, just as a slave is never superior to the slave-master. It is sufficient for the student to aspire to become a teacher, and for the slave to aspire to become a slave-master." This "Jesus" accepts slavery, and also accepts the rights of slave-masters.[5]

In *Matthew* 13:12, "Jesus" directly instructs his disciples, that, in the Kingdom of Heaven, "The person who has something will be given still more, until he possesses more than enough; but the person who has nothing will find even that taken away from him."

In *Matthew* 25:29-30, "Jesus" tells a parable of the Kingdom of Heaven, a realm where: "To every person who has something, even more will be given, until he possesses more than enough; but the person who has nothing will find even that taken away from him. And unproductive slaves will be thrown outside into the darkness, where there is want and weeping."

---

[5]   This isn't unusual. As Jefferson Davis, President of the Confederacy, said before the U.S. Civil War over slavery, in his 18 August 1849 letter to Malcolm D. Haynes, "We rely on the Bible as authority for the establishment of slavery among men."

He wasn't referring there just to such Old Testament passages as *Numbers* 31:15-18; *Deuteronomy* 2:34-35, 3:3&6-7, 7:1-6, 13:12-18, 20:16-17, and 25:19; *Joshua* 6:21, 8:26, and 10:28&30&32&33&35&37&39&40; *1 Samuel* 15:3; *Isaiah* 13:11-16; *Jeremiah* 48:8-10; and *Hosea* 13:16. In the New Testament, *1 Peter* 2:18 says, "Slaves, submit to your masters with full respect, not only to those who are good and kind, but also to those who are harsh." Additional support is in such passages as *Ephesians* 6:5, *Colossians* 3:22, and *1 Timothy* 6:1. The abolition of slavery occurs not because of the Bible, but despite it. In fact, Adrian Desmond's and James Moore's 2009 *Darwin's Sacred Cause: How Hatred of Slavery Shaped Darwin's Views on Human Evolution*, documents that, "Darwin's starting point was the abolitionist belief in blood kinship, a 'common descent.'" Darwin's belief in the brotherhood of Man, and even in the brotherhood of *all* animals, led him to the search that produced his discovery of evolution. His grandfather Erasmus Darwin was similarly motivated, and had earlier proposed the theory of evolution, but didn't perform research to test out the theory. (He was terrified of the inevitable rejection from religious people.)

In 2 *Thessalonians* 3:10, "Paul" says: "Whoever refuses to work must not be permitted to eat."

On the side of the poor, are these passages:

In *Matthew* 6:24, "Jesus" says: "No one can serve ... both God and wealth."

In *Matthew* 19:21, "Jesus" says: "If you wish to be perfect, sell all your possessions and give the money to the poor."

In *Matthew* 19:24, "Jesus" says: "It is easier for a camel to go through the eye of a needle than for a rich man to enter the Kingdom of God."

In *Luke* 6:20, "Jesus" says: "Blessed are the poor, for theirs is God's Kingdom."

In *Luke* 6:24, "Jesus" says: "Woe to you rich, for you have already received your comfort."

Thus, in order to understand the will of Jesus, or otherwise to carry out God's will, one must actually first discard one's ego, so as to avoid believing *merely* what one *wants* to believe. One must start this quest by *accepting* the reality that the Bible *contradicts* itself. Rather than merely assert "The Bible says" this or that (as is usually done), one must open-mindedly seek a coherent, *non*-self-contradictory, *explanation* of its self-contradictions. The alternative – to *choose* this or that *side* of a given biblical contradiction (such as rich/poor) – is only to follow one's *own* will, *not* to follow the will of *God* (if God exists). Whoever does that, carries out solely his personal preference, whenever the Bible contradicts itself – as it often does.

A primary purpose here will be precisely this: to *explain* the Bible's contradictions, and not merely to endorse this or that – and to oppose that or this – in the Bible. Explaining the Bible's contradictions entails indicating *where these contradictions came from*. The *basic belief of Christianity* is that *the entire New Testament comes from God and Christ*, but the present work does not confirm this belief; to the contrary: it *disconfirms* Christianity, by scientifically finding that the New Testament was actually created by enemies of the Jewish sect that Jesus had started.

For this reason, fundamentalist Christians will tend to ignore the findings here. However, if this work is true, then it is fulfilling the intention of Jesus, who has thus already been misrepresented for two thousand years, and who would definitely not wish to *continue* being so misrepresented. In a situation such as this, Jesus would want *every* Christian to read and consider the present work, because he would oppose misrepresentations of himself, and he would thus want any such misrepresentations to be exposed. Consequently, a fundamentalist Christian, who presumably wishes to follow the will of Jesus, is *obligated* by his commitment to Jesus, to keep an *open mind* to the *possibility* that Jesus is misrepresented in the New Testament. And, if this work turns out instead to be false; and if Jesus did, after all, start Christianity (and so himself said *both* sides of the contradictions that the New Testament attributes to him); then the reader, after finding a falsehood in this work which discredits this work, will have thereby come to know Christianity's truthfulness *with even higher certainty than before,* as a direct outcome of having found such a falsehood in the most rigorous case against Christianity. In that case, the contradictions that are attributed to Jesus came from Jesus. Even if this means that Christianity is morally ambivalent, Christianity's *basic* belief is confirmed. The belief that Jesus advocated Christianity will then have survived its stiffest test; and, to paraphrase *Matthew* 16:19, even the gates of hell will then not be able to hold out against Christianity's truth. However, you cannot make this judgment *unless* you have first considered this case.

In *either* eventuality, the will of Jesus will have been served, and the truth will win out. As *John* 8:32 says, "You will know the truth, and the truth will set you free." What you believe after you've been freed will depend upon what you find in this search.

However, even at the present stage, this much is clear, and it's substantial: The words of "Jesus" in the New

Testament contradict themselves on core issues, such as rich and poor, and the Trinity itself. Such self-contradiction insults Jesus (*if* he existed – and the investigation presented here will confirm that he did, and that scholars who allege otherwise haven't put forth a single valid argument for their position). A "Jesus" like that is obviously not worth taking seriously, much less worshipping (if he even *intended* to be worshipped). He is his *own* opponent, on important matters. What would the *real* Jesus think of a self-styled "Christian" who cares so little about the alleged religion that "Christian" holds, as not to investigate whether those words, and the other words attributed to Jesus in the New Testament, *misrepresent* what he said, and what he stood for; and as to care so little about whether these words might even have been placed into Jesus's mouth by Jesus's actual *enemies*? If an alleged believer doesn't care enough about the religion he professes, so as to investigate whether its Scripture lies about the person's very object of worship and basic beliefs, then what would Jesus – or anyone else – think of such an individual? That's yet *another* reason to consider this investigation.

This work is written for *anyone* who seeks a scientific investigation of Christanity. If its findings are true, Jesus would passionately want Christians to read it. If its findings are false, Jesus wouldn't care whether Christians read it, because the self-contradictions that the New Testament attribute to Jesus would then reflect Jesus, not distortions of him by enemies, and such a Jesus would nullify himself.

Introduction: The Methodology

Methodology is even more important than findings, because it *determines* the findings. This work differs from others on earliest Christianity because its methodology is different – far more rigorous.

Any reader who is interested in a straight historical account of Christianity's start will find that in the next section ("Summary: The Findings," starting on page 30), but this book is not like others about history; it's not presenting (except on those pages) merely a story that is *alleged* to be nonfictional. Except for those fifteen pages, this work is a historical, real-life, who-done-it (and when, and where, and why, and how) *investigation*, laying out the evidence to the reader in a very systematic way, like in a court of law, so that the reader can judge *for him/herself*, what the history was, that's "told" *by this evidence*. The evidence *itself* will tell the story. (That fifteen-page narrative merely summarizes the broad outlines of this history.) The reader will therefore be reading history here in a different way – the way that a jury reconstructs, *from the evidence*, a history of how and why and when and where, and by whom, a crime was committed, and renders a verdict saying that this is the history (of the crime), and that any other alleged account (of this event) should be considered to be partly or wholly fictional, on the basis of the evidence.

However, a verdict is rendered not *only* on the basis of the evidence; it's rendered also on the basis of the *methodology*, which here is legal/forensic methodology – what's used in courts of law in democratic countries. Legal/forensic methodology is the scientific methodology for reconstructing history from evidence; and, on this basis, you, as a juror, will be reading, *directly* from the evidence, the actual history – no mere story, no fiction at all – the event that, *in fact*, started Christianity.

Being a responsible juror requires immense attention and care, far more than does simply reading a mere narrative "history" of an alleged event. In the present instance, investigating what might possibly have been the biggest deception in all of history requires a degree of intellectual concentration that will greatly sharpen the mind. Anyone who is prepared to engage in such an analysis will find the process itself to be rewarding, not merely because of the new information and understandings that result, but also because the methodology, that's used in this discovery, possesses wide applications, far outside courtrooms. A skill in recognizing liars (and their lies) protects one against deception, no matter what the subject might happen to be; and this increases one's intellectual capacities. The same process of discovery can be applied (for example) to such things as identifying when politicians are lying, or when an advertising claim ought to be discounted – and when to discount it to zero.[6] However,

---

[6]   Thus, for example, Sharon Begley aptly headlined in *Newsweek* on 8 November 2010, "Wanted: BS Detectors – What Science Ed Should Really Teach," and she wrote: "It is time to stop cramming kids' heads with the Krebs cycle, Ohm's law, and the myriad other facts that constitute today's science curricula. Instead, what we need to teach is the ability to detect Bad Science – BS, if you will." She went on (in a truth about legal/forensic methodology and every other scientific methodology), "Understanding what counts as evidence should therefore trump memorizing the structural formulas for alkenes" or any other supposed or alleged "finding" *from* "evidence." She consequently closed: "Science is not a collection of facts, but a way of interrogating the world." This way (the way of science) will be how the New Testament will be "interrogated" here. For example, rather than simply assume that the canonical Gospels constitute the most reliable evidence about how Christianity started, we'll open-mindedly examine: What *is* the most reliable evidence here?

perhaps its greatest usefulness is to disentangle faith from fact, which happens to be the objective in the present instance.

A full discussion of this methodology will be presented in the final chapter, the "Conclusion," where it can be consulted as you go along in this work, if you should happen to have any methodological question about how this history is being documented. Since methodology is even more important than the findings (in *any* scientific work, not *only* in this one), that explanation will culminate this work. Methodology is king here. However, a summary of this methodology will now be presented, up front, so that you will know, right at the start, the evidence on which this historical account is based, and what the basic rules of modern legal/forensic methodology are, which will produce this history from this body of evidence:

The highest-ranked source here, which is considered by scholars to be the gold standard of authenticity regarding earliest Christianity, is Paul's letter to the Galatians. (The reasons why it's considered #1 are discussed more fully in our final chapter, the Conclusion.) This document is recognized by virtually all scholars as having been written before not just the canonical, but *all* (including *non*-canonical), accounts of Jesus's life. Furthermore, *Galatians* is entirely a first-person account, not based upon hearsay but instead providing authentic witness testimony. Part One of this book will thus be a line-by-line analysis of *Galatians* – the first such analysis ever to employ modern legal/forensic methodology, which is the scientific methodology for interpreting documents (and the methodology that's described in detail in our Conclusion). This will be the first occasion anywhere in which Paul's testimony is, essentially, being cross-examined, by using new legal/forensic methods for interpreting documentary evidence. For example, Paul's honesty will not be assumed here. Nor will there be any assumption here that Paul is lying. No assumption whatsoever will be made regarding these and other matters which, in a standard scholarly analysis, are loaded with such assumptions. Though this evidence has existed for thousands of years, this methodology for interpreting it is new.

The second-highest-ranked sources, which will be used here to explain additional details of the meaning of *Galatians*, are the 6 other letters by Paul that scholars consider authentic: *Romans, Philippians, 1&2 Corinthians, 1 Thessalonians,* and *Philemon.* These 7 documents (including *Galatians*) are the 7 earliest-written documents pertaining to earliest Christianity, the ones written closest to Jesus, and written only to people who definitely had access to representatives from Jesus's disciples – individuals who might criticize anything that was inaccurate in them – and all are furthermore virtually universally accepted as being authentic first-person accounts of the people and events they describe. No other evidence about earliest Christianity is at all like this.

In addition, whenever a given assertion that Paul made was paraphrasing a passage from the Old Testament, for authority, that source-passage also is 2nd quality – unimpeachable for interpreting Paul, but still not *Galatians* itself.

All other evidence (including *Matthew, Mark, Luke, John, Acts,* Josephus, etc.) was written after Paul, might have been influenced by Paul, and is lower-ranked (#3). Its only usefulness is for expanding upon (or filling in gaps of) the historical narrative, or "theory of the case," that is constructed from the best evidence. Such expansions are not as reliable as is the theory of the case itself, but are likely true, rather than likely false.

Speculation by scholars (or anyone else) about what Paul was trying to say, or about the meaning of any document, is speculation, *not* evidence, and therefore cannot be cited here at all (except to point out *that* it's *not* evidence). Only the evidence is evidence, and only the reader/juror will interpret it; no scholar can serve that function (of interpretation). Scholars can serve to *authenticate* documents, and these documents have been authenticated by them; but only you can *interpret* the evidence. The present work is intended merely to assist you in interpreting, by providing you the relevant evidence, which no one can interpret *for* you, *except* you. The only aspect of the evidence that you cannot evaluate for yourself is its *authenticity*; scholars' opinions are thus accepted as constituting expert opinions on matters of authenticity, but differences of opinions among these experts will be noted, where applicable (such as, for example, regarding the authenticity of the passage 2:13-16 in Paul's letter *1 Thessalonians*, which some scholars consider to be a later addition – not authentic). Where there are such differences of opinion, modern legal/forensic methodology will be applied to make the final determination as to authenticity. (In this example case, 2:13-16 will be demonstrated to be authentic.) However, you will always be the final *interpreter* of the evidence. That's a juror's function. Any reader who would rely upon some "authority" to interpret the evidence excludes himself from this (or any) case.

As was noted, modern legal/forensic methodology does not (like scholarly methodologies do) assume whether a given writer wrote with the intention to inform, rather than to deceive: the honesty of the documents will not be assumed, nor will their dishonesty. Instead, the honesty/dishonesty of each given statement will be investigated here, in the light of the *other* evidence. On this basis, an *explanation* will be presented, of any *contradictions* within the evidence.

In a nutshell, then, this is the methodology:

(1) Assume as little as possible.

(2) Always rely on the best (most reliable) evidence.

(3) Explain (instead of ignore) any contradictions within the evidence.

Summary: The Findings

(Everything from this point onward in this book is intended only for readers who accept the methodology, which has just been summarized in the Introduction – and which is more fully described in our final chapter, the Conclusion. Since that methodology is basic to this work's findings, and since no previous work has applied this methodology to historically reconstructing the start of Christianity, anyone who doesn't accept that methodology would be simply wasting time to read any further here. On the other hand, readers who accept that methodology will find the following history of Christianity's start to be amply documented in this work. This summary encapsulates the historical narrative that that methodology will be documenting from the evidence:)

TIME-LINE OF KEY EVENTS

c. 30: Jesus, the founder of a Jewish sect, is executed for sedition against Rome.

c. 32-33: Paul, an enemy of Jesus's sect, joins them after alleging that he was told to do so by Jesus's ghost.

35 or 36: Paul, for the first time, meets two of Jesus's disciples in Jerusalem. He receives two weeks training from Peter, the disciple who headed the mission to the uncircumcised or Gentiles; and he also is introduced to Jesus's brother James, the leading disciple.

49 or 50: James orders Paul to return to Jerusalem so as to defend his practice of accepting into Judaism uncircumcised men, in blatant contradiction of Judaism's signature commandment, *Genesis* 17:14, in which God had allegedly told Abraham "No uncircumcised male will be one of my people." At the end of this council in Jerusalem, James rules that, at least for the time being, Paul's followers will continue to be accepted as Jews despite that blatant violation.

49 or 50: Shortly afterward, James sends Peter and other representatives to Paul's Antioch headquarters to tell Paul that *Genesis* 17:14 must be enforced after all. Paul refuses and announces that God's religion is no longer Judaism (obedience to God's laws) but Christianity (faith in Christ). James decides not to expel Paul's followers from the sect, and Paul decides not to tell his followers that they aren't really Jews.

After 50: Paul tells his followers, in *Romans* 13:1-5 and elsewhere, that the ultimate lawmaker and enforcer of the laws is the Emperor, and that the Emperor is actually God's representative on Earth to perform such legislative functions.

Jesus of Nazareth started a new sect in Judaism. He was then crucified by the Romans in approximately the year 30. The Romans crucified him because he claimed to be the King of the Jews. The Romans crucified everyone who made that claim (there were others who made this same claim). All of these men were crucified because the Romans had appointed solely the Herodian family to that kingly position. For anyone else to claim this title was automatically viewed as being – and it actually was – sedition against Rome. This is why Jesus was crucified by the Romans, for sedition. (Though the Gospels say that Jesus was crucified for violating Jewish blasphemy laws, that was a lie, as will be documented and explained in this work.)

Jews were at that time a conquered people, who had lost their independent nation of Israel, and who were being ruled by these kings appointed by Rome. Moreover, Jesus taught that the Law came from God, not from Rome's Emperor or Caesar, and this made his sedition especially threatening to Rome's continued rule over Jews.

Consequently, if for no other reason, Rome actually had little other choice but to crucify Jesus, as a public example and warning to any Jew who might similarly challenge Rome's authority to make the laws, and to appoint the kings.

Furthermore, according to Josephus's *Antiquities* 18:2:2, Rome appointed not merely the Jews' kings but also the chief Jewish priest, in Jerusalem, Caiaphas. If Caiaphas advised his people to tell (his actual employer) Pilate to kill Jesus, as is alleged in *John* 18:14, then this wouldn't have been done "so that one man should die for all the people," as that Gospel alleged, but instead done to halt and block any spread of such sedition. And it also wouldn't have been done to suppress "blasphemy" against Jewish laws, as is alleged in *Matthew* 26:65 and *Mark* 14:64. Pilate's job wasn't to assure "that one man should die for all the people," nor to suppress blasphemy against Judaism; it was simply to crush sedition. Moreover, Jesus did not blaspheme against Judaism; he taught Judaism; he was, in fact, a recognized rabbi. He never abandoned Judaism. The idea that he did was created, starting twenty years after his death, by enemies of the sect that he had established.

Jesus's disciples were followers of this convict who had been executed by Rome for sedition. Rome was wary of them.

Furthermore, Jesus's disciples were poor people, not serving or affiliated with the owners of most wealth, the ruling Roman authorities.

This historical background is essential in order to understand why Jesus's remaining followers, in Jerusalem, were vulnerable both politically and economically.

Shortly before Jesus's crucifixion, he appointed his brother James to head the young sect. (Though the Gospels say that Jesus appointed Peter as the group's new leader; this, too, was an intentional falsehood, documented and explained herein.) James took over leadership of this Jewish sect. Within approximately three years after Jesus's crucifixion, Paul joined the sect. Then, three years after joining, Paul traveled to Jerusalem, in order to receive missionary training specifically from Peter, who was the sect's chief missionary selling this sect to Gentiles, or to *non*-Jews.

Peter had had only modest success converting Gentiles to join this Jewish sect, but Paul became the star missionary or salesman to the Gentiles. In fact, Paul brought in such a great number of new members, so that soon most of the sect's members were actually Gentiles who had been converted to Judaism by Paul.

As the years went by and Paul brought more and more Gentiles into this sect throughout the Roman Empire, he was bringing into the sect a wealthier and less threatening-to-Rome class of members, people who hadn't been raised to believe that God and not Rome was the ultimate arbiter of the laws. Paul collected funds from these higher-social-status people to maintain and support the very weak-status disciples in Jerusalem. Consequently these disciples grew increasingly dependent upon Paul.

However, this soaring number of new members who hadn't been born as Jews created a problem for the members who had been so born: These new Jews weren't circumcised. According to the Jewish legend, which as Jews they all believed to be history and not myth, Judaism had started at *Genesis* 17:12-14, with God telling Abraham: "Circumcision will be your signature on our agreement [God's agreement with the Jews], a physical sign that our covenant is eternal." In *Genesis* 17:14, God said: "No man who is uncircumcised will be one of my people." God's agreement was thus *only* with circumcised men; no uncircumcised man would be one of God's people. Then, in *Genesis* 17:19, God made clear that this would never change; he said: "This agreement will extend through all future generations – everlasting." Abraham

complied, and thus the Jewish covenant began, according to
the Jewish legend. In ancient cultures, and in cultures that are
pre-literate or maybe just becoming literate, "signing" a
contract (like the contract with God, which is the Jewish
covenant) was sometimes done "in blood"; and the signature
in this case was done on a private part of a man's body, a part
which moreover represented the future; it represented coming
generations: the penis.

So, the question is: were these new men, whom Paul
had brought in, *actually* Jews? Not according to the
commandment that started Judaism: they certainly weren't.
Circumcision was Judaism's signature commandment; a man
didn't even qualify to be a Jew unless he had first signed the
covenant with God by becoming circumcised, and Paul's men
had *not* signed. This was in black and white, in *Genesis*. It was
undeniable.

By the time of the 17th year of Paul's employment with
the sect, 14 years after his first visit to Jerusalem, Paul's
congregations included so many members, that James called
Paul back again to Jerusalem. In *Galatians* 2:2, Paul said that
what was at stake in this Jerusalem conference was the success
or failure of all of his missionary work up to that time. The
crucial moment for him had finally come.

If circumcision were to be imposed upon his men, Paul
would have lost almost all of them, and the reason for this was
quite simple:

Anesthesia didn't yet exist, and therefore any medical
operation was a living terror. This is why few medical
operations occurred that weren't absolutely necessary. The
circumcisions of male Jewish infants on their eighth day, in
accord with *Genesis* 17:11, were exceptions. Those infants
didn't even choose it; this was something that their parents
did to them. Paul's converts, by contrast, were grown men.
They would have been terrified to be subjected to that
requirement. Most would have refused.

In addition, antibiotics and antiseptics didn't exist;
germs weren't even known to exist; the microscope hadn't yet

been invented. Consequently, the death-rate in any type of operation was very high, due to infections. When death occurred to an infant, it was no major concern, because infants possessed no property, and thus no power. But adult males possessed all the property, and so all the power in society, and therefore Paul knew that he would lose his life's success if he demanded that his men become circumcised.

All scholars have ignored these determinative realities about circumcision during the First Century, and many scholars have even said that circumcision was only a small concern to those of Jesus's followers who were trying to convert uncircumcised adult males. For example, Harvard's Krister Stendahl said (in his 1963 *Paul Among Jews and Gentiles*, Part 6) that "circumcision ... was not a barrier to Christianity but quite attractive to Gentiles, who were enamored of what was Oriental. ... Even ritual laws like those from the Old Testament were not a liability but an asset – as any reader of Galatians can see." He provided no documentation for that opinion regarding circumcision, because none exists: You'll be investigating *Galatians* yourself in the pages here to follow, and you won't find anything in *Galatians* to support this commonly held scholarly opinion of the innocuousness (if not attractiveness) of circumcision during the First Century – nothing whatsoever there. Scholars don't have to document their opinions, because (unfortunately), even without evidence, scholars are deemed to possess authority of their own. Only scientists are obliged to cite evidence for their views. (We're not doing it here in this Summary, but we do it throughout the rest. Even a scientist may summarize.)

James understood that if he demanded that Paul's men become circumcised, then he'd lose most of his members; and so James, too, didn't want to do that. Furthermore (as has been noted), Jesus's disciples were poor people; they were Jerusalem Jews, who had been defeated by Rome, and almost all of the rich people were associated with the Roman regime, and they were Gentiles – uncircumcised. Paul's congregations were thus contributing money to the upkeep of these poor

Jews in Jerusalem. James strongly wanted this financial
assistance to continue.

Paul wrote in *Galatians* 2:10 that at the conclusion of the
conference James required only that this money keep coming.
Paul seemed, at first, to have had his way.

But then, only shortly after Paul returned to Antioch,
Peter came, and, later that same day, other agents from James
also came, and they told Paul that James had changed his
mind, and that Paul's men would have to be circumcised, after
all. According to Paul's account in *Galatians* 2:14-21, Paul
responded by saying that the covenant was at an end as a
result of Jesus's crucifixion, and that "a person is viewed
favorably by God only by means of possessing Christ-faith,
never by following God's laws [which are set forth in the
covenant in the Torah, the first five books of the Bible]." In
other words, Paul said that the agreement that God had with
the Jews was now replaced by Paul's "gospel of Christ," in
which a faith that Jesus was the Messiah is all that God
requires, in order for a man to become one of God's people
and so go to heaven instead of to hell after death. Paul said, in
Galatians 2:21, "If a person is put right with God by adhering
to the covenant, then the Messiah died for nothing!"

That was the first time this doctrine, Christianity's basic
doctrine, personal salvation by means of faith instead of by
the Jewish means (which is via obeying God's
commandments), had been stated anywhere. It occurred in the
year 49 or 50. That's the occasion when Christianity actually
started: the doctrinal break away from Judaism, the creation of
Paul's gospel of Christ. Paul was virtually forced into it, by
circumstances, or else he would fail in life; his entire prior 17
years as the sect's best salesman would have gone down the
drain, if he had required his men to go under the knife. In
Philippians 3:1-2, he warned his men, "As I've said before, I am
concerned about your safety," because "those evil people,
those dogs, who insist upon cutting the body," are wrong, and
(*Philippians* 3:8) the entire covenant is "garbage" (or "dung"),

which the Messiah's death has made superfluous. Judaism
was here trashed.

Paul knew that discarding circumcision meant discarding the covenant to which it signed. (A contract doesn't exist
unless it's accepted; and, according to *Genesis* 17:10-14, God's
contract wasn't accepted unless it was signed *via* circumcision.) But Paul couldn't afford to tell his men that he was
rejecting the covenant on account of rejecting the circumcision
requirement – and that he wasn't *really*, as Paul claimed,
rejecting the circumcision law on account of rejecting the
covenant. Paul understood that, if he were to say to his men,
"I reject the covenant because I reject the circumcision law,"
then his phenomenally successful sales career would end. He
would be confessing his own fraud. His followers would reject
his fraud, and he'd soon have no followers. An honest statement of his concerns here would have transformed him from a
success to a failure in his own eyes, because of this loss of his
followers. He would have told them, in effect: For you to be a
member of the Jesus (or, indeed, of *any*) sect of Judaism, you
must *first* become circumcised, because no uncircumcised man
is one of God's people; no uncircumcised man is a Jew *at all*.
They would have left not only Judaism but also his congregations, in order to avoid the terror and danger of an operation.
So, Paul never told them this.

Galatians 2:11-21 presents an embarrassed and nervous
Paul recounting to the Galatians the event that had actually
started Christianity (as noted, he couldn't afford to admit to
them that this occasion *was* its start); and, in this account,
Peter simply lacked the stomach to inform Paul of the bad
news from James. Peter instead sat down to dinner at Paul's
headquarters, with Paul's uncircumcised followers. Then,
James's backup team suddenly arrived, and saw that Peter
was dining with Paul's uncircumcised men, not telling Paul
that they needed to become circumcised before they could be
authentic followers of Jesus. Peter backed away from the table
and seconded James's demand. This precipitated the blow-up,
which caused Paul to assert 2:16-21 – Christianity.

Paul, in *Galatians*, didn't mention that James had changed his mind and had decided that *Genesis* 17:14 needed to be imposed after all in order for Paul's men to continue being members of the Jesus sect of Jews. Paul simply couldn't bring himself to admit this, because if his Galatian readers were to be *informed* that the sect's leader, James, now demanded circumcision, then those Galatians would be made conscious that by their staying in Paul's congregations they'd no longer *be* members of the Jesus sect, and they'd then abandon *both* James and Paul. They'd abandon the Jesus sect on account of refusing to go under the knife in an era without anesthesia, antibiotics, and antiseptics; and they'd abandon Paul's congregations because they'd know that Paul's congregations were in violation of Jesus, and weren't even Jewish *at all*; they'd learn that this was really just a hoax. (The case presented in this work will be that Paul perpetrated not just an "error" but a hoax when he created Christianity – that he was *intending* to deceive; that his deceptions here were the result of careful planning and scheming, not of mere sloppiness on his part. That will be our case.)

Paul and James were now locked in the equivalent of a bad marriage that couldn't be ended. Divorce was too painful for either to carry out. If James were to announce publicly that Paul's men were no longer his followers, then James's poverty-stricken group in Jerusalem would no longer continue to receive the financial contributions coming in from Paul's far better-off Gentile congregations throughout the rest of the Roman Empire. James's desperate followers had simply become financially too dependent upon the far larger number of Paul's followers. Thus, James remained quiet about his change-of-mind. And Paul, for his part, continued telling *his* followers to continue contributing to the group in Jerusalem, because Paul needed the at-least-tacit acceptance by James's group to continue for a long enough time for Paul's new faith to be able to go out ultimately publicly on its own, as an entirely new religion, abandoning its Jewish status. If Paul were to become *publicly* known as being no longer Jewish, then his claim to be a follower of the Messiah would be blatantly fraudulent, since no *non*-Jewish context yet existed for even the very concept of the Messiah ("Christ"). Paul walked a fine line: he had to preach a new religion, by using terms that *seemed* to his contemporaries to be consistent with an established religion, when he was actually *negating* the latter.

James's group faded away. But Paul's blossomed and thrived. One reason why Paul's group grew was that Paul was telling people that they don't need to go under the knife in order to win an eternity in heaven; just Christ-faith (as described in *Galatians* 2:16-21) will do the job. In other words, Paul said that God changed everything after Jesus's crucifixion, so that heaven was now on sale at a far lower price than in Judaism. No longer did one have to follow Jewish Law in order to go to heaven, but now mere faith in Jesus's being the Christ was sufficient.

Another reason Paul's group grew was that in *Romans* 13:1-7 and elsewhere, Paul and his followers told their followers that the laws they should adhere to weren't the ones from Judaism's God, but were instead the ones from the Roman Emperor of the time. *Romans* 13:1-7 and other passages presented Rome's Emperors as, in effect, God's agents upon Earth, imposing God's will, and legislating on God's behalf, so that, as *Romans* 13:5 put it, "You must obey the political authority [the Emperor] not just because, as God's agent, he'll punish you for violating the law, but also as a matter of conscience." This teaching by Paul and his followers was enormously helpful to the Emperors; it served as a huge inducement for Emperors ultimately to impose Christianity throughout their realm.

When it's understood that the four canonical Gospel accounts of Christ were written not by Jesus's followers but by Paul's, both the truths and the lies in the New Testament become fully explained, and make 100% sense. Even the NT's internal contradictions now make sense, without any exception whatsoever.[7] Reality makes sense; only myths do not.

Paul, in his account in *Galatians* 2, had been faced with an extraordinarily painful choice: either he would carry out his instructions from James and demand that his perhaps thousands of men become circumcised, or else he and his congregations would leave the sect and go off into the future as an entirely new religion, which renounces the Jewish covenant (wherein, following God's laws is a person's

---

[7] A legal/forensic analysis is perfect only if it explains not just the evidence, but any contradictions between and within different items of evidence. An ideal theory of the case explains *all* of the evidence, and this means explaining why any contradictions exist among the evidence. An ideal theory of the case doesn't depend upon there being no contradictions within the evidence. For example, Paul's *Romans* 3:28 contradicts both his 3:31, three lines later, and his earlier 2:6. New-Perspective-on-Paul scholars tend to ignore (or else to twist beyond recognition) 3:28, and Old-Perspective-on-Paul scholars tend to ignore (or twist) 3:31 and 2:6. Any explanation that is selective among the evidence, on any basis other than the relative degrees of reliability of those items of evidence, is necessarily prejudiced. Lawyers, as lawyers, are prejudiced in the only (and very narrow) way that science accepts: as a proponent, either for or against, any hypothesis or theory is expected to be in any scientific controversy.

Scholars are not violating science when they ignore contrary evidence, but any juror would be violating science who preferred a theory of the case that fails to explain all the evidence, over an alternative theory of the case that succeeds at explaining all of the evidence. *Only* jurors are in a position to weigh the opposing arguments; contending lawyers are not. Similarly, in any scientific controversy, each and every observer of that controversy must make the decision for himself, as to which hypothetical explanation of the data is the more comprehensive, or explains the greater share of the given body of evidence. Presumably, an unprejudiced jury (which is the ideal in any trial) might be split if the two contending theories of the case are approximately equally unsuccessful at explaining all of the evidence (including contradictions that may exist within the evidence).

However, if one of the contending two theories of the case explains all of the evidence (including any contradictions within it), and the other theory does not, then any juror who preferred the latter would be prejudiced. To be prejudiced is anyone's prerogative, in the sense that it cannot be penalized, but it violates a juror's obligation to the court, and to the state, and to the entire society. Whereas the court expects a lawyer to be prejudiced for his own side, the court expects a juror to be as impartial to both sides as it is possible to be. Courts have procedures to minimize prejudice in the selection of jurors, and not only to minimize prejudice in the judgments by jurors (such as by sequestering a jury, in some extreme circumstances). However, no way exists to eliminate prejudice entirely. Even the most scientific procedures cannot absolutely guarantee that the conclusions that are reached will necessarily be truthful.

pathway to an afterlife in heaven), and which replaces that by
Paul's Christian "gospel of Christ" (in which Christ-faith is
Paul's *new* pathway to heaven). Replacing Judaism – Jesus's
own religion – would be traitorous to Jesus. But remaining
Jewish would have led here to Paul's oblivion, because few of
Paul's men were willing to risk their lives (via circumcision) in
order to stay with him. Paul took the path to his personal
success, rather than to his personal oblivion. This is what
caused Paul to start an entirely new religion, which was
custom-tailored by him to become the world's largest, because
it placed heaven on sale, and also because it created for the
Roman Emperors a new universal or "Catholic" religion to
replace the old parochial and merely local Roman gods.

   Already before Paul's time, the Emperors had been
struggling with the inadequacies of their old religion: the
Roman gods provided *no moral authority for the laws the
Emperors dictated;* and these gods were also *purely local tribal
Roman deities, who possessed no authority outside of Rome anyway.*
Paul's solution to both of these pressing problems provided
the only way to make the Emperors' subjects – not just in
Rome but elsewhere, throughout the Empire – follow the
Emperors' commands as if those commands came from God.
(E.g.: *Romans* 13:1-5.) This solution emerged to become a
powerful inducement for the Emperors ultimately to adopt
Christianity.

   However, in order for Paul and his followers who
wrote the Gospels to win support from the Emperors, a way
also had to be found to explain Jesus's crucifixion by the
Roman authorities. After all, no Roman Emperor would ever
endorse a religion that worshipped a man who was *acknowledged* to have been executed by one of the Emperor's *own*
predecessors. Paul and his followers came up with a solution
to this problem, too: They alleged that the Jews (despite
having been conquered by the Romans) somehow (and they
didn't say how) managed to force the supposedly reluctant
Roman authorities to crucify Jesus for "blasphemy" *against
Jewish Law.* This lie didn't only present in a frighteningly

bad light the very thing (Jewish Law) that Paul in *Galatians* 2:16, *Romans* 3:28, and elsewhere, had said that God was now abandoning in favor of Paul's gospel, Christ-faith. More to the point here, this lie *freed the Roman Emperors from any Deicide charge, that they had killed God.* Without this lie, Paul and his people would have stood no chance at all of ultimately winning over the Emperors.

Thus, securing his support from both the mass base and the Imperial elite, Paul emerged to become the most powerful person in history, the creator of the world's largest religion, just as he hoped. Paul said, in *1 Corinthians* 9:24-25, "Run life's race so as to win the prize." For him, winning was everything. "Every athlete in training submits to strict discipline in order to win a prize that will not last; we, however, do it to win a prize that will last forever." And so he did: his prize has already lasted 2,000 years.

The people who penned the four canonical Gospel accounts of "Christ" wrote into his mouth words expressing the agenda of Paul, not necessarily of Jesus.

And that's how the moral base of Western Civilization was created: as a hoax.[8] This is how Paul dealt with a threat that would otherwise have destroyed what had been, up till the moment, his phenomenally successful 17-year-long career: he overcame it in the only way that was even possible. Moreover, subsequent millennia have demonstrated that his career not merely succeeded, but that it turned out to have been the most successful career ever, because the organization he thereby started became the largest in history, just as he was hoping it would.

---

[8]   Calling it a "hoax" is what I infer that it would be called by Jesus if he believed the sort of thing that he was quoted in *Matthew* 5:17-20 as having said, including "Do not think I have come to do away with the Law of Moses, ... for it will be eternally binding."

This and other statements attributed to Jesus obviously contradict Paul in *Galatians* 2:16, *Romans* 2:28, and elsewhere, negating the continued applicability of the Law. Paul's saying, in *Romans* 3:31 and elsewhere, "We uphold the Law," is itself a lie, as this work will demonstrate. Paul can't really have it both ways: on the one hand, Paul argues at length that the Law is dead; on the other hand, he says

Even the Trinity, and the Resurrection, are fully
understandable, and will be explained in the following pages,
as outcomes from this decision by Paul. (That is to say: those
beliefs were essential to the success of Paul's hoax; and this is
why he introduced them, and it's why his followers fleshed
them out in their narratives about "Jesus.")

Even the word-choices by Paul, and by his followers
who wrote the four canonical Gospel accounts of "Jesus,"
were carefully calculated by them to fool future generations,
and not only their own. For example (as was previously
noted), they presented their "Jesus" as having established an
"ekklesia" (which is today translated as "church," though it
actually meant in their own time *any* kind of an assembly,
which could also have included its being a synagogue or
"sunagoge") rather than as his having established (as they
might *otherwise* have called it) either a *"threskeia"* (meaning a
religion – which would have made their hoax obvious to their
own generation, since everyone in their time knew that Jesus

---

that he didn't say that. It will be for you, the reader, to decide whether or not Paul
was a con-man, as this work describes him as being. This work lays out all the
evidence on the case; but, ultimately, only you, the individual juror, can decide what
it actually means. No one else can decide that for you.

An essential part of the prosecutor's burden in this case is (as was
previously noted) to explain contradictions within the evidence, such as the
contradiction (earlier pointed out) between *Matthew* 5:17-20 and *Matthew* 28:18-20.
This will be done here. Paul's defense attorneys, the scholars, have the same
burden – to explain instead of to ignore contradictions – but they often ignore the
contradictions, and they always ignore their obligation to explain the contradictions.
The prosecutor here acknowledges, instead of ignores, this obligation to the juror,
and accepts it.

Consequently, no assumption will be made here that Jesus actually *said*
"Do not think I have come to do away with the Law of Moses, ... for it will be
eternally binding." However, regardless of whether the author of *Matthew* was
accurately (or even knowledgeably, or even honestly) reporting this, our
investigation will establish, from better quality evidence – documents that were
written earlier than any of the canonical four Gospels – that Jesus did *believe* that
way: that Jesus was 100% committed to, and preached only, Judaism, and that the
statements in the New Testament which assert or suggest that Jesus had anything
to do with starting Christianity are purely bogus: parts of a hoax. This hoax will be
described and documented here.

hadn't started any religion), or else a *"sunagoge"* (which would have made their hoax obvious to future generations, such as to ours, since future generations weren't intended to know that Jesus had lived and died as a devout Jew). Paul was the source of *all* of these brilliant tricks. (E.g., the decision to refer to Jesus's organization as an *ekklesia,* and not as a *sunagoge* or *threskeia,* predates the canonical Gospels: "ekklesia" is the term Paul used in all seven of his authentic letters.)

Some supporters of religion might consider this to be too harsh an account of the creation of the Christian faith. However, the actual distinction between this account and all others isn't its harshness, but rather its methodological foundation: namely, that this account is based upon a legal/forensic analysis of the evidence.

This history of the origins of the hoax we recognize as Christianity is documented with full details in the following, in which the people who created that hoax wrote and displayed not only their hoax, but also – under the first-ever legal/forensic analysis of their writings – how and why they did it. Without necessarily assuming their testimony to be honest, but rather "cross-examining" this testimony by placing it under a legal/forensic logical microscope, which exposes both the overtly explicit and the logically implied assertions in these documents, and which distinguishes between these two levels of assertion, this history becomes revealed with stunning clarity, as we shall now see, starting with the first-ever legal/forensic analysis of the most reliable of the Christian scriptures, *Galatians,* in which Paul exhibits far more than he asserts, and in which his testimony even demonstrates/proves some things that outright contradict, and that thus disprove, some of his claims.[9]

---

[9]   Methodological issues will be addressed in depth, not in the main text (except the Introduction and the Conclusion), but in the footnotes to it, which will provide epistemological commentary upon the text's ontological account. Like all history, the history in the text is ontological, describing the documented events. The epistemological commentary in our footnotes will probe more deeply into *how* these events are *being* documented.

The Evidence, Part One:
Paul's Letter to the Galatians

Decoding the 'DNA' in what turns out to be the confession of the man who started Christianity

1. Paul Prepares His Readers: Analysis Up to 2:10

"O, what a tangled web we weave,
When first we practise to deceive!"
Sir Walter Scott, 1808, *Marmion*, Canto VI, Stanza 17

This book's thesis is that Paul's letter to the Galatians describes not just the event that created Christianity, but also what led up to and caused this event, and also what this event's immediate consequences were – including the changes it caused in Paul's teachings about Jesus's life and death. Consequently, the first three chapters here are devoted to a legal/forensic analysis of this single item of evidence, *Galatians*.

What you will be experiencing here is like what jurors in a major white-collar-crime trial experience when documentary evidence is placed before them and there is no assumption regarding whether the people who wrote those documents were trying to inform the recipients, or whether these writers' intentions might have been, in some instances, instead to mislead or even to deceive those recipients. A juror might take interpretive shortcuts, such as always believing that everyone communicated honestly, and this might make that juror's interpretive job easier, but not if inconsistencies exist within the evidence – as often does happen. Whenever such inconsistencies are found, this juror may discover that an assumption of a person's honesty will actually complicate his understanding, so much as to make any rational verdict impossible. Thus, in many cases, a juror's job can end up being a slow and careful evaluation of a given body of evidence, to reconstruct a history from that evidence, so as to meet the given standard of proof (such as a preponderance of the evidence, or beyond a reasonable doubt), while at the same time *explaining* whatever contradictions exist among the evidence, instead of *ignoring* those contradictions. This is how an authentic *history* can be produced, from evidence, *even when there are evidentiary contradictions*. This is how a juror can come to know history, slowly and carefully from the evidence, with a degree of rational confidence that vastly exceeds any other method. We use *this* method – modern legal/forensic methodology – in cases that are consequential enough to make worthwhile the coming to know their history slowly and carefully, because their stakes are high. The kinds of cases that are considered in courts tend to *be* high-stakes cases. So, too, is the case here: reconstructing, from the evidence, the event that created Christianity.

In or around the year 54, Paul wrote a letter to be read aloud to the congregations of Jesus-followers he had started in Galatia. He was afraid of losing some of his men to Jesus-followers who disagreed with Paul, and he wrote with such urgency and passion that one might even think he was fighting here for the success of his life's work – because he actually was. These high stakes were the reason Paul put into his letter everything he had, hoping to persuade those followers to stay with him, in his congregations.

Of course, this letter to the Galatians wasn't like, say, Sophocles's *Elektra*, or Aeschylus's *Oresteian* trilogy: it was no fictional tragedy, with dramatic effects in sex, family relationships, and murder, and with royal principal characters, whose lives and deaths held intrinsic interest to large masses of people. This letter, in fact, described events that took place among real people, who were obscure in their own time.

But Paul's letter to the Galatians is a tragedy, nonetheless. It doesn't merely describe, it also participates in, a *non*fictional tragedy, in which virtually all of us today perform roles, though unknowingly (until now).

The role of the legal/forensic investigator is simply to expose this real-life drama accurately – even to others of its unknowing participants, two millennia afterwards, whose world has been shaped both by the events that this letter describes, and by Paul's stunning success at winning over its recipients to his side in the conflict it joined.

So: let's start as did this letter's author, Paul, at the very beginning, when he took up a pen, which was made of either quill or reed, and dipped it into ink; this is how he applied ink to papyrus (parchment being too expensive, and thus not commonly employed for letters). All of those parts – the pen, the ink, and the papyrus – are long since gone, and only what Paul wrote has come down to us. Paul said, in *Galatians* 6:11, "Notice how large my letters are as I write this in my own hand." But it's all mere dust now; only what he wrote survives, to provide the crucial evidence. Two-thousand years later, in our own emerging Age of Science, we might hope that this ancient piece of evidence will bring forth the ultimate undoing of the tragic story, the story this letter both begins and reluctantly describes.

In the present analysis, *italics* will be employed not to provide emphasis, but to provide clarity to the reading of the text. Words are italicized so that the reader will understand the given passage at once, not need to *re*-read it.

This clarity will be especially helpful in the present chapter, because this chapter requires by far the greatest concentration of all chapters in the book. Afterwards, everything is pretty much a breeze to understand. The reason this chapter is difficult is that it provides the basis for understanding the passage that constitutes the climax of *Galatians*, 2:11-21, Paul's description of the actual creation of Christianity. On this basis, the second chapter will provide the full details, from Paul, about Christianity's creation – the event that Paul describes there. The present chapter is Paul's description of the circumstances that led up to his creation of Christianity, and is thus the foundation for understanding everything.

Any reader who finds this chapter too taxing, might at any time skip forward to our second chapter, which describes the event that started Christianity, and then page back to this chapter wherever Chapter 2 refers to the lines discussed here: 1:1-2:10. However, the analysis in the present chapter provides the best case-study of how to become empowered to read documentary evidence so as to reconstruct from it the actual circumstances that caused it to be written as it is. Purely for the methodology of understanding written forms of persuasion (such as *Galatians*), this chapter is the prime one.

Perhaps you'll want to get your Bible out now, and turn to *Galatians*. (You'll also find the crucial part of *Galatians*, from the start up through 2:21, reproduced herein complete as the Part One Appendix, starting on page 287, just in case you don't happen to have a Bible. You might want to read it through there once or twice before proceeding, so as to get your initial bearings on it.[10]) That's the document; it will place Paul now onto the witness stand before us, facing a cross-examination, and legal/forensic analysis (below), which Paul never knew when he was alive, nor since (till this very moment).

---

[10]   An initial read-through of Paul's text here will serve the function, for the reader/juror, of "direct examination" of a defendant in court, which is the defendant's direct, or first, testimony. In court, it's followed by "cross-examination," which is the questioning of this witness by the opposed attorney, the prosecutor. The reason why the reader here is advised to view Paul's testimony before reading the cross-examination of his testimony (which is to follow herein) is that this will provide the reader a closer approximation to a juror's experience in court. In some

Paul's Opening Greetings to His Friends

As was the custom with letters (or "epistles"), *Galatians* opens abruptly, with 1:1, a succinct identification of the letter's writer. He is:

1:1 [From] Paul, whose call to be an apostle came not via man or by means of man, but via Jesus Christ and God the Father, who raised him from the dead.

Right off the bat, Paul simultaneously prepares the way here for FOUR of his important strategic objectives, each of which he will develop throughout the letter:

First, he's saying that his own status as an "apostle" comes via the authority of not MERE MORTAL MEN, but of both God and Christ. Note especially that, right away, Paul has here, implicitly, CORRECTLY identified his target market (his readership whom he aims to convince) as consisting of RELIGIOUS people: people for whom the most persuasive forms of alleged evidence are *not* natural ("from man or by means of man"), but rather *supernatural* (supposed miracles, in this case by God and Christ). He starts off by asserting his own claimed

---

instances, in a courtroom, the defense attorney returns and this witness is questioned yet a third time, in "redirect," which is a defense attorney's elicitation from the defendant of testimony to undo any potential damage to the defendant's case that might have been engendered by the prosecution's cross-examination of him. Scholars have served that function of redirect, even though there hasn't yet been (until what you are about to read here) any cross-examination of Paul's testimony. Scholars have presented what they think Paul would have said in response to what they think might be misunderstandings of his testimony. Some footnotes that will follow here reply to such redirect. Thus, the reader can experience fairly completely a modern court proceeding into Christianity's creation.

Since this evidence is a document instead of actual oral testimony, there's no issue here regarding a defendant's right to refuse to testify. Paul's testimony, the direct examination of this witness, already exists and has been entered into evidence. What has not existed till now is the witness's cross-examination, which is here.

authority to speak for Jesus ON THIS SPECIFIC BASIS; that is to say, on the basis of his target-audience's underlying religious, rather than scientific, EPISTEMOLOGY (or criteria for determining truth/falsity). (As a juror, you'll examine this line in *Galatians* for yourself, and commit yea or nay on your concurrence with this observation about it, before proceeding any further. Throughout, the comments made here are only statements about the evidence, and aren't themselves evidence. These comments are intended only to *assist* you in your reading/understanding of the evidence, *nothing more*. Paul's text is itself the *evidence* being examined, and – for you – *only* you can interpret it. Someone *else's* interpretation, such as that of either the prosecuting attorney or the defense attorney, can, at best, only *assist* you, by calling your attention to, or else explaining, particular aspects of the evidence. To the extent that any attorney does more, it's improper: either distracting or outright deceptive. A judge is supposed to prohibit that.) The underlying assumption he is putting forth here – what he is implying without explicitly asserting – is that supernatural authorization is better, of better quality, more authoritative, than natural authorization ("by man, or by means of man"). Paul is here implicitly claiming supernatural authority from his now-popularly-referred-to "Damascus road experience" of the Risen Christ that he mentions later in 1:16, and that Paul also mentions in *1 Corinthians* 9:1, 11:23-25 & 15:3-11; and *2 Corinthians* 12:1-7; and that's further described in *Acts* 9:3-9, 22:6-21 & 26:12-18.[11] This claim of supernatural authorization immediately distinguishes Paul's authority as being (from the standpoint of his religious target market) allegedly *superior* to

---

[11]   Some scholars debate whether all of these passages refer to the same experience. Nothing in any of the passages indicates that they do not. (Later herein will be discussed some of the differences between these passages, differences that reflect, among other things, the different stages in Paul's own development as he looked back upon events in his life, but no actual differences in the event that these particular passages refer to.) However, proving a negative (such as that these passages don't refer to different experiences; that they all refer to the *same* experience) is so difficult as to be often impossible. [continued]

that of the people whom he'll soon be implicitly identifying as his opponents, whose apostleship is assumedly MERELY "from man or by means of man." Paul's position here is, indeed, an extraordinarily authoritative one to present to such a religious audience, for whom Jesus's disciples, who knew the man "in the flesh" rather than *purely* "from [the resurrected] Jesus Christ and God the Father who raised Him from death," would thus stand in a far less authoritative position. Paul understood the importance of identifying and appealing to his target market, even though the field of technical marketing research didn't exist until thousands of years later. He exhibits here a sophisticated intuitive understanding of the marketing challenge he faced, and of how to overcome it. As a person who admittedly had never met the living Jesus, Paul needed somehow to overcome the authority, about Jesus, that could be wielded by his opponents who *did* know Jesus "from man or by means of man." Paul, after all, was only a relative late-comer to joining the group – he had joined it only after Jesus's

---

Challenging the widespread view that all of these passages refer to the same alleged event provides a means by which scholars become enabled to add unnecessary confusions to the reading of the evidence. These unnecessary confusions are superfluous assumptions. The only purpose they serve is to empower each scholar to attack any interpretation with which he happens to disagree. The methodological rule that will be followed here is instead to *minimize* the number of assumptions. The hypothesis that these passages refer to different alleged events increases the number of assumptions. To increase the number of assumptions beyond what's necessary in order to explain things is to violate the earliest-established rule of science, which is known as Occam's razor. Among the legal/forensic applications of Occam's razor is the principle asserting that irrelevant (or "immaterial") evidence or assumptions aren't admissible. Irrelevant information can be prejudicial, and is not informative in any way that's acceptable to a court in a democracy.

No assumption will be made here that Paul encountered or claimed to have encountered Jesus's ghost on only a single occasion. This might have been so, or it might not. Whether or not Paul claimed to have met Jesus's ghost on more than one occasion is irrelevant to our reading of the evidence. It's immaterial to the theory of the case that is to be presented here.

All that will be assumed regarding the matter at hand is that Paul alleged to have joined the Jesus-following group as a consequence of having encountered Jesus's ghost. That's how we're interpreting this part of *Galatians* 1:1.

death, whereas the disciples were members and had
supported Jesus while Jesus was alive. Paul immediately faces
this immense challenge head-on: right at the letter's start, he
implicitly *acknowledges* lacking his opponents' kind of
authority; while, IN THE SAME BREATH, he also implicitly places
his authority ABOVE that, as purely supernatural and even
divine in character, supposedly uncorrupted by matters of the
flesh. This is a very important tactic for Paul's persuasive
purposes. At the letter's start, where, by custom, the writer
was to identify himself, he identifies himself as having
received his authority directly from God and Christ, and not
at all from any man. As we'll soon see, this assertion of purely
divine authorization will be repeated/reinforced numerous
times in *Galatians*. Modern marketing, both research and
practice, likewise recognizes the crucial effectiveness of
repetition. So, the first thing that Paul is doing in this opening
line is to *distinguish himself from his competitors*, by means of
carefully chosen words that implicitly place him at a
competitive advantage in the eyes of his target market. Scholars
don't mention such things as Paul's "target market," or
"competitive advantage," but no legal/forensic analysis can
proceed by thus ignoring a letter-writer's intended audience
or target market, and what he's selling or trying to achieve,
and how he's doing it. The standards of a court of law within
a democracy are set by science, and not by less-demanding
mere scholarship. So, the target market, and the means of
competitive advantage, are discussed here, because this
investigation has to be scientific[12] for legal-forensic standards.

---

[12]   Similarly, a court of law restricts as narrowly as possible any reliance upon
"expert opinion," and attempts, as much as possible, to empower the jurors to
decide upon the basis of only the facts that are presented to them during the
course of the trial. (It's like physicists or chemists describing the experimental
situation they had employed in their experiment, so that their readers in a technical
journal can replicate the experiment for themselves and verify the results which are
there being reported. Readers and jurors are thus empowered to make their
judgments on the basis of facts, not of *anyone's* opinions.) "Experts" are brought in,
for example, to authenticate documents, but *not* to interpret them – the latter
function (interpretation) must be as unprejudiced as possible, and can be done only
by the jurors themselves, and only upon the basis of the evidence (facts) set forth

during the trial. Interpretation is the jurors' job. Sometimes, but rarely, jurors are sequestered to enforce this avoidance of prejudicial outside input. Any field of science relies upon the individual to interpret findings *on his own*. A theoretician merely offers an interpretation to consider as possibly fitting the facts, and must base his theory not upon *other people's* theories (which may be false, or may even be based upon tampered "evidence" that hasn't been admitted by the court into evidence), but upon *only* the facts of the case (the evidence that the court *has* authenticated). In legal/forensic practice, just as in all other areas of scientific practice, a clear distinction is thus drawn between opinions and facts. Opinions (theories) are never facts, but are instead to be formulated *upon the basis of* facts; "an unprejudiced trial" consists of exactly this.

Consequently, *no one's* opinions regarding what Paul meant are cited as evidence in the present work. Only Paul's statements are cited here as *evidence* regarding that. A legal/forensic presentation of the evidence must be restricted to *only* the evidence, and not to anything that might prejudice jurors' opinions *about* the evidence. The judge's function in a trial is to police this, to enforce scientific standards in the courtroom; and the function of both the prosecuting and the defense attorneys is to behave in accord with that. The prosecuting attorney is supposed to present facts which he believes support the defendant's guilt (this is the prosecutor's theory of the case); the defense attorney is supposed to present facts which he believes support the defendant's innocence (which is the defense attorney's theory of the case); and jurors, having been presented with both sets of facts (which usually include much crossover between them – facts both sides find necessary for their respective presentations), are then supposed to make the *ultimate determination* as to the defendant's guilt or innocence, applying the given standard of proof.

The highest standard of proof that's required in any courtroom is that of a criminal trial, in which the defendant is presumed innocent unless proven guilty "beyond a reasonable doubt." This doesn't mean that a defendant has to be proven guilty beyond *any* doubt; a scientist recognizes that *absolute* certainty exists *only* in such fields as mathematics, and *never* in empirical matters. [continued]

So, a court of law in a democracy strives to produce judgments that are entirely warranted by the epistemology recognized as being science. And this is the objective here, where you are the jury, I am Paul's prosecutor, and scholars have already performed the function of Paul's defense attorneys (who have, however, routinely *broken* court rules by citing not just Paul but each others' opinions as "evidence"). (Whether scholars intentionally performed this pro-Pauline function is immaterial; they've performed it, and their interpretations execute it.)

In this trial, the prosecuting attorney has accepted, at the start, what the defense attorneys have previously identified as constituting the best evidence, and diverges from them in actually *applying* their choice in this regard – which has not previously been done, not even by themselves.

As regards what the prosecutor aims here to prove beyond a reasonable doubt, it is, in brief, this: Paul was a traitor to the cause of Jesus, whom he never knew, and was a traitor to the billions of people Paul deceived in his own and subsequent generations to believe that they were followers of Jesus, when they

Second, in this same line, Paul separates Jesus from all
men, and thus, especially, from Jesus's true apostles (the
people who were Jesus's followers during his lifetime, who
will soon appear here as Paul's opponents). Paul presents
Jesus as being different from other humans: part of God. Paul
does this by explicitly introducing the DUALITY of God, in the
Father and the Son. This is a remarkable concept that he
restates in 1:3; and more explicitly in 1:16, 2:20, and 4:4. He'll
add yet the THIRD Trinitarian element, of Spirit (the Holy
Ghost), in 3:14, 4:6, 5:16-18, 5:22, 5:25, and 6:8. But, even in this
letter's FIRST line, Paul is already going BEYOND the Jewish
unitary monotheistic God, to a dualistic God, in which Paul's
"Christ" transcends being merely a prophet who RECEIVES the
Law (like Moses; or, conceivably here, like Jesus's own
authentic APOSTLES, Paul's opponents, could become); and
Jesus, as Paul's "Christ," is here JOINED TO GOD HIMSELF as,
essentially, the co-lawgiver or otherwise the direct CO-GRANTOR
of covenant (or of God's agreement with, and promise to,
God's people). Paul thus is enabled to cast himself as being
this new covenant's DIRECT RECIPIENT (through his supposed
Damascus-road "revelation" of "Christ"), bypassing his
opponents' authority from the living Jesus "from man or by
means of man." Why, then, does Paul grant his "Christ" godly
co-authority, along with the Jewish God the Father? Nothing
LESS than such a Pauline claim for this "Christ" can provide
Paul's "Christ" the degree of authority that's required in order
for Him to be able to authorize Paul to speak (or here, write)
for Him and for God (such as Paul will do in the climactic line,
2:16). Paul's sole alleged authorization came from this Christ
after Jesus's death (Paul's claimed personal conversion-event),
and so cannot possess any higher status than does *that* Christ,
the supposed *after-death* Jesus. Paul needed to boost this
"Christ" as high as possible, and that meant for this Risen
Christ to adjoin God. That split of the Jewish God into at least

---

were actually followers of Paul. Paul is now on the witness stand being cross-
examined on this charge.

two parts will thus construct the essential platform from which Paul will be enabled, ultimately in *Galatians* 2:16, to overthrow the Jewish covenant, the Law of God. No MERE prophet *possesses* such high authority; nor did Jesus's apostles, Paul's foes, possess the authority to replace, or even to change, the covenant, nor did they claim such authority; Paul was here actually manufacturing that authority for Jesus, as the worshipped "Christ,"[13] precisely so as to enable Paul to sell his own (and, as we'll see, equally manufactured) "*gospel* of Christ," by representing himself as this Christ's supposedly chosen (by no less than God and Christ) "apostle." In Islam, EVEN Mohammed is never claimed to have possessed an authority to SUPERSEDE God's laws/commandments given in the covenant. Paul is here implying that Christ Himself DID; and, subsequently, Paul will even make that claim for Christ explicit. Paul will (in *Galatians* 2:16 and 3:10-14, as well as in *Romans* 3:24&26) present a God who replaces His previous covenant with a new one in which the sole requirement is to have faith in His Son. Yet this Son is, miraculously, also an actual part in Himself, and so this God will, supposedly, be demanding faith in Himself, but ONLY THROUGH one's having

---

[13]   There exists no evidence from *prior* to Paul that indicates belief in Jesus's divinity. Although some scholars (such as Larry Hurtado) assume that this belief went all the way back to Jesus's time, no evidence prior to Paul exists or has ever been cited for that (unfounded) assumption. The assumption is routinely made that Paul was a follower of whomever Jesus appointed, or of whomever was serving, as the Jesus-group's leader. That, too, is an unfounded assumption, and it's coextensive with the unfounded assumption that Paul was, in this and other passages, merely representing the views of that person (which the myth says was Peter) in his attributing divinity to Jesus, and didn't himself *invent* Jesus's divinity. No consistent understanding of the New Testament has ever resulted from these and other unfounded assumptions about Christianity's start. A consistent understanding of the New Testament will result here from *eliminating* unnecessary assumptions – such as that Jesus was worshipped prior to Paul, or that Paul wrote with an entirely honest intention to inform, rather than with a sometimes dishonest intention to persuade, his readers. No court of law in a democracy can accept such unfounded, prejudicial, assumptions. Myths, not history, are based upon them. This is a work of history, not of myth. Paul was the first person to assert Jesus's divinity. As we shall see, he did it very carefully, so as to minimize its being noticed during his own time. This permitted him to go about collecting Gentiles, while he avoided, as much as possible, generating adverse attention from Jews.

faith in His Son. Therefore, Jews, who worship MERELY the
Father (and, in Judaism, *even* the mashiach wasn't supposed to
be WORSHIPPED, since that would violate the First of the Ten
Commandments), but who don't worship ALSO the Son (i.e.,
Paul's NON-Jewish version of "the Messiah" in the personage
of Christ), are consequently NOT accepted by this Diune, even
if not as yet Triune, now distinctively *Christian* God. This will
place unconverted, or *non*-Christian, Jews, *outside of salvation*
according to Paul's new Christian faith. Paul hasn't yet stated
this here; he has, however, here laid two important
FOUNDATIONS for it: first, that he, Paul, possesses the highest
authority to speak (or, here, write) for Christ; and, second, that
Christ's authority is sufficient to consign NON-Christian Jews
to damnation. Furthermore, it's also important to note that, by
means of Paul's construction of this "Christ" as a component
in a multi-parted, Diune or even Triune, God, Paul has also
separated Jesus from his disciples, Paul's own opponents, and
simultaneously has, yet again, claimed FOR HIMSELF an
especially privileged, purely supernatural, authority, by
which he, Paul, can represent (or speak and write for) this
now-*godly* version of the historical Jesus. All of this, and we're
still only partway through 1:1! That's how packed with
"subliminal sell" Paul's writings actually were.

    Third, and connected to the point just discussed, Paul
here is implicitly challenging the Jewish covenant, the very
same covenant that he'll be explicitly *overthrowing* in 2:16
when he says that "a person wins God's approval only by
means of Christ-faith, never by obeying God's
commandments." He does this here by implicitly violating the
four parts of the first three of the Ten Commandments (*Exodus*
20:3-7; *Deut.* 5:7-11), which he does by placing "Jesus Christ
and God the Father" (his Diune pair) in one and the same
category as *joint* suppliers of his own authority or commission
to be an "apostle." The covenant-violations in this line are
direct against the First and Third Commandments, and are
indirect, merely door-openers to such direct violations, in
respect to both of the two parts of the Second Commandment

("Do not make idols," and "Do not pray in front of idols").
That is to say: In this line, Paul directly violates the First
Commandment against having other gods (such as "the Son"
or Paul's deified "Jesus Christ"),[14] indirectly violates the
Second Commandment's first provision, against making
images of God (such as of the crucified Christ), and the
Second Commandment's second provision, against bowing in
prayer before such idols; and then he yet again directly
violates the Third Commandment against misnaming the one
unitary God (via Paul's *renaming* it into those two, Diune,
parts, of Father and Son, as being his own *co*-authorizers,
which the *mono*theistic Jewish faith could never accept). This
is, therefore, in total, an extremely severe break with Judaism
or "the Law"; which is to say, violation against the covenant
that *constitutes* Judaism. Essentially, Judaism's monotheism is
here being challenged twice outright, and twice yet again by
means of door-openers to the making of idols, and then to the
use of idols in worship as intermediaries or symbols of God –
both of which Judaism roundly condemns, and which
Christianity readily and quickly instituted as Christian
practice, such that Christians everywhere today take for
granted as routine both kinds of violations of the Second
Commandment. (In keeping with the Second and Third
Commandments, Jews were prohibited even from
pronouncing God's name; so, it was spelled "YHWH," to be
as unpronounceable as possible.) Consequently, even in this

---

[14]   Notice that he says here "Jesus Christ *and* God the Father," not "Jesus
Christ *or* God the Father." The word for "or" existed in his language, and he used it
elsewhere (such as a few lines later, 1:8, "we or an angel"), but Paul is very clear
here that his authorization came from *both*. If Paul had used the word "or" here,
one might reasonably infer he meant it in the sense of "that is to say," the sense of
"otherwise known as," the sense of two names for one individual, the sense of
synonyms, as opposed to the other common sense, "either/or"; but he chose not to
do that. He chose to indicate here that he was authorized by two gods, each of
which possessed full authority to say yes or no to his appointment, and each of
which agreed with the other that he was to be appointed. So: as a logical certainty,
these are two gods, not one, he was referring to. Furthermore, he says "God the
Father, who raised him from the dead," and thus clearly, yet again, refers to two
deities, not to one: the Father *raised* the Son from the dead.

his introductory line, Paul is implicitly and very strongly casting down the gauntlet to "the Law" (including the Ten Commandments) which he will more *explicitly* attack in the climax that will be forthcoming, in 2:16.

Fourth, there's yet MORE in this meaning-compressed line: Paul's crucial *emphasis* upon Jesus's DEATH, as opposed to his life, appears at the line's end ("the Father, who raised Him from the dead"). This emphasis also REINFORCES in a very subtle way the FIRST-mentioned point: namely, that Paul in this letter will be presuming to his readers that his OWN knowledge of *only* the Resurrected Christ (UNCONTAMINATED by knowledge of the living Jesus "from man or by means of man") is superior to, or takes PRECEDENCE over, his opponents' knowledge that includes and is supposedly contaminated by their having known the living Jesus. However, whereas that first distinction categorizes supernaturally acquired knowledge as being superior to naturally acquired knowledge, this distinction focuses instead on Jesus's death as being more important for winning a person's salvation than was His life. Paul is implicitly anticipating, here in his opening line, a key feature of his Christianity (subsequently to be explicitly stated by him in the climax, 2:16-2:21), which is the centrality of Christ's death to the believer's personal salvation in heaven; Jesus's life is not. Paul is, thus, *and in yet another way*, implying that his *purely* after-death contact with Christ places Paul in a privileged position to represent this *purely godly*, and supremely salvific, Christ. Paul's theological emphasis upon the higher salvific importance of Christ's Crucifixion/Resurrection than upon that of His life and words, might help to explain why Paul's letters said only little about the latter, even though there existed plenty of stories then-circulating about Jesus's life that Paul could have picked up on and parroted as an "apostle" if he had wanted to do so. Yet another reason, however, why Paul didn't, is simply that Paul knew, quite well, that, if he were to do so, then he would be competing against his opponents, the disciples, on terrain where it was *they*, and not he, who would possess the overwhelming advantage. He certainly didn't want[15] to precipitate a situation in which they would compete against him by pouring forth with voluminous first-person recollections of the historical Jesus, and of what he had said, since Paul simply couldn't compete against such living-Jesus authority. Moreover, it's striking that when Paul finally will reach the point to which he's building (2:16-21), he'll be referring solely to Jesus's death, and not at all to His life. Paul could have taught not only any PR/advertising executive, but any general in any war. One basic rule of war is to choose, if at all possible, the battleground where you have the greatest advantage, or at least the smallest disadvantage, as against your opponent. Paul did precisely that here. Not only is his Christ purer than what his opponents know and had known, but this is the *only* Christ that can save the reader a place in heaven.

So, Paul has said all of this – mainly by means of *implication* instead of by explicit assertion – in merely the first line of *Galatians*. Paul's sales-letter has, in four distinct ways, opened by positioning himself, and what he has to sell (which

---

15   Paul's motivations are sometimes stated explicitly by Paul, such as when he asserted, in *1 Corinthians* 9:24, "Compete so as to win," or asserted in *Galatians* 2:2, "I refused to lose," indicating, in both of those passages, a strong competitive motivation. However, even when Paul has explicitly asserted that he had a certain motivation, interpretation is necessary in order to attribute this motivation to him as part of his basic beliefs or personal constitution. Interpretation is needed even in order to determine whether such an explicit assertion by Paul was intended by him to inform, or to disinform/deceive. In other words, our saying here, that, "He certainly didn't want" to lose – where this describes Paul's personality or motivations, instead of a specific explicit statement that he made in the cited context – is *interpretive*; it's part of our theory of the case, part of our explanation of the events. It's not part of *Paul's description of events*. Paul did not *say*, in *Galatians* 1:1, that he was aiming to avoid precipitating his losing to his opponents. Instead, his argument *displayed* it. In legal/forensic practice, interpretation is just as necessary as it is in other fields of science.

        Scientists continually interpret reality; that's what a scientist is supposed to do. No science exists without theory, which is interpretation. Description is one of two parts of what scientists do; the other part is interpretation, or theory. What distinguishes a scientific interpretation of reality, from a religious or faith-based one, is solely the epistemology: the criteria for truth-falsity.

he'll soon call his "gospel"), at a competitive advantage, as against his opponents. (The term "gospel," incidentally, meant "good news"; and most successful salesmen claim to be promoting *some* type of "good news.") What's especially interesting here is that in not just one but four different ways, Paul has, in this line, prepped his readers for the climax yet to come in 2:16-21, wherein he describes (after carefully veiled language in 2:1-2:15) the exact occasion on which Christianity (which he in 1:6-9 calls his "gospel") was actually *first asserted*, and wherein he essentially defines Christianity without using the term "Christianity."

(If the reader happens to have encountered other exegeses of *Galatians*, then note might be made here that the present analysis differs from others in its methodology,[16] and

---

[16]   Above all, the explanation that you've just read of the meaning of this, the first line in *Galatians*, doesn't (1) make any reference to opinions which have been written by others about what this line means, and (2) assume that what Paul is saying is true or even honest.

My rejection of the routine scholarly practice, in which they employ, within their interpretations of a given textual passage, the interpretive opinions that have previously been expressed by other scholars regarding the passage, has elicited contempt from scholars. Whenever I have asked a given scholar to explain to me the reason for this reaction, none has answered, and this has greatly puzzled me.

My rejection of the assumption that Paul wrote truthfully and honestly has likewise elicited from scholars contempt, and sometimes even anger. Though I am not assuming that Paul wrote falsely or dishonestly – though I instead insist upon there being no assumption at all on this – scholars have simply assumed that Paul was both truthful and honest, and they demand that I start with that same assumption. However, to start with that assumption is to start with the assumption that Paul was right and that his opponents were wrong in the conflict that Paul is referring to. Scholars have been advocates for Paul, and they will not allow him to be challenged. They insist that Paul's opponents have no lawyer to represent them. They insist upon a kangaroo court.

In any event, the ultimate judgment as to what Paul is saying here rests with you, the juror, and not with me, nor with anyone else. The interpretation of what Paul means here is being explained via statements that Paul made, and secondarily via statements from *Acts* and other sources which were less reliable about Paul, which here supplement Paul's evidence about Paul. In the present line from *Galatians*, as in all lines of Paul's text, you are the only ultimate interpreter, and (as was previously noted) I am merely providing assistance to a juror who is performing his interpretive job. My hope is to enrich each line of Paul's text by

not in its translation. Although translation issues will occasionally be raised, in applying legal/forensic methodology to *Galatians*, the difference between this exegesis and others lies not in the translation, but in that methodology itself, as our footnotes explain. In fact, though the interpretation you have just read of 1:1 is worlds away from any previous one, no translation-issues whatsoever separate it from those others; only methodology does.)

> *1:2 And [this letter comes also from] all brethren who are with me, [and it is addressed] to the churches ["ekklesiais"] in Galatia:*

1:2 tells his readers that they have presumably numerous "brothers" in Paul's operation, and, thus, that his

---

means of pointing out other lines from Paul (and sometimes from the other, lesser, evidence) that might possibly help to clarify what Paul is conveying here. Also (and also as has been noted), wherever appropriate, I cite lines from the Torah, the Jewish Scripture, which evidently constituted the reference-points or authorities for the members of Jesus's movement. Sometimes, Paul explicitly cited as his authority passages from the Torah; but, in other instances, such as has been pointed out here regarding this first line, Paul didn't explicitly refer to any Torah-passage, but instead he actually violated some of the Ten Commandments, which are within the Torah. All of these matters are facts, which you, as the juror, have access to and can verify in your Bible, which here is treated no differently than any other group of written works or documents are routinely treated in a court of law in a democracy; i.e., as evidence, neither more nor less. Although I am also presenting my own interpretive opinions here, I am doing all I can to construct those opinions, brick-by-brick, only from the evidence, and never from anyone else's interpretive opinions, since no one's interpretive opinions are evidence; only evidence is evidence. Even if scholars find this approach to be offensive, it is what a scientist routinely does whenever theorizing, or interpreting evidence; and this is the way that a court of law in a democracy is also supposed to produce verdicts.

A scientist tries to maximize the role of facts, and to minimize the role of interpretive opinions; and a court is supposed to do likewise. However, no scientist, and no legal/forensian, would deny the crucial role of interpretive opinions. The question therefore isn't whether interpretive opinions are necessary; they are. The question is whether those interpretations are based on the best evidence, or, contrarywise, whether they're based (in whole or in part) on other interpretive opinions (which aren't *evidence* at all). The building of interpretive opinions, upon other interpretive opinions, produces a conceptual pyramid scheme, no solidly grounded structure.

Galatian readers possess a substantial community there, amongst which the letter-writer himself is likewise a "brother" to these readers, and so is, in an important sense, a member of their very own personal family. If Paul's readers are ultimately going to be leaving the organization, the Jesus-following sect of Jews, that they originally joined, and to commit themselves instead to Paul's new, *non*-Jewish, religion (which he had conceived of about four years prior to this letter, at the incident that he'll be retelling here in 2:11-21), then they had better be sold on something that will be even MORE attractive to them than the Jewish sect Paul had originally sold to them. Paul here implicitly promises them precisely this. But there's also another important point made in this line, and this second issue is even more significant: Paul here greets these people not just as "brothers," but as "the EKKLESIAIS in Galatia"; and "EKKLESIA" was a very CAREFULLY selected term, which (as has previously been noted here with regard to *Matthew* 16:18) referred to ANY kind of assembly, Jewish or otherwise, though Christians today translate it as "church," as if it referred to a specifically Christian and specifically religious assembly, which isn't at all what the term referred to. (And Christianity, the doctrine that Paul will assert in 2:16-21, didn't even exist until the event that he'll be describing there; so equating "ekklesia" with Christianity is ahistorical, thoroughly false.) As we shall subsequently discuss in more detail, Paul's Galatian readers believed themselves to be members of the Jesus-sect of Jews, rather than of any NON-Jewish religion; these men (women didn't count in the value-system of that society: they couldn't own property; they *were* property – *of* men) had originally been converted by Paul to this Jewish sect. Christianity hadn't been invented until the event Paul will be describing in 2:11-21, an event that (as was mentioned) occurred only about four years prior to this letter; and *all* followers of Jesus, up till that time, were simply Jews. Not all of Jesus's followers had been born as Jews, but they all *were* Jews, because *only* Jews believed in the mashiach.[17] And yet these men, Paul's

---

[17]   The mashiach, or "Christ," had no reference outside of Judaism, and was solely a Jewish concept, because it was tied in with the restoration of the House of David reigning over an independent Israel. The very concept of the mashiach was simply nonsensical outside of Judaism. Thus, the followers of Jesus, being people who considered Jesus to *be* the mashiach, necessarily *believed in* Judaism; they *were* Jews; there was nothing else even *possible* for them to be.

A common false assumption, made by many scholars, is that the recipients of this letter, and the other followers of Jesus after his death, not only worshipped Jesus, in blatant violation of the first three of Judaism's Ten Commandments, but viewed themselves as constituting a "church" in something *other* than a Jewish sense; in other words, these scholars simply assume that Jesus's followers saw themselves not as constituting a synagogue or a Jewish sect, but as being instead already a different religion, *not* Judaism.

As with the common false assumption that Jesus was worshipped prior to the event that Paul refers to in *Galatians* 2:11-21, a legal/forensic analysis cannot support such a belief as an assumption, but must instead examine the evidence *without* prejudices.

In a court of law in a democracy, assumptions must meet various tests in order for an attorney to be permitted by the judge to present them to a jury, but these aren't tests that pertain in scholarship, and therefore scholarly writings about the start of Christianity are rife with such totally unfounded assumptions, as that the Jesus-followers constituted, already at that early time, a new religion. Scholars want to push it all the way back to Jesus, so that Christianity was started by Him. The contrary conclusion, to be presented here – that Christianity, as a new religion, started actually approximately twenty years after Jesus's death, and that it started specifically at the event Paul elliptically describes in *Galatians* 2:11-21 – isn't expected to be taken on faith, since a court of law in a democracy is based upon science instead of upon any faith at all. Instead of taking anything on faith, this conclusion will (as was explained in the Introduction) be derived from the evidence throughout *Galatians* and the New Testament and all of the other evidence that will be cited here, but especially from the best evidence of all, which is *Galatians*.

On 23 July 2007, Adam Liptak headlined in *The New York Times*, "Study of Wrongful Convictions Raises Questions Beyond DNA," and he reported that, "Brandon L. Garrett, a law professor at the University of Virginia, has, for the first time, systematically examined the 200 cases, in which innocent people served an average of 12 years in prison. In each case, of course, the evidence used to convict them was at least flawed and often false – yet juries, trial judges and appellate courts failed to notice. 'A few types of unreliable trial evidence predictably supported wrongful convictions,' Professor Garrett concluded in his study, 'Judging Innocence,' to be published in the Columbia Law Review in January. The leading cause of the wrongful convictions was erroneous identification by eyewitnesses, which occurred 79 percent of the time." Overwhelmingly, the false convictions occurred against minorities; personal prejudices played a big role. Historians who seek to get beyond scholarship, to reach science, will acknowledge that they too must eliminate their prejudices. Courts in democracies are constantly improving their legal/forensic methods and so reducing the ambit for prejudice. It's hard-won scientific progress.

That study showed the intrinsic unreliability of witness evidence: witnesses' prejudices or personal agendas enter too readily into the answers they give. This is why witnesses are cross-examined in court. However, until recent decades, no comparable legal/forensic methodology existed for testing the truthfulness of, and interpreting, written evidence – documentary evidence – such as the documents that comprise the New Testament.

Only after about 1950 did the types of legal/forensic methods that are being applied in the present work start to be applied, in the analysis of white-collar-crime cases, contract disputes, and other primarily business-related cases. Before that time, the old purely faith-based, scholarly, approaches to reconstructing a sequence of events from documentary evidence pertaining to them, were rarely challenged anywhere. Only starting in the late 18th and early 19th Centuries did faith-based "history," of the start of Christianity, so much as *begin* to be even questioned. The concept of "white collar crime" didn't even exist before it was introduced in 1939 by sociologist Edwin Sutherland. When Yale University Press in 1983 finally issued the uncensored version of his classic 1949 *White Collar Crime*, the Introduction by Gilbert Geis said that Sutherland's having discovered the concept of "white-collar crime" had "altered the study of crime throughout the world in fundamental ways." Legal/forensic methods of analyzing documentary evidence began to develop and to be applied in courtrooms starting with the trials of war criminals at the Nuremberg Military Tribunals in 1945-49, and started being applied in U.S. courts during the following decade. From that time to this, these methods have not yet been applied to the reconstruction of historical events, by historians. But now, methodologies that have previously been applied to those white-collar-crime cases are finally being applied to reconstruct how a major historical event occurred, rather than how an alleged criminal violation of law occurred.

Paul's letter to the Galatians doesn't *say* that he's trying to switch them from the Judaism he had originally sold to them, to an entirely new faith, Christianity. Instead, it *demonstrates* this, as will here be argued.

If a juror were to challenge a lawyer's theory of the case, then clearly, mine here could be challenged as blasphemy, which, for any juror who did that, would settle the entire matter, and the trial would effectively be over before it could even begin. But how could scholars' cases defending Paul be challenged? Scholars haven't been united on their theory of the case defending Paul, but his defenders have all agreed on one central thing: Paul didn't start Christianity, and this means that converts to Christianity worshipped Jesus as a god even before Paul entered the picture. A juror could thus challenge any one of those lawyers: What meaning are you assuming that the concept of the Messiah possessed for these Gentile converts? What evidence will you offer that any concept of the Messiah at that time even existed, at all, outside of Judaism, to provide a specifically *non*-Jewish framework for these converts to be able to interpret or understand Jesus? What evidence can you provide for your assumption that these converts didn't, in fact, think of themselves as *being* Jews? Since you assume that they weren't Jews, what do you think that they were saying to Jews whom they tried to convince to convert to their new, supposedly *non*-Jewish, religion? How will

audience, weren't OFFENDED here to be referred to collectively by Paul's term ("*ekklesiais*") which represented, to them, ANY kind of assemblies, not just synagogues, but even NON-religious assemblies, such as political assemblies. In other words, these men simply weren't aware, when Paul addressed them as an *ekklesia*, that he was intending to remove their synagogue or Jewish designation and change them to an entirely new religion, which he had started only about four years earlier. The care in Paul's word-selection here is exhibited especially by Paul's having NOT referred to these people as constituting *sunagoge* (which they actually WERE) in Galatia, which would have, gratuitously AGAINST Paul's core strategic objectives, REMINDED his readers of their own chosen pre-existing JEWISH identities – identities to which he, Paul, had converted them. A *sunagoge* referred SPECIFICALLY to a *Jewish* religious assembly. It was a Jewish *ekklesia*. Paul's followers knew themselves as being members of a *sunagoge* started by Jesus (into which Paul had inducted them), but Paul doesn't employ that term here; and the reason he doesn't want to remind them that they're Jews is that Paul is now aiming to *remove them* from Judaism; he had only recently created Christianity, the doctrine to be explicitly stated in *Galatians* 2:16-21. This letter concerns Paul's transitioning these men from Jesus's Jewish sect to Paul's entirely new "church," the religion that believes in the profoundly non-Judaic – even *anti*-Judaic – 2:16-21. Paul has to do this inconspicuously so that

---

your theory of the case account for the cagey language that Paul employed, such as his using "*ekklesia*" instead of "*threskeia*" or "*sunagoge*" when referring to the group (as will immediately be discussed herein)?

If a hoax exists, it's not overcome by merely *wishing* it didn't. It's overcome *only* by science, specifically in this case by legal/forensic methods of analysis of the evidence. And if a hoax doesn't exist, then science won't threaten anything, but will instead simply confirm allegations. No allegation can be confirmed without first being tested by scientific means. That's what a court is supposed to do – test assertions – and that's what *any* scientific profession is *supposed* to do.

Only frauds and follies are threatened by science.

they don't know it's even happening. (If they had noticed that
it were happening, then Paul's effort would have failed; his
opponents would have won. Paul thus needed to be extremely
careful.) Similarly (as has been noted), Paul's follower who
subsequently wrote *Matthew* 16:18, also placed into the mouth
of Christ Himself the founding of an "EKKLESIA," so as to avoid
there explicit ACKNOWLEDGMENT that what the historical Jesus
had ACTUALLY founded, which everyone even in Matthew's
relatively late time knew to have been the case, was a *Jewish
sect*. It could have been called, by Matthew's Christ, a
SUNAGOGE, but this would have destroyed forever the FUTURE
myth that Jesus had founded a separate, NON-Jewish, religion;
and thus, the avoidance of "*sunagoge*," here, displayed the
intentions of Paul and of his follower who wrote *Matthew* to
fool FUTURE generations, rather than just their own. It COULDN'T
have been called by Matthew's Christ a THRESKEIA, meaning
actually a religion, because then everyone, in Matthew's *own*
generation, would have recognized that 16:18 was a
FRAUDULENT "Jesus"-statement. Everyone, even in that
relatively late era, knew that Jesus hadn't founded any
THRESKEIA. (In fact, if Jesus had ever broken from Judaism, he
would thereby automatically have renounced any claim to be
the mashiach, since only a Jew could even *qualify* to be the
mashiach: according to the legend, God would never anoint a
person who wasn't one of God's people to be the leader of
God's people.) The avoidance of "*threskeia*" here thus
exhibited their intentions to fool the people of their own time.
Matthew's word-choice of "*ekklesia*" was safe, for him, because
Paul had EARLIER used the same word, in a similar context,
successfully, such as here. Thus, Paul truly invented the fraud
that Jesus had founded Christianity as a separate, non-Jewish,
religion;[18] his followers merely EXPANDED upon it. (Paul will

---

[18]   A typical example of scholars simply *assuming* that Paul was *honest* and
that Jesus started the Christian "Church" instead of a Jewish sect, is Duke
University's James M. Efird, who published in 1980 his introductory New Testament
textbook, *The New Testament Writings: History, Literature and Interpretation*, which
stated on its very first page: "The church itself came into existence as a result of
certain events which took place in Palestine basically in the early years of the

present era, ca. 25-30 A.D. Those events revolved around the life and ministry of a man from Galilee, Jesus from Nazareth." (Efird made no note that, even in the original Greek of the myth, this "church" which Jesus allegedly founded was merely an assembly, *not* – as Efird's gulls would naturally assume – a religion.) Among the recommended "New Testament Introductions" listed at that book's end is his fellow Duke professor James L. Price's 1961 *Interpreting the New Testament*, which starts its first page: "The interpretation of the career of one man gave rise to the Christian Church and sustains its mission in the world today. Who was he, this Jesus who is called the Christ?" (Again, "Church" there went unexplained.) In both works, the assumption is baldly made that Jesus, and not Paul, started Christianity – though the question of when and how he did this, is ignored, simply not discussed, so that the reader is left with what the Gospels say, as constituting "history" on those subjects. If scholarship were at all scientific, then there would be no assumption whatsoever regarding the identity of the first Christian and the founder of the Christian faith. Such matters would instead be addressed without prejudices. Leaving those issues to be decided upon the basis of inferior evidence – in this case, the Gospel accounts – violates the best-evidence principle. Those authors opened by implicitly validating the Gospel accounts *as though* those documents constituted the best evidence available on this matter – an assumed *falsehood*.

One of the most influential scholars leading up to the "New Perspective on Paul" was C.H. (or Charles Harold) Dodd, who started his career at Oxford, and ended it retiring from Cambridge; and whose final book (1970) was *The Founder of Christianity*, which dealt not with Paul, but with Jesus, as that supposed "Founder."

Even in the rare instances where a particular Scriptural writer's honesty is placed in question, the *assumption* is made that any shading of truthfulness is done to serve a high purpose, not for a selfish reason. (See, for example, Mark D. Given's 2001 *Paul's True Rhetoric: Ambiguity, Cunning, and Deception*, which assumes that Paul wanted only to be the best teacher he could.)

If the students of those professors had known that they were studying in a glorified Sunday school, instead of in a scientifically respectable institution, then would those students have registered in those courses? Probably not. But some of them graduated and became the following generation of "authorities" overseeing the Ph.D.'s of yet the next generation, transmitting the same unexamined assumptions.

And so it goes; and so this hoax continues generation after generation. At the present point in our argument, a juror would neither accept it nor reject it, but would instead recognize when an assumption (such as by those scholars, that Jesus's followers considered themselves to be members of a new religion, rather than to be Jews) is actually *unsupported* by evidence; and would consider the evidence carefully; and, finally, would formulate conclusions upon *only* the evidence, not upon *any* prejudices at all.

The use here of such terms as "fraud" and "hoax" to describe what Paul has done isn't asserting that this conclusion is, *as of yet*, proven in accord with whatever may be the requisite standard of proof, but is, instead, asserting only that the theory of the case that is here being presented will explain what Paul has done implicitly tell us, in *Galatians* 2:11-16, when and where he did it; and, in 2:1-10, why. Then, in 2:16-21, he'll state the new religion – what it believes, which hasn't changed in 2,000 years.)

1:3 May you all be granted grace and peace by God our Father, and by the Lord Jesus Christ,

1:3, as previously mentioned, reinforces God's Duality (Father and Son). Again, Paul makes the Jewish God, God the Father, co-equal with Jesus in authorizing Paul. In addition, Paul here pretends to be in a position to communicate to his readers the blessings from both. This, yet again, implies that Paul is the agent for his Diune God. Yet again, Paul is implying that his alleged encounter with Jesus's ghost conveyed, to Paul, a joint authorization from both God and Jesus.

1:4 Who sacrificed himself to free us from our sins during the present evil age, in accord with the plan of God the Father.

1:4, very subtly, anticipates or prepares the way for the coming climax in 2:16-21, Paul's assertion of what will REPLACE the Jewish covenant: it previews what Paul will subsequently refer to as his "gospel of Christ," or "gospel of the Messiah," which is (2:16-21) faith in the Messiah's or Christ's, crucifixion and Resurrection, as being the sole basis for personal salvation, "to free us from our sins," or to free believers from

---

(such as his using the term *ekklesia*) as being a part in a fraud, instead of as being (such as scholars merely assume) a part in an endeavor by Paul to describe truthfully the origins of Christianity.

In other words, any conclusional terms (e.g., "fraud") employed at this early stage in our presentation, at the very start of the argument, aren't claimed to be *proven*, as of yet, but are instead employed here *only* to describe our theory of the case. This book presents a large accumulation of facts, all from the best evidence; and the requisite proof will rely only upon that substantial accumulation of facts, which is here starting.

being punished by God for their sins. "Christ" is the English version of the Greek term, "Christos," for the Jewish mashiach, or Messiah, and Paul wrote in Greek; thus, from "Christos," we now have "Christ" and "Christianity." However, 1:4 doesn't employ the phrase "gospel of the Messiah" (or "gospel of Christ"); that phrase makes its entrance at the end of 1:7. What we're getting in 1:4 is just a quickie-version of that gospel's *definition* – Paul's initial statement of what he's selling (which will be more FULLY presented in 2:16-21). Notice especially that this preliminary version of the definition emphasizes that "Christ gave Himself," or was crucified, precisely "for our sins," which, in short form, is the preparatory part, within the coming lines 2:16-21, for Paul's conclusion in 2:21: "But if a person is put right with God through obedience to the Law, then Christ died for nothing!" By Paul's pre-encapsulating here his rationale, he's preparing the reader's mind to ultimately assent to the more-fully-developed case that he'll be presenting in 2:16-21. What Paul has to sell – his "gospel of Christ" – will be fully described in that climax.

Paul closes 1:4 by saying that the *reason* "Christ gave himself" was "obedience to the will of our God the Father," thus implying that the Father is the top God, above even Christ the Son; and Paul thereby communicates to his followers that Paul is no different from Jews: he places God at the very top. Paul carefully avoids mentioning a crucial fact – that Jews hold only one God, and that the Jews' god is not just unitary but has *no family at all.*[19]

---

[19] This refers, of course, to biblical Judaism, not to pre-biblical or purely tribal "Judaism," which was polytheistic. In Paul's time, Judaism was the biblical faith, not its polytheistic precursor. Jesus's followers worshipped the God of the Torah, and accepted the Torah as a work about history, and not merely as a myth. First Century Judaism was the monotheistic faith that is today known as "Judaism," but without any reformist or other modernistic sects: all varieties of Judaism in that era believed the Torah to be literally true.

Paul is implicitly contradicting himself here, by insinuating that God is at least diune, and by insinuating that God is unitary. Just as Paul is relying upon his market's religious and not scientific epistemology, he relies also upon his market's

1:5 To God alone belongs all glory, forever and ever! Amen.

1:5, equally subtly, reassures Paul's readers (who had thought that he had converted them to a Jewish sect) that the monotheistic unitary God, which they had originally been converted to worshipping, APPROVES of Paul's message – a message that is supposedly for this very same God's glory, in accord with Judaism's First Commandment (*Exodus* 20:3 and *Deuteronomy* 5:7). This, therefore, equally subtly, also reinforces in yet another way the point that was differently made in more than one way in 1:1, to the effect that Paul speaks for God. Paul, quite evidently, feels confident that his Gentile readers, whom he himself had brought into this Jewish sect, are thereby sufficiently unknowledgeable about Judaism, so that they won't even have noticed his Diune God in 1:1 and 1:3, as being in violation of Judaism, and thus in violation of the God he's honoring here in 1:5. The present line's end praises pointedly *only* God the Father, which is the Jewish God, unitary and *not* comprising within itself also the

---

insensitivity to self-contradiction. (One key feature of *scientific* epistemology is total sensitivity to logical structure. That's not a feature of the *opposite* epistemology: faith.) Consequently, Paul was directing this letter to people who didn't even notice the logical tension, if not outright internal contradiction, between the joint reliance upon both the Father and the Son that's exhibited in 1:3, versus the clear subordination of the Son to the Father that's exhibited in 1:4. To a scientist, this tension is immediately perceived, and is a likely sign that its author (Paul) is either stupid or manipulative. *Galatians* presents ample subsequent evidence, which will answer that question, as the juror will see.

Paul has claimed authorization *solely* via the Son, the Risen Jesus. Unlike such prophets as Abraham and Moses, no meeting with *God* was alleged regarding Paul. Consequently, given Paul's implicit acknowledgment in 1:4 that God is *supreme* over Christ, Paul hasn't even alleged authorization to be a prophet of, or message-carrier from, God; he never *met* God. And yet 2:16, the letter's climax, presents himself as being exactly that – he speaks there *for God*. The line that's immediately to follow here, 1:5, will help lay the groundwork for him to do that, even without his claiming any authorization *to represent* God, which would be the *logical prerequisite* for him to do it. Presumably, Paul thinks his audience won't have any idea what's going on here. He's relying simply upon their being people of faith, for him to be able to manipulate them toward his ends.

Son. Consequently, Paul's real message in this line is that *the God of Judaism* has no objection to, and is even glorified by, Paul's teachings. Paul is thereby using to his advantage his earlier teachings to these people, that the Jewish God is the *sole* judge and basis for a person's salvation. To employ the vernacular here (and with poetic license): Paul is now taking the Jewish God's knife, and stabbing it into the Jewish God's chest. (He's doing this in front of an audience of new Jews who wouldn't recognize the Jewish God even if it were to walk right up to them with that knife and command them: "Become circumcised!" So, Paul is safe to treat his people with such contempt: He had largely engineered the superficiality of their involvement with Judaism, and he now merely aims to harvest the fruits of their ignorance and gullibility – which he will harvest plenteously.)[20] Likewise, subsequently in the letter (e.g., 2:16), Paul will refer to salvation being based upon how God views a person, rather than upon how Christ, or the Son, does; the role that the Son will play in salvation is instead the Son's serving as the *object* of the believer's faith: the Father judges men, as in Judaism; but *what* He judges is whether or not a person has faith *in the Son*; that's to say, Christ-faith. This

---

[20]   No one who reads Scripture by applying faith to it is going to accept even the possibility that its author was a con-artist, but in a court of law in a democracy, jurors who have such prejudices regarding a defendant or other testifier (in this case, that Paul was *not* a con-artist) are supposed to be barred from serving on a jury. This lack of prejudice is the epistemological rule that is being applied here.

In a theocracy, prejudices are instead obligatory, and anyone who approaches things with an open mind is an anathema; faith is demanded of people, and the systematic skepticism that constitutes science is barred there. The object upon which faith is based is Scripture. Obviously, if a theocracy happens to be imposing the *Christian* faith, then taking Paul's testimony at face value is obligatory, since Paul's testimony is *in* Scripture. If a Christian theocracy exists, then the present investigation is banned there, simply because this investigation is *not* prejudiced.

In an aristocracy, prejudices are also obligatory, and everything depends not on Scripture but on genealogy and "who you know," so that a person's identity, rather than (as in a democracy) his behavior, determines the way he's treated; and the object upon which faith is based is "the right connections." Instead of a faith founded upon Scripture, it's a faith founded upon geneology: ancestor-worship. [continued]

will also distinguish the Christian version of salvation as
against salvation via adherence to Judaism's First
Commandment, which demands the believer's faith in the
Father, *not* in any Son. Judaism entails God-faith, *instead of*
Christ-faith. In fact, the Messiah, in Judaism, was *never* an
object to be worshipped. (Similarly, as was previously noted,
Mohammed is not an object to be worshipped in Islam:
Mohammed was presented as merely God's prophet, not as a
part of God.) To worship the mashiach would have violated
the first Three of the Ten Commandments. Jesus's disciples
would never have done such a thing, nor would any
purported mashiach have condoned doing it.[21] By contrast,

Mankind is proceeding through four successive phases: Prehistorical
(which we don't discuss), Tribal, Religious, and finally Scientific. The three historical
phases are distinguished from each other by their respective epistemologies. The
Tribal phase assigned authority to the aristocracy. The Religious phase assigns
authority to Scripture. The Scientific phase will deny that authority exists:
everything will be subject to a certain form of systematic skepticism, which is
science itself.

[21]   The reason is that the mashiach was always viewed as an *enforcer* of
God's Law, including of the First Commandment, which bans worship of *anyone*
but God, the Father. However, the mashiach wasn't actually important in Judaism,
not basic to the faith anyway. It was a strictly Jewish concept, *but not important
even in Judaism*. The mashiach isn't even mentioned at all in the Jewish Scripture,
the Torah, the Pentateuch, the first five books of the Bible – the scrolls that carry
Judaism and that occupy the position of honor in a synagogue. Some passages in
the later books of the Tanakh or Jewish Bible are said by scholars to be referring to
the mashiach, mainly in *Isaiah* 11, but even there he isn't to be worshipped, but is
merely to serve God as His anointed king, who is yet to come from David's line,
and who is to re-establish an independent Israel and then to conquer other nations
and to impose Judaism in every land he conquers; that is, to impose God's Law,
the commandments in the Torah (including, of course, the Ten Commandments),
over a wider realm. So, by definition, the mashiach was going to be a great
enforcer of God's Law, and certainly not someone who would *condone* people's
violating it – much less serve as some kind of justification himself for his supposed
followers to ignore God's Law. Paul's conception of the Christ went far outside
anything countenanced in Judaism. This is one reason why Paul won only few
followers from among Jews. But, until the event he recounted in *Galatians* 2:11-21,
which occurred in the year 49 or 50, Paul stayed within Judaism and preached the
mashiach, not Christ. So, it was only *after* this date that Paul bolted and became
isolated from, and was clearly rejected by, Jews. This will be documented here.
[continued]

But actually, the entire Old Testament never even once employs the *term* "Messiah," nor "Christ," nor any equivalent. The concept of the mashiach, in any form, was sufficiently insignificant in Judaism, so that even the Old Testament passages that scholars claim to be referring to the Messiah don't actually include any such word. The only *phrase* in the OT even close to the *term* (or *word*) "Christ" in Christianity is the Hebrew phrase "the anointed [one]," referring to God's anointed king, which appears thrice in *1 Samuel*, and once in *Psalms*. (It's in *1 Samuel* 2:10, 12:3, and 16:6; and also in *Psalms* 2:2.) That's all; this phrase doesn't appear anywhere in *Isaiah*, which is where Christians are most often referred as foretelling "Christ." Nor does it appear anywhere else – and it *never* appears in the entire Torah.

The reason why Jews in Jesus's time were far more interested in the mashiach than were Jews in previous eras, is that their land, Israel, was at that time militarily occupied by the Romans, and that the war that the Jewish historian Josephus called the biggest war in history was raging then between the Jews and this Roman occupying force. In other words, the mashiach (without being called "mashiach" or anything like that) was predicted in the Jews' Tanakh to be the person who would re-establish an independent Israel, winning freedom for these Jews, freedom at that time specifically from Rome's tyranny.

The mashiach was the expected liberator of Jews from foreign rule. Jews during that period thus craved the mashiach, for this political reason, not for any religious reason separate from it.

This is also why Jesus became a much harder sell among Jews once he was crucified; all that then remained of interest to Jews was this rabbi's reputation as a wise man, but such wisdom was only a lesser attribute of the foretold mashiach; the main attribute of the mashiach was his being a *conqueror*, and this was now gone, except among the few Jews who expected a second coming of Jesus. (The model for the mashiach was King David, the greatest-ever Jewish warrior, who started out by killing Goliath in *1 Samuel* 17, and who then went on to major battlefield victories throughout *2 Samuel*.)

The situation for Jews was tragic. This was the historical background, before Paul created Christianity: the Jews were a conquered people, whose rebellions against the Roman conquerors were soon to culminate in their mass-slaughter by Roman forces in the year 70.

Possible evidence of a pre-Christian, even pre-Jesus, Jewish belief in a suffering Messiah appear in some fragments of the Dead Sea Scrolls, as interpreted first in Michael O. Wise's 1999 *The First Messiah: Investigating the Messiah Before Jesus*, and then in Israel Knohl's more carefully argued 2000 *The Messiah Before Jesus*. These fragments suggested to Knohl that, during the years immediately preceding Jesus's birth, a Jewish community in Qumran believed that an Israeli freedom-fighter whom the Romans had recently caught and executed would be resurrected and go to heaven on the third day after his death. Then, on 19 April 2007, Knohl headlined in Israel's *Ha'Aretz*, "In Three Days, You Shall Live," interpreting in a similar way the inked inscription upon a recently discovered stone slab from that same period, right before Jesus. A scholarly version of Knohl's article appeared in the April 2008 *Journal of Religion*. Whether or not such specula-

Christianity *demands* Christ-faith: Christ is the *focus* of faith –
Paul asserts (in 2:16, as well as in *Romans* 3:24&26, and
elsewhere) that this is what God *requires* in order to grant a
person salvation in heaven. So, Paul in 1:5 is subtly
transitioning his followers *away* from Judaism (personal
salvation via obedience to God's laws or "commandments") into which he had originally converted them, to their
adopting instead Christianity (personal salvation via faith that
Jesus is Christ), which he's now selling (as 2:16 will make
clear). He's here saying that the Jewish God, whom he had
originally converted them to worship, will *approve* of their

---

tions have bearing upon the beliefs that were held by a broad cross-section of Jews
during the years leading up to Jesus's birth is currently unknown. The canonical
Gospels assert that Jesus was resurrected three days after his crucifixion, so that
the inscription, "In Three Days, You Shall Live," might have shaped the account the
Gospelists wrote.

But regardless: neither the Qumran documents nor the stone document
provide any evidence of belief by Jews in a Messiah in the Christian sense, and
there's sound reason why not: any Jew who believed in such a Messiah couldn't
possibly have been any longer a Jew, because worship of anyone other than the
unitarian God was prohibited in the Torah.

Christian scholars ignore all of this, and deflect onto Jewish scriptures
supposedly referring to the mashiach without any particular word even referring to
the concept of the mashiach. For example: many Christian apologists allege that
Genesis 3:15 refers to the mashiach, when it says that Satan will have an enemy,
and that Satan and this unidentified enemy will "hit" each other.

Many Christian apologists also allege that, when *Psalms* 72 says, in line
5, "May your people worship you," and when it says in line 11 that "all kings shall
fall down before him, and all nations shall serve him," the "you" in line 5, and the
"he" in line 11, are both referring to the Messiah, *not* to the Jewish God – despite
line 1 having *already made clear* that the entire Psalm is addressed to "God" and to
no one else (and despite the Psalm's final three lines *reaffirming* that).

Perhaps one might credibly speculate that *Genesis* 3:15 refers to Jesus,
but there is no reason to think that it *does*; similarly, there is no reason to think that
Psalms 72:5&11 refer to Jesus, instead of to "God." In other words: apologists have
nothing but speculation to support their Trinitarian allegations, but the Torah is
remarkably consistent in *demanding* a unitarian God. The repeated demands of the
Torah thus stand starkly opposed to the numerous speculations of Christian
apologists. And *Galatians* proves that Christianity is nothing more than a hoax,
which Paul started in the year 49 or 50.

leaving Judaism to join Paul's Christianity. Paul is explicitly saying that "God's glory will be forever, amen," and is implicitly saying that Paul represents and supports *this* God – the Jewish God. It's a way of suggesting to his Gentile converts, to a Jewish sect, that he's not aiming to convert them to something else – which, however, is exactly what Paul is trying to do.

In fact, though a faith that Jesus was the mashiach wasn't necessarily inconsistent with Judaism, any *worship* of Jesus, as Christ or anything else, is repugnant not merely to individual Jews, but to Judaism itself. Jews, as signatories to their covenant with God, are committed to obey the covenant, and thus aren't permitted to worship *any* person: not even Abraham, nor Moses, nor King David – the latter of whom is viewed as being the very model for, and the defining ancestor of, the prophesied mashiach. Worshipping the mashiach would have seemed just as repulsive to Jesus's followers as would worshipping King David. It was and is prohibited. In Judaism, *only* the unitary creator-God was worshipped during Jesus's time, exactly as in ours, because that's what the first three of Judaism's Ten Commandments *demand*. Paul here *pretends* to be respecting that.

As was mentioned previously, the Jewish God has *no* family – no "Son," no wife, no brother, no relative of *any* kind. The Jewish legend asserted instead that He has *only* a People, Jews, who are comprised of each signatory of His covenant to obey His commandments, so long as the given signatory *does obey* those commandments and thereby fulfill the contract, the Torah laws. Pagan gods (such as Zeus or Jupiter) had family, and so Paul could pull the pagan wool over the eyes of his Gentile "converts," but that's all it actually was. Upon the basis of their previous pagan gods, Paul could fool these men. He knew his market, and he took advantage of that knowledge in order to get them to do what he wanted, which was to remain his followers, even if this would now have to mean their no longer being followers of James, which meant their no longer being followers of Jesus.

Paul Says His Enemies Should 'Go to Hell'

1:6 I am shocked that you are so quickly abandoning the one who called you by the grace of Christ and that you are turning instead to another gospel.

1:7 But of course, there isn't really any other gospel, and it's only a perversion of the gospel of Christ, and has been offered by some others, so as to mislead you.

1:8 However, even if we or an angel from heaven were to proclaim a gospel contrary to the one which we have taught you, then such a person should be condemned to hell!

1:9 I shall repeat what I've said before: If anyone preaches to you a different gospel, he should go to hell!

1:6-9 introduces Paul's as-yet-barely-defined "gospel of Christ" (1:7) as being somehow opposed by as-yet entirely anonymous others, who should (Paul twice says, first in 1:8, and then REPEATED for emphasis in 1:9) "be condemned to hell!" Paul's war is now drawing closer; the sound of his rhetorical artillery is here growing distinctly audible. But yet his enemy still remains invisible in the distance, and will remain, in this letter, unheard-from in any EXPLICIT way. (Paul never quotes or otherwise presents his opponents' COUNTER-arguments to his own). (Fortunately, their counter-arguments are implicitly clearly reconstructible, and will here, for the first time, be reconstructed.) Paul's terminological usage of the phrase "gospel of the Messiah," referring to what he's preaching, intentionally avoids making explicitly clear to his Galatian readers that Paul is aiming to wean them AWAY from Judaism; this is why the phrase, "gospel of Christ," or "gospel of the Messiah," was *acceptable* to his readers: that phrase sounded, to people of its era, very much like the belief-system of a JEWISH sect, especially because the "Messiah" was, itself, a thoroughly Jewish concept. Consequently, Paul was able to preach this "gospel" even while not EXPLICITLY informing his readers that he was aiming to convert them AWAY from the

religion that he had initially converted them TO. Another very
important point, which Paul is introducing in this passage, is
1:7, "There is only one gospel of the Messiah, but there are
some people who are trying to change it," and then, he repeats
twice in 1:8 and 1:9, "whoever would preach to you a gospel
that is different from the one that we have preached to you,
should be condemned to hell!" Paul's implication here is that
his "gospel of the Messiah" has never changed and is the
thing he has always preached unchanged to them. We make
special note of this, because, in our upcoming discussion of
2:11-16, we'll demonstrate that an earlier letter from Paul, *1
Thessalonians*, testifies in its passage 4:1-8, that Paul's "gospel
of the Messiah" had, in fact, been different then, and CHANGED
subsequently (after the council in Jerusalem, which is referred
to in *Galatians* 2:1-10), so that what Paul is now saying in
Galatians 1:7-8 is actually false, and he had to know that it was
false – a lie. This is one of the reasons *why* Paul is *not* here
DEFINING what his actually NEW gospel of the Messiah IS. He's
holding that off till later in this letter, in 2:16, which is far
enough separated from 1:7-8 so that probably none of Paul's
Galatian readers will even NOTICE that there's a *difference*
between his new "gospel of Christ" in 2:16, and his previous
teaching (as in *1 Thessalonians* 4:1-8). All that his Galatian
readers know *thus far* about Paul's gospel is what he has told
them in 1:4, which is sufficiently skeletal a definition, so that it
applies to BOTH his previous, *and* his new, versions of it: 1:4 is
so *vague* a "gospel," that it describes Paul's previous *Jewish*
version, AS WELL AS his current and future *Christian* one. In this
sense, the present passage, 1:6-9, serves the function of a
subtle, indeed imperceptible, but still crucial, psychological
transition, both to prepare his Galatian readers to hate his
enemies (who "should be condemned to hell!"), and to
transform those readers from membership in his enemies'
Jewish sect, into becoming members of his own entirely new
religion. He's making this transition imperceptible to his
readers, because if he were to be direct about it, he'd lose
them. By the time he actually states his gospel of Christ, in

2:16-21, his audience probably won't even remember that here in 1:6-9 he had asserted that this "gospel" hadn't changed. What Paul is doing in 1:6-9 is to accuse his opponents of changing their "gospel," which was Judaism. But Paul is actually changing *his* "gospel" from the Judaism he had originally preached, to Christianity; and he's doing this in a way that he thinks his gulls won't even notice. (Scholars don't notice it, either, but we must, and we'll document all details of this change when discussing 2:11-21.)[22]

1:10 Do you think I'm just trying to please people? It's only God I'm trying to please. If I were pleasing people, I wouldn't be serving Christ.

1:11 For I want you to know, my brethren, that the gospel I teach isn't of human origin.

1:12 For I didn't receive this gospel from a human source; I received it from a revelation by Jesus Christ.

---

[22]   This exhibits the legal/forensic principle of distinguishing between what a person's statements assert, and what those statements exhibit. Paul is now asserting or claiming that his gospel of Christ has never changed, and that his enemies have changed the gospel and are trying to persuade the Galatians to join them in this changed gospel. But what Paul *demonstrates* or *exhibits*, in his very own writings, as we shall soon be discussing, is that his gospel of Christ did, in fact, change, and that it changed quite substantially. A microscopically close logical examination of Paul's statements proves the truth of some things he asserts not to be so, such as here, that his own gospel of Christ *had* changed. Similarly, in 1:5, Paul has implied that he champions the Jewish God, but yet he had already actually championed, in 1:1, 1:3, and 1:4, the utterly non-Jewish Diune God, which he subsequently preaches at length in this letter. And similarly, he violates Jewish Law, such as when he broke the first three of the Ten Commandments which prohibit worshipping anything other than the unitary Jewish God, but yet he claims or asserts in *Romans* 3:31, "We uphold the Law." A close logical examination of a witness's statements can thus prove some things that contradict what the witness asserts. A witness can say "X is true," even when his own assertions *demonstrate* that X is false. That's what is happening with Paul's testimony, which comes to us via documents, instead of by words spoken upon a witness-stand. The result is the same either way: a virtual cross-examination of a witness, only in this case it occurs by means of his documents, instead of via his oral testimony. A close logical analysis can expose lies. Physical presence of the witness isn't the *only* way to expose his lies.

1:10-12 constitutes the first of the many reinforcements that Paul will bring to bear upon his initial claim, in 1:1, that his own authority is divine. Paul's argumentative tactic in this is always the IMPLICIT one: that his enemies, even those who were known by his Galatian readers to have been PERSONAL ACQUAINTANCES of the living Jesus, had received their authority MERELY "from man or by means of man" (1:1). 1:12 states that Paul had received his commission "from a revelation by Jesus Christ." Unlike 1:1, there is no mention here of "God the Father, who raised him from death." In 1:1, Paul had added the mention of God, under an assumption that Christ wouldn't have appeared to Paul in his "revelation," *unless* God, who had raised Jesus from the dead, had *wished* it. In 1:10, Paul employs a different means of identifying God as the authority he's trying to please: He asserts directly, "It's only God I'm trying to please." This recapitulates 1:5. Paul is saying that the *way* he aims to please God is by "serving Christ." In Judaism, one pleases God by obeying His commandments, but Paul in 2:16 will present an alternative.

Paul Says His Former Judaism Made Him Evil

1:13 You've probably heard how I behaved in my earlier life, as a Jew, how I persecuted mercilessly the church of God, and tried to destroy it.

In 1:13, we learn from Paul "how I used to live when I was devoted to the Jewish religion" (which implicitly means that Paul once WAS a Jew, but also that at the present stage of his claimed followership of Jesus, Paul has renounced Judaism and now no longer considers his Christianity – his "gospel of the Messiah" – to be a sect of Judaism; i.e., HIS BREAK WITH JUDAISM HAS ALREADY OCCURRED, *and yet he doesn't* EXPLICITLY

INFORM *his Galatian readers of this*); and also, "how I persecuted without mercy the church [EKKLESIA] of God and did my best to destroy it" (which brings into focus his implicit view that Jews are hostile to Christianity – an important theme that Paul IMPLICITLY REITERATED in numerous contexts, and explicitly stated in *1 Thessalonians* 2:15). It might also be noted here that, since Paul has already previously (in 1:2) addressed his readers as being members of an "ekklesia," his REPETITION of that term in the present context is very subtly informing his readers that, WHEN he himself had BEEN Jewish, he had been persecuting people who were LIKE THEMSELVES. This is yet another tactful way of his informing them – only implicitly, not at all explicitly – that Jews aren't actually like THEY are, but are, instead, DANGEROUS to people such as they. In germinal form, this is a charge that the Roman Catholic Church and its "Saints" historically developed at length: that Jews are DANGEROUS to Christians. (For example, St. Justin Martyr, at around the year 160, wrote, in his *Dialogue with Trypho the Jew*, Ch. 133, [in one widely available translation] "For verily your hand is high to commit murder, because ye slew the Christ, and do not repent of it, but so far from that, ye hate and murder us who have believed through Him in the God and Father of all, as often as ye can.") Paul is here implying that he knows, from his personal experience, that this is true; he's here implicitly using his own former Jewish faith very skillfully as a RHETORICAL WEAPON against Judaism ITSELF.

   This line conclusively proves, by logically necessary implicit declaration and not by any explicit or overt assertion (which would have drawn negative attention to him from his readers, whom he had previously converted *to* Judaism, and so he here avoids *explicitly* stating this), that he's *no longer* a Jew. He says here that he used to be a Jew, but implies that he isn't one any longer. The passage also says that, when he was a Jew, he "persecuted without mercy" people such as his readers are. Paul, in other words, is here setting his readers up *to fear Jews*. He's not only saying that he no longer is a Jew, but that his readers would reasonably fear people who are. This is a remarkable achievement from a man who had converted these same readers into this Jewish sect; he couldn't achieve it if he were to have stated *explicitly* that Jews are hostile to people who accept Jesus as the Jewish Messiah. His readers know that the disciples in Jerusalem, their own religious leaders, who were followers of Jesus while Jesus was alive and who have continued as Jesus's followers and supporters, are all Jews. And that's why Paul states this *only* implicitly. However, the assertion is no less categorical on account of its being logically implicit rather than explicit: it's an unequivocal assertion, just as if it were stated in overt terms. But it's also a belief that he cannot admit to his readers that he holds: he's out to manipulate, not to inform, them, and this is *how* he does that.

1:14 I was more advanced than many Jews of my age in the practice of Judaism, and was much more devoted to Jewish traditions, the traditions of my ancestors.

In 1:14, Paul now EXPLAINS this "without mercy": "I was ahead of most fellow Jews of my age in my practice of the Jewish religion, and was much more devoted to the traditions of our ancestors." He's here stating exactly what had caused the mercilessness of his early opposition to the Jesus-followers. He's implying that, whereas Jews are his readers' enemies, the most devout Jews are mercilessly so. Clearly, Paul is here implying that Judaism leads, or inspires, its believers to attack Christians. This assertion, even though implicit and not explicit, is the hate-mongering anti-Semitic original,[23] subsequently to be embellished in many Christian

---

[23] Some scholars have objected to my calling it so, and have said such things as "Sympathetic engagement with one's subject is an important element in the dialectic of interpretation," but such a prejudice against actually seeing a hate-

myths that Jews are dangerous to Christians. A common
Medieval myth thus emerged that Jews killed Christians and
drank their blood. Such behavior was widely suspected of
Deicidists. *Acts* 8:1-3 provides a tale of the PRE-Christian Paul,
as "Saul," having approved of the murder of one Christian,
and of his having dragged others and thrown them into jail.
Paul is now saying that the REASON why he was so especially
dangerous to followers of Jesus – followers such as the readers
of this letter, of course, are themselves – is that he was even
MORE Jewish than were other Jews. Neither Paul nor *his*
followers (such as the author of *Acts*) ever explicitly
mentioned that those Jesus-followers whom Paul then
persecuted were themselves Jews who had been born Jews:

---

mongering assertion as what it is – which in the present case might even be the
historical original of a myth that generated the medieval anti-Semitic pogroms, and
the earliest significant historical precursor to the Holocaust – is simply
unacceptable from the standpoint of legal/forensic methodology; no court of law in
a democracy can accept such prejudice, regardless whether that prejudice is
favorable or unfavorable toward the given document's writer.

Classical scholarship tends to view the authors of these documents as
being questionable only as regards whether what they said was true, but not also
as regards whether the given author possessed and exhibited in the document
character-attributes today's scholars might happen to despise. This is especially
the case with respect to "sacred" texts.

As a scientist, any reader will approach each document without such
prejudicial assumptions, and will read it instead with a minimum of assumptions,
which, regarding the present letter, are mainly that Paul was trying to *persuade* his
readers. That is the methodology pursued here. We are describing his persuasive
techniques.

If Paul exhibited some "un-admirable" character traits (or so they are now
widely viewed, but as recently as Martin Luther's time they were not), such as, in *1
Thessalonians* 2:15, saying that Jews are hated by God, and in *Philippians* 3:2-8,
saying that Jews are superficial and that Judaism is garbage, then a scientist will
acknowledge it and not tie himself up in circular arguments that start and end with
denying that Paul said such things. The present passage in *Galatians* wasn't
isolated; it has to be understood within the context of everything that Paul said, and
any assumption that Paul couldn't possibly have initiated a historical chain of
events culminating in the Holocaust is rejected as extraneous. The evidence Paul
created is there; let's see where it leads us, as scientists, applying a minimum of
assumptions, and applying no extraneous assumptions such as scholars routinely
do.

Paul is now setting forth onto a second and far more damaging round of doing the same thing to the followers of Jesus/James, but this time as the originator of these attacks, instead of as a mere operative for someone else (perhaps he had even been an operative for the same Roman authorities who had crucified Jesus for sedition), if he indeed was someone else's agent in those earlier incidents. This omission might have been serving for Paul a directly PERSONAL psychological function: to help him deal with feelings of GUILT he might have then been experiencing on account of his having "persecuted without mercy the church of God" and done "my best to destroy it." Given that he now alleged to feel this way about what he had previously done, it's very possible that (unless he was now lying) he felt deep pangs of guilt about what he had done. He here allays that shame, by transferring this blame away from himself personally, and onto his previous religion, Judaism. He does this by his attributing that outrageous behavior to his having been exceptionally "devoted to the Jewish religion" and "the traditions of our ancestors." In his own mind, he could sincerely have held that Judaism was to blame: He could have thought that the chief rabbi of the Temple's having been appointed by the Roman occupying authority constituted, for him, "the traditions of our ancestors," and he could sincerely have blamed *Judaism* for this recent tradition, even though that would have been factually false (since it wasn't at all among "the traditions of our ancestors"). This implicit condemnation of strict Jews would have been blaming the victims, and would be entirely in keeping with Paul's basic outlook on life as reflected in his letters, his worship of the very personification of Power, The Almighty. Paul is, in any case, here setting his readers up for his coming onslaught against "the traditions of our ancestors"; i.e., against "the Law," which is to say against Jewish belief *itself*, which had supposedly caused him to be "without mercy," and he's now favoring instead faith and grace – the salvation-doctrine that he will soon (in 2:16-21) be introducing *instead of* Judaism. This obviously serves a practical purpose in Paul's program, *irrespective* of how he rationalized it to *himself* at the time. Consequently, in his present view (again assuming that he wasn't lying here), the more strongly that he now *separates* himself from "the Jewish religion" and "the traditions of our ancestors," the better and purer a Christian he will be able to become and be. He is, then, now attacking Judaism not only in order to drive a wedge separating his followers from it, but also in order to absolve *himself* of those pangs of guilt – blaming Judaism for his own prior cruelty.

Importantly, he's also signifying to his readers that any followers of Jesus who continue to assert Jewish Law could, themselves, become dangerous to his readers, in the same way that Paul used to be dangerous to the followers of Jesus. (Presumably, he's referring here to incidents such as *Acts* 8:1-3 describe, when Paul was called Saul and persecuted Jesus's followers, before he supposedly joined their group.) This is not only a warning for his readers to avoid taking Jewish Law – that is, Judaism – too seriously, but it's also a warning for them to avoid the people who do so, possibly including, as he had already instructed the Galatians twice in 1:8 and 1:9, "whoever would preach to you a gospel that is different from the one that we have preached to you, should be condemned to hell!" Paul is thus employing several devices to make his readers *fear and hate Jews*, who hold "a gospel that is different."

It might be noted here that *Galatians* presents Judaism (the covenant) in so clearly negative a light, so that probably no born Jews were in the Galatian congregations; they were probably all Gentiles, uncircumcised people, whom Paul had converted to Judaism; specifically, to the Jewish sect that Jesus had started. No indication is provided in *Galatians* that Paul felt any need to mollify the circumcised. By contrast, Paul's later letter written to the Roman congregations seems to have been addressed to congregations that included a significant number of born Jews. For example, *Romans* 9-11 appeals to members of the Roman congregations by presenting a God who accepts everyone who possesses faith in Jesus as the prophesied mashiach, and this includes born Jews as well as the Gentile converts to Jesus's Jewish sect. (However, even there, Paul said of *non*-Jesus-following Jews, in *Romans* 11:28, "Because they reject the gospel or good news about Christ, which was granted for your benefit, the Jews are God's enemies, even though God loves them on account of their ancestors."[24]) *Galatians* exhibits no such concern to placate born Jews within these congregations – it presents as being dangerous, to the Gentile converts, the born Jews who are

---

[24]   This is one of two instances in which Paul called Jews God's enemies, the other being *1 Thessalonians* 2:14-16. Yet scholars say that Paul wasn't anti-Semitic.

On 23 March 2010, the *Journal of Applied Social Psychology* (v. 40, #3) headlined "The Scientific Impotence Excuse: Discounting Belief-Threatening Scientific Abstracts," and Geoffrey D. Munro summarized: "The scientific impotence discounting hypothesis [alleging that science cannot address certain questions] predicts that people resist belief-disconfirming scientific evidence by concluding that the topic of study is not amenable to scientific investigation. In 2 studies, ... participants reading belief-disconfirming evidence indicated more belief that the topic could not be studied scientifically." This article was discussed five days later by John Timmer at arstechnica.com, under the headline "When Science Clashes With Beliefs? Make Science Impotent," and he pointed to the problem that closed-minded people, when they encounter evidence of the falseness of their views, simply decide "that, regardless of the methodological details, a topic is just not accessible to scientific analysis."

Scientifically, there can be no doubt that Paul, during the late period of his career when he wrote his letters, tried to get his followers to believe that Jews (any who didn't convert to his new religion) hated God. He never said that Gentiles who didn't convert to his new religion hated God – *only* Jews. Here in *Romans*, Paul sugar-coated his manifest hatred of Jews by saying that God did not return their hatred, but instead "loves them on account of their ancestors," in other words that God loves Israelites *despite* Jews' hatred of Him. The closed-mindedness that scholars exhibit, in denying Paul's anti-Semitism, might be an example of "the scientific impotence discounting hypothesis"; but, whatever it is, it's widespread among them, and it isn't only non-scientific, it is profoundly *anti*-scientific; it is reality-denial, because a theist's allegation that Jews hate God *is* anti-Semitic, especially if this allegation is applied selectively to *only* Jews, and not equally to *other* non-Christians as well.

Furthermore, an earlier (and now-classic) study had shown that "People who hold strong opinions on complex social issues are likely to examine relevant empirical evidence in a biased manner." This study, "Biased Assimilation and Attitude Polarization: The Effects of Prior Theories on Subsequently Considered

committed to the entire Jewish covenant.

Galatians 1:13-14, in other words, tells the letter's audience: Judaism, the covenant *itself*, is dangerous to you; and that's why I, Paul, was dangerous to you before I abandoned it and joined you.[25]

Evidence," appeared in the November 1979 *Journal of Personality and Social Psychology*. Its three researchers, Charles G. Lord with Lee Ross and Mark Lepper, studied attitudes toward capital punishment. It was well summarized by Boysen and Vogel in an online follow-up, on 9 September 2007, "Biased Assimilation and Attitude Polarization in Response to Learning About Biological Explanations of Homosexuality." The authors here wrote: "In the original attitude polarization study, Lord et al. (1979) selected participants for their extreme views on capital punishment and had them read summaries of fictional studies about the effects of capital punishment. The studies were identical except for the results, which were manipulated so that they either supported or refuted the effectiveness of capital punishment. ... Participants tended to rate the study consistent with their attitudes as more convincing and also indicated that their attitudes actually became stronger because of the evidence presented to them." Boysen and Vogel found that the same result occurred when the issue was homosexuality instead of capital punishment: "Individuals with positive attitudes toward homosexuality tended to see biological evidence as reason for acceptance [of homosexuals], and those with negative attitudes tended to take the exact opposite view."

Attitudes toward Christianity (or any other religion) can therefore be expected to be reinforced by whatever people read about the given subject. This is the self-reinforcing effect of faith itself, regardless of whether the faith happens to be in Christianity, or in some other religion, or in atheism, or in anything else. Only by setting aside all faith, in anything, can science come to shape one's opinions. This is true regarding everyone: not just the general public, but also scholars. Faith blinds anyone.

[25] No previous exegesis of *Galatians*, or published discussion of these two lines in it (1:13-14), points this out. The aggressive approach that Paul takes here against people who seek to promulgate the Jewish covenant (or in other words against preachers of Judaism) is ignored in all of the discussions of *Galatians* by scholars.

Even this early in the reading of *Galatians* here, your attention is being drawn to important and previously undiscussed truths about Paul which come from the interpretation of Paul's written words, and not from Paul's explicit statements. Paul doesn't explicitly *say* "Jews are dangerous," but he describes his own background in a way that *exhibits* or *displays* this dangerousness, to anyone who accepts the truthfulness of Paul's account here (which we don't necessarily do). [continued]

What this showing – as opposed to mere explicit claiming – itself demonstrates, is the overriding importance of applying the correct methodology when interpreting a text. Scholars apply a different methodology to the task of interpretation. (E.g.: they merely *assume* that Paul would not intentionally deceive.) The first problem a scientist faces, when challenged to interpret a document so as to reconstruct from it the events that caused it to be written as it is, is to determine what scientific methodology is appropriate for such an interpretive task. The appropriate scientific methodology, in such cases, is not (for example) some chemical experiment or other application of physics, but is instead legal/forensic analysis of the given text. Understanding this methodology is even more important than the findings (or the "history") that result from its application, because the findings *do* result from the application of this methodology to the evidence.

There are a million different ways to misunderstand any subject, but there is only one way to understand it, and science is that one way; but what's especially difficult in any given field is to determine *which* scientific methodology is able to solve the problems *in that given field*. Within the field of history, legal/forensic methodology is the one that does the job.

Unfortunately, the big challenge for the reader to overcome at the start when reading the present work is this methodology, because if the reader doesn't first understand this methodology, then this book can only be, to him, yet another repackaging of myths, or even of myths about myths, just like all other works that have been published about earliest Christianity. The methodology is the entrance-way to the findings, and only science can produce *scientific* findings. Legal/forensic methodology is the applicable scientific methodology for interpreting documentary evidence.

One thing that's important in any legal/forensic analysis of the evidence regarding a person's motivation is a pattern of behavior exhibited by that person, in contradistinction to merely an anomalous or non-patterned behavior from the individual. Paul exhibited a pattern of behavior here in his insinuating and avoiding explicitly asserting that Jews are dangerous to "us." For example, elsewhere, in *1 Corinthians* 11:23, he introduced the idea – later picked up on in all of the Gospel accounts of "Jesus" – that Jesus was "betrayed" (presumably by some Jew). As William Klassen noted in his 1996 *Judas: Betrayer or Friend of Jesus?* (pp. 47-51), the Greek word that Paul introduced there, and which the Gospel-writers subsequently used, "*paradidomi*," actually meant "handed over," not "betrayed," but might have had a *secondary* usage to mean "betrayed." Klassen also pointed out that the Greek language had several *other* terms, which would have been *specific* for indicating betrayal ("*prodidomi*," "*prodosia*," and "*prodotes*"), but that Paul avoided those (just as we have earlier noted that Paul avoided "*threskeia*" and "*sunagoge*," and instead used the vaguer "*ekklesia*").

So, just as Paul carefully avoided saying, even while he could explicitly have said, that Jesus started a religion (since Jesus didn't), Paul carefully avoided saying, even while he could explicitly have said, that Jesus was betrayed (since Jesus wasn't). Paul insinuated falsehoods about Jesus, while maintaining deniability to protect himself in his early era when there still remained some people around who knew the facts and could upbraid him on the deception if it were explicit. He was a serial dissembler and deceiver, and the Gospel-writers learned

More of Paul's Autobiography

1:15 But when God, who had cast his grace upon me before I was born,

In 1:15, he's claiming that "God chose me even before I was born," and he's thus setting up the reader to accept Paul's authority on a basis so high that only Jesus Himself had previously possessed such lofty authority for the reader. (Paul can do that with these people, because he had introduced them to the Jesus sect.) This statement reinforces 1:1, 1:11, and 1:12; Paul obviously was intent that the reader mustn't miss this point, of his super-authority. And even now, he's not done with his repeating of it. At many crucial points in this letter, and also in his other authentic letters, he comes back to this allegation of his super-authority, again and again.

---

their tricks from him; and the overwhelming majority of scholars (unlike Klassen) do all they can to avoid even mentioning such realities. (However, even Klassen, in his "Anti-Judaism in Early Christianity," in the 1986 *Anti-Judaism in Early Christianity, v. 1*, said [p. 19] "It is not good historical method to find classical anti-Semitism in the New Testament." That view, in which the supposed findings *come before* the methodology, instead of *follow from* the methodology, unfortunately characterizes all of scholarship, and enables scholars, including Klassen, to contradict themselves right and left. The idea that "findings" can precede methodology is rejected by science, and this is the basic difference between scholarship and science: scholarship accepts it.)

The commitment reflected within the present work is not to Christianity nor to any other religion, not to any faith at all, but only to science. This is an epistemological commitment, and therefore it doesn't reject any specific faith such as the Christian faith; it instead rejects faith *itself* – an epistemology that's inconsistent with the opposite epistemology, which is science. Faith and science are not complementary subject-areas, but are instead mutually contradictory epistemologies, and there is no reason why a scientific investigation of a particular given religion (such as Christianity) would be impossible to achieve. The aim here is, in fact, to achieve that. The aim is to apply science to the Christian faith, since that faith in particular has produced Western Civilization, which is *our* civilization.

1:16 Saw fit and was so pleased with me as to reveal His Son to me, in order that I might proclaim Him among the Gentiles as the gospel [the good news of personal salvation], I didn't then seek counsel from any human being,

In 1:16, he's implicitly recapitulating yet again 1:1, that this letter comes "from Paul, whose call to be an apostle did not come from man by means of man, but from Jesus Christ and God the Father, who raised Him from death." In fact, he both starts and ends this line by reinforcing that even though he had never personally met Jesus, nor heard Him speak "from man by means of man" as 1:1 had put it, such as did Paul's now-enemies the Jerusalem elders in the Jesus-sect of Jews, who had known and lived with and spoken with, Jesus, over years of intimate contact with Jesus, Paul was nonetheless authorized, on even better grounds – directly from God Himself and from the resurrected Jesus – to speak for and on behalf of Jesus: "I went to no mortal for advice" on this, but only to God and God's Son, to receive his mission. (Paul wasn't shy; he was brazen enough to belittle his teachers who had, back then, provided his authority to preach now to these Gentiles. If the disciples in Jerusalem had rejected him back then, Paul would now be nowhere, and he wouldn't be writing as an authority to these Galatians. But he was nonetheless writing here dismissing those teachers and saying that *only* God and "His Son" had authorized and taught him.) Paul is here claiming also that his *"gospel,"* or *"good news,"* was authorized by none other than both God and Christ – that it came from them. His mission assigned by Them was: "that I might preach of Jesus and proclaim Him [as the Christ] among the Gentiles" – namely, to his readers.

Importantly, this line is the first in which Paul *unambiguously* refers to Jesus as *being* God's unique *"Son,"* and thus as possessing a distinctive status which Jews and Judaism never asserted nor could possibly assert for the mashiach, who was to be instead merely a king, a prophet, and a revered rabbi. (The Gospel-writers referred to Jesus as *specifically* a "rabbi" in *Matthew* 26:25&49; *Mark* 9:5, 11:21, 14:45; and *John* 1:38&49, 3:2, 4:31, 6:25, 9:2, 11:8, and 20:16.)[26] In this line, 1:16, and also in 4:4 to come, Paul *explicitly* introduces the Diune God, two thirds of the ultimate Christian God. This Diune God is an anathema to Judaism, a faith based on a monotheistic and entirely unitarian God, and which prohibits as the gravest violation worship of any other God.

Paul here asserts that the Resurrected Jesus was God's "Son" in a way no one else is, because "I received my authorization from no human being." Unlike Judaism, where (*Psalms* 89:26 and *Isaiah* 64:8) a mortal human can refer to God as "Father," and so can be a "son of God" even though a mortal human, Paul claims here to have been authorized by an explicitly *non*-human "Son of God." Paul's Diune God – which was, until now, logically implicit – has thus now become explicit. This doesn't make it any likelier true, but merely displays Paul's technique of first implying something as an assumption and then, later, (sometimes) asserting it as "true."

> *1:17 Nor did I go to Jerusalem to those who were apostles before me, but I immediately travelled to Arabia, and then returned to Damascus.*

In 1:17, Paul closes in on the coming issue by stating, "nor did I go to Jerusalem to see those who were apostles before me," referring here, for the first time directly, to the

---

[26] Scandalously, many translations of the Bible *mistranslate* the "rabbi" word there from the original Greek (Strong's # 4461, "rhabbi," which was pronounced "hrab-bee" and was used specifically to refer to any respected teacher of Judaism, like "rabbi" is today) as merely "teacher," or "master." They do this despite the fact that on 31 additional occasions in the four canonical Gospels, Jesus's disciples are presented as referring to him as "didaskalos" or "didaskale" (Strong's # 1320), which meant *any* type of respected teacher or master of any subject whatsoever. There's no excuse for mistranslating "rhabbi." If the more generic term were *always* used in the texts, then translating as "teacher" here wouldn't be misleading, but on these 13 of this total of 44 separate occasions, "rabbi" *is* the word in the oldest surviving manuscripts, and translators know that.

apostles, now Paul's own foes, who had actually met and intimately known and for years conversed with Jesus, rather than having supposedly encountered Him *only* in a "revelation." These are the same people that Paul is setting his readers up for Paul to be breaking away from and standing against in 2:11-21, the New Testament climax, which describes the conception of Christianity. Paul certainly doesn't want to grant his enemies respect. He's now simply reinforcing by implicit means a central point: that Paul wasn't speaking on behalf of those who had known and suffered along with Jesus but were still living and able to state from their own personal recollections what Jesus had actually said and done. By Paul's here re-emphasizing that he hadn't so much as even just consulted with these people, he implicitly reiterates his *dis*respect for their authority, and thus, yet again, helps to set the reader up to accept his own *superiority* over them in the coming, climactic, disagreement (2:11-21).

1:18 Three years after returning, I finally went to Jerusalem, to make the acquaintance of Peter, and to stay with him for fifteen days.

1:18 indicates that three years into his ministry, "I went to Jerusalem to get to know Peter [Cephas], and I stayed with him for two weeks." In *Acts* 10:34-11:18, whose real core is the line 11:2 stating what all the rest was actually all about, Peter at around this same time is described as having successfully been preaching to the Gentiles; and (11:2) "those who were in favor of circumcising Gentile male converts criticized him," but Peter managed at least temporarily to allay those concerns. In *Galatians* 1:18, Paul is finally coming to Jerusalem to receive acknowledgment and advice from his senior in his mission to the Gentiles, and he stays with Peter for two weeks of, essentially, missionary training from the man who presumably was the founder of the sect's outreach program to convert non-Jews. Peter himself left no writings; the two letters attributed to him in the New Testament were actually written by followers of Paul, after Peter's death.

1:19 But I didn't see any other apostle, except for the Lord's brother James.

      1:19 states, "I did not see any other apostle except James, the Lord's brother." Finally, Paul here meets the leader of the Jesus-sect of Judaism – the man who is ultimately to be his nemesis in 2:12, and in *Acts* 21:21 forward. But at this stage in *Galatians*, there's not yet a split between them. This might be the same visit to Jerusalem that's reported, very differently, in *Acts* 9:26-30, which says that the disciples were, at first, extremely suspicious of him, presumably because of his prior violent opposition to the Jesus-following movement. However, in Paul's account, no indication is given of any suspicions by the Jesus-followers that he may actually be an enemy agent whose real motive is to infiltrate and thus to harm the movement. (After all, Rome had crucified this movement's very *founder*.) Paul's account of his initial meeting with Jesus's disciples omits any such reference, inasmuch as it would have been contrary to his objectives to gratuitously *remind* the Galatians that such suspicions of his motives existed at all. As with any great rhetorician, Paul's omissions were just as skillful as his assertions. Unlike the account that's presented in *Acts* 9:21-30, in which the suspicions against Paul were supposedly that he might be a secret Jewish agent, any suspicions that might *actually* have existed against him on the part of Jesus's people would probably have been that Paul was a secret *Roman* agent, trying to infiltrate the followers of this man whom Rome had executed for sedition, and thereby to suppress any ongoing sedition-threat that these followers might still be posing to Roman authority.[27] However, Paul in

---

[27]   Even the canonical Gospel accounts of Christ, despite their clear anti-Jewish slant, say that Jesus was crucified for claiming to be "King of the Jews," which was a seditious claim since the Roman Imperial regime had designated the Herodian family as ruling Judea, and crucified everyone (there were others besides Jesus) who asserted or was believed to be the "King of the Jews." [continued]

his letters leaves out any hints that the Jesus disciples had any suspicions of him at all; and whether the disciples did or didn't cannot be confidently established. The scholar Robert Eisenman, in a 1996 article on the internet, "Paul as Herodian," argues that Paul was probably a Roman agent from the very start, a Roman spy/saboteur aiming secretly to do to Jesus's movement what Rome had already publicly done to

---

Acts 1:6 asserted that Jesus's disciples expected Jesus "to re-establish the independent sovereignty of Israel," which the Romans would necessarily take to mean that Jesus was expected by his followers to overthrow the Herodian kings and thus to end Roman rule of Judea and to re-establish the Davidic kingship. If that assertion in *Acts* was true, then all of the Gospel-writers' assertions that Jesus was crucified for Jewish rather than for Roman reasons had to be lies. Furthermore, supposedly, the King Herods hated and feared Jesus (*Matthew* 2:1-18; *Mark* 3:6, 8:15 & 12:13; and *Luke* 9:7-9 & 13:31). Thus, the possibility that the Roman Imperial regime had agents inserted among the followers of Jesus after Jesus's death cannot be ruled out. Indeed, it's a reasonable assumption. One possible reason for the suspicions against Paul is that Paul, according to *Acts*, was a citizen of Rome, and that he might have been feared to be an undercover Roman agent who had infiltrated the Jesus movement.

Moreover, *Acts* 26:9-18 directly quotes Paul as describing himself as saying that his Damascus-road encounter with the resurrected Jesus (or Holy Ghost) had come soon after he had "received authority from the chief priests and placed many of God's people into prison, and joined in sentencing them to death."

He was even quoted there as asserting, "I went to Damascus under the authority and orders from the chief priests," and that on the Damascus road he had encountered the Holy Ghost telling him to devote the rest of his life to converting Gentiles (quoting now the Holy Ghost's words, being quoted by Paul, being quoted by Paul's follower Luke, who was the actual *writer* of this) "'so that through their faith in me [Christ] they will have their sins forgiven and join God's people.'" The author of *Acts* wrote that he had accompanied Paul during the incident at which Paul said that he had been serving the chief priests when he was persecuting Jesus's followers.

So, even Paul's follower Luke wrote that he had witnessed Paul admitting that he had persecuted Jesus's followers because of "authority and commission from the chief priests." (NOTE: According to Josephus's *Antiquities* 18:2:2, the Roman Procurator, Pilate, appointed the chief priests.) Though this isn't as solid evidence as it would be if Paul himself had written it, it nonetheless strongly suggests that, prior to Paul's alleged Damascus-road experience, Paul was an agent of the chief priests (who were agents of the Roman Emperor, who was behind the crucifixion of Jesus for sedition).

Jesus himself, and was thus a Roman intelligence-operative in Rome's war against the Jews, which ended when Rome destroyed Jerusalem and its Temple in 70 CE. It's an interesting possibility, entirely consistent with the documentary record (such as *Acts* 22:5), but not proven by it. What can be proven is that Rome was at war against the Jews, that Paul favored the Romans, that the Romans crucified the Jew Jesus, and that Paul hated both Judaism and Jews (as will be further documented). It's quite possible that Paul's hatred of Judaism and Jews began only after, and as a consequence of, the Council in Jerusalem and its immediate aftermath (the incidents recounted in *Galatians* 2), rather than prior to his entrance into the Jesus-sect; and, if this is true, then Eisenman's theory here is false.[28]

Regarding Paul's reference to "James, the Lord's brother," many scholars have questioned whether this phrase meant what it said. Preferring to believe that no Jesus-disciple was physically related to Jesus – much less, perhaps, Jesus's appointed successor – these traditional Christian-apologetic scholars have hypothesized that Paul meant only that James was a disciple of Jesus, and that *all* such disciples were "brothers," in a broader sense. However, those scholars are

---

[28]   If Eisenman's theory here is true (which is to believe this aspect of *Acts* 22:5 & 26:9-18), then Paul might have joined the Jesus sect with the goal in mind of bringing into it so many Gentiles, who were loyal to Rome, so as to reduce the danger the Jesus sect would pose to Roman rule over Judaea. If that was the case, then Paul's refusal, twenty years later (as will be discussed in our next Chapter), to obey James's command for the circumcision of his Gentiles, would have been consistent with what had been Paul's intention all along. For Paul to disobey James here was for him to take these Gentiles away from Judaism altogether.

Paul's thinking, in that case, would have been that this *coup d'état* would not only fulfill his initial reason for having joined the sect, but it would produce a new religion which would be better for Rome and which would also be far likelier to continue growing after Paul's death. Was Paul so wise in the ways of the world? All the evidence from his letters indicates that he was. Consequently, I agree with Eisenman's theory in "Paul as Herodian." Nonetheless, the only direct support for it rests outside Paul's authentic letters, and thus this additional detail does not quite meet the requisite standard of proof for it to be included as part of the theory of the case expounded here.

clearly wrong: no other prominent Jesus-disciple was commonly referred to as "the brother of the Lord," or as "Jesus's brother." Above all, Peter, whom these apologists like to think of as having been the group's leader, was not the leader (as will be proven here). Furthermore, it wasn't *only* Paul who referred to James in this remarkable way. The other earliest writer concerning James, which was Josephus (in his *Antiquities of the Jews*, 20:9:1), likewise called this James Jesus's brother, and even several of the subsequent Church-historians did. "James" ("Jacob") was at that time a common name, and clearly the modifier that this James was "Jesus's brother" was intended to indicate *which* James was being referred to by the given writer. Josephus was even clearer than that, by identifying this particular "Jesus" (also a common name) as "the so-called Christ." Some scholars question whether "the Lord" in Paul's phrase "James, the brother of the Lord," referred to Jesus, but Paul's authentic letters frequently employed the phrase "the Lord" as a synonym to refer to Christ or to Jesus (such as in *Galatians* 1:3, "God our Father and the Lord Jesus Christ"), and no basis exists to assume otherwise. Furthermore, the earliest of the canonical four Gospels, *Mark*, at 6:3, says that Jesus was "the brother of James, Joses, Judas, and Simon," and that Jesus also had (unidentified) "sisters." None of the contortions by scholars provide reason to read "James, the Lord's brother" as anything other than Jesus's biological brother. So, Paul undoubtedly referred here to a James who was *biologically* a brother of Jesus, not *merely* to a disciple of Jesus. Ancient Greek, like many modern languages, used the term for "brother" in two different senses, one biological, and the other – as in *Galatians* 1:3 – metaphorical (merely collegial), but the meaning here was clearly the biological one, and there is no reason for thinking otherwise.[29]

---

[29]   The Greek term for brother, "adelphos" (in its various forms), appears in the New Testament 343 times, and 60% of those references are unambiguously genetic/familial. Of the 40% that are "colleagues," all are the writer referring to his

1:20 In writing this to you, I swear to God, I'm not lying!

1:20, "What I say, I swear to God I am not lying!"
shows that, when Paul was writing, there had evidently been
a contrary account of some sort circulating. The likely
prospect here is the evident contradiction with *Acts* 9:26-30,
which has Paul meeting with all of the elders. If Paul here in
1:20 is referring to the same event, he's asserting that he did
not; that he spoke only with Peter and James. However, in any
case, Paul couldn't have been intending here to contradict
something said in *Acts*, since *Acts* hadn't yet been written;
instead, the *Acts* account would have been based upon the
contrary story then circulating, which Paul was here
contradicting.

If Paul, on that occasion, met only Peter and James (and
there's no reason for us to believe otherwise), then why would
this have been so? One possible reason would have been that
Paul was already, by just his third year, aiming to convert
Gentiles to this sect, and that Peter was the senior person in
that mission, as Peter was described to be in *Acts*. Paul wanted
to spend some time with Peter in order to obtain from him
advice as regards what methods Peter had found to be the
most effective for interesting Gentiles in conversion to
Judaism and for closing the sale to them. As regards Paul's
reason for meeting with James – and Paul didn't say that he
had stayed with him for two weeks, as he had with Peter, but
only that he "saw" James – the likeliest reason would have
been that James led the group, and that the group's leader was
"seen" by almost everyone who was rising within the
organization. However, Paul doesn't explain *why* he "did not
see any other apostle except for James, the Lord's brother."
Perhaps one reason why he didn't explain this is that Paul

---

own colleagues, like *Acts* 22:13 "Brother Saul," or *Acts* 15:13 "Brothers, listen to
me"; none are referring to someone *else's* "brother." *Whenever* someone *else's*
brother is referred to (such as here, "the Lord's brother," or *Acts* 1:14 "Mary, the
mother of Jesus and of his brothers"), it's *always* familial, not *merely* collegial.

preferred to focus attention upon supernatural "explanations" for his actions, such as his saying in 1:15 that "God chose me even before I was born."[30] Again: Paul *knew* his market, and he honed in on it, with total, even obsessive, discipline. As he said in *1 Corinthians* 9:26-27: "I do not run uncertainly, as one unfocused upon the finish line. I'm no boxer who merely flails the air and loses focus upon his opponent. I'm like a boxer who handles his body roughly, disciplining and subduing it, so as to avoid failure."

1:21 Then I went into the regions of Syria and Cilicia.

---

[30] The farther that we proceed into the Scientific Age, the less credibility such assertions have, and that's a major reason why only since the time of Samuel Reimarus (the 18th-Century figure who was to historiography what Copernicus was to physics) has such a statement, as this one from Paul ("God chose me even before I was born"), come to be questioned regarding its truthfulness. To question its truthfulness isn't as skeptical as to question its honesty, and now even the honesty of such a statement becomes subject to open-minded examination.

Science and faith are not compatible with one another, because they're epistemological opposites. The present work is thoroughly scientific. A court of law in a democracy does everything it can to adhere to science. The situation is different in a dictatorship, which demands prejudice.

An epistemology is a meta-methodology of knowing things, and not a methodology of doing things. A methodology of knowing things is comprised of criteria both for evaluating the credibility of evidence (so as to determine facts), and for drawing conclusions from evidence (so as to render verdicts upon the basis of facts). It concerns criteria not only for assumptions, but also for conclusions. An epistemology consists of criteria for determining the truth/falsity of *all* statements. By contrast to a methodology of knowing things, a technology is a methodology of doing things. A scientist is an individual who applies the epistemology that is science, and an engineer is an individual who applies a technology that is based upon science.

Galatians is a sales-letter. A sales-letter is driven by its agenda, and not only by its alleged subject matter. A religious or faith-based reading will not question its honesty, but a scientific reading will, and does. And the reason it does is that only by penetrating *past* the document's agenda can the document's subject matter become scientifically known. This doesn't mean that a sales-letter inevitably lies, but only that it can lie and that it can also falsify with honest intent; even an honest writer might be mistaken, depending upon his use of faith-based methodology, or depending upon delusions, or depending upon other factors. A scientist avoids assuming the truth or falsity, or the honesty or dishonesty, of *any* assertion, and simply reads the evidence as a scientist does.

1:22 And throughout this time, I remained unseen by the churches of Christ that are located in Judea.

1:23 They only heard people say, "The man who formerly persecuted us is now proclaiming the very faith he had tried to destroy."

1:24 And so, because of me, they glorified God.

1:21-24 acknowledges suspicions against himself not by Jesus's disciples, but by their followers, who "did not know me personally; they knew only gossip about me." Thus, Paul is here telling his Galatian readers, by implication, that if they've heard anything bad about himself, it's merely gossip, nothing based on actual knowledge of him: he hadn't even met them. This is a pre-emptive defensive device on his part, since Paul cannot possibly have known for certain whether, or what, his Galatian readers might possibly have heard about him from his enemies. Paul couches this passage very carefully, just in case any of his Galatian readers might have heard critical comments against himself coming from any of the disciples in person; Paul was judicious in 1:19 to indicate that likewise the disciples themselves didn't really know him very well. Paul has thus completed his rhetorical preparation that's necessary in order for him to be fully defended, in advance, against anything that his Galatian readers might possibly have heard against him coming from either the disciples or their agents. He presents himself as being superior in status to his enemies, and yet of equal status to them as being *all* "apostles" of Jesus, which he himself *actually* was not, since he, unlike his enemies, had never known the living Jesus. And he has also warned his readers in advance against their believing anything negative against himself that they might possibly have heard coming from his enemies. Now, he'll describe his conflict with his enemies; yet, also with full carefulness, totally exclude from his account of it what his opponents' side in this dispute was, or even that it was a conflict at all. In other words, in what's next to come, Paul is extremely careful to give away to his readers nothing more than he absolutely must reveal in order for him to be able to win them. Not knowing whether, or what, they might possibly have already heard about this conflict from his enemies, Paul is at great pains not to do any of his enemies' work for them, but to do only his *own* work here. No direct historical record survives of his enemies' statements. Fortunately, however, we'll be able to reconstruct their argument on the basis of Paul's refutation of it, and of the Old Testament passages whose meanings were in dispute.

It might be noted that 1:22 indicates that the supposed visit by Paul to Jerusalem that Paul's follower Luke alleged in *Acts* 11:30 & 12:25 is fictitious. Paul asserts that his second visit to Jerusalem was the one he will be describing in *Galatians* 2.

2:1 Then, after fourteen years [away from Jerusalem], I went again to Jerusalem, this time with Barnabas and Titus.

2:1, "Fourteen years later I went back to Jerusalem,"[31]

---

[31]   1:18 states that in his third year of ministry he first went to Jerusalem; and here in 2:1 he's saying that fourteen years afterwards he again went to Jerusalem, so that the climactic Jerusalem conference recounted in 2:1-10 occurred in the seventeenth year of his ministry – and this letter to the Galatians was written after that.

Consequently, though scholars commonly write such things as that the available information "would not tell us whether it [*Galatians*] came early or late in Paul's career," Paul himself tells us that it came sometime after his 17th year in the ministry, which certainly was not "early." I would date the events recounted in 2:1-21 as occurring in either 49 or 50 CE, and *Galatians* as having been written sometime afterwards, perhaps in 53 or 54. *Acts* cannot be used for such dating, because its reliability is far less than Paul's. For dating Pauline letters and events, *Acts* must be simply ignored wherever it contradicts the Paulines.

Additional chronological-biographical details of Paul are provided in 1:17, indicating that in his first three years of mission he "travelled to Arabia, and then returned to Damascus"; and in 1:21, indicating that after his then visiting Peter and James in Jerusalem, he "went into the regions of Syria and Cilicia." Up through the moment of his writing *Galatians*, that's all we know of Paul's missionary travels: He had started in Damascus, then travelled in Arabia, then visited Jerusalem, then went into the regions of Syria and Cilicia, then visited Jerusalem a second time in the year 49 or 50, and then he went back to his office, which was now in Antioch. Again, anything that might be inferred from *Acts* to contradict these chronological-autobiographical details of Paul can be simply dismissed out-of-hand. [continued]

indicates the passing of so very long an interval of time, that it seems inconceivable that the passing of yet *more* time would have been required in order for Paul's ongoing admission and

---

Rainer Riesner's 1998 *Paul's Early Period: Chronology, Mission Strategy, Theology* discusses (pp. 10-28) "Abandonment of the Framework of *Acts*," and he concludes by saying that chaos reigns over scholars' attempts to choose between *Acts* and Paul's own letters when dating events that they both refer to. Riesner fails to address the way legal/forensic methodology interprets documents, namely formulating the theory of the case (the reconstruction of history from the given body of evidence) upon *only* the best evidence (such as *Galatians*), and then citing inferior evidence (if at all) *only* to the extent that it's *consistent* with that superior evidence. It's the approach employed here; and the reason Riesner ignores it is that it has never before been done in historiographical writing.

Citing *Acts* to date events in Paul's life is a basic violation of legal/forensic methodology, because the far superior evidence from Paul's authentic letters – especially *Galatians* – is available. Such inferior evidence that contradicts this shouldn't even be considered. On 18 March 2009, John Schwartz in *The New York Times* headlined "As Jurors Turn to Web, Mistrials Are Popping Up," and he described the struggles of courts to keep the evidence-pool clean in an age when jurors have access to the indiscriminate display of evidence over the internet. He noted: "Jurors are not supposed to seek information outside of the courtroom. They are required to reach a verdict based on only the facts the judge has decided are admissible, and they are not supposed to see evidence that has been excluded as prejudicial." Scholars are like judges who promiscuously violate legal/forensic rules, and like jurors who reach verdicts upon the basis of those anti-scientific instructions and guidances from prejudice-reinforcing judges. All prior works about the start of Christianity have been products of that anti-science; none have been products of science.

However, as has already been stated, scholars' datings of documents are accepted here, to the extent that those datings are consistent with legal/forensic methodology. For example, any dating of a Pauline letter is invalid if the dating is based upon *Acts* in violation of the 7 authentic Paulines. (This means that datings from many scholars are ignored here.)

In order to relate Paul to Jesus chronologically, Riesner might again be noted, when he concludes his discussion of "The Most Probable Date" for "The Crucifixion of Jesus" by saying (p. 58) that, "the fourteenth of Nissan (7 April) of the year A.D. 30 is apparently in the opinion of the majority of scholars ..., far and away the most likely date of the crucifixion of Jesus."

Scholars who date the start of Christianity to the Resurrection, which supposedly occurred three days after the Crucifixion, are therefore alleging that Christianity most likely started on 10 April 30; however, as will be made clear herein, no scientific reason exists to believe that, and overwhelming scientific reason exists to date the start of Christianity approximately twenty years afterwards. (Paul is about to describe the exact occasion here.)

accumulation of uncircumcised males into the sect to produce the crisis that's reported (correctly or not, we don't know) in *Acts* 15. This line is absolutely crucial for any authentically historical account of Christianity's start. Anyone who writes about the start of Christianity and who fails to take into account this line in *Galatians* is no historian but only a mythologist.

Paul hasn't yet told us the reason why he went back to Jerusalem. He tells us this in the next line. But after fourteen years, Peter has been (2:7) reassigned "the task of preaching to the Jews"; Paul has now taken over Peter's former assignment in a higher capacity than before, if not as being himself now the lead evangelist to the Gentiles, then as being at least higher in that assignment than Paul had *formerly* been. Evidently, Paul was also more successful in this assignment than Peter had been. Paul was thus rising in the organization. Furthermore, Peter's reassignment to preach to the Jews has evidently been in force now already for some time, and therefore we can reasonably assume that Peter has at least been *starting* to feel the pressures from circumcised Jews to require *all* male converts to the sect to adhere to the covenant-forming commandment, **Genesis 17:14**, in which God said to Abraham, **"No uncircumcised male will be one of my people."** Thus, it was taken for granted that every male Jew was circumcised, and the sentiment on the part of these men to exclude any men who weren't circumcised – to exclude anyone who violated God's law *Genesis* 17:14 – was certainly understandable. The question in the sect, during all of these years, has therefore been: are all of these now possibly thousands of uncircumcised adult Gentile male "converts" *actually* converts; are they actually members of the Jesus sect of Jews, or not? The covenant-forming commandment, *clearly*, says no – they're not. But, obviously, these "converts" themselves believed that, yes, they *were* Jews. And, according to *Acts* 11:2, Peter himself had accepted them as being so; Paul was merely continuing along that line. However, now, after fourteen years of this definitional limbo, a critical mass of

sheer numbers of these "converts" had evidently accumu-
lated, and so the question could, it seems, simply no longer
continue to be postponed. Obviously, on the one side of the
issue, just as in *Acts* 11:2, were adherents to the covenant.
These were Jews – defined as *being* adherents to the covenant
– and Jesus was their Jewish mashiach or "Messiah." What
other answer could there be for these people? The language of
Genesis 17:14 couldn't possibly have been clearer. Furthermore, this passage wasn't only a commandment; it was *the
covenant-forming commandment*, the statement from God as to
what it means to *be* one of God's people; it means, if you're a
male, that you *must* be circumcised; none who aren't can be so
much as considered even *possibly* for inclusion among God's
people.[32] Yet, there were now all of these maybe thousands of
adult Gentile uncircumcised men who believed, and who had
been told, *otherwise*. What should be done about them?
Probably by this time, after 17 years of Paul's work, they
constituted even the *majority* of the sect's membership. Yet
there obviously were Jews within the sect, and *all* Jews outside
it, who believed in the *necessity* of enforcing the covenant-
forming commandment. Procrastination can continue for only
so long. It had continued for at least seventeen years. And so
now the confrontation finally came.

---

[32]   Some scholars argue that this isn't so, and that what was at issue here
wasn't whether these Gentiles were Jews, but was only whether these Gentiles
adhered to "the seven Noahide laws." However, "the seven Noahide laws" didn't
even exist until hundreds of years later; they first appeared during the Third
Century CE, in the Gemara, or Babylonian Talmud. The Torah doesn't assert these
laws to be sufficient for a person's acceptance by God as being one of God's
people, and so these "Noahide" laws *aren't* membership-criteria. Those scholars'
argument is like the argument from some other scholars who say that Paul's
opposition to the Law pertained only to Judaism's "ritual" laws, and not to
Judaism's "moral" laws – another distinction that postdates the First Century events
these scholars are claiming to explain, and that doesn't appear in *Galatians* nor in
any other of Paul's writings after the year 50. After Paul invented Christianity in the
year 49 or 50, he was consistent in asserting that, as he said in *Galatians* 2:16, "no
one will please God by adhering to God's laws." Paul wasn't distinguishing between
some of God's laws versus other of God's laws, but was instead distinguishing
between salvation via obedience to God's laws (Judaism), versus salvation via
Christ-faith (Christianity). [continued]

Paul Is Called to Jerusalem

2:2 I went because of a revelation, and I presented the gospel that I preach among the Gentiles. I presented this privately, to the reputed leaders. I didn't want to have been running, and to be running, in vain.

2:2 is hardly to be believed when Paul asserts, in reaffirmation of 1:1&11&12&15&16, that he took only from God his instructions to come to this conference; the conference was, in fact, *called by James*, the man who is to reach the ultimate decision on this matter of circumcision, first at the end of the conference, in both *Acts* 15:13-21 and *Galatians* itself 2:10, and subsequently in 2:12 when James will abruptly change his mind on the matter. Obviously, the ultimate decider was the real leader; and the real leader was the ultimate decider. But we're getting ahead of ourselves: Paul in this line says only, "I went because God revealed to me that I should go. In a private meeting with the supposed leaders I

Furthermore, the only base in the Torah for a supposed "covenant" before the time of Abraham was *Genesis* 9:1-17, in which God commanded all men not to eat bloody meat and not to kill people, and promised that, if *no one* violated either of those two commandments, then "a flood will never again destroy *all living beings*" (my emphasis). This command to a collectivity wasn't a "covenant" in the sense of *Genesis* 17, which was an agreement between God and *each individual man* who signed it (by his becoming circumcised). No individual signed or agreed to anything in *Genesis* 9, which was instead merely a commandment, no agreement with anyone. This was God's "covenant ... with all creatures, including your animals," not with God's people or any specific religious community. Moreover, those two commandments failed to include even such basics as the ten commandments, including worshipping only God, and avoiding sexual immorality – things which Paul's letters show that he enforced upon his congregations. In fact, Paul never even so much as referred to Noah. So, *no* Noachic laws were objects of debate between Paul and James.

More is said following, about the Noahide laws, in our fn. 51, the lone footnote to the sub-chapter of Chapter 2 that's titled "2:14-21 One Unitary Quotation." It starts on page 180.

explained the Gospel message that I preach to the Gentiles. I did not want the race that I have been running to have been run in vain; I did not want my life's work for the past seventeen years to end up being a waste." (His literal construction here was the incredibly brief "lest I have run and am running in vain," the kind of super-cryptic expression to which Paul typically resorted when he was saying something that was both specially important, and especially potentially embarrassing, to him. This phrase here employed a key Pauline metaphor about the importance of success or of "winning the race" in life, a concept that was given its lengthiest exposition in *1 Corinthians* 9:24-27, in which he urged his people to "run to win."[33]) Paul is here saying that

---

[33]   Paul's emphasis that one should "Run in such a way as to win the race," which was stated or referenced by him several times, in *1 Corinthians* 9:24, and *Philippians* 2:16 & 3:14, as well as here in *Galatians* 2:2, exhibits the importance of the point that was made earlier, at the end of the discussion of the first of the four strategic objectives Paul was aiming at in 1:1 – namely, that Paul cannot be accurately understood outside the context of his intense competitive drive to beat his opponents; in other words to win. As stated earlier, "the first thing that Paul is doing in this opening line is to *distinguish himself from his competitors*, by means of carefully chosen words that implicitly place him at a *competitive advantage* in the eyes of his target market."

One might debate whether Paul's ultimate motive was to serve God or to serve his own career-success; one might even assume that those two objectives were really one in Paul's mind. However, the fact stands that in *Galatians* 2:2 Paul admitted that the success or failure of his career was at stake for him in the upcoming conference. One may reasonably assume that Paul came to this crucial conference prepared, which would mean that he was informed in advance of what would be debated there – especially because it centrally concerned his own career. If he was informed in advance, then certainly Paul's saying in 2:2 "I went because God revealed to me that I should go" would have to have been a lie, because Paul would have been motivated, in any case, to salvage his career, to do everything possible toward that end.

Whichever way one interprets Paul's motivation for success – whether it was ultimately to serve himself, or to serve God – Paul made powerfully clear that he possessed a laser-like focus upon success. This would have made a lie of Paul's saying "I went because God revealed to me that I should go." Paul's statement here in 2:2 is like his having said in 1:1 that his authorization "did not come from man or by means of man" but supernaturally from God and the Risen Christ – Paul was laying it on thick. Paul repeatedly appealed to his audience's underlying assumption that the supernatural possesses higher authority than natural explanations.

everything was at stake for him in this conference; his success or failure over the prior seventeen years' hard work was now to be determined. But he has opened this line by artfully implying to the *contrary*, that the authentic disciples had *not* required him to come to this conference, that only God Himself told him to come. This, of course, is intended to hide the fact that this conference, which was to decide his fate, had been called by James *precisely* in order to decide this question that had been postponed for so long. After all, Paul's Galatian readers are also at stake for Paul in this. The account of the matter given in *Acts* even opens (15:1-2), "Some men came from Judaea to Antioch and started to teach the believers, 'You cannot be saved unless you are circumcised as the Law of Moses requires.' [Actually, this law preceded Moses, and was Abrahamic; this was the Law of God, not of Moses at all, and this passage reveals that Luke didn't know the Torah and must therefore have been a Gentile. Any Jew would have recognized that the attribution in this passage in *Acts* was false; any seriously believing Jew could be routinely expected to know that the circumcision law was Abrahamic not Mosaic. By the time *Acts* was written, Christianity had evidently already pretty much abandoned the effort to convert Jews, and was concentrating almost exclusively upon converting Gentiles.] [It might also be noted here that there's debate among scholars as to whether *Acts* 15 even refers to the same council in Jerusalem as does *Galatians* 2. All of that debate is just more irrelevant scholarly speculation.[34] The interpreta-

---

[34]   Not only that, but the debate amongst scholars, as to whether the "south Galatian theory" or the "north Galatian theory" for interpreting Paul is true, is undeterminative on this matter of whether *Acts* 15 refers to the same conference as does *Galatians* 2, because even if Paul was writing to the north Galatian "churches," *Acts* 15 could still be referring to the same conference as *Galatians* 2, but some earlier passages in *Acts* would then be false, which is widely regarded to be the case anyway, regardless. [continued]

tion being presented here is based upon *Galatians*, regardless.]
Paul and Barnabas got into a fierce dispute [with the disciples
and their followers] about this [necessity of circumcision], and
it was therefore decided that Paul and Barnabas and some of
the others in Antioch ought to go to Jerusalem to discuss this
issue with the elders." Yet, even this late in his letter, Paul
hasn't so much as even just *mentioned* circumcision, which is
its key issue, soon to transform everything. After all, Paul
doesn't know how much his Galatian readers might have been
informed about this particular event. He obviously is hoping
that they don't even know that circumcision *is* the central
issue in it. But he can't afford to take any chances on this. Now
he is, at last, going to tip his hand on this matter, but even
when he does so, circumcision will be skillfully kept in the
background, only implicitly as being an issue at all, never
explicitly as being what it implicitly actually *was*, the central
issue and the reason, not only for the council in Jerusalem he's
here about to describe, but even *the reason for his writing this
letter at all* (as we shall subsequently document in our third
chapter, when discussing 5:2-12).

Paul's admission in 2:2, that his life's work, up to that
moment, was at stake for him at the impending conference in

The problem with scholars speculating about "the south Galatian theory"
versus "the north Galatian theory" is those scholars' underlying false assumption
that *Acts* provides a truthful chronological *sequence* of events. It doesn't. The only
valid basis for citing here *anything* from such chaotic documents as *Acts* or the
Gospels is to refer to events that are mentioned in those documents but that are
taken outside of any chronological sequence imposed upon them by those
documents; essentially, to cite those alleged events, if at all, only within a
chronological context that's superimposed upon them by Paul's authentic letters,
not by *Acts*, *Matthew*, or etc.

No assumption will be made here regarding "the south Galatian theory" or
"the north Galatian theory"; but, due to the similarities between the council in
Jerusalem as described in *Galatians* 2, and the council in Jerusalem as described
in *Acts* 15, a likelihood will be accepted here that both documents are probably
referring to the same event. Wherever those two descriptions contradict each other,
the description in *Acts* 15 is false. *Galatians* reigns above all other evidence. *Acts*
is nothing but a string of anecdotes, which needn't necessarily have happened at
all, and whose sequence indicates nothing, except where the sequence makes
sense within the context drawn from *Galatians*.

Jerusalem, is absolutely stunning; especially because he doesn't explain this shocking admission, not in the least. Scholars for two thousand years didn't press him on it – they didn't dig here, at all, to find out *why* his career-success was on the line in this event. They didn't even note that Paul's admission of this stood in direct contradiction to Paul's own immediately accompanying claim that God, and not James, had "revealed to me that I should go" to this conference, instead of what was clearly the fact: James's having *demanded* that he come to this crucial conclave to defend the non-circumcision of his congregants, their violation of *Genesis* 17:14. But why would Paul's attorneys throughout the ages – that is, why would scholars – have probed into this? They *wouldn't* have. They *ignored* it. If their institutional function was to defend Paul, and to prevent the public from knowing that he was a con-man and that Christianity is a hoax, then, clearly, they'd have gone easy on this admission that he needed to come to this conference, not probed it (as a prosecutor would do) so as to understand *why* he had to come. Thus, for two thousand years, Paul's testimony simply wasn't cross-examined.[35] But finally, it will be, here. Paul's *implicit*

---

[35]   The typical interpretation from scholars of this passage has been that, as Ronald Y.K. Fung put it in his 1988 *The Epistle to the Galatians* (p. 90), Paul's concern here was only "for the unity of the Church," in order to avoid "a rupture of the one Church into two separate branches of Jewish and Gentile Christianity." In any case, scholars haven't, at all, questioned Paul's motives, as a prosecutor would do. Fung, and other scholars, simply assumed that Paul's motivation was not self-interested; that it was "for the unity of the Church" or for some other supposedly selfless reason.

Scholars have, in other words, been rank authoritarians who've accepted blindly the saintliness of Saint Paul, the honesty of his statements, because to do otherwise would quickly expose Paul as a con-man and Christianity itself as his hoax, as we shall see.

To the exact contrary of the common scholarly interpretation that Paul's concern here was to prevent "the one Church" from splitting "into separate branches," the historical reality, which will be documented extensively, is that Paul *created* the split, and that he didn't split "one Church" but Jesus's Jewish sect, and that he split it not into "two branches" but instead into two separate faiths, one being the original Jewish sect that the Jew Jesus had founded, and the other being the entirely new religion, Paul's own Christianity, which wasn't only anti-Judaic, it was even intrinsically anti-Semitic, as will be shown here. Scholars for thousands of years have merely assumed the contrary, but their assuming it can never make Paul's lies true. Those lies are now scholars' lies also, and have been accepted on faith alone, because there's no other real basis for believing them than faith.

This prosecutor will show that the defense attorneys have been defending a con-artist, that their defense of him can be accepted only on faith, and that this con-artist is provably such and isn't merely "maybe" a con-artist. In other words, the defense attorneys' case is full of self-contradictions (including Paul's own, such as his saying that he came to this conference voluntarily, but that all his work for the prior 17 years was somehow nonetheless mysteriously at stake in this supposedly voluntary conference: even Paul admitted that the stakes for himself were enormous here); and, by contrast, the prosecutor's case is entirely consistent, and it will even explain the inconsistencies in the New Testament, as will be shown.

Consistent with the methodological principles that were stated in the Introduction, the citation here of a scholar's (Fung's) interpretation of Paul's meaning is presented not as constituting evidence for the case that is here being constructed, but instead only as an object of attack, since the evidence is only the evidence, and no one's opinion about the evidence – including mine – constitutes evidence, at all, in a legal/forensic case. A lawyer presents evidence, for his theory of the case; the jury then judges that theory, upon the basis of the evidence thus presented – and the jury also judges the theory from the opposed attorneys (such as Fung), upon the same basis: the evidence only. And so, at last, the public will now have a prosecutor's case to consider, while the defense case has always been widely available in numerous different forms (from scholars).

This isn't to claim that legal/forensic procedures are necessarily scientific, as they currently are practiced. To assert such a thing would be like asserting that current methods and theories in physics are necessarily scientific; essentially, to imply that the practice of physics has reached an end. But instead, science itself is the end, which scientists in every field do their utmost to reach. The difference between scholars/religionists on the one side, and scientists on the other, is the end or goal, which, in the case of scholars/religionists, is to argue for some existing cultural belief; and, in the case of scientists, is to find truth – irrespective of what anyone has said or written.

Paul W. Kahn's 1999 The Cultural Study of Law: Reconstructing Legal Scholarship describes some of the fundamental ways in which the entire field of legal practice is, even today, scholarly or "theological," instead of scientific. For example, he observes (p. 28): "The law review article characteristically begins by identifying an alleged error in a recent appellate court opinion. The outcome should have been different, according to the scholar. The argument that follows consists largely of a review of prior Supreme Court opinions. ... The only authority that the scholar can hold up to the Court turns out to be the Court itself." Kahn might as well have been describing there the way scholars write exegeses of Galatians, and of other texts. In the legal field, the inevitable result is also the same: rotten opinions that are based upon rotten opinions, rather than upon evidence. However, it's important here to note that this is a characteristic of appeals court practice, decisions about the law; not of trial court practice. For example, the U.S. Supreme

statements will fully and convincingly explain how and why his life's work for the prior 17 years was at stake for him in this conference (as we shall now see).

    2:3 Moreover, even Titus, who was with me, wasn't required to be circumcised, though he's a Greek [who isn't circumcised].
    2:4 False brethren had been secretly smuggled in to spy on the freedom [from Judaism's commandments] that we enjoy in Jesus Christ, and they wanted to enslave us [to those commandments].
    2:5 But we stood our ground, so that the truth of the gospel would be protected for you.

    2:3-5 reports the scheming of Paul's opponents to force his Gentile companion, Titus, to be **circumcised**. *Finally*, Paul mentions the circumcision-issue, and only at the very start of the council in Jerusalem; he recesses this issue as much as he can; he doesn't want his readers to know of its centrality to the council meeting in Jerusalem if they haven't already been informed of that by his enemies. However, in the account of the council's start that's presented in *Acts* 15:5-6, it says, "Some believers who belonged to the party of the Pharisees

---

Court makes decisions about the law that are based not on the U.S. Constitution, but on prior decisions interpreting that document. The anchor in the Constitution can thus easily become lost with the passage of time.

    So, the present work is no attempt to apply to the study of historical questions today's majority practices, the practices specifically by the majority of today's legal and forensic practitioners, including of today's judges and jurors. No statistical survey is being offered here, to determine what those "majority practices" are, much less is any assumption being made here regarding that question. Bad lawyers, judges, and jurors, are *not* what this work is based upon, nor what guides it.

    What guides the present work is instead science *itself*, namely the *goal* science – here, as in physics, and as in any other field of investigation that has by now reached the stage at which the given field deserves to be characterized by this term, understood as the term referring to the highest of all epistemological stages. This is the methodological ideal toward which courts in democratic countries aspire, regardless of the extent to which it yet is being achieved in any particular country.

[thereby implicitly acknowledging that despite all of the Gospels' blanket condemnations of the Pharisees as Jesus's enemies and even crucifiers, at least *some* of the Pharisees were actually "believers," Jesus's *supporters*] stood up and said, 'The Gentiles must be circumcised and told to obey the Law of Moses.'" *Acts* followed this with a speech from Peter in defense of Paul's practice against imposing circumcision, and then by James's decision on the matter. But here in Paul's account, circumcision isn't even mentioned as having been a point at issue in the conference; Paul mentions circumcision only as if this conflict about whether or not to circumcise Titus had been an incident that just *happened* to have preceded the conference itself. And scholars for 2,000 years have gone along with Paul's tactic here, ignoring its centrality.[36]

---

[36] The centrality of circumcision to this council in Jerusalem is essential to understanding what's going on here. One cannot understand this council at all unless this incident's relationship to that conference is understood truthfully. Viewing as merely incidental to the conference the struggle over whether or not Titus would be required to be circumcised is normal; that's a common scholarly understanding of the situation here; but is that a true understanding of this situation?

Understandings can be either true or false, just as facts themselves can be. For example, Paul's allegations here are facts, but whether they are true or not is a matter of interpretation, or theory, or understanding. To assert that what Paul said is true, or that it's false, is interpretive, and interpretations can be either true or false, just as factual allegations can be.

The difference between a fact and a theory (or between knowledge and understanding) is identical to the difference between a language and a meta-language. In formal languages, a clear distinction is drawn between, on the one hand, a logic or mathematics, and, on the other hand, a meta-logic or meta-mathematics. However, in common languages, the concept of meta-statements doesn't ordinarily appear; it's not present, because the structure of thinking is not a subject that is commonly discussed in ordinary languages. However, though the present investigation is of ordinary language statements, and is also about ordinary language statements, this investigation is scientific; and, therefore, the distinction between statements and meta-statements is constantly kept in mind. Quantitative sciences entail not only logic but also mathematics, and so they require formal language and not only ordinary language. However, qualitative sciences entail only logic, and formal language is optional in logic; but the distinction between statements and meta-statements is never optional in science and exists irrespective of whether or not a given language has been formalized. Thus, even in *non*-quantitative fields of scientific investigation, such as history, the distinction between fact and theory (or between data and interpretation) needs to be constantly kept in

Though circumcision isn't mentioned as having been at issue in the conference, 2:5 does admit one revealing fact about this incident's relevance to his readers: that the reason he had stood his ground there against the circumcisers was "to protect the gospel for you." In other words: he here *implicitly admits* that the point at issue in this conference was whether or not the circumcision-commandment, *Genesis* 17:14, is binding *upon Paul's followers.*

Paul has laid most of the groundwork now for his war against the continuing applicability of *Genesis* 17:14. However, an important part of his war is his denigration of the authority of his actual superiors in the organization, because it is those people against whose argument he is actually fighting. And he still has some work to do, in order to diminish their authority.

---

mind, so as to exclude confusing the levels of discourse (which leads to false understandings).

The assertion that the issue of circumcision here is essential to understanding the council in Jerusalem, is interpretive, but this doesn't imply that this assertion is undecidable as to its truthfulness or its falsity. In science, separating true facts and theories from false ones is always essential, and the person who ultimately does it is oneself, no one else. But that doesn't imply it cannot be done. A scientist always believes that it can be done, and searches to find the way to do it. That's what science is all about.

Any scientific research does this by exploring hypotheses or speculations, in order to test them to find the one that explains the most facts and that contradicts the fewest facts. That one is then a theory; and if no fact contradicts it, this theory is then the theory of the subject, and it constitutes the scientifically established explanation (or interpretation, or theory) of that phenomenon.

The deficiency of scholarly hypotheses is that no way exists to get beyond such hypotheses to reach theories; much less does any way exist to get beyond theories to reach the scientific theory of the given phenomenon. In other words, scholarship inevitably is mired in contending speculations. That's not the case with science. Science is distinguished not by its being mathematical, but by its being scientific. For example, Darwin's writings were scientific, but they were not mathematical. And Milton Friedman's writings were mathematical, but they weren't scientific. Regardless of whether a given field of scientific research is quantitative or qualitative, the means are established there to get beyond hypotheses to reach theories, and even to get beyond contending theories to reach the scientifically established theory of that phenomenon.

The Council at Jerusalem

2:6 The supposed leaders – and what they actually were makes no difference to me, because God doesn't judge by such outward appearances – made no new suggestions to me.

2:6, "But those who seemed to be the leaders – I say this because it makes no difference what they were," performs two functions. First, it raises yet again the question in the reader's mind as to whether or not these people, who will soon be Paul's opponents, really *were* the leaders, and so it reinforces, yet again, Paul's previous implications in 1:1&11&12&15&16 & 2:2, that Paul was himself at *least* as high in status within the organization as were the authentic Jesus-disciples. Second, it restates by implication that Paul's own "leaders" were only God and Christ, no "mere" mortals, and so Paul was oblivious as to whether or not anyone in Jerusalem was or wasn't a "leader"; Paul stood *above* such concerns. "God does not judge by outward appearances," likewise serves two rhetorical goals: First, it, yet again, identifies Paul with the "authentic" followers of God, so that the people who knew Jesus "from man or by means of man" (1:1) and who therefore would have had more authority to speak for Him if one were to "judge by outward appearances," possess a *diminished* claim to holding such authority. Second, with supreme subtlety, it yet again sets the reader up for the coming assault against judging by actions (here supposedly to be equated with "outward appearances"), versus faith (supposedly, inward reality, as opposed to "outward appearances"). Paul is insinuating here that circumcision (such as of Titus, in 2:3) concerns *only* "outward appearances"; this is thus yet another implicit dig against *Genesis* 17:14; Paul is saying, of each Jew's signature upon that individual Jew's contract with God – which *is* his circumcision – that it makes no difference but is merely "for show" (and in 2:16 upcoming, Paul will say *why* it makes no difference: God has *replaced* that contract with a *different* one).

"Those alleged leaders, I say, offered no new suggestions to me," equally subtly, likewise achieves multiple simultaneous objectives for Paul: First, by his employing here the concept "suggestions" instead of "demands" or "commands," from the "alleged leaders," this verbal construction is implicitly placing Paul, yet again, as being equal in rank to his actual superiors within the organization.[37] Second, what the council issued to Paul, whatever it was, was here supposedly not issued at all, but was rather "offered," like a request is "offered." What's "offered" can be declined; a command, however, must be obeyed. So, by Paul's using "offered," he reinforced his insinuation that James, Peter, and the other disciples, were not superior to Paul in the organization. If this

---

[37]   When a court of law in a democracy investigates an organizational or white-collar crime, that court needs to understand the organization, so as to be able to understand why the actors in the organization behaved the ways that they did; this is essential in order to understanding the actors' motives, as well as to understanding what person was responsible for what; it's essential in order to be able *scientifically to reconstruct what happened.* By contrast, many scholars have little or no interest in understanding the organization of the Jesus-followers, little if any interest in such questions as: Where did Paul fit on the organizational chart? Was James the leader, or Peter the leader, or were they co-equals? A person who has a strong need to believe in the supernatural – so as to be able to believe in an afterlife, or for any other reason – can make psychological sense ignoring the organization here, but cannot make legal/forensic sense; a scientifically inclined investigator is necessarily very concerned to understand the organization, and a legal/forensic theory of the case must include the organization. (Prior to Edwin H. Sutherland in 1939 introducing the concept of "white collar crime," courts exhibited little to no interest in understanding the organization.)

Whereas some scholars assume that the organization here was flat and that Paul was equal in status to James and to Peter, or even equal to the members of his own congregations, other scholars make different assumptions regarding the organization, or else they ignore it altogether. The Jesus-followers are thus often viewed as having been a purely God-inspired group, who each imbibed the Spirit spontaneously. However, the evidence, as analyzed here, is clear that James led the group, and that Paul did everything he could to avoid drawing attention to that fact. There are numerous instances in Paul's letters where the subordination to himself of Titus and Timothy and others is indicated clearly, even though Paul always blurred his own subordination to James; it was only where Paul was the subordinate that he *denied* the organization. Paul's intention to manipulate, rather than to inform, his readers, was demonstrated in a multitude of different ways, all of which are studiously ignored by scholars; and this is one.

encounter is the same one that's reported in *Acts* 15, then Paul might here be referring to the Jerusalem leaders ultimately accepting (*Acts* 15:19) "that we should not trouble the Gentiles who are turning to God," and that, therefore, only the easier-to-comply-with commandments (dietary, etc.) should be enforced upon the Gentile converts. However, Paul's account of what was demanded of him, given in 2:10 below, will be even more minimal than that.

2:7 On the contrary, they recognized that God had assigned me to carry the gospel to the uncircumcised, just as Peter had been entrusted with spreading the gospel to the circumcised.
2:8 For God had given each of us our assignments.

2:7-8, "On the contrary, they saw that God had given me the task of preaching the gospel to the uncircumcised," reasserts Paul's authority as having been granted *not* by mere men, such as was that of James (appointed by Jesus) and the other disciples (likewise appointed by the human Jesus); but instead granted directly by God, the Father and Son. "... just as He had given Peter the task of preaching the gospel to the circumcised," which the Galatian readers probably assumed anyway, since Peter possessed far higher seniority within the sect than did Paul. Peter's authority for these readers was unquestioned; Paul's implication here that he possessed equal status with Peter was, by contrast, a palpable *boost* in Paul's status. Furthermore, Paul's assertion that Peter had received from God and not from James authority to preach to the Gentiles constitutes yet another implicit denigration of James as the sect's leader. Paul is here implicitly denying that James had assigned Peter the mission to the Gentiles; Paul is skipping over James to attribute Peter's authority directly to God. (Similarly, Paul here attributes his own authority to God instead of to James. Paul does it in both instances, so as to, yet again, equalize himself to Peter, as *both* being appointed by God. This writes James out of the picture – a brilliant tactic of deception – and implicitly places *only* Peter and Paul as being

God's appointees to carry Jesus's message. Paul here is thus implicitly demoting James from being Paul's boss – which we shall soon see that James *was* – to being Paul's and Peter's subordinate, and Paul is falsely identifying Peter as being Paul's ultimate opponent in the dispute that is next coming.) Also worthy to note in this line is Paul's referring to Jews as "the circumcised," and to Gentiles as "the uncircumcised." This implicitly acknowledges the unique role of the circumcision-commandment, *Genesis* 17:14, because it was the covenant-forming commandment, the basis of Judaism, and so, too, the basis for the distinction that Paul is drawing here, between the two missions, one the mission to Jews, and the other the mission to non-Jews, distinguished solely by the presence or absence of circumcision in those two communities, not distinguished by the presence or absence of circumcision in the respective "gospels" that are taught. Paul will, in fact, just a few lines later (2:15-21), be making clear that there is only one *single* gospel, which is a point that he already has emphasized earlier (1:7-9). Consequently, Paul is emphatic that there's only one gospel; the *same* gospel is being preached to *both* groups within the Jesus-sect. This also means that the decision at the council in Jerusalem affected the teaching *throughout* the sect, and not only the teaching by Paul and by other evangelists who were carrying the message to the Gentiles. Even though Paul's work among Gentiles had precipitated the council, the subject to be decided at the council was to extend universally throughout the sect. In fact, it may very well have been the case that what had finally forced James's hand to convene this meeting was that, over the course of 17 years, two different "gospels" were indeed *beginning to emerge* within the sect and so to create a schism within it. There's no indication that two separate and different "gospel messages" were acceptable to the sect, but only that two different groups of people now constituted the sect, and that, contrary to the sect's aim, those two groups were becoming separated by two different "gospels."

"For God had given each of us our assignments" even
more emphatically places Paul into a context here in which
Paul and Peter are on the same high plane of authority within
the sect – something that actually never was so, not only
because Paul had been Peter's student, but also because Peter
had personally known Jesus and worked with him whereas
Paul had not; and, finally, also because Paul (not only
according to *Acts* but also by his own admission in his letters)
was an enemy of Jesus's Jewish sect before joining it.

   *2:9 James, Peter, and John, the reputed leaders, recognized
my divine assignment, and offered, to me and Barnabas, the right
hand of fellowship, and agreed that we should work among the
Gentiles, while they worked among the circumcised.*

   2:9, "James, Peter, and John, who seemed to be the
leaders," again recapitulates the question as to whether these
leaders really *were* the leaders; 2:6 is thus reinforced. "…
recognized that God has given me this special task," reinforces
yet again that Paul's authority comes *directly* from God rather
than from his own merely mortal enemies in Jerusalem. Paul
implicitly repeats that his authority is higher than that of his
enemies, because his enemies knew Jesus (1:1) "from man or
by means of man," while Paul did not. "… and so they shook
hands with Barnabas and me, as a sign that we were all
partners," not only communicates, yet again, that Paul's status
within the group was at least equal to that of the authentic
disciples, but asserts that Paul's practices were *validated* by
these supposed colleagues of his, at the council, so that Paul
was fully accepted there as the "partner" of these individuals
"who seemed to be the leaders" (2:6&9). "… and we agreed
that Barnabas and I would work among the Gentiles and they
among the Jews," very subtly boosts Paul's status yet again;
instead of his saying here "… and *they instructed us* that
Barnabas and I …," he yet again implicitly denies what's
clearly the *fact*: that the Jerusalem elders *were* Paul's "leaders,"

little though Paul wanted *explicitly* to admit this. This passage also informs us that Paul and Barnabas were equals within the organization; probably the Galatians already knew that Barnabas's status was at least as high as Paul's; Paul was never one to *downplay* his status. Subsequent Christianity knows little of Barnabas; he has nothing in the canon, and only one epistle attributed to him in the apocrypha. However, it's quite possible that Paul wasn't even the leading evangelist to the Gentiles; we've no way of knowing independently of Paul and his followers, and these sources aren't to be trusted on this. Paul's implication here is that God made Paul the leading apostle to the Gentiles, and made Peter the leading apostle to the Jews. However, a later-written letter, *Romans* 11:13 (written to a congregation Paul hadn't started, and which included some born Jews) claims only "I am an apostle to the Gentiles." He doesn't say there that he is "the" apostle to the Gentiles, because that sort of lie wouldn't fly in Rome, where the congregants knew it's not true. Paul was almost certainly the most successful salesman to the Gentiles, but there's no indication he actually held authority over all other salesmen to Gentiles. However, unlike in Rome, probably the Galatians consisted virtually entirely of Gentiles who had no *direct* contact with Jesus's disciples. So, they didn't know. Paul was constantly expoiting their ignorance.

It should be pointed out here that the clause, "… that we should go to the Gentiles and they to the circumcised" repeats the respective assignments; and that – as in 2:3&7&8 – the important implicit *equation* is asserted here, of "the circumcised" with "the Jews," and of "the *un*circumcised" with "the Gentiles"; thus again demonstrating that circumcision was the *central* point at issue in the climax to come. Paul, in 2:3&7&8&9 refers to Jews as "the circumcised," and contrasts them to the Gentiles. This is crucial: it consistently and repeatedly shows that the basic issue discussed at the council in Jerusalem was circumcision.

Another important feature of 2:7-9 is that this passage asserts that Paul would not be allowed to preach to the circumcised – that is, to born Jews – but *only* to people who were not. Wayne Lamar Harrington, at Harrington-sites.com, in his essay "Sacrificing Paul's Credibility to Rescue Acts," notes that this agreement is sufficient reason to disregard the numerous scholars who assert that *Galatians* 2 describes a different Jerusalem conference than does *Acts* 15. Harrington observes that, "To argue that *Galatians* 2:1-10 occurred during Paul's alleged [in *Acts*] Jerusalem visit in *Acts* 11:27-30 & 12:25 is to completely dismiss what was agreed to in *Galatians* 2:1-10. For after that alleged visit the Paul of *Acts* continues to 'go unto the circumcision,' a clear violation to what is agreed to in" *Galatians* 2:7-9. (He cites there passages such as *Acts* 13:5, which assert that Paul and Barnabas "preached the word of God in the synagogues of the Jews" – which would clearly have violated Paul's agreement with the disciples that's indicated in *Galatians*.) Harrington also cites other evidence to show why any scholarly work that quotes *Acts* in preference to Paul's authentic letters should be simply ignored as non-credible. He argued there as a legal/forensian instead of as a scholar. In any event, the only way *Acts* may permissibly be quoted when interpreting one of the authentic Pauline letters is when the given passage in *Acts* is entirely consistent with everything in those letters. Clearly, *Acts* 15 (to the extent that it possesses any historical value at all) refers to the same Jerusalem council as *Galatians* 2. Therefore, after the council in Jerusalem that's referred to in *Galatians* 2, Paul wasn't visiting congregations of born Jews, except possibly to defend the missionary work he was doing among Gentiles.

2:10 They requested only one thing: that we ought to keep in mind the poor in their group, and this was something I was actually eager to do.

2:10, "All they asked was that we should remember the needy in their group, which is the very thing I have been eager to do," contrasts strikingly with the four conditions imposed upon Paul's converts in *Acts* (repeated thrice:

15:20&29 and 21:25); however both versions, Paul's and Luke's, agree on the single critical issue, which is that circumcision, the subject of the debate, was *not* imposed. What we're told is that James (and the other elders, in Paul's account here) decided, *at least for the time being,* not to prohibit Paul from accepting into the sect uncircumcised males. Paul's Gentile converts would be required, according to Paul's account, to adhere to *none* of the covenant; Paul is claiming that the Jerusalem community had capitulated totally, and that Paul's Gentile converts were totally freed from Jewish Law or covenant. By contrast, *Acts* says that Paul's Gentile converts must adhere to the food and sexual laws of *Leviticus* 17 and 18, as well as to the food-law of *Exodus* 34:15 against eating food (meat) that has been sacrificed (slaughtered) in worship of idols, but that (*Acts* 15:19) "we should impose no irksome requirements upon those of the Gentiles who are turning toward God," or, in other words, that these converts need not go under the knife. Also, Paul, in other documents which have much higher credibility than *Acts*, informs us that (*1 Corinthians* 5, 8, and 10) he had, in any case, been *imposing* upon his converts at least *Leviticus* 18 and *Exodus* 34:15; he accepted the food and certainly also the sexual laws, but definitely *not* the "irksome requirement," as *Acts* 15:19 put it. Thus, it seems reasonable to assume here that if *Acts* 15:19-29 is truthful and *Galatians* 2:10 is false, then Paul was probably being required to impose only what he already was, and long had been, imposing upon his converts. Obviously, if *Galatians* 2:10 is true, then, yet again, Paul didn't have to change a thing. So, according to *both* versions, there was no parting of the ways here. But, as was logically implied by the immediately following lines, James subsequently changed his mind in any case, and he and Paul promptly split apart into two different organizations and religions, one being James's Jewish sect that faded from history, and the other being Paul's Christian religion, that became the world's largest.

From this point on, the tone in Paul's account changes suddenly and dramatically; with no explanation from him as

to why, his mood changes from one of cooperation to one of
fierce hostility and outright war. No scholar has ever
explained why; few have even tried to, or so much as even
noted the striking and sudden change in tone; but you can see
it for yourself; it's blatant. The likeliest explanation for this
abrupt souring of Paul's tone is that he skips here a key
intervening event: after Paul returns to Antioch, the debate
within the Jerusalem community probably continued; but, in
any case, James *definitely did change his mind*, for whatever
reason, and he sent agents to Paul to instruct him that he must
no longer accept the uncircumcised: They must be circumcised.

2. Climax: The Event, 2:11-21

2:11 But when Peter came to Antioch, I opposed him in public, because he was clearly wrong.

2:12 Before some men who had been sent by James came, Peter was dining with the Gentile brothers, but when these men arrived, he withdrew from the table and refused to dine with the Gentiles, because he feared the circumcision party.

2:13 The other Jewish brothers joined Peter in this cowardice, so that even Barnabas joined their hypocrisy.

2:14 When I saw that they weren't honest [in expressing their support for the gospel of Christ], I said to Peter, in front of them all:

"You are a Jew [i.e., circumcised], yet you have been living like a Gentile [i.e., as if you weren't a Jew]. So, how can you try to force Gentiles to imitate [born] Jews?

2:15 "Although you and I are Jews by birth and not Gentile sinners [i.e., not non-signers to the Jewish covenant, under the signatory law Genesis 17:11&14],

2:16 "We know that a person is viewed favorably by God only via Christ-faith, never by following God's Law. Even we [you and I] have believed in Jesus Christ in order to be viewed favorably by God via Christ-faith, instead of by adhering to God's Law. For no one can please God by following God's Law.

2:17 "However, if our effort to please God by our union with Christ causes us to sin as the Gentiles do [since they didn't even sign the covenant], does this mean that Christ is assisting us to sin? Of course not!

2:18 "For, if I were to rebuild the system [the Law] that I have torn down, then I would violate the [purpose of the] Law [which is personal salvation].

2:19 "I am dead to the Law, killed by the Law itself, in order that I might live for God. I have joined Christ's death on the cross,

2:20 "So that it is no longer I who live, but Christ, who lives in me. I live this life by faith in the Son of God, who loved me and gave his life for me.

2:21 "I don't nullify God's grace; for, if God views a person favorably upon the basis of a man's following God's Law, then Christ died for nothing!"

This passage receives less attention from the general public than the passages in the canonical Gospels that allege to be quoting Jesus. The reason is: it's not about Jesus, but instead concerns Jesus's apostles/followers two decades later. However, this passage is actually far more important than those "red letter" passages. Unlike any of them, it was written earlier, and by an actual participant in the event it relates; and moreover it describes, in first-person witness testimony, a difference of opinion among top people within the Jesus-followers (e.g., between Peter and Paul). Paul is clashing here with Peter and with James's other agents, concerning Jesus, whom both Peter and James knew, but whom Paul had never even met. (He claimed in 1:1 to have met *only* Jesus's ghost.) This event *really happened;* it's not like the mere allegations about "Jesus" in the Gospels, which are evangelical hearsay at best; this is instead actual witness testimony, by a participant. Paul's slant on this event may be entirely untrustworthy, but will be stripped away regardless, so that a legal/forensic analysis will reconstruct from Paul's account (and from all of the supplementary evidence in this case) a remarkably detailed and thoroughly reliable historical narrative of what actually occurred in this event.

Paul here explicitly condemns Peter, whom the Gospel-writers say was the leader of the Jesus-followers. Furthermore, the subject of this disagreement is whether or not God, after the Crucifixion, changed his mind about the Jewish covenant ("the Law"), and replaced it with Paul's gospel of Christ – Christ-faith being Paul's *new* path to personal salvation – since (2:16) "no one wins God's approval by obeying God's commandments [the Law, the Jewish covenant]." Paul states his case here, against Peter and the agents from James, concerning, essentially, the teachings of Jesus (whom, as we've noted, they had met, and Paul had not). The views of Peter and of James concerning these matters can far more reliably be reconstructed by means of a legal/forensic analysis of this passage than by means of any analysis of the letters in the New Testament that are attributed to Peter and to James, because the actual authorship of those letters from "Peter" and from "James" is unknown, and many scholars consider the letters from "Peter" and "James" to be bogus: written by anonymous forgers, after the deaths of both men. By contrast, this letter from Paul is virtually unanimously accepted as being authentic. So, here we not only possess the definitive statement regarding Paul's position in this seminal conflict, but we also possess the most reliable evidence with which to be able to reconstruct, from this account, *the opposed position*, of both Peter and James, against which Paul is here arguing. Although subsequent Christianity (as canonized in the New Testament) stands with Paul, and against Peter and James, in this seminal dispute, and thus accepts Paul's doctrine of salvation-via-Christ-faith, and repudiates as no longer valid the Jewish covenant (salvation-via-obedience-to-the-Law), serious question exists regarding whether that position accurately reflects Jesus's views, because both Peter and James had known Jesus, while Paul – the proponent of this *new* covenant – had never met him.

2:11-21 doesn't just state what Paul wanted his Galatian readers to believe, but it – more importantly for historians – recounts the first occasion at which Paul had asserted this startling doctrine (of salvation by mere faith), and presents this within the context of the circumstances (1:1-2:10) that *had led up to and caused* this first-ever assertion of it by Paul. This passage thus comprises his account of the climactic Antioch break with the Jerusalem community of Jesus-followers, the event – occurring during the year 49 or 50 – at which Paul's followers and James's followers were drawn to opposite poles, into communities with (as subsequent history has shown) drastically different fates: oblivion for the Jewish Jesus's Jerusalem-oriented group led by James, and ultimate global dominance for the Rome-oriented group created and started from this point onward (not from the point of telling, but from the point being told about) by Paul. This passage culminates in 2:16, which announces "A person is viewed favorably by God only by possessing Christ-faith, never by obeying God's commandments." Paul there is rejecting Judaism (salvation via obeying God's commandments) and replacing Judaism by Christianity (salvation via Christ-faith). Here he describes the circumstances that led him to do this – to introduce Christianity. For mysteriously unexplained reasons, Peter comes to Antioch, and Paul opposes him in public, concerning a subject that likewise remains tantalizingly unidentified. But, given 2:3-5, there can now hardly be doubt about what it had been that had driven Paul to confess, at the end of 2:2, "I did not want my work in the past and in the present to be a failure." (Literally: "I did not want to have been, and to be, running [my race] in vain." Paul resorted to such cryptic and obscure phraseology whenever he hoped that his audience wouldn't understand what he was writing about. By his employing such phraseology, anyone who unfortunately already knew the truth couldn't object and would credit him with being truthful, and anyone who didn't would remain in the dark, as he wanted. So, no one would object, and yet he would actually yield nothing. This left him safe, and served his cause either way.) Furthermore, 2:3 makes clear that the thing that had aroused such intense opposition from Paul as to make him call his teacher Peter "hypocritical" and a "coward" was the threatened imposition of the *circumcision-commandment* (specifically, *Genesis* 17:14). And when Paul in 2:4 went so far as to charge, "They wanted to make slaves of us!" by *imposing* circumcision, the danger against his winning the race (2:2 and also *1 Corinthians* 9:24, as well as *Philippians* 2:16 and 3:12-14) was starkly cast. Peter, in 2:11-12, is at first portrayed here as accepting of Paul's uncircumcised "converts," at least until (2:12) "some men who had been sent by James arrived." Likewise mysteriously, Paul never states why James had sent them, or even what they did when they arrived. All that we're informed of by Paul is that Peter "drew back and would not eat with the Gentiles, because he was afraid of those who were in favor of circumcising them." But who were these "those"? Again, Paul doesn't say; he leaves all of his meaning in this passage *behind* the lines, virtually none *on* the lines (which is the level that scholars have restricted themselves exclusively to). But, clearly, "those" refers here to the "agents from James." This reveals a great deal; it reveals that *James actually precipitated this blowup.* And the law that Paul's men were violating, the circumcision-law, had been the focus of the dispute at the council in Jerusalem leading up to this climactic moment. And the particular law that Peter was caught here by James's men to have been violating might well have been *Exodus* 12:48-49, the law against ceremonially dining with uncircumcised men. Or else, Peter might have been considered by James's men not to have been breaking any law at all; it's enough that James's backup team caught him dining with Paul's men *as if they were fellow members,* when he was supposed to have been instead demanding them first to *become* members by being *circumcised* – not to treat them as if they were, until they were. What seems clear here is that Peter was caught violating his assignment from James. (If your Bible happens to be one that mistranslates this key passage of 2:12, to indicate Peter here fearing not proponents

CHRIST'S VENTRILOQUISTS

of circumcision, but instead fearing anyone who happens to be Jewish or "circumcised," then you'll probably find of interest the following box, "A Fine Point of Translation." Otherwise, you might prefer to skip it.)

A FINE POINT OF TRANSLATION

When we read Paul (or any other translated source for that matter), part of that reading is necessarily of the translation itself. Paul wrote in ancient Greek, one of the two languages (the other being Latin) of his era's power-elite, with whom Paul personally identified (as opposed, say, to Jesus's own Aramaic tongue, which was dominant among the Jewish poor). Here we shall explore the single biggest translation-problem in the New Testament, which concerns a phrase at the end of *Galatians* 2:12. Specifically, the question to be answered here is: Did Peter draw away from the dinner table because it was serving non-kosher foods, or did he withdraw from it because his dining partners there, Paul's men, were not circumcised? It may sound like a small point, but it's actually huge, because if the correct answer was the latter, then the issue here was whether or not Paul's men were complying with the covenant in terms of their own personal identity – whether or not these men *were* Jews and thus could be members of the Jesus sect at all. On the other hand, if the issue was merely whether or not the food fulfilled Judaism's kosher laws, then only Paul's own compliance with Judaism was at stake, and not whether or not his men were being rejected by Peter, and by James's other representatives, as being not members of the Jesus-sect of Jews. In other words, if food was the issue here, then only Paul's compliance with Judaism was being challenged by James's men; but if circumcision was the issue, then the compliance, and even the Jewish identity, of Paul's men was the issue, and Paul's violation would have been not that his food was un-kosher, but that he had not commanded his men to become circumcised. Consequently, a truthful translation of this line, 2:12, will tell us what was really at issue in the council at Jerusalem just prior to it. If what was at issue in 2:12 was Paul's non-compliance with the kosher laws, then his disobedience here of James's final decision after the Jerusalem conference would mean that that final decision was that Paul must serve only kosher food. This wouldn't have meant that Paul's congregations weren't members of the Jesus-community. But if 2:12 concerned instead circumcision, then James's final decision was that all of Paul's men must be circumcised – a matter of their personal identity.

This is the key to whether or not what Paul is describing here was the incident that created Christianity. Obviously, people who see themselves as Christians and who don't think that they're members in a Jewish sect, wouldn't want to view this passage as being about circumcision, *Genesis* 17:14 – and Christian scholars don't see it as focusing around circumcision. But does it?

It does.

People who see this passage as focusing instead around the kosher laws haven't a leg to stand on: there's no indication anywhere in the New Testament that Paul's congregations, during his lifetime, weren't required to adhere to, and did not adhere to, the kosher laws. But there are numerous clear indications in the New Testament that they weren't being required to adhere to the circumcision law.

Galatians 2:12 represents Paul's account of the greatest turning-point in its writer's life: the moment in which he gave up on Jesus's Jewish sect and set forth boldly into the future to found his own new faith worshipping Jesus Himself, in direct violation (as we have previously explained) of Judaism's first three of the Ten Commandments (*Exodus* 20:3-7 and *Deut.* 5:7-11): the First Commandment against having other gods (such as "the Son"); the Second against making images of God (such as of the crucified Christ), and against bowing in prayer before such idols; and the Third against misnaming the one unitary God (via renaming it into three parts, the Trinity – and even *Galatians* 1:1&3&4 had introduced the *two*-part God). This gross violation of Paul's own former Judaic faith is crucial to understand in order to have a sense for the possible embarrassment that Paul might well have felt in recounting here to his Galatian readers the event that had driven him to abandon that faith and to create his own religion to replace it. This was a momentous step for anyone to take – even Paul. It inevitably would have elicited in him very mixed emotions, if only because he knew that he was violating the instructions of Jesus's religious organization that he had worked for during the prior 17 tumultuous years, for which violation alone he would naturally have felt extremely embarrassed; yet he also probably felt immensely proud to be pioneering an entirely new religion that he was convinced stood a far better chance than did Jesus's sect, of enshrining Jesus's name into the hearts and minds of perhaps billions of people in future generations. Thus, Paul's understandably conflicted emotions about this momentous event produced from him an ambiguous expression here to describe it. Furthermore, Paul didn't want to "give away" to his Galatian readers any more than he necessarily had to tell them in order to respond to charges that they might already have heard from his enemies, James's men, concerning this incident. Therefore, for two very powerful reasons, Paul couched in enigmatic, obscure, terms, his description of this event; and, as a consequence, bible-translations of this key passage vary significantly in their meaning.

The biggest single variance in translation concerns the meaning of the end-part of 2:12, in which the Greek original can in a generic sense be said to refer to Peter's fear of the party of circumcision, which could possibly be interpreted either as fear of the circumcised ones, namely of the Jews; or else as fear of the proponents of circumcision, irrespective of whether or not they might have been Jews or Gentiles. On the first of these two interpretations, Peter was afraid of the agents from James because they were Jews; on the second, he was afraid of them because they were advocating circumcision. Although the context (e.g., *Galatians* 2:3 & 3:6-10 & 5:2-7; *Acts* 15:1-3 & 15:19; etc.) indicates quite clearly that proponents of circumcision, not Jews themselves, were Paul's adversaries in this climactic incident, Paul in 2:12 skillfully avoided employing words that made clear what the meaning was, and this has provided scholars with a welcomed opportunity to avoid dealing with the unpleasant reality that stands behind Paul's words here. This opportunity was further enhanced by means of Paul's passing reference in 2:12 to Peter's having been *dining* with Paul's Gentile followers, so that one could conceivably, if one wanted to do so, interpret the cause of this tumult to have been the Jewish dietary laws, even though those laws were never an issue; but Peter could, nonetheless, conceivably still have been backing away from the table here because James's men had caught him dining at a perhaps un-kosher table, rather than because the other diners there had not been circumcised. This would change the meaning of the entire passage, confuse that meaning, and thus de-fang the passage's implications, and scholars have therefore overwhelmingly selected this (Christian-apologetic) interpretation, that only Paul's violation of kosher laws was the issue here; but how likely is it to be true? There's substantial evidence against, and no evidence in support of that interpretation. Here is why:

   According to Paul's account (*Gal.* 2:10), the Jerusalem sect of Jesus-followers demanded of Paul only that he keep in mind the poor among their Jerusalem community, not that Paul's people adhere to any of the laws of the covenant, neither to the dietary laws, nor to the circumcision-law, nor to any other. And on the basis of *Acts* 15:29 (& 15:20 & 21:25), the only requirements were to adhere to the dietary and sexual laws, but (considering 15:19) to permit violating the circumcision-law. Consequently, according to *both* accounts (*Galatians* 2:10, and *Acts* 15:29), the standard scholars' interpretation of *Galatians* 2:12, that "table fellowship" at an un-kosher meal is what had been violated here by Peter, makes no sense at all: if Peter was being caught dining at an un-kosher table, then that wouldn't have been violating *Galatians* 2:10, and there would have been, according to Paul's account there, no issue whatsoever in 2:12, yet there clearly *was* an issue; and furthermore, the only violation of *Acts* 15:29 (etc.) would have been that *Paul* (not Peter) would have been violating his promise to impose the kosher laws upon his followers, but in that case Paul's charge of Peter's "cowardice" (*Gal.* 2:13) here wouldn't make any sense; it wouldn't even be an issue at all, yet Peter's "cowardice" clearly *was* an issue to Paul. Furthermore, according to *1 Corinthians* 8, Paul's regular practice was to urge his followers *not* to violate the kosher laws in any event (even though for reasons other than the kosher laws themselves), and so it is *extremely* unlikely that Paul's dinner table serving Peter on this occasion would have *been* un-kosher. Even more striking, a few lines earlier in the same letter, 7:19 instructs his Corinthian followers, "Whether a man is circumcised is unimportant; the only important thing is to obey God's commandments." That line, which was clearly written *prior* to the split, proves that the *only* law that Paul's men were *not* being instructed by him to follow was the *circumcision* law, *Genesis* 17:14. Paul therefore served a kosher table. The food laws, consequently, could not have been an issue at all in *Galatians* 2:12. The *only* explanation that makes sense under *either* scenario (*Gal.* 2:10 or *Acts* 15:29) is that the issue between Paul and Peter here was that Peter was caught by James's representatives dining with uncircumcised men, after James had changed his mind immediately following the council and sent first Peter, and then those other representatives, to demand Paul finally to impose circumcision, and that Paul was now shocked to see Peter side *with* James against himself, when Peter had done the very same as Paul when Peter had been proselytizing to the Gentiles (*Gal.* 2:14 and *Acts* 11:2), and even though Peter had just a few days earlier *defended* Paul's doing the same (according to *Acts* 15:7-11). The only thing that Paul has told us about James's men is that they were "of the party of circumcision," so that circumcision clearly was at issue here; only Paul has not told us *how* it was at issue, because he doesn't want to tell his readers how it was, if they don't already know how it was; he doesn't want to present his enemies' case here, but *only* his own. Fortunately, however, the application of a little logic makes unambiguously clear *how* circumcision was at issue: *James changed his mind on the circumcision-issue.* This is clear because clearly the entire tumult was precipitated by the arrival of James's men in 2:12: James had sent, as his first representative to Paul, Peter, in 2:11, starting the confrontation with Paul. Peter was selected by James as the best possible person to lay the bad news upon Paul, because Peter had been Paul's own mentor and senior in the Gentile mission. But, evidently, Peter was meek and didn't press the issue. Perhaps he was just too soft a person for such a hard assignment. In any case, a backup team from James evidently entered by surprise only a few hours later, to check up on Peter's work so as to *verify* Peter's enforcement of this changed order from James. Peter's shocked backing-away from the table now in 2:12 makes sense: not only was Peter caught here violating James's instructions to him, by his evidently not having stood firm in his presentations to Paul and his men; Peter might even have been felt, by James's strict Jews, to be violating not only James's assignment to him, but God's will, the principle that's set forth in *Exodus* 12:48-49 against Jews ceremonially dining with *any* non-circumcised males, such as Paul's men here were known to be. In *Acts* 11:3, Peter had years earlier been caught in the same violation; but way back then, James hadn't yet made up his mind on enforcement of the circumcision-commandment. Now he quite clearly had finally done so.

Further evidence that circumcision was the issue here is that throughout *Galatians* 2:2-9, "the uncircumcised" is synonymous with "Gentiles," and "the circumcised" is synonymous with "Jews," and *not* with "those who dine kosher" or etc. Yet further evidence is that in *Galatians* 2:3-5 and 2:12 in the incident itself, and in 5:2-12 concerning the very reason for Paul's having written this letter, circumcision was the *only* point at issue; and also that in *Acts* 15:2-3&5&19, likewise describing the council in Jerusalem, yet again circumcision was the only point at issue. In other words, the evidence that the majority of scholars are wrong in their interpretations here is both consistent and overwhelming.

Some, but by no means all, of the standard Bible-translations reflect this studied obtuseness by the scholars. For example, in *Galatians* 2:12, the King James, New King James, New Catholic Edition, New American Bible for Catholics, New Jerusalem Bible, New Century Version, Contemporary English Version, and Revised English Bible, all present Peter (who himself was a circumcised Jew), like an anti-Semite, as fearing simply Jews, rather than as fearing *advocates* of circumcision, in this passage. The New International Version is thoroughly ambiguous on this vital point – undecided as to what Paul was referring to. The Revised Standard Version, New Revised Standard Version, English Standard Version, New American Standard Bible, and Amplified Bible, all tilt in the direction of Peter's fearing advocates of circumcision instead of Jews *per se*. And, admirably, the New English Bible, Good News or Today's English Bible, New Living Translation, and Jerusalem Bible, all get the reference right here: they portray Peter as fearing proponents of circumcision, not as fearing Jews *per se* as an anti-Semite. The standard scholarly, directly anti-Semitic, false, interpretation of this passage (as also of *Titus* 1:10 and of *Acts* 11:2) has absolutely no justification, and no excuse whatsoever.

Paul's followers in *Galatians* 2:11-14 are indicated to be violating the covenant somehow; the only issue is which law they are violating.

But if the kosher laws were at stake here, and circumcision was not, then would it really be the case that Christianity didn't start at this occasion? If the kosher laws were the issue, then the New Testament makes no coherent sense at all; and thus, this incident would constitute merely another piece of nonsense in a Scripture so hopelessly loaded with self-contradictions that the only basis upon which one can accept it is to willfully accept self-contradiction, and to base one's morality upon it. This is to reject Jesus and to accept the people who wrote such nonsense about him and his movement.

However, not only do scientists shun individuals who accept a scripture on blind faith, but most scholars do as well. Or, at least, many scholars are averse to seeing themselves as people of faith.

This passage describes the founding of "Christianity." The significance of getting the answer *right* here is that *only* if the answer is right, can Christianity's founding event be understood. If one doesn't wish to understand the founding of Christianity, then one won't wish to get the answer right here. However, there's no justification or excuse for getting it wrong. The evidence concerning which law was being violated is clear, it's entirely consistent, and it is overwhelming: Paul's men weren't circumcised; they were in violation of *Genesis* 17:14. Peter's violation here was his violation of James's assignment to him to lay down the law to Paul and to Paul's inauthentic "converts." (Peter might also have been felt to have been caught in violation of *Exodus* 12:48-49; he was dining with these *uncircumcised men.*) It's important to understand these things, in order to be able to understand the creation of Christianity – *if* one wishes to understand that.

One can accept Paul's account at face value, but only upon the basis of faith – not upon the basis of science. According to science, Paul was a salesman who would do anything in order to succeed – even desecrate the will and the intention of the man (Jesus) whose beliefs he *claimed* to be championing.

What was actually going on here? There is obviously a lot that's *hidden* behind these lines. Let's peel off the outer layer that scholars focus upon, and get to what's really important: Paul doesn't explicitly state why Peter had come to Antioch. Paul doesn't explicitly state what the issue was between himself and Peter. Paul doesn't explicitly state what the emissaries or agents from James had come this long way for. *These are the basic things that must be understood in order to be able to understand this crucial passage,* but Paul doesn't explicitly answer ANY of these essential questions. Fortunately, however, they're all IMPLICITLY answered, and not only by Paul's text's having offered *mere* SUGGESTIONS of what the actual case MIGHT have been, concerning which Paul was writing, but by LOGICALLY NECESSARY IMPLICATION indicating what the case *actually and incontrovertibly* WAS. (For a text to logically imply "x" is not for it to merely suggest "x" or indicate that "x" is probably the case, but is instead for it to assert that "x" *is* the case, no less powerfully than if the text explicitly asserted "x." However, the differences between assertions that are explicit and assertions that are logically-necessarily implied will be discussed here subsequently.) We'll now be developing this incontrovertible case.

But first: what can possibly explain Paul's reasons for his not having *explicitly* ADDRESSED these central issues in his

letter to the Galatians? And what can explain his having
mentioned this blowup *at all*? What could have motivated him
to have mentioned the incident to them, and yet NOT to have
explicitly ANSWERED these BASIC questions about it for his
Galatian readers?

To this matter, there's only *one* answer that is at all
likely to be correct:[38] Paul knows or believes that his Galatian
congregations *might* have received, from the sect's
headquarters in Jerusalem – that is, from James's emissaries –
accounts of this event. Paul isn't necessarily certain that his
Galatian followers have been informed of the event by James's
people, but he can't afford to take any CHANCES on that; he
must ASSUME that they've been informed of the event, and *by
his* ENEMIES. And he has to place his own spin on it here, yet
without telling the Galatians anything more about the event
than they probably already know of it from James's people.
Paul therefore has to walk a rhetorical tightrope here: he has
to talk about this (to him) extremely embarrassing event, yet
without explicitly saying just *what it was*; and he has to do it in
such a way, or with such spin, that the *only* thing that
explicitly comes out about the event, is HIS side of the dispute.
Paul has to refer to a dispute without making explicit even
that it really WAS a dispute; and, at the same time, he has to
make explicit exactly what HIS side of that argument was. The
letter to the Galatians has masterfully built up to this point,
and the letter's follow-through will be equally masterful, as
we'll see.

---

[38] This inference – that Paul believes that the Galatians might possibly
already have heard of this blowup from James's agents – is *not* logically-
necessarily implied, such as is for example the inference that James's agents
precipitated the blowup here. But it fits with everything else that Paul says in
Galatians, and no other explanation for Paul's having mentioned the blowup does.
In that sense, this inference (that Paul mentioned the blowup because he knew that
the Galatians might already have heard of it from his enemies) is drawn by a
process of elimination of alternative possible explanations for Paul's having
mentioned the blowup. [continued]

The Enormous Challenge Paul Faced

But the situation for Paul here is even dicier than this:
he cannot afford to say anything against his actual opponent,

The *likeliest alternative* possible explanation for Paul's having mentioned it would be that Paul was just rambling there, that he was verbally wandering, and not headed toward some persuasive goal in his mentioning of this blowup. However, that explanation would contradict everything else that's *demonstrated* by Paul in this letter – it's all stunningly goal-oriented. So, this option can simply be dismissed.

Might Paul have mentioned the incident because James's verdict at the end of the conference *allowed* Paul's men to continue being uncircumcised? Paul could then instead have said in 2:10 something like, "The verdict at this conference was that you're Jews even though uncircumcised." The reason he *didn't* is that Paul didn't want to tell any of his followers who didn't already know it, that their *non*-circumcision was an issue of great concern among Jesus's disciples. He didn't want to tell them that their membership was being challenged, much less why. He was never explicit about circumcision's being an issue at all in Jerusalem. Only *implicitly* was that displayed. If he had *informed* his followers that Jesus's disciples were disturbed at their being uncircumcised, Paul would have had to deal with the question, "Why are they concerned about this?" He wanted *no such question*.

Could one reasonably assert that the hypothesis is "speculative" that Paul mentioned this blowup on account of his having thought that word of the blowup might *already* have reached one or more of the Galatians from James's agents? Hardly: this hypothesis about why he mentioned it is established almost as certainly as if it were a logically necessary inference from the text (such as is the inference that James's agents *precipitated* the blowup). It meets the "beyond a reasonable doubt" standard, though not the "beyond a doubt" standard (such as does the latter). In criminal trials, the highest requisite standard of proof for anything is "beyond a reasonable doubt"; no court of law demands proof that's "beyond a doubt."

Speculation is avoided as much as possible here, but not necessarily 100%. By contrast, scholarship on Paul's letters is rife with speculation, not even meeting the weaker "preponderance of the evidence" standard in matters of textual interpretation, which is why there are so many different scholarly interpretations of what Paul meant. Scholars build their interpretive opinions not upon Paul, but upon the interpretive opinions that other scholars have published about Paul. Scholars selectively cite other scholars who happen to agree with their own interpretation of a given line of text, and they assert this arbitrary selection as if they were thereby arguing for their own interpretation on the basis of evidence, when their argument is instead based only upon a selection of other people's opinions, and not upon actual evidence at all. Traditional scholarship is thus very speculative, indeed. The purpose of a legal/forensic analysis is to *reduce* speculation as much as is humanly possible, and this is the goal here.

James, explicitly, because he knows that his congregations look up to his opponent as possessing (for his readers) higher authority than he himself does. 2:12 indicates that the "representatives of James" carried such high authority as to be able to cause even Peter to back away from the table and join them against Paul. Peter, far from being the head of the sect, could even be called "cowardly," "hypocritical," and "wrong" by Paul, and everyone would accept his saying it; Paul wasn't then attacked in return, for being insubordinate, even though he was denigrating his own teacher (according to 1:18), Peter. Paul could publicly attack Peter, but could not publicly attack James. Paul, as was previously documented, had been converting Gentiles into James's Jewish sect, not into Paul's new religion; and Peter had come here on a mission from James. James's people had caught Peter violating this mission in some way. Paul's challenge now was to defend his ground against James, who could not be attacked, and also against Peter, who could be attacked; so, Paul attacked Peter. This is also the reason for all of Paul's earlier references, *leading up to* his description of the actual event, in which he had asserted that perhaps the acknowledged leaders weren't *really* the leaders in the eyes of God (e.g., 2:6). Paul needed to tear down the leaders' authority as representatives of Jesus, but to do this job in such a way that he wouldn't invite being attacked in return. Likewise, in *2 Corinthians* 11:5 & 12:11, he twice told his congregants (only in a different geographical region), "I am not at all inferior to those special 'apostles' of yours." No one would have replied "Yes you *are* inferior to them!" which would have seemed to his congregants a cruel rebuke to the very man who had brought them into the sect.

    In other words: Here were "agents from James," and Peter – Paul's own *teacher* in the mission to the Gentiles – and Paul is telling his readers who are followers in the mission to the Gentiles, in essence: I, who brought you into this group, had a disagreement with those men who preceded me and who even taught me, and they were wrong and I was right about Jesus.

The rhetorical burden Paul faced here was almost impossible to overcome, but subsequent history proves to us that he nonetheless *succeeded* and overcame it.

Since Paul's "converts" had originally seen themselves as having converted *not* to *Paul's* organization, but to *James's*, Paul now had to work very hard, AFTER the split, in order to keep these nominal "converts" to the Jesus-sect of Jews, as ACTUAL converts to his own NEW religion (which is represented here by 2:16-21). He had to make the process, of conversion *away* from Judaism, as imperceptible to them as possible. Implicitly, Paul had been working, up to this point in his letter, repeatedly upon his Galatian readers, to get them to doubt that James really DID possess higher authority than himself. Now will come the PAYOFF from all that work.

Consequently, too, while Paul is here criticizing Peter explicitly, he still can't lay a rhetorical *hand* on James explicitly. The emissaries from James appear explicitly in Paul's account almost as only an incidental detail (in 2:12), rather than as the MOTIVE FORCE in this entire incident that they IMPLICITLY clearly were. People with a weak sense of a given text's internal logic[39] will hardly even NOTICE from Paul's account here that James's agents are important, much less, *central*, to what's going on in this passage – nor that this

---

[39]   Scholars are like this, because they've been encouraged to be, by the wider society, which wants to believe in the prevailing myths. By contrast, lawyers in a court in a democracy are encouraged to win; this means that the incentives in legal/forensic practice are to *expose* falsehoods, instead of only to *protect* them.

As is noted in the Conclusion, the stakes in court proceedings are high, whereas the stakes in academia are low – essentially, only the careers of the profession's practitioners (the professors) are at stake in academia, whereas the stakes in a court of law are not just the lawyers' careers but even more directly their clients, and are far larger for the clients, so that even the client's life or death can be at stake in court. Those high stakes drive courts to apply science, and not faith, as the underlying epistemology there. Consequently, the adversarial system is established in order to assist the truth to result, and it does this by providing an incentive for each side to find and expose any falsehoods on the other side. [continued]

passage is the most important one in the entire New Testament, as we shall here prove. Paul would probably have loved to have poured out here his hatred against James's agents, but he couldn't very well have done that, since this letter's Galatian readers knew that these "agents from James" were from their own sect's head. Later, however, in 4:17-21, Paul can SAFELY make negative reference to such agents who had been sent NOT to him, Paul, but, on that *other* occasion, to THEM, his congregants. He's under no such constraint in THAT case, because, there, to malign James's agents isn't explicitly to set Paul himself against the readers' own sect's leader; the opposition in 4:17-21 is instead implicitly between, on the one hand, the Galatians themselves, and on the other, James's agents as *their* enemy. Yet more implicitly, in 4:17-21, if the

---

By contrast, in academia, especially outside the established sciences in which clearly recognized standards of truth/falsity exist, collegiality is a far bigger determinant of career-success than is the quality of one's work, and often the best practitioners die obscure. The best practitioners in the law are paid well for winning, and are immediately known for their skill, not only by their professional colleagues, but by the general public. Similarly, in scientific research, the best practitioners rise to recognition, from both their colleagues and the general public, by means of advancing truths and discrediting falsehoods, and the falsehoods that are discredited in this process are ones that have been hypothesized by other scientists. All of science is an adversarial system.

(We are still only early in the shift from the Religious Age to the Scientific Age, and therefore even the supposedly established scientific fields *remain*, unfortunately, significantly corrupt and authority-based; but that's not to condemn science, which is the ideal; it is to condemn the failure yet to achieve it – to condemn faith, *not* to condemn science. Faith is *always* the enemy of progress.)

In other words, the incentive system in scholarship has encouraged the keeping-hidden of Paul's hoax, and that's why scholars have botched these matters, from a scientific standpoint. To achieve anything like legal/forensic excellence within academe, professors would have to be rewarded on the basis of their exposing and discrediting (meaning not just attacking, but convincingly disproving) defects in the works of their colleagues. At present, a professor, especially outside the hard sciences, instead places his career at risk by exposing the incompetence or deceit of his colleagues – especially if the malefactor who is thereby exposed is influential – and this system inevitably perpetuates myths.

A go-along-to-get-along culture stifles, instead of supports, the truth. That's why scholars haven't even noticed that James was the driver behind this, the most important passage in the New Testament.

Galatians themselves thought of those agents as being representatives from James – which is likely – then Paul is here painting James as actually HIS READERS' OWN ENEMY, without Paul's so much as even MENTIONING James's name: as was noted, he couldn't lay a rhetorical hand against James. And so he did not. Paul's behavior here is supremely tactful.

Paul in 4:17-21 portrays these agents from James ever-so-gingerly as sneaky and downright evil, by saying, "Those other people show a deep interest in you, but their intentions are not good. All they want is to separate you from me, so that you will have the same interest in them as they have in you. Now, it is good to have such a deep interest if the purpose is good – this is true always, and not merely when I am with you. My dear children! Once again, like a mother in childbirth, I feel the same kind of pain for you until Christ's nature is formed in you. How I wish I were with you now, so that I could take a different attitude toward you. I am so worried about you!" Paul here skillfully analogizes himself to their own *loving* MOTHER, and his concern for them as being like a mother's natural concern that some evil-intentioned person (James) will take the child away from her. But never does Paul explicitly MENTION James in such aspersions – only James's *agents* – and the reason is simply that, until the event that Paul recounts in 2:11-16, Paul had himself been selling these same Galatian readers *on James's organization*. So, now, he has to wean them AWAY from that, and to portray James's agents as, essentially, loose wheels, yet without ever explicitly indicating to his readers that this is what he's trying to do to them. Also in *1 Corinthians* 3:1-2, he reminded the Corinthians that when he first converted them to Judaism, "I had to feed you milk and not solid food, because you were not ready for it. And even now you aren't, because you still focus more on this world than on the next." (His reference there, to "the next," exhibited his emphasis, shown in *Galatians* 1:1 and elsewhere, on the afterlife, above real life.)

Paul had, perhaps just a few years prior to this Galatian letter, employed a similar tactic with the Thessalonians, saying

in *1 Thessalonians* 2:7-8, from this Thessalonian letter that
many scholars date immediately prior to the one Paul wrote to
the Galatian community, "When we were with you, we were
gentle, like a mother taking care of her children. Because of
our love for you, we have shared with you not only the Good
News [the gospel], but ourselves. You are so dear to us!"

Then, just a few lines later in this Thessalonian letter, in
2:14-16, he spoke of "the Jews" (UNNAMED of whom being
PRINCIPALLY James) who "even tried to stop us from preaching
to the Gentiles [including to these very same readers] the
message that would bring them salvation," etc. That "stop us
from preaching" line was referring PRECISELY TO THIS EVENT
recounted in *Galatians* 2:11-16. That's why *1 Thessalonians* 2:14-
16 was so impassioned; it referred to this recent climactic
event in Paul's life. In fact, when Paul said there that "the Jews
... even tried to stop us from preaching the message which
would bring salvation to the Gentiles," he was referring to
James and the "agents from James" in *Galatians* 2:12. This was
the only place in all of Paul's writings where he referred to
James's change-of-mind about the necessity of imposing
Genesis 17:14 upon Paul's "converts" to Judaism. Even here, he
veiled what he was saying, and the reason is clear: He
couldn't afford to be *explicit* that James *had* changed his mind
about this.

Paul Faces Even Bigger Challenge Now

Furthermore, fascinating additional supporting
evidence of the development of Paul's thinking is provided in
1 Thessalonians, which is the only surviving whole epistle that
Paul is generally considered to have produced before
Galatians. According to the scholarly consensus, *1
Thessalonians* was written in or about 50 CE, only shortly after
the council in Jerusalem. If that view is correct, then this letter
would have exhibited Paul's thinking SOON AFTER THE SPLIT, but

yet possibly BEFORE his outright *war* against Judaism had
started. The hostility would have been there, but it would
have been *held in* CHECK if there still were felt to remain some
possibility of an ultimate rapprochement between Paul and the
Jerusalem elders. And *1 Thessalonians* does reflect *precisely*
such a transitional state. Paul, in this letter, doesn't attack
Judaism at all. (He restricts his attacks there to Jews, in 2:14-
16, but – unlike in his much later-written *Philippians*, in its line
3:8 that calls Judaism itself trash – he doesn't attack Judaism,
because what he had initially SOLD these people on, just so
SHORT a time before, was itself a VARIETY of JUDAISM: THE NEW
SECT JESUS HAD STARTED.) To the contrary, in 4:1-12, he reminds
the Thessalonians, "you have learned from us how you should
live in order to please God," and he then proceeds to tell them
that, if they will adhere to the Jewish covenant, they WILL
please God. 4:7-8 even says, "God did not call us to live in
immorality, but in holiness. Therefore, whoever rejects this
teaching is rejecting not man, but God." That's Judaism, pure
and simple, he was preaching there (salvation via adhering to
God's commandments), in this earliest of his surviving letters,
written right after the split. But, just a few lines later, in 4:15-
17, Paul informs the Thessalonians of "what we are teaching
you *now* [the emphasis here being mine]," which is, 4:16,
"Those who have died believing in Christ will be the *first*
[again, my emphasis] to be raised to eternal life" on Judgment
Day; and this, of course, is Paul's *new*, Christian, covenant,
NOT the old, Jewish, one. Only it's an importantly different
version from the one he subsequently taught (such as in
Galatians 2:16): it's not yet a *supersessionist* one (though
trending in that direction – i.e., toward *replacing* the Jewish one
– on account of his placing it "first"). When Paul wrote this to
the Thessalonians, he wasn't saying that the Jewish pathway
to heaven has been superseded by the Christian pathway, but
that it co-exists with the Christian pathway. Implicitly, then, *1
Thessalonians* presents a two-covenant, or two-pathways,
theory of salvation, even though a two-pathways theory that
gives the new, Christian, pathway *first preference* in the Pauline

God's view.

Here, then, is important documentary evidence of the evolution or development of Paul's teaching, changes that were exquisitely calculated by him to meet his changing tactical challenges, and where he outsmarted not only his enemies, such as James, but even his friends, including scholars right down till the present day. Scholars, even today, remain so balled-up in their controversies about what Paul's message was, that they don't realize that – and how – Paul's message changed, both over time, and to different audiences (Christian and Jew). The reason for this confusion is that scholars haven't had legal/forensic methodology. (Most scholars thus used the vastly inferior evidence, *Acts*, to track Paul's development, and this has caused endless confusions in their interpretations of Paul.)

Prior to the split, Paul's challenge was to make his followers think that circumcision was optional in Judaism; after the split (once he had finally lost that challenge), his challenge was even bigger: to bring these people over into Paul's own, entirely new, religion, yet without letting them know that he was doing this to them.

Another indication that tends to date this letter, to the Thessalonians, soon after the council in Jerusalem, is the letter's opening with 1:1, "From Paul, Silas, and Timothy": *Acts* 15:40-16:3 says that Silas and Timothy JOINED Paul for a missionary journey that took place SOON AFTER the council in Jerusalem; and so, if that's true, Silas and Timothy accompanied Paul shortly after the council in Jerusalem. Also, 16:3 indicates that Timothy wasn't circumcised, but that Paul REQUIRED HIM TO BE CIRCUMCISED in order to join Paul on this trip. If this is true, then Paul probably felt confident that Timothy's commitment was sufficiently strong for Timothy to be able to accept the intense pain and danger that circumcision entailed. Paul's alleged requirement of circumcision here provides strong external support to *1 Thessalonians* reflecting Paul's *transition* from the split to the war. The circumcision of Timothy makes sense ONLY within the context of Paul's having been in transit between those two phases. That would likewise fit perfectly with Paul's transitional two-gospels message in *1 Thessalonians* 4:1-16. However, *Acts* 17:1-2 implies that this journey was Paul's first that took him to Thessalonica itself; and this superior evidence, Paul's own letter *1 Thessalonians,* indicates that's incorrect; Paul had converted these Thessalonians to James's Jewish sect years earlier than his follower "Luke" (the author of *Acts*) knew.

Even the Gospel that was written the latest, and that is generally considered to be the most anti-Semitic, *John*, had to acknowledge, in the late period in which it was written, that Jesus was passionately a Jew: *John* 4:22 quotes its "Jesus" as asserting "[only] we [Jews] know whom we worship, because salvation comes from the Jews." And, of course, Matthew similarly quoted Jesus as asserting to his disciples (*Mat.* 10:5-6), "Go nowhere among the Gentiles, ... but go instead to the lost sheep of the house of Israel." (As was earlier noted, Matthew quoted the after-death Jesus as changing his mind on that, in *Matthew* 28:19-20.) Again: Paul's followers could go far in their lies; but, even for them, limits existed on just how far they could *safely afford* to go.

Paul's Immediate Response to the Challenge, Basic Changes It Wrought in Paul's Thinking

It's interesting that, if *Acts* was correct about Paul's having Timothy circumcised in 16:3, then Paul's immediate response to James's command was, at least to that extent, to make this concession to it. Such a concession would suggest that immediately after the event recounted in *Galatians* 2:11-21, Paul accommodated that command to the extent he thought necessary in order to avoid provoking James into proclaiming publicly that Paul's followers weren't Jews and therefore weren't followers of Jesus (because they weren't circumcised). Paul was now set upon gradually removing his followers from the Jesus sect. By Paul's moving only *gradually* away from the covenant, he avoided providing James a public provocation that might have compelled James to expel Paul from the sect before Paul could stand as an authority on his own, amongst his own. Evidently, by the time Paul wrote *Galatians*, he felt sufficiently confident to do this – to tell his followers that they would be lost to Christ if they became circumcised. (In fact, in *Galatians* 5:4, Paul says precisely this: "If you seek salvation through obedience to the Law, you will be severed from Christ and from God's favor.") What he had said in the incident he recounted in *Galatians* 2:11-21 was thus now suitable, approximately four years later, to repeat to these men *as being* "the gospel of Christ." No one in human history has been so effective a strategist and tactician as was Paul; his sense of timing was like a finely crafted timepiece, inside a bomb.

Further indications of the changes in Paul's message over time are provided by the two *Corinthians* letters, both of which are mixtures of more than one letter written at different times to the Corinthian congregations. The editor(s) who assembled these letters did so in patchquilt fashion. *1* 7:19 has to be from the period prior to the split, even prior to *1 Thessalonians*, because Paul here instructs his people, "Whether a man is circumcised is not important; only obeying God's commandments is important." That directly contradicts *Galatians* 2:16. In this *Corinthians* passage, Paul displays himself from the period before the blow-up, the period when he was collecting uncircumcised converts and telling them to follow the Law but that the circumcision law was an exception and could be ignored. This is further *conclusive evidence that Paul's "gospel of Christ" did indeed change over time*, and that Paul is brazenly lying when he says in *Galatians* 1:7, "there is only one gospel of Christ, but others are trying to change it," and in the following two lines, "Anyone who preaches a gospel different from what I taught you should go to hell!" Paul is there consigning himself to hell, because he had, indeed, earlier taught that *only* the circumcision-commandment is invalid, and that the *rest* of the Jewish covenant remains in force, even after Jesus's death. Paul's having asserted in *1 Corinthians* 7:19 "Whether a man is circumcised is not important; only obeying God's commandments is important" provides further proof to our central point that Paul in *Galatians* 2:16 is actually rejecting the covenant because he rejects *Genesis* 17:14, and isn't, as he claims there, rejecting *Genesis* 17:14 because he rejects the covenant – in other words, it's further proof that Paul in *Galatians* 2:16-21 was simply lying to Peter and to James's other representatives, and to Paul's own men, and that his Christianity is thus nothing but a hoax built upon his understandable *refusal* to impose circumcision on his followers. Christianity's fraudulence is there incontrovertible.[40] In this passage *1 Corinthians* 7:19, Paul

---

[40]   This technique of deception by Paul has been used also by other master-liars, such as, for example, Italy's wealthiest man and Prime Minister, Silvio Berlusconi, as reported by Britain's *Telegraph* on 15 November 2009, headlining "Silvio Berlusconi Uses Food Summit as Excuse to Miss Trial." Nick Squires in Rome reported that, "The prime minister has chosen not to travel to Milan for the first day" of his corruption trial, "which was reactivated after Italy's highest court ruled that a law giving him immunity from prosecution was unconstitutional." Berlusconi "said he could not attend the hearing because he was welcoming more than 60 world leaders to the start of the three-day World Food Summit [in Rome], organized by the UN's Food and Agriculture Organization." Instead of Berlusconi's saying that he was hosting the FAO meeting in order to avoid his trial, he said that he was avoiding his trial in order to host the FAO meeting. "Leaders of the Group of Eight club of rich nations were 'snubbing' the summit. ... Mr. Berlusconi, as host, will be the only G8 leader to attend." Moreover, Mr. Squires noted that "His conservative government last week unveiled a plan to radically reform the notoriously slow Italian justice system so that trials could last no longer than six years," which would cancel all of the cases against Berlusconi, since they had been postponed by passing laws granting him immunity from prosecution, and by other stalling tactics. "The effect of the reforms, which critics say are a cynical attempt to help the prime minister wriggle out of his two corruption trials, would be 'devastating,' according to the Italian magistrates' association. They would bring to an abrupt halt 100,000 trials over the next two years, including some cases in which tens of thousands of small investors are trying to recover their money from companies which fraudulently declared bankruptcy. ... 'In order to block justice for one individual, they are blocking it for 100,000,' said Carlo Taormina, a lawyer who served in a previous Berlusconi government." Whereas Paul was lying that he opposed the circumcision-law because he opposed the covenant, Berlusconi was lying that he avoided the trial in order to host the FAO meeting. Furthermore, Berlusconi claimed that he shouldn't be prosecuted because no one should have to

obviously hasn't *yet* been compelled to apply *Genesis* 17:14 as
being one of God's commandments; James hasn't *yet* made the
decision to enforce it. Paul's gospel after the split became
exactly the *opposite* of "only obeying God's commandments is
important." His new "gospel" is instead Christ-faith; not at all
"obeying God's commandments." What Paul said in *1
Corinthians* 7:19 was that the circumcision commandment can
be ignored and the believer can *still* be "obeying God's
commandments." That, of course, is precisely the position of
the *pre*-split Paul. According to *Acts* 11:2-18, it was also
precisely Peter's position prior to Peter's abandoning the
mission to the Gentiles and his leaving that to Barnabas and
Paul. Moreover, *1 Corinthians* 7:20 completes this statement by
adding "Everyone should remain as he was when he accepted
God's call." In other words, yet again: One doesn't have to
become circumcised in order to be "obeying God's
commandments." The tensions within the sect, over
circumcision, had obviously not *yet* come to a head then.
When Paul wrote this, he and James and Peter were all of a

---

face a court in a case that was first brought many years earlier. But Berlusconi had
delayed the cases against himself. Many Italians possessed faith in Berlusconi
because he owned or controlled almost all of Italy's major "news" media, and many
Christians possess faith in Paul because they are surrounded by his propaganda.

As had been widely expected, nothing was achieved at the international
"Food Summit" Berlusconi hosted. Then, on Thursday, 11 March 2010, the *Wall
Street Journal* bannered "Berlusconi Can Delay Trials Under New Law," and Stacy
Meichtry in Rome reported that, "The Italian Parliament on Wednesday approved a
law that temporarily shields Italian Prime Minister Silvio Berlusconi and top
members of his government from criminal trials." The rationale for this legislation
was "that potential appearances in court would interfere with their governing
duties."

This is mentioned here because it shows that recognizing Paul's tactics
can help to free people from voting for, or otherwise supporting, individuals who are
merely exploiting them by appealing to their faith, such as, in Berlusconi's case, to
his appealing to their respect for his power or etc. In other words: understanding
Paul's tactics can help to reduce the frequency with which psychopaths gain and
retain power. This is one of many ways in which the scientific examination of Paul's
tactics can help to improve things, by weakening/disempowering hoaxers in the
future.

single mind on this, that these uncircumcised men *were* Jews. It was the easy way to collect Gentiles. And even *2 Corinthians* contains some pre-split lines. 2 12:1-6 says (12:2) that Paul's conversion to Jesus (the mythological account of this Damascus-road experience being famously provided in *Acts* 9:3-22) had occurred 14 years prior, which would certainly date this particular passage of the second Corinthian letter three years *prior* to the split, and thus, also, even earlier than *1 Thessalonians*. This fascinating early-written passage, providing us a window into Paul's teachings before the split, alternates between first-person and third-person references to his subsequently-made-famous Damascus-road conversion experience. It even admits that that experience might not have been authentically supernatural or revelatory at all (such as he subsequently implied it to be, and such as Luke in *Acts* 9:3-19 asserted it to have been). Evidently, at such an *early* period in Paul's ministry, when he was still loyally following James's leadership and functioning in the Jesus-sect rather than in his subsequent Christianity, Paul was willing to admit then that the "revelation" he had had from the Risen Christ might have been purely imaginary or delusional. Only *after* the split, when, as the founder of an entirely *new* religion, it was *absolutely essential* for him to claim *direct* authorization from the Risen Christ (inasmuch as he had always previously *admitted* that he had never known the *living* Jesus), did Paul insist, as in *Galatians* 1:1, that his authorization *definitely* came "from Jesus Christ and God the Father who raised Him from death." However, back again to *2 Corinthians*, line 3:6 was clearly written *after* the split, saying that, "the new covenant consists not of a written Law but of the Spirit. The written Law brings death, but the Spirit gives life." (The King James Version mistranslates this "new covenant" as "new testament," but the new testament didn't even exist until it was canonized in the 4th Century, so Paul couldn't have been referring to it. Moreover, even the KJV elsewhere translates the very same term here from the original, "diatheke," as "covenant," such as in *Galatians* 3:17, and in *Romans* 11:27.)

This "new covenant" reflects *emphatically* the supersessionist, Christian, Paul; he more commonly calls this supersessionist covenant the "gospel of Christ." 2 11:13-15 is probably also from after the split, if it implicitly condemns both James and his followers as being agents of Satan. However, it doesn't *necessarily* include James in its denunciation here, because only James's *followers* are directly attacked (James didn't visit the Corinthian congregation; only his agents did), and it's possible that these followers weren't presenting James's position but only their interpretation of it – there was, as yet, no definitive statement of what James's position on circumcision was, until after the council in Jerusalem and its final decision reflected in *Galatians* 2:11-13, which changed everything. Until that time came, it remained possible for James's followers to *disagree amongst themselves about whether or not uncircumcised men could be followers of Jesus – members of the Jesus sect of Jews.* Clearly, 2 *Corinthians* 11:13-15 exhibits Paul's being at war against *some* of James's followers, but we cannot tell for certain from that passage whether Paul was at war against *all* of James's followers at the time. Also after the split was such a passage as 1 *Corinthians* 15:56-57, "Death gets its power to hurt from sin, and sin gets its power from the Law. But God deserves our gratitude for granting us victory over death via our Lord Jesus Christ." So, whereas in 1 15:56, "Sin gets it power from the Law" (i.e., from the commandments), 1 7:19 tells us that, "Only obeying the commandments is important." 1 15:56 condemns "the Law" (the commandments) as the *enabler* of sin, and this intellectual contortion was a direct outgrowth of the event Paul describes in *Galatians* 2:11-21. Also, the passage that opens 1 *Corinthians* is clearly from *after* the split: 1 *Corinthians* 1:2-3 is similar to *Galatians* 1:1 in its placing Jesus with God.

Nonetheless, despite the obvious patchwork nature of the two canonical *Corinthians* letters, each of them provides useful information, not otherwise available, concerning Paul's position prior to the split. Each of these two letters contains some material that clearly pre-dates the split. And this material is exceptionally valuable from a historical standpoint, because none of Paul's other surviving letters does. One can only speculate as to why such passages survived – perhaps it was because the Corinthian congregation was Paul's first, and because the members were proud to be asked by Rome, long afterward, to supply whatever they still possessed from Paul, and the person or persons to whom this task was assigned had available to him only incomplete shreds and tried to form continuous letters from them, and this is the best that he could achieve with the shreds he still had at hand. Perhaps he furthermore recognized that, if he failed to do a credible job of this, then Rome wouldn't include *anything* from Paul to the Corinthians in the final collection. Here was an opportunity for this man to shape future world history. He did what he could toward that end. In any event, whoever performed the task succeeded: the Pauline materials he supplied were accepted and ultimately canonized.

Contrast *1 Corinthians* 7:19 versus *Galatians* 5:2-4. In the former, from prior to the split, "whether or not a man is circumcised means nothing; what matters is to obey God's commandments." But in the latter, "if you permit yourself to be circumcised, ... you are outside God's grace."

And there we have it: incontrovertible testimony, even from the pre-split Paul – Paul's testimony from prior to his invention of Christianity – proving beyond any reasonable doubt whatsoever, not only that Paul lied when he said in *Galatians* 1:7-9 that he had never changed his gospel, but also that Paul invented Christianity at the event he described in *Galatians* 2:11-21, and that "table fellowship" and other distractions upon which scholars focus there, had nothing to do with 2:11-21, but that circumcision had *everything* to do with it. Scholars want to believe, virtually as much as preachers do; and, in any case, there hasn't been any significant distinction between those two professions: both are anti-science. What's the difference between a professor of New Testament at a seminary and at a university? Legal/forensic analysis of the evidence proves conclusively that Christianity is simply a hoax, which started at that specific occasion, in or around the year 50, at Antioch.

This contrast also proves, yet again and with finality, that circumcision, not the food laws, constituted the only part of the Law that Paul *hadn't been imposing* upon his followers. In other words: yet again, there's simply no question that the debate in 2:11-21, between Paul on the one hand, and Peter and the other agents from James on the other, concerned whether or not *Genesis* 17:14 remained binding after the crucifixion.

This interpretation of the evidence is consistent with *all* of the evidence. By contrast, the scholars' interpretations are *not*. No interpretation which assumes that Paul was honest is consistent with all of the evidence. The assumption of Paul's honesty isn't only extraneous: it's false. It certainly wouldn't be admissible in court as an assumption, but would require proof; and the proof runs *in the opposite direction*, as shown here.[41]

---

[41]   Why, then, is Paul's honesty so widely assumed by scholars? (As will be explained in the third footnote in our Conclusion, very few scholars, such as Hyam Maccoby, and Robert Eisenman, have been exceptions – they didn't assume Paul's honesty – but those scholars lacked the legal/forensic methodology that's necessary in order to challenge Paul's honesty in a scientific way, as has been done here.)

The answer to this question started to become clear in 1947, when the scientific psychologists, Jerome Bruner and Cecile Goodman, reported, in their "Value and Need as Organizing Factors in Perception" (*Journal of Abnormal and Social Psychology*, v. 42, pp. 33-44), that children overestimated an object's size dependent upon how much they wanted the object. Subsequently, other scientific psychologists, Emily Balcetis and David Dunning, found, in their "Wishful Seeing: More Desired Objects Are Seen as Closer" (*Psychological Science*, 17 December 2009), that adults overestimate how close an object is, to the extent that they desire the object: "Five experiments demonstrated that perceivers tend to see desirable objects ... as physically closer to them than less desirable objects." In other words, "wishful seeing" is a normal if not a virtually universal distortion of people's perceptions.

Perhaps this "wishful seeing" is especially characteristic of people whose epistemology is faith instead of science. If that's the case, then it would be understandable that scholars of Paul, in a Christian culture, will be *especially* likely to overestimate Paul's honesty. [continued]

Scholars, when they interpret a text, usually ignore instead of explain contradictions that it contains. This alone suffices to disqualify their interpretations, from a legal/forensic standpoint, because a case built from evidence that contains *unexplained* contradictions is nonsense. And, in order to make 100% sense, a case must credibly explain *all* contradictions within the evidence. So, that's the goal here. No previous "historical" work on earliest Christianity has come anywhere near to meeting this basic standard of legal/forensic acceptability. They're all merely myths that are based upon myths.

Describing the Event
That Created Christianity

What, then, can we say about the event itself – what actually happened at the event that created Christianity?

Circumcision is the issue before the event, and the issue after it; circumcision is also the issue in the event itself.

In 2:11, Peter is coming to Antioch, shortly after James at the council in Jerusalem had produced his initial judgment on the circumcision-issue, a judgment that, whatever its specifics (which are uncertain), did, at least for the time being, permit Paul to continue with his uncircumcised "converts" as being, at least for the time being, actual converts. We know, however: whatever Peter at Antioch said in 2:11, disturbed

Obviously, the idea that Christianity is a hoax will encounter enormous resistance in a culture that is predominantly Christian. Furthermore, a culture that is predominantly religious (regardless of *which* religion) probably will also not wish to know that the world's largest religion is a hoax, because, if it's a hoax, then the likelihood that other religions are honest will also probably appear to be reduced. If even the world's largest, most successful, religion is a hoax, then what is to prevent smaller religions from being hoaxes? Therefore, although other religions might find attractive the idea that Christianity is a hoax, there will probably be a far larger countervailing prejudice in any religious culture, against accepting that idea. Consequently, Jewish scholars, Islamic scholars, etc., will probably also be predominantly prejudiced *against* the thesis here; and this explains why scholars are reluctant to place Paul's honesty into question.

Paul greatly, and Paul opposed Peter about this matter in public – that is to say, in front of his own followers. Even though it was an embarrassing thing for Paul to have to admit to the Galatians, that he had been standing opposed to his onetime mentor Peter on this occasion, he probably *had* to admit it, out of fear that they might already have known as much from James's representatives who had been sent to their OWN congregations. We know that James had, in fact, sent representatives to the Galatian congregations, because Paul refers to those agents in 1:6-9, 4:17-21, and also in 5:2-12 (which will be discussed here subsequently). But even if Paul hadn't known about and referred to those agents, there would have been no way for him to have known for certain that his enemy had *not* sent any. Paul therefore simply couldn't afford the risks he would have faced if he had altogether avoided referring to this climactic incident, despite his strong desire not to do so; and this is the reason why he refers to it. (This explains why the proof of Christianity's being a hoax, *Galatians* 2:11-16, *exists*; this explains why Paul mentioned the incident at all in this letter. This thus also explains our extreme good fortune now, which enables a Scientific Age world to recognize the hoax, after 2,000 years of Paul's unremitting success in it.)

Then, in 2:12, Paul explicitly states that, whatever this dispute was between Peter and Paul, Peter nonetheless did sit down to dinner, presumably that same evening, to dine with Paul and his uncircumcised "converts." We know that these "converts" had *not been* circumcised, because James at Jerusalem had ruled that, *at* LEAST *until* he might subsequently decide otherwise, no such circumcisions would be REQUIRED. We can infer from Peter's sitting down to dinner with Paul and his "converts," that, whatever the point-at-issue between Paul and Peter might have been, the two had subsequently calmed down and emerged from their dispute in at least a civil accord, even IF the point-at-issue here remained unsettled between them. From 2:12, we learn explicitly that while Peter was dining with these men, emissaries from James arrived, and that their arrival is what precipitated Peter's sudden withdrawal from the table. If these emissaries were actually a backup team that was sent by James in order to make certain that Peter – despite (according to *Acts* 15:7-11) his having SUPPORTED Paul's position against circumcision at the just-recently-past council in Jerusalem – would, in fact, *now* be "laying down the law" AGAINST Paul's position, and making clear to Paul and his "converts" that, finally, these men must all be circumcised, then these emissaries would probably have been SHOCKED to see Peter actually DINING with these very same *uncircumcised* "converts." In Judaism, dining is an act with much religious significance (God had legislated about it: the kosher laws), and a strict Jew, especially in that ancient era (when strict Jews were even stricter than they are today), might well have considered it to be improper to dine with NON-Jews, especially at ceremonial meals, or else at meals on especially Jewish-significant occasions – which this event certainly was for members of this Jewish sect, since the Jewish identity of these men is what Peter was now challenging and what Paul was defending. This question of Jews dining with non-Jews was no personal rejection of non-Jews; Jews (like members of almost every religion) were, and are, customarily EAGER for others to *join* their religion. This rejection of co-dining reflected Jewish Law, the covenant, in this case the principle that, unless a person had ALREADY JOINED their faith, dining with non-believers was of doubtful obedience to God, perhaps by extension from the principle emphatically set forth in *Exodus* 12:48-9, regarding the celebratory Passover meal: "If a foreigner lives amongst you, and wants to observe the Passover to honor the Lord, all his males must first be circumcised, and then he may come near and observe it, and he will even be as one who is born Jewish – for no uncircumcised person may join in the meal. The same law will apply to the native-born as to the foreigner who is a friend amongst you."

Consequently, given the specific background of this climactic occasion, James's emissaries would almost certainly have felt that they were catching Peter "with his pants down," as it were; and Peter, very understandably, thus drew himself away from the table in embarrassment, to reassert here his loyalty to James.

Now, we come to what the issue here was, and this is the issue that's addressed in detail in the preceding box: this issue was Peter's having been caught dining WITH UNCIRCUMCISED MEN. (The issue was *not* Paul's having set an un-kosher table, as scholars assume.)[42] Of course, Peter had himself done the very *same* thing many times before, in his youth, when he had been Paul's predecessor and subsequent mentor in the mission to the Gentiles (such as in *Acts* 11:3), and had done, in that capacity, just as Paul was now doing – accepted non-circumcised men as members. But that was before the question had been finally *decided* by James, and it was also many years ago; and what Peter was now doing, on this occasion, was a direct VIOLATION of the reason for which James had SENT Peter to Antioch. James's wisdom in having sent a BACKUP team, to arrive a few hours after Peter, was thereby confirmed: Peter exhibited himself to be *not* a man who could be depended upon.

When scholars, as they wrongly but widely do, assume that the reason why Peter withdrew from the table was that James's men found him dining at an un-kosher table (in violation of Judaism's laws regarding food), they depart entirely from the evidence. Their assumption here is that Paul favored fellowship with people who violated the food laws, whereas James didn't and tried to impose here the food laws.

---

[42]   The scholars' assumption, that kosher laws (or "table fellowship") were the issue here, doesn't indicate anything about the evidence, but does indicate something about the people who hold the assumption: it displays their desire to accept without question Paul's claim that he rejected the circumcision-law because he rejected the covenant, and not *vice versa*. In other words, this assumption indicates something about the culture that Paul created, which affects us all, especially because Christianity is the world's dominant faith. To explain this assumption is a task for scientific cultural anthropology, examining scholarly culture, and not a task for scientific historiography, examining this document, *Galatians*.

Exodus 12:48-49, the law against ceremonially dining with uncircumcised men, had nothing to do with the food laws, and yet even at as late a time as Luke's writing of *Acts* 11:3, there was evidently widespread public recognition that during that era Jews considered dining with uncircumcised men to be sinful, a violation of God's Law, perhaps a violation of *Exodus* 12:48-49. And so, the mere assumption by scholars that the food laws were the source of the disagreement motivating *Galatians* 2:12, is utterly unwarranted: there's no basis for it *at all*.

Now we proceed to 2:13, which explicitly states that Paul's group at the table included not only Gentiles, but Jews (who had been circumcised as infants), and that these people joined James's side in this dispute, and that EVEN Paul's important co-worker (and possibly boss) Barnabas joined the James side. Here, then, is the IMPLICIT situation: It was, now, on the one side of the conflict, Peter, and the other agents from James, and Barnabas, and even those men who were born Jews but who were in Paul's own operation; and, on the OTHER side, there was ONLY Paul, accompanied by his leading Gentile "converts." This was, in other words, a microcosmic model of the same great schism that the event itself PRECIPITATED – a schism that, for the first time ever, now publicly rocked Paul's Antioch headquarters.

2:14 explicitly presents Paul arguing against Peter, since Peter is the senior-most person present. Peter is here no longer Paul's mentor, but rather his FOE. Paul reminded Peter that what Peter was doing here was in direct violation of Peter's OWN *practice* when Peter had been evangelizing to the Gentiles, and was also in violation of what Peter had been standing for till this very moment. (Note here that *Acts* 11:2-3 asserts that the issue decades earlier, when Peter instead of Paul was ministering to the Gentiles, concerned circumcision and *not* the food laws. The assumption by scholars that for some unstated reason this *changed* and now the food laws had become the source of friction, has no other basis than scholars wanting to interpret 2:14 in this unfounded way; it is simply and quite clearly false.) We can reasonably assume that Peter would likely have retorted to Paul *something like*, "That was then, Paul, and this is now, and James has finally decided against that policy, and I am therefore honor-bound, as a follower of Jesus, to obey the mashiach's appointed successor, James,[43] and so to separate myself from you on this matter." Would Peter have gone the very next step, to have asserted the ultimate *split* between the two of them, "If you do not comply, Paul, then you and your people are no longer a part of our sect"? Would a vacillating, accommodating, man, such as virtually all accounts of Peter describe him to have BEEN, have been likely to say such a thing? Hardly. Furthermore, his FAILURE to have said that is probably *why* Peter had sat down to dinner with these people in the first place, and so been

---

[43]   *Matthew* 16:18, and the other passages indicating that Peter and not James was the group's leader, were written after *Galatians*, and are inferior "evidence" from a legal/forensic standpoint, and therefore cannot be relied upon here. The writer of *Matthew*, furthermore, was not writing for an audience of contemporaries who were able from their own personal experience to verify or disconfirm what *Matthew* said. By contrast, Paul, the writer of *Galatians*, was. Paul thus was subject to a check against his lying, which "Matthew" was not. *Matthew* 16:18 isn't evidence against *Galatians*; it's disproven by *Galatians*.

The only one of the four canonical Gospels not to mention Peter's primacy (and it didn't mention anyone's primacy) is the earliest-written one, *Mark*. When *Mark* was composed, James's primacy was too fresh, too well-known, for the fraud saying that Peter was the group's leader to be able to work.

But *Matthew* 16:18, *John* 21:17, and *Luke* 22:32, all have Jesus appointing Peter as the group's leader. Those Gospels were written late enough for the fraud to succeed that made Paul's teacher, and Paul's predecessor in the mission to the Gentiles, Peter, retrospectively into Jesus's successor, and the first supposed Pope.

As will subsequently be discussed here, James had been Jesus's successor since the crucifixion: it's not the case that Peter was the successor and that somehow James rose under Peter to replace Peter and to become Peter's boss. (Furthermore, the Roman Catholic Church, which produced the lie that Peter was appointed, doesn't list James as the second – or *any* – Pope.) The Gospelists who asserted that Jesus appointed Peter and not James to lead the group were lying, as will soon be explained here.

"caught with his pants down" on this matter. Peter didn't confront them. But Paul's account doesn't – not ever – give his OPPONENTS' side on this supremely important matter; a con-artist *does not* DO such a thing unless he's stupid, and Paul was anything but stupid: he was as cunning as anyone in all of history.

Scholars have widely picked up on Paul's accusation in 2:14 that Peter was trying to force Gentiles to imitate Jews ("ioudaizein"), and scholars have used this sole occasion on which Paul employed that term ("ioudaizein") as constituting their supposed justification to label Paul's opponents as having been "Judaizers," which means people who try to convert others to Judaism, but that's not what Paul was alleging, not even on the *sole* occasion in which he used the term "ioudaizein." He didn't call Peter a "Judaizer" in this line, nor did he ever employ any such term anywhere; i.e., he never alleged that Peter – or anyone – had preached for Jesus by demanding that a listener must "Judaize," or become a Jew who preaches Judaism to others. In fact, that's not the way *anyone* preached for Jesus in those times. Among Jews, the missionary message during Jesus's life was that Jesus was the prophesied mashiach; and, after Jesus's crucifixion, it was that Jesus had been a Jewish prophet. Among Gentiles, the missionary message during Jesus's life didn't even exist, and the message after the crucifixion was that Jesus had been the Jewish prophet who represented God for those – and all future – times. As long as the latter message didn't require a listener to subject himself to the medical operation of circumcision, it was acceptable to Gentiles, and was far more acceptable to them than the message of the vast majority of missionaries of Judaism, who (in accord with *Genesis* 17:14) did require circumcision as a pre-requisite for salvation. All of Jesus's disciples were Jews and remained Jews, just as Jesus himself was and did; and, in their time, it was taken for granted that anyone who preached for Jesus among Gentiles was hoping to convert them to Judaism, because that was the religion Jesus had preached and they were preaching. For

Paul to have accused Peter of Judaizing (i.e., of preaching Judaism) would have been ridiculous, because until this moment that's what *all* people – including both Peter and Paul – who claimed to be preaching for Jesus were doing. Instead, Paul accused Peter here of his trying to make Gentiles *imitate Jews* or *practice Judaism* – which is what *"ioudaizein"* meant. To understand how this would have been understood by his readers: Paul's followers were born Gentiles who thought that they *were* practicing Judaism except for the circumcision-commandment, and Paul's argument here was that *that suffced* – and *this* was the issue in the dispute here, *not* whether Peter (and James's other representatives) were "trying to force Gentiles to Judaize," or to force them to preach Judaism, which is a wildly fictitious translation of this Greek word. The only reason scholars here interpret "ioudaizein" that absurd and false way (as preaching – rather than as practicing – Judaism) is that this tactic has been central to their various defenses of Paul: i.e., that his opponents were "Judaizers" – a concept one doesn't find anywhere in Paul's writings. When Paul said that Peter was trying to make Gentiles *imitate born Jews,* he was understood by everyone present to mean here that Peter was trying to make Gentile followers of Jesus become *circumcised,* because that was the *only* law of Judaism Paul's men weren't *already* following. But Paul didn't want to *say* this *explicitly* – he didn't want to *name* circumcision as the *specific* Jewish law that was at issue – because he didn't want his followers to know that circumcision had been *the* issue *at the just-completed council in Jerusalem.* So, he used instead this more-general term, "ioudaizein," as if the issue there had been whether or not one must follow Jewish customs, in a *generic* sense. Like the greatest of salesmen, Paul calibrated each word he used. And, as advocates for Paul, scholars might have, as their chief (or even *only*) reason for alleging that Paul's opponents "Judaized" among the Gentile converts, that this allegation – though it's entirely unsourced in all of Paul's writings – enables scholars to avoid recognizing that Paul's opponents demanded that his followers become circumcised in accord with *Genesis* 17:14 as a pre-condition for membership in Jesus's (or *any*) sect of Judaism. The allegation, from scholars, that Paul's opponents "Judaized," leaves the door open for interpreting the cause of the council in Jerusalem in 2:1-10, and of the ensuing conflict in 2:11-21, as having been disputes over *other* commandments from God, *not* over the circumcision-commandment. But if Paul had accused his opponents of forcing people to "Judaize," he would have been laughed at by his readers in his own time.

Furthermore, 2:14 provides two high quality evidences that the Roman Catholic Church outright falsifies (and that its Gospel Scriptures mislead) that Peter was the first Pope: first, Peter was being upbraided here by Paul, which obviously wouldn't have been accepted by anyone present, if Peter were, in fact, the *leader* of Jesus's followers; and, second, Peter was described here by Paul as preaching Judaism (or, according to the many "Judaize" scholars, even as preaching the preaching of Judaism), which clearly wouldn't have been done by the first (or any) Pope. Is Roman Catholicism a *sect* of Judaism? Obviously *not*. Yet, even as late as the year 50, Jesus's disciples (and, according to the myth that Peter was the leading disciple, even the *leader* among them) were preaching Judaism – *not* Christianity, *not* Roman Catholicism. So: Peter wasn't the first Pope, such as the Roman Catholic Church claims; and Peter preached Judaism, instead of Christianity, and so the Roman Catholic Church has no *authentic* connection whatsoever to Jesus's disciples. 2:14 thus proves, yet again, that Christianity is a hoax. 2:14 displays this, and doesn't merely assert this; it is conclusive. 2:14 destroys Roman Catholicism, and leaves Christianity no foundation except lies. 2:14 is dispositive against Roman Catholicism in particular, and against Christianity in general.

But Paul now goes on to give us even *more*: He proceeds to announce the end of what had actually been Jesus's religion, Judaism, and its *replacement* by Paul's own new religion, Christianity:

2:15-16 continues with what was almost certainly what Paul had said next in his self-defense – and in defense of his viewpoint – on the occasion he was now recounting: "Indeed, we are Jews by birth and not 'Gentile sinners' [meaning people who can be PRESUMED to be violators of the covenant, because they've not *signed* the covenant – via circumcision – to BECOME Jews]. Yet we know that a person is put right in the view of God only by means of Christ-faith,[44] and never by doing what the Law [the commandments of God] requires. We, too, have believed in Jesus Christ, just so as to be viewed favorably by God through our Christ-faith, and never through obeying the Law. For no one is put right in God's view by obeying God's Law."

---

[44]   Often in Paul's writings, it's unambiguous that Paul is speaking about faith as being the basis for a person's salvation, such as in *Romans* 3:27-28: "[Salvation comes] by the principle of faith. Thus, we conclude that a person is justified by faith, not by following God's Law."

Another example is *Philippians* 3:9, which asserts that to be viewed by God as being right is based not on one's "obeying the Law," but on "the righteousness that comes from God and is based on faith." Paul's contrast there of faith vs. law, or belief vs. obedience, is clear. Yet another such example is *Galatians* 3:23-25, which says that, "Before the time came for faith, we were prisoners to the Law," but now "we are all justified by [our] faith."

However, in other passages, such as the present one, *Galatians* 2:16, there appears, instead of the clear "faith in Christ," a phrase that might also be translated as "faith of Christ," which might possibly mean faith about Christ (or faith that Christ is the Messiah), which is the same thing as faith in Christ; but it also might possibly alternatively mean Christ's faith, which would be Judaism – Jesus having been a rabbi and having been held to be even the Jewish mashiach. Judaism was (i.e., it consisted of) belief in salvation via obeying God's Law, and so any interpretation of "faith of Christ" as being Judaism, or "the Law," instead of as being salvation via possessing faith, would contradict everything that Paul said against salvation via following the Law, and everything that Paul said in favor of salvation via possessing faith.

Clearly, then, "faith of Christ," if that is how one would translate those passages, was being used by Paul interchangeably with "faith in Christ," and so I use here simply the phrase "Christ-faith," to indicate that it's (some kind of) faith, as opposed to (any kind of) obedience, as being what God requires for a person's salvation. [continued]

Moreover, *Romans* 3:26 directly asserts that "everyone who believes in Jesus" will be saved; there is no question at all that Paul is saying that Christ-faith is faith in Jesus, *not* faith of Jesus.

Regardless of the different ways in which Paul said this, his message was the same, and this message – Paul's preaching that salvation comes via faith instead of via obedience – was what Paul elsewhere referred to as "the gospel of Christ," or what we know as Christianity. That's what makes Christianity different from Judaism; and, otherwise, Christianity would be merely a sect of Judaism, not a different religion. It's the pathway to heaven that sets the two religions apart.

Furthermore, if one were to assume – as some scholars do – that Paul meant to say that what causes a person to be viewed favorably by God is Christ's own faith, not an individual's faith in Christ, then what would be the meaning of passages such as *Galatians* 3:9-14&24 and 5:4, and the numerous other Pauline passages which assert that any individual who tries to achieve salvation via following the Law will go to hell? Clearly, Jesus possessed faith just the same, either way. Thus, Paul, either way, was communicating to his readers that the covenant ended after the crucifixion. "Whoever seeks salvation by following the Law will be rejected by God." Any imputation of contrary meaning to Paul, so as to deny his supersessionism, makes no sense whatsoever, and certainly cannot comport with Paul's meaning to his readers in the context of the dispute, between Paul and James, which so concerned Paul's letters.

Moreover, any scholar who interprets Paul as asserting that Jesus's faith, which is Judaism, is the path to salvation, cannot coherently address the basic questions about *Galatians*, such as what precipitated Paul's writing of the letter, and how that objective on his part determined his argument in it.

Moreover, in passages such as *Galatians* 3:9-12, Paul sets the Law opposite to faith without even mentioning Christ at all, and so the entire question as to whether it might have been Christ's faith, Judaism, which was being endorsed here by Paul, doesn't even arise. Incontestably, those passages are asserting that salvation is attained only by faith of some sort, and not by obedience of any sort.

Why, then, do some scholars persist in interpreting Paul in this ridiculous way? Because Paul, in some passages, employed vague terminology, and because, in the wake of the Holocaust, most Christians don't want to believe that Christianity is intrinsically both anti-Judaic and anti-Semitic, and because many scholars are people of faith, which means that they believe whatever they want to believe (which, after the Holocaust, is usually *not* Paul's anti-Judaism and anti-Semitism). That's all; those scholars have nothing to stand upon; they're dancing all over the head of a pin that doesn't even exist.

Why didn't Paul employ clearer terminology? Because he was determined to avoid giving his opponents an easy time arguing that Paul was saying that Judaism was no longer valid. He didn't want to give his enemies such a clear argument to attack. When Paul used a phrase such as "Christ-faith" (or *pistis Christou*) he left himself the possible retort: "Look, I am preaching Judaism! After all, the faith of Christ was Judaism." Paul prepared such a fictitious ballroom upon

That's the core of Christianity; Paul continued, until 2:21, to connect it to the crucifixion and supposed subsequent Resurrection, for the reasons we presented in our discussion of 1:1. Furthermore, when Paul said "no one is put right in God's view by obeying God's Law," this was clearly supersessionist; he clearly was asserting that Christianity replaces Judaism, and isn't merely another pathway to salvation, but now the *only* pathway to salvation.

How do we know that this assertion was the start of Christianity? One cannot know when Christianity started unless one has first *defined* "Christianity," such as has been done here (as salvation via Christ-faith). Furthermore, inasmuch as the start of Christianity is necessarily the event in which some members of the Jesus sect of Jews broke away from Judaism to create "Christianity," one must *also* have first defined "Judaism," as has also been done here (as salvation via obeying God's commandments). For, if "Judaism" hasn't

---

that fictitious pinhead of a distinction, precisely so as to enable his lawyers now to dance there. It's all he gave them, and thus scholars are dancing on it like crazy.

At the end of 2006, in the journal *Novum Testamentum* (#4), Roy A. Harrisville III's "The Objective Genitive as Good Greek" reviewed the ways in which other ancient Greek writers (Aeschines, Euripides, Herodotus, Demosthenes, Plato, Lysias, Thucydides, Hyperides, and Xenophon) employed this same verbal construction that Paul used in such places as *Galatians* 2:16; and Harrisville concluded: "'faith in Christ' is good, if not excellent, Greek." In other words, scholars who have insisted upon translating "*pistis Christou*" as referring to anything like Jesus's faith (or "faith of Christ") aren't really interested in Paul; they're interested only in "arguing" a case to deny that Paul broke away from Jesus's Judaism and created his own religion, Christianity. Theirs is solely a scholarly "case," not a scientific case at all; it hasn't got a scientific leg to stand on – none whatsoever. It's simply inadmissible in court. It's not a theory of the case; it's an entirely unsupported speculation, which directly contradicts some of the evidence, and which thus makes Paul's meaning – his theology – incoherent throughout. It does not explain contradictions within Paul, but only adds contradictions to Paul.

However, in order to avoid those Christian apologists, I employ merely "Christ-faith" here, so as to focus upon what's important, which is that what Paul is opposing to the Law here is *some type* of faith.

been defined, then there's no way, there's no criterion, to determine precisely *when* "Christianity" *broke off from* "Judaism," as something that's *not* Jewish. We have, indeed, defined Christianity here, as the belief that a person gets to heaven by possessing Christ-faith (what Paul asserted in *Galatians* 2:16); furthermore, we have defined Judaism as the belief that one gets to heaven by following God's laws. Clearly, these are two different faiths; by definition, they're *entirely* different. Paul, in 2:1-10, has described the precise events that *led up to* the exact occasion at which he first asserted Christianity, to his former teacher, Peter, and to other "agents from James." 2:11-15 has described this occasion; and even Barnabas and some of the others in attendance, were shocked at hearing this, and disagreed with this religion, which Paul was then introducing. Paul said "the circumcision party, even including Barnabas, joined in Peter's cowardice" of supporting this demand from the "agents from James." And 2:16-21 describes *precisely what Paul asserted there, which they were rejecting: Christianity.* (Moreover, as was pointed out, Paul – as in *1 Corinthians* 7:19, "Whether or not a man is circumcised is unimportant; what's important is to obey God's commandments" – had previously *shared* their view. Until now, circumcision had been the exception, but Paul now created the rule from it, and he thereby created Christianity: 2:16.)

2:21, and the other lines concerning the cruciality of the Resurrection to the personal salvation of Christians, constitute an integral part of Paul's new religion. Without the Resurrection, Christianity is nothing. Thus, too, in *1 Corinthians* 15:14, Paul states flatly, "If the Resurrection did not occur, then we have nothing to preach, and you have nothing to believe." Paul founded his new faith not upon the living Jesus, but only upon the Resurrected Christ – that is, upon the Being whom Paul claimed to have met, and not upon the person Paul's opponents had served and whom they continued to serve after Rome's regime had killed him. The Christian Christ was concocted by a total stranger, two decades after the Jewish Jesus was crucified. The reason Paul had opened *Galatians* with 1:1, indicating that he had received his authority from the after-death Christ, has already been discussed; and here, this is culminated.

So, *Galatians* 2:16-21 is a complete statement of Christianity. It starts with 2:16, which is the core, Christianity itself, the belief in salvation via Christ-faith; and it ends with 2:21, which is an argument for the cruciality of Jesus's death *to* Christ-faith.

In no way is this new faith consistent with Judaism; and, in 2:16, this new faith actually constitutes a nullification of Judaism when Paul states that salvation comes "never by doing what the Law requires. For no one is put right in God's view by obeying God's Law." That unequivocally asserts God's *replacement* of Judaism by Christianity.

So, we now know how it happened that though Jesus died as a Jew in about the year 30, he became verbally resurrected by Paul as a Christian in about the year 50. One cannot understand this unless one understands the personal predicament that Paul faced.

Evolution of the Resurrection Story

Note that our account here doesn't imply anything in regards to the existence or not of the Resurrection: that is, nothing is said here regarding the question of whether some ghost of Jesus actually went to one or more of his followers after Jesus was believed, by some people, to have died.[45] However, more basic than that question is the question of

---

[45] As regards whether there actually *was* a "resurrection" of Jesus, that question is even more nebulous than is a question regarding any modern ghost-story that concerns an alleged ghost-sighting by witnesses now living. Furthermore, the answer similarly rests upon answers regarding the sanity, sobriety, and truthfulness, of each individual witness, because even if an alleged ghost-sighting is sincere, it might be delusional. [continued]

whether or not any ghost-story is ever true, an issue that can be safely addressed in the negative, because even the very possibility of such a phenomenon is, to put it generously, improbable. Standard religious theories about the supposed continuation of someone's consciousness, or of "a person," after the physical source of consciousness – a functioning nervous system – has terminated in that particular body which has thus transformed into a corpse (or, in other words, theories about ghosts), possess no basis in fact. They are false theories. Speculation cannot be presented here about the

---

Paul, who left us the earliest-written of all allegations of the resurrection of Jesus, which are consequently the least tampered-with and the ones that are the least likely to be totally fabricated, said in 2 Corinthians 12:1-7 that "I do not know whether this actually happened." (He phrased this by saying that he didn't know whether the thing he saw was really there in front of him, or merely "inside the body" – an imagining inside the head.) He wrote this, according to his own account there, only 14 years after his alleged sighting of Jesus's ghost, and this means that he wrote it no later than the year 47, which was two or three years prior to the event that he recounts in Galatians 2:11-21. He was still a Jew then; he hadn't yet created Christianity, which he created at the event he describes in Galatians 2:11-21. Before he created Christianity, he had no need to assert as a certainty that he had seen the ghost of Jesus – Paul was willing to acknowledge that this experience might have been only his "vision," and not a real ghost that he had experienced on that alleged occasion. This account of the Resurrection is the earliest and the least fraudulent of all, and it is also the only surviving account that acknowledges: the alleged ghost-sighting might have been purely imaginary.

Ethan Bronner headlined in The New York Times on 6 July 2008, "Ancient Tablet Ignites Debate on Messiah and Resurrection," and he reported that, "A three-foot-tall tablet with 87 lines of Hebrew that scholars believe dates from the decades just before the birth of Jesus is causing a quiet stir in biblical and archaeological circles, especially because it may speak of a messiah who will rise from the dead after three days," as Jesus was alleged to have done. This scholarly debate concerned both what the stone tablet actually said, and also whether it prophesied such a mashiach. Paul and his followers might have been using such a prophesy to construct their own subsequent Resurrection-accounts.

Suffice to say that no evidence exists that the Resurrection actually occurred, and that, even if some ghost stories might possibly be true, no scientific reason exists for including the Risen-Jesus stories among the possibly-truthful ghost-stories. Anyone who believes in Christianity on account of believing in the Resurrection is basing his or her morality upon what is actually nothing more than a myth. No scientist would believe such an unfounded allegation. (That is to say: Anyone who believes in the Resurrection is violating science, and isn't violating merely findings from the application of science.)

reality of ghosts in any case, much less about any theory to explain ghosts, much less about Jesus's ghost in particular, since no theory about the physical cause of disembodied consciousnesses has been put forth, and since all scientific understandings of the cause of consciousness refer instead only to a functioning nervous system; none relates to a corpse as causing consciousness, even though ghosts are alleged to retain the physical appearance of the deceased (even when all that's left of the *actual* corpse is bones). There is no scientific evidence for ghosts, and so there is no scientific theory to explain ghosts. Scientists simply don't attempt to explain things that haven't been demonstrated to exist. Consequently, no explanation of the resurrection of Jesus is presented here, and the only explanation that's actually needed, for our purposes, is an explanation of the belief, "the Resurrection of Jesus." That belief is now explained.

The reason why, for Christians, the belief in the Holy Ghost – the Resurrected Jesus – and not only a belief in both the Son (the holy Jesus) and in the Father (Judaism's God), is an essential part of their faith, is that Paul, the faith's inventor, had claimed to have *met* the Holy Ghost, whereas Paul never claimed to have met either the Father (God) or the Son (Jesus). He claimed to have met *only* the Holy Ghost. Thus, though God the Father and God the Son are both explicit in *Galatians* 1:1, God the Holy Ghost is implicit there, and is just as essential to Paul's new faith as the two Trinitarian components that are explicitly mentioned there; the entire Trinity is present even at the start in 1:1. Paul needed the Resurrection, regardless of whether or not the Resurrection happened. In 1:1, Paul was implicitly assuming, and was implying to his readers, that he wouldn't have seen the Holy Ghost if God hadn't wished him to see it. The Holy Ghost was Paul's claimed connection to *both* the Father *and* the Son, and that's why the Holy Ghost is part of his Trinity. Paul had supposedly received his commission "from Christ and God the Father" *via* the Holy Ghost he had allegedly encountered on the Damascus road. That's what he was referring to when he said in *1 Corinthians* 9:1, "Have I not seen Jesus our Lord?" Inasmuch as Paul stated in *Galatians* 1:1 that he hadn't received his commission "from man or by means of man," his claim in *1 Corinthians* 9:1 was to have "seen Jesus our Lord" *only after* the Crucifixion. In *1 Corinthians* 15:8-9, Paul added that, following the Resurrection-appearances to all the apostles, "Finally He [Christ] appeared to me also, ... the least of the apostles."[46] Whereas Paul asserts that the other apostles knew both the Son and the Holy Ghost, Paul asserts that he himself had met *only* the Holy Ghost, the Risen Christ. This is also why, in *Galatians* 1:12, Paul said "It was [only] Jesus Christ who revealed it [the gospel] to me." This referred not to the living Jesus, but to the Holy Ghost, otherwise referred to as the Resurrected Jesus, or as Jesus Christ. It's more than just a "Spirit" (such as later in *Galatians* 4:6), because it appeared *physically* to Paul; this was a "spirit" that was a ghost. Implicit within Paul's view is that Jesus became the Christ only upon the Crucifixion, which crowned Him as the King, the Messiah. (To Jews, this concept of a mashiach would have seemed nonsensical, since the mashiach was to be demonstrated by his defeating the military occupier of Israel and restoring Israel's independence – *not* by his being defeated and killed by Israel's

---

[46]   Jesus was crucified in about the year 30 (as was mentioned in the footnote to 2:1), and the alleged Resurrection was just a few days afterward, on which occasion Jesus allegedly appeared to the disciples. Paul, according both to his own accounts, and to the account of his follower who wrote *Acts*, violently persecuted Jesus's followers during an extended period of time after that Crucifixion and Resurrection, and a reasonable date for Jesus's alleged Resurrection-appearance to Paul would be around the year 33, at which time Paul supposedly abandoned his enmity toward Jesus and became instead a follower of Jesus. Based upon *Galatians* 1:18, a reasonable date for Paul's first visit to Jerusalem would be around the year 36. Based upon *Galatians* 2:1, a reasonable date for the decisive council in Jerusalem, and for the creation of Christianity immediately following that, would be around the year 50.

Consequently, if there was a Holy Ghost (which no credible evidence indicates occurred), it would have appeared on at least two occasions, separated by about three years, in 30 and then in 33, so that rather than refer to Jesus's alleged Resurrection, one should refer to his alleged Resurrections.

occupier.) Prior to that, Jesus had been only the Messiah-in-waiting; and Jews *now* (after his crucifixion) could view Jesus only as having been no Messiah at all. That left as the prime prospects for conversion to Christ only Gentiles – Paul's specialty. By asserting this implicit structure, Paul was cementing his authority as being higher than that of the authentic apostles, who had known the living Jesus. Paul thus, yet again, was implying that his authority came from a *purer source than theirs*. And so, 2:21 climaxes the argument that 1:1 had begun.

The transmission of the Ten Commandments by God to Moses is purely a religious belief; and so, likewise, is the Resurrection of Jesus a purely religious belief. Such beliefs can be taken *only* on faith. They are not scientific.[47] But, in the latter case – that is, concerning the Resurrection – at least the

---

[47]   If the reader happens to believe that he/she has seen a ghost, then this proves nothing at all about whether or not Paul did. Nor does it prove anything about the reality of ghosts. Many people have delusions, and one of the functions of science is to distinguish between facts and delusions. Religion provides no means of distinguishing between the two, and therefore religion intermixes the two, and preachments promoting faith encourage intermixing the two.

The results of intermixing the two extend outside the sphere of clergy and affect the entire society. To cite two prominent examples: without this intermixing of facts with delusions, people would never have voted for such politicians as Adolf Hitler or George W. Bush, and so fascism would never be able to emerge from democracy anywhere.

Clergy are professionally committed to encourage faith and to discourage science. (Science, after all, is itself a form of systematic skepticism, and therefore scientists are professionally committed to repudiating faith, in anything.) No scientific understanding of politics during the Religious Age is possible without understanding how religion actually functions. The present work scientifically explores this question, of the interrelations between religion and politics, during the early years of Christianity.

If a reader has had a delusion, that delusion isn't admissible evidence in a court in a democracy; it's not admissible evidence about anything in the case that is being presented to the court.

Clergy teach that the Resurrection should be accepted on faith. However, in a court in a democracy, nothing can be taken on faith. Of course, in a dictatorship, faith is a requirement, because otherwise the public wouldn't believe in the leader. But not in a democracy. [continued]

circumstances which *led* to that particular belief are *now clear*.

Each of the four canonical Gospels (*Matthew, Mark, Luke,* and *John*), at the Gospel's respective end, alleges that Jesus's tomb was empty after the Resurrection, but Paul doesn't say this, and Paul's accounts, which were written earlier and without such embellishments, were more along the lines of the standard model of a ghost story, with no concern about what happened to the deceased's corpse. Paul said nothing about Jesus's corpse. Paul even asserts in passages such as *Galatians* 3:5 that the "Spirit" inspires Christians, and that "God gives you the Spirit ... because you hear the gospel and believe it." Paul's "Spirit" is there reduced to being a mere inspiration; it doesn't even require a ghost. Paul alleges that God gave to Christians Jesus's inspiration, but that this inspiration comes *only* to people who possess Christ-faith.

Furthermore, as has been previously noted, 2 *Corinthians* 12:1-7, a passage which asserts itself to have been written three years before the event that Paul describes in *Galatians* 2:11-21, and whose writing therefore predated by three years Paul's invention of Christianity, presents Paul *admitting* that his having seen Jesus's ghost might have been merely a delusion or an illusion. Only *after* Paul invented Christianity did Paul need to claim that it wasn't *merely* imaginary. He now needed this ghost not in order to convince his readers that Jesus's ghost appeared, but in order to convince his readers that Paul possessed some kind of miraculous authorization. Paul needed this ghost originally in order for Paul to impress people regarding Jesus; that's all. Paul in that pre-year-49 period was selling Jesus's sect, and he was doing this by selling Jesus. But by the time of the event which Paul describes in *Galatians* 2:11-21, Paul needed to assert that Jesus's ghost really did exist on the Damascus road,

---

The political and religious indoctrinations of people throughout their lives during the Religious Age have encouraged them to believe in delusions and frauds about ghosts. But delusions and frauds are not admissible as evidence in a court in a democracy.

and that it authorized Paul; this allegation, of his seeing an actual Resurrection, now became part of his "gospel of Christ," for the reasons we delineated when discussing 1:1. Previously, it hadn't been, as *2 Corinthians* 12:1-7 demonstrates. (That pre-Christian account of Paul's encounter with Jesus's ghost served a very different and more modest function.[48]) The Trinity was developed subsequently, as a happenstance of Paul's predicament in the event he describes in 2:11-21. And so, clearly, nothing of Christian doctrine predated the event that Paul describes in 2:11-21, an event occurring in the year 49 or 50. Prior to that, Paul was a Jew. And after that, he was a Christian – the *first* Christian.

In *2 Corinthians* 12:1, Paul clearly said that he was writing about "visions and revelations I have had from the Lord." But then promptly in 12:2, without explanation, he switched to third-person: these apparitions had appeared instead to someone else. And furthermore, Paul now said he didn't know whether this actually happened, and he didn't even make clear precisely what he was referring to – *all* of the "vision," or only *part* of it, and (if the latter) *which* part (e.g., "the third heaven"). Moreover, he now was speaking not of "visions and revelations from the Lord," but of being "elevated to the third heaven," a phrase which literalist Christians could take to mean possibly something different from "visions and revelations ... from the Lord." Furthermore, he now was writing about experiences "inside the body" versus experiences "outside the body," and a literalist reader might again not equate that contrast with the contrast between "visions and revelations" versus reality. He couldn't possibly have written this passage more ambiguously – and this is the

---

[48]   Paul originally had cited this vision merely in order to persuade people to join a religious organization (a Jewish sect) that had been founded by an amazing man who inspired visions. But after Paul started Christianity, Paul's own authority to represent Jesus became the most pressing issue – Paul now needed to claim that the vision he had seen was real, not even possibly just imaginary. Paul's purpose in *2 Corinthians* 12:1-7 was thus to assert merely that Jesus was so amazing as to have given Paul this stunning experience.

earliest description that survives concerning the Resurrection; so, it's key. If Paul happened to be a skilled liar, then such vagueness from him would have been understandable as a means to avoid being asked questions which could expose his entire account there as a lie. (Perhaps when Paul wrote this passage, in the year 46 or 47, any allegation that the ghost of Jesus appeared after his death would have been too baldfaced a lie to assert clearly and unambiguously without one's being considered crazy.) However, what's clear from 2 *Corinthians* 12:1-7 is that 14 years after those "visions," Paul *wasn't* asserting to be a certainty his "visions" on that occasion, as having been anything more than that. Simple logic makes clear that Paul indeed *was* writing here about the same person, namely himself: Right after his miraculous references in the third person, he switches immediately back again, in 12:5, to the first person; and, by the time he gets to 12:7, he's even boasting about "the many wonderful things I saw," while he simultaneously denies that he is boasting about anything. That is clearly first person: Paul was writing, throughout 2 *Corinthians* 12:1-7, about himself. The mark of the dissembler is all over this passage. The contrast between this account and Paul's subsequent categorical references to his "visions" is also striking.[49]

---

[49]   That contrast is the reason some scholars deny that this passage refers to Paul's conversion-experience, and hypothesize that the reference is to a different incident in which Paul encountered Jesus's ghost. As has been remarked in one of our earliest footnotes (the first footnote to the explanation of *Galatians* 1:1), the assumption that Paul encountered Jesus's ghost on multiple occasions makes easier the defense of Paul; and scholars have been serving as Paul's attorneys, so this multiple-encounter theory attracts them. However, there is no sound reason for assuming that 2 *Corinthians* 12:1-7 refers to anything other than Paul's conversion-experience, his commonly-called "Damascus road encounter with Christ."

The argument in the present work stands regardless of whether this passage refers to Paul's conversion-experience, but people who think of Paul as having been an honest man do not generally like to think of him as having modified his testimony to serve changing argumentative needs. People don't like to think of themselves as having been conned. But the more that a person resists recognizing having been conned, the likelier it will be that the person has been conned, because this reluctance is itself a force that increases the likelihood of the person's being deceived. [continued]

Among Paul's subsequent accounts of his having seen the Resurrection, the most detailed is *1 Corinthians* 15:4-8, which says that three days after the Crucifixion, the Holy Ghost appeared repeatedly to Peter and James, and perhaps repeatedly to all of the disciples; and that He also "appeared to more than five hundred believers at one time, most of whom are still alive." Whereas in our era, crowd counts are debated even when an event is captured on film, Paul's 500+ estimate was totally unconfirmable in his era, but it conveyed a tone of gravitas to his account. Paul also fudged the chronology so as to give the impression that Paul experienced the Resurrection shortly after the disciples and the "more than five hundred" did; but all evidence suggests that for about three years after the crucifixion, Paul was hounding and perhaps even helping to kill Jesus's followers until Paul allegedly saw this ghost on the Damascus road. When Paul wrote about Christ's having appeared simultaneously to 500+ followers, Paul had not been among those followers, even if that happened; he was not writing this as eyewitness

---

The more resistance someone puts up to understanding the truth, the likelier he is to become wrapped in a cocoon of lies. The more complete this cocoon becomes, the harder escape from it is. Faith thus acts like an addictive drug.

However, the case that *2 Corinthians* 12:1-7 refers to Paul's alleged conversion-experience is virtually conclusive. Paul cites the incident here by saying (in 12:5), "I will boast about this man, but I will not boast about myself." He clearly was trying to convey that the incident was something to boast about.

In numerous other passages from Paul (such as *Galatians* 1:1, 1:11-12, 1:15-16, and 6:14), Paul boasted about his conversion-experience. Furthermore, the most detailed description by him of his alleged conversion-experience, *1 Corinthians* 15:1-10, ends with his alleging that, "By God's grace, I am what I am, and the grace that he gave me was not without effect." Paul was consistent at least in his alleging that his conversion-experience was the most important thing in his life, and that this experience transformed him and was the source of whatever authority he possessed. Therefore, the idea that *2 Corinthians* 12:1-7 referred to a different experience (or alleged experience) than the experience he alleged in his other passages regarding his alleged conversion, embodies the implicit claim that Paul's conversion-experience wasn't one experience but rather a number of experiences, which occurred at different times during his life. This is stretching things, even for scholars.

testimony, regardless whether it was true. No eyewitness account, no first-hand description, of the Resurrection exists, except Paul's account of his own alleged Damascus road encounter – an account that solidified only after the year 49, approximately 16 years following the alleged event, and which still remained quite vague. That vagueness is especially remarkable because of Paul's assertion, just a few lines later, in 15:14, that, "If Christ has not been raised from the dead, then we have nothing to preach, and you have nothing to believe." Paul said the Resurrection was the most important thing ever – but it wasn't important enough for him to mention except vaguely, in passing.

To create the Holy Ghost, Paul readily accessed, from Jewish belief, the concept that God's will, or God's spirit, or the Holy Spirit, occasionally intervened in human affairs; and Paul's Gentile audience didn't even notice that Paul's alleged third element of his Trinity – the worship of a ghost – was actually *adding*, to this Jewish belief, still another Christian violation of the first three of the Ten Commandments: a violation on top of worshipping Jesus.

Other than in Paul's writings, the earliest-written account of the Resurrection would have to be in one of the Gospels, but *not* in the *first*-written Gospel, *Mark*. The earliest two of all currently surviving manuscripts of *Mark* – the *Codex Vaticanus* and the *Codex Sinaiaticus*, both of which were written during the Fourth Century – did not include *Mark*'s reference to the Resurrection (*Mark* 16:9-20), which constitute the final eleven lines of the *Mark* that's in today's bibles. Someone after approximately the year 350 added those lines to *Mark*, presumably in order to bring *Mark* into line with *Matthew*, *Luke*, and *John*. Consequently, other than Paul's references to the Resurrection, the earliest-written reference to the Resurrection would have to have been one from among those three Gospels. The earliest-written of the Gospels, *Mark*, did not mention any appearance of Jesus's ghost, to anyone.

The author of *Luke* was even smart enough to write that the resurrected "Jesus" denied that he was a ghost. *Luke* 24:39

presents "Jesus" saying to His disciples, "Look at my hands and feet, and see it is I myself; feel me and know, because a ghost does not have flesh and bones, as you see I have." However, if an apparition in a person's hallucination asserts "Look at me; I'm solid flesh," this doesn't necessarily indicate that the apparition is real. A fantasy is a fantasy, no matter how "real" it seems to the person who is fantasizing it. Though one's perceptions can often be equated to reality, sometimes the two are not actually one: appearances can be deceiving. When the author of *Luke* wrote "Jesus" as saying He wasn't a ghost, that writer might have been retelling the delusion of someone who thought that he had heard this, or else that writer might have been knowingly passing a fraud; but, either way, there's no credibility to it.

Paul himself, at the very end of *Galatians* 2:11-21, admitted in 2:21 that "Jesus died." The only question was whether he "died for nothing." Any later implication, by Luke or anyone else, that Jesus didn't die, was false.

Like other aspects of Pauline or "Christian" theology, the Holy Ghost was, in later Church writings, built into a magical being who had always existed and who interceded in Jesus's life. Christians writing after Paul imagined anything they wished about this "Spirit," so long as it remained consistent with the entity Paul had constructed so as to *authorize* Paul's apostleship of Jesus.

It's worth emphasizing here that, when Paul said, in *1 Corinthians* 15:14, "If Christ has not been raised from the dead, then we have nothing to preach, and you have nothing to believe," the reason this was true, for him *personally*, was that if Jesus had *not* been resurrected to Paul, then Paul would have possessed no authority *whatsoever* amongst his own followers. As Paul said in *Galatians* 1:1, and elsewhere, he had been authorized *only* by the Holy Ghost. If Paul had not seen, and been instructed by, the Holy Ghost, then Paul wouldn't have been authorized by anyone at all. For him to have admitted that maybe Jesus had not been resurrected, would have been for him to admit that the *only* people who were authorized to speak for Jesus were Jesus's disciples – now Paul's enemies – who had been Jesus's followers when Jesus was *alive*. Paul would have simply had to quit.

Paul struggled hard to win his "converts" over to his view. They seem to have challenged him on it, because his letters battle such push-back. Paul had to fight especially hard to persuade his "converts" that the Trinity was acceptable *from a Jewish standpoint*. For example, 1 *Corinthians* 8:4-7 subtly uses his followers' own prior polytheism as an argumentative knife to cleave Judaism's very monotheism in two, when he rejects there "the many gods and lords that people believe in [which his followers had *already* abandoned, so he was using this reference as a mere doctrinal bogeyman to build his audience's sympathy], because there is, for us, only one God, the Father, who created all things, and one Lord, Jesus Christ, who is the means through which we experience all things." Paul here pretends to *reiterate* Judaism, by his repudiating his followers' original polytheism, while what he is *actually* doing is to take up the common practice in the Torah of referring to the Creator both as the one-and-only "God" in some places, and as the one-and-only "Lord" in other places, and to transform that Jewish practice, of two synonyms for *the same object*, into *two separate objects* in his new Christian religion, which are as different from one another as are a father and a son – definitely *not* the *same* person. Only an extremely careful reader (or listener) would have recognized Paul's deceptive tactic here, of changing a pair of synonyms ("God" and "Lord") into separate and distinct objects, as distinct from each other as are a father and his son. Whereas in Judaism, "God" and "Lord" refer to the same thing; "father" and "son" aren't synonyms; and, in fact, they are defined *by their relationship to each other*, so that they can *never even possibly* be the *same* person. For example, although "physician" and "artist" *sometimes* refer to one and the same person, "father" and "son" *always* refer to two *different* people. By contrast, for example, the phrase "God the Lord" appears together ten times in *Genesis* 2, not to mention the numerous other instances in which the Torah uses those synonyms in immediate succession. *Genesis* 2 uses the term "Lord" once without "God," and *Genesis* 1 uses the term "God" 32 times, and doesn't use the term "Lord" even a single time. Judaism couldn't possibly be clearer that "God" and "Lord" are synonyms. For Paul to use those two terms here, to refer respectively to the "Father," and then to something that's definitely *not* "the Father" (the "Son"), was pure deceit from him. Moreover, God isn't actually referred to even *once* in the Torah as *being* "the Father." Only twice is God the Father referred to in the later parts of the Old Testament, in *Psalms* 89:26 and *Isaiah* 64:8. Paul picked up simply from that skimpy base, to make Jesus into God's Son, but he did this in a sense which was alien even to *Psalms* and *Isaiah*, where God was portrayed as being *every* person's Father, not just as Jesus's (since the Jewish God, unlike pagan gods such as Zeus and Jupiter, has no *relatives* at all, and thus *no* distinctive "Son"). And, of course, *Psalms* and *Isaiah* didn't even constitute Scripture for Jews, since they're not in the Torah. So, Paul's distortions and misrepresentations of Jewish Scripture occurred on numerous levels. (And Paul also deceived routinely about his Trinity. For example, in *Galatians*, 1:1 says "God the Father ... raised Jesus Christ from the dead"; 1:4 says Jesus "sacrificed himself ... according to the will of God the Father"; and 1:16 says that God "revealed his Son to me." So, this "Father" and "Son" are *two* beings, *not* one, and worshipping both of them is therefore polytheistic if the term "polytheistic" has meaning at all.) This piling of deceit upon deceit is how Paul split the Jewish God in two (and then, from there, in three, so as to reach the Holy Ghost, which he *claimed* to have met, and whose existence he was actually striving to establish by all of these gyrations). In other words: Paul *knowingly and with great care* confused and misled his readers, in order to be able to win his arguments. He even admitted, in *1 Corinthians* 9:20-27, that he would do whatever was necessary in order to win. He virtually admitted there, to his "converts," that they were his tools, who believed him at peril of becoming his dupes. He said that he was doing this to them in order to save them, but (like everything else in his statements) he had to contradict both the Torah and even himself, in order to present his arguments, since he was actually lying. The only basis for believing him was faith; and he kept violating that faith, whenever he contradicted himself, and also whenever he cited the Torah while contradicting the Torah.

In short: Paul deceived *repeatedly*, so as to argue for his Resurrection-based Trinity.[50]

---

[50]   The difficulties with Jews continued after Paul's death, and therefore the latest-written of the four canonical Gospel accounts of "Jesus" finally introduced, at *John* 10:30, the Christian Godhead, with "Jesus" saying "The Father and I are one," and, repeating it, eight lines later, with, "The Father is in me, and I am in the Father," and repeating that yet again in 14:11.

This last-written (and thus least reliable) Gospel is largely constructed so as to reinforce that separation from Paul's Trinity, that subtle twist in the original version of it, perhaps so as to deal with Jewish rejections of Paul's Trinity, in order to enable Christians to persuade Gentiles that the Jewish God and the Christian God were the same, and that Jesus was merely its personal appearance, a different name for it (and thereby to overcome Jewish accusations – based upon Paul and his followers prior to that Gospel – that they weren't the same God).

John even quoted its "Jesus" as saying, in 8:58, "Before Abraham was born, I am," retrojecting "Jesus" far back in time. This three-synonyms-as-one, eternal, Godhead became the basis for the Chalcedon Creed in 451, but it actually originated later than Paul, and later than Paul's immediate followers.

However, *John* 14:28 also quoted its "Jesus" as telling his disciples, shortly before his crucifixion, "If you loved me, then you would be glad that I am going to the Father, because the Father is greater than I." This blatantly contradicts "The Father and I are one." Christian theologians are thus trapped by the sloppiness of the Scripture that they've committed themselves to believe – nonsense, like so many other hoaxes. The anonymous author of *John* loaded his Gospel with self-contradictions, and therefore left even Godhead Christians floating within an intellectual miasma.

Of course, Paul himself was full of such miasma. *Philippians* 2:5-11, in fact, is so messy, that many scholars argue that this passage – which opens by saying that Jesus knew that equality with God the Father would be impossible for anyone to achieve – asserts that Jesus had always been and was God the Father. (The passage opens by referring to Jesus's being "in God's form," referring to *Genesis* 1:27; and scholars take this to mean that Jesus was *identical to* God the

2:14-21 One Unitary Quotation

Interestingly, many translations of *Galatians* don't place
between quotation marks the entirety of the passage in which
Paul set forth his gospel of Christ, from that statement's start
in the middle of 2:14, extending straight through to its end
2:21. (There are NO quotation marks in the *original*, because
ancient Greek didn't *have* quotation marks.) Perhaps these
translators wanted not to make EXPLICIT that, until the event
he's recounting here, Paul had actually NEVER PREVIOUSLY
ASSERTED what subsequently emerged to become his "gospel of
Christ" – namely, the SUPERSESSION of the Jewish covenant by
faith-and-grace – and that he DID assert it, and that he asserted
all of it, up through 2:21, on this cardinally important
occasion, right after the council in Jerusalem. (Prominent
EXCEPTIONS, biblical translations that got this RIGHT, and that
placed all of Paul's gospel of Christ in quotation marks,
include the New King James Version, the New International
Version, and the Contemporary English Version.) But there's
actually every reason to believe that, prior to the event
recounted in 2:11-16, Paul had been accepting obedient Jews
as saved without question, and had been converting all of his
Gentile "converts" to a Jewish-Law-abiding system that added
faith-and-grace for violations by Gentiles, as the means by
which Gentiles could win the very SAME salvation that any
obedient Jew does. (That's the system Paul had been teaching
in *1 Corinthians* 7:19-20 and throughout his missionary work
until the event he recounts in *Galatians* 2:11-22. But, as we've
also previously mentioned, *1 Thessalonians* 4:1-17 exhibits a
transitional two-gospels approach, because it was written so

Father.) Furthermore, many scholars have assumed that this passage was lifted by
Paul into his letter from some pre-existing source or "hymn" and therefore "proves"
that Jesus was worshipped before (and thus independently of) Paul – even though
not a single item of historical evidence exists or has ever been cited for that
assumption. Scholars grasp at such intellectual straws, and tie these into knots, to
rest upon, in beliefs that can provide them neither rest nor truth.

soon after this event. And after this event and the brief
transitional period following it, Paul was the Christian
recognized by "historians.")

There is, in other words, every reason to believe that
these "converts" by Paul considered themselves to have
belonged, AS Jesus-followers, to a Jesus-following SECT OF
JUDAISM. The only Jewish law which Paul and the leaders in
Jerusalem considered to be so dangerous to impose so that
faith-and-grace, really God's mercy, would be the only hope
for Gentiles' salvation, was *Genesis* 17:14 – the circumcision
law, Judaism's signature-law. And it's understandable,
therefore, that this is where the split *ultimately emerged.*

We possess good reason to infer that the statement of
Paul to Peter that starts in 2:14 actually ends at the very end of
the second chapter – at the end, that is to say, of 2:21 – because
Paul's argument to Peter flows SMOOTHLY all the way through
to the chapter's end, and it's furthermore all of a single piece,
culminating in the centrality of the crucifixion, without which
the earlier parts of this statement would have made no sense
at all. After this event; that is, after the event recounted in
2:11-21; Paul was – as here now in *Galatians* – trying to wean
his followers GRADUALLY AWAY from that Jewish sect, into his
own, entirely new, faith, which he called simply "the gospel of
the Messiah," or "the gospel of Christ." As was previously
noted, this phrase sounded, to people in Paul's time, like the
belief of a JEWISH SECT. Only in subsequent decades did Paul's
new gospel start to be called "Christianity," by Paul's
followers in Antioch. This was at sufficiently LATE a period so
that the split away from Judaism had now *become* OVERT. Paul
wanted to retain his association with the Jerusalem
organization for as long as he possibly could, so as to continue
borrowing from their pre-established credibility for as long as
possible. But, ultimately, that became no longer practicable.
By that time, perhaps there were more members in Paul's
organization than there were in James's.

How do we know that, PRIOR to this event, Paul had
never asserted that Judaism was superseded; had never said

(2:16) "For no one is put right in God's view by obeying God's Law," and also that he DID say it ON that occasion? How do we know that Christianity was originally conceived on this occasion, and thus that this event was the most important event in all of human history – the event that created Western Civilization? If Paul had not actually stated this on that occasion, he wouldn't then have had *any* rationalization whatsoever for his side of this crucial argument against Peter and the other agents from James. Paul never expressed any OTHER argument for this position (the core of which is 2:16).[51]

---

[51]   Some scholars assert, without providing evidence, but only as being a supposedly plausible hypothesis, that Paul's argument for the non-necessity of circumcising the Gentile Jesus-followers was instead based upon a supposed tradition within Judaism of accepting uncircumcised Gentiles who adhered to the Noahide laws, the seven laws that the Talmud set forth as being demanded by God of all mankind and not only of Jews. Their "explanation" is an alternative to the one that Paul provides, and so simply ignores 2:16-21. These scholars assert that circumcision wasn't included among the seven Noahide laws, and that, supposedly therefore, Paul was probably arguing here upon the basis of this set Noahic tradition, and that Paul was saying that God accepted these uncircumcised men despite *Genesis* 17:14 on account of these men supposedly adhering to the seven Noahide laws. According to these scholars, 2:16-21 wasn't really Paul's argument. Substituting a merely plausible explanation (if it is that), without any evidence, in the place of an explanation that's documented by the best evidence (*Galatians*), and that's supported by all of the other evidence, would be prohibited to present as a theory of the case to a jury in any democracy, because such a theory of the case would violate the best-evidence principle; it would be barred as being purely conjectural, under the best-evidence principle.

However, actually, this scholarly speculation of a Noahic Paul is even worse than that: It presumes that the Talmud held such high authority among Jews, that it trumped even the Torah. But the reality was that, in Paul's time, the Talmud didn't even exist, much less did it possess such high authority.

The Talmud consists of two parts, the Mishna which was formed during approximately 70-200 CE, and the Gemara or "Babylonian Talmud" which was completed by around the year 500. If Paul didn't possess a time-machine, then he couldn't have argued upon the basis of the Noahide laws.

The "seven Noahide laws" were first written in around the year 300, in two parts of the Babylonian Talmud: Sanhedrin 56a; and Tosefta, Aboda Zara 8:4-6. [continued]

And if Paul had stated this argument PRIOR to that occasion, then his split away from the Jerusalem community, and the riots against him by not just Jesus-sect Jews, but by all Jews, that were portrayed in *Acts* 21:21 forward, would have started occurring earlier, even PRIOR to the council in Jerusalem – but there's no reason to believe that to have happened. 2:16 asserts that the Jewish covenant has been terminated by God; that Judaism is DEFUNCT. For Paul to have asserted this, was for him to negate the Jewish religion, to say to Jews that God no longer viewed favorably people who adhere to the Jewish faith and who do not believe that Jesus of Nazareth was the Jewish mashiach. Paul was here implying (and he made explicit in *Romans* 3:20&23) that God had concluded that circumcision and other obedience to the covenant were too high a price for people to have to pay for an admission-ticket into heaven, a price that too few people (Paul even said that "no one") were willing or able to pay, and that this God had therefore now placed heaven on sale, to be purchased instead by mere faith in Jesus's being the mashiach. Paul was saying that therefore circumcision and all the rest of the price Jews had already paid for heaven were henceforth a total waste, or "sheer trash" according to *Philippians* 3:2-9. Jews had overpaid; they wouldn't get any refund on their overpayment; and, from now on, Gentiles were successfully going to buy heaven for far less, they'd get a much better deal and become God's new "Chosen People" (*Philippians* 1:1, *1 Corinthians* 1:2, *2 Corinthians* 1:1). All of this was already implied in *Galatians* 2:16. Thus, those were fighting words not only to Jesus-sect Jews, but to non-Jesus-sect Jews. These were fighting words to *all* Jews; and this is why, if Paul had said such a thing PRIOR to this event, then the Jewish riots against him (recounted in *Acts*

The straw of reality upon which such scholars grasp is that Jews, in Paul's time, did often try to bend the Torah rules in order to accept into Judaism Gentiles who wanted to join. However, these accommodations were viewed as only temporary measures, not permanent. What *Galatians* 2:11-21 describes is Paul's argument when he heard from Peter and from the other representatives of James, that finally this temporary accommodation had *ended* in the case of Paul's men.

21:21 forward) would have started prior to this event; and no evidence even suggests this to have been the case.

If what Paul said on that occasion included everything from 2:14 through 2:21, then the "agents from James" were communicating from James that he rejected 2:16-21 as representing what Jesus had stood for. Paul was calling Peter hypocritical for changing his mind and joining in with James there. In other words, Paul was necessarily implying in lines 2:16-21, but was not explicitly asserting there, that Paul had, on that occasion, in the year 49 or 50, shocked everyone present, by having asserted a doctrine (namely 2:16-21) which *contradicted what Jesus had stood for*. Obviously, if Paul were to have *explicitly* admitted in these lines that Jesus would have opposed the doctrine 2:16-21, then Paul would promptly have lost all his followers, and his career as an "apostle" of Jesus would have ended *as a direct result* of this admission by him. This is why he didn't *explicitly* say that 2:16-21 was anti-Jesus and that James and Peter therefore rejected it. But his *implicitly* asserting this makes even more certain that it's so, and that Paul had, indeed, *first announced* Christianity (2:16-21) on that very occasion. This is the reason scholars devote little ink to the subject of whether Paul's statement on that occasion was *only* 2:14, or was instead *all* of 2:14-21: this matter is too important, too central to a *scientific* understanding of the creation of Christianity; too threatening to a scholarly interpretation of Christianity's start. So, scholars drip buckets of ink onto other, far less important, "issues," while virtually ignoring this smoking gun and the fingerprints that cover it. Even the scholars who assert that Paul's entire statement in 2:14-21 was made on that occasion, ignore the massive implications of this assumption – an assumption that a scientific analysis of *Galatians* finds to be established with no authentic reason to doubt.

Although Paul in this passage refers to Jesus (as "Christ"), he does not quote Jesus as having said anything that *authorizes* what Paul is saying here: the replacement of salvation-via-obedience-to-God's-commandments (Judaism), by salvation-via-Christ-faith (Christianity). If Jesus had said any such thing, then it would have been the most prominent of all of the statements attributed to him, and Paul would certainly have been intelligent enough in *Galatians* to have *cited* it here, but Paul didn't cite Jesus at all. The radical innovation Paul was introducing was thus *new* to everyone present at the time – and had *especially* never been asserted by *Jesus*.

Scholars wish to avoid the negative implications for the legitimacy of Christianity that arise from acknowledging that Paul on that occasion said to Peter not only 2:14 but the *entirety* of 2:14-2:21. So, they place in quotes *only* Paul's remark in 2:14; they are implicitly assuming that Paul, in *Galatians*, failed to state what his response was to Peter, other than to label Peter (his own teacher) a hypocrite. How likely is it that, in Paul's response on this occasion, Paul failed to present an *argument* against Peter and the other agents from James? Such a failure, on such an occasion, would have been entirely out of character for Paul.

Furthermore, 2:15 – the first of the lines that those scholars are alleging to pick up *after* Paul's account of the incident in Antioch – is clearly *a part of* the incident in Antioch, because 2:15 addresses Peter, saying *"we"* are "Jews by birth"; and the Galatian readers of Paul's letter were *not* that, but Peter clearly *was*. So, without a doubt, the statement that Paul had made to Peter on that occasion was 2:14-2:21, not *just* 2:14.

A random sampling of 17 popular translations of the Bible shows most of them to be incompetent in this regard. 10 translations were *grossly* incompetent, in that they ended this quotation at 2:14: English Standard Version, New Century Version, New Catholic Edition, New American Bible for Catholics, Jerusalem Bible, New English Bible, Revised English Bible, Revised Standard Version, New Revised Standard Version, Today's English Version. 2 translations ended it at 2:17: Living Bible, New Living Bible. 1 translation fudged this question entirely: King James Version. 1 translation fudged whether the quotation ended perhaps at

2:15: Amplified New Testament. Only 3 translations (as previously listed) ended this quotation correctly, at 2:21: New King James Version, Contemporary English Version, and New International Version. So: only 3 out of 17 translations were competent. 10 of these 17 translations were *grossly* incompetent, clearly ending at 2:14, despite the general recognition – even by scholars – that only few-to-none of Paul's members in Galatia had been *born* as Jews (and so, that 2:15 was *logically necessarily a part of* the quotation that starts with 2:14). Evidently, then, one crucial reason why scholars have not understood that 2:11-21 represented the event that actually started Christianity is that even the most elementary logical ability is simply absent in the majority of scholars. Moreover, if a person's logical ability is weak, then it's very easy for that person to believe whatever he or she wants, which isn't likely to be that Christianity is a hoax. Scholars will therefore probably continue to resist this conclusion, quite regardless of the evidence.

Clearly, from *Galatians* 3:1 onwards, Paul is addressing his Galatian readers directly, no longer recounting what had happened at and immediately after the council in Jerusalem. Thus, he opens 3:1 by addressing the Galatians *personally*. By contrast, 2:14-21 presents Paul's account of what his response had been when Peter and James's other men challenged him over *Genesis* 17:14. This quotation definitely *ended* at 2:21.

The Fictitiousness of *Matthew* 16:18, Etc.

What *else* can be said, at this point, about what's not explicit in 2:11-21, but about what's IMPLICIT in it?

To begin with, high significance attaches to Paul's having considered to be acceptable, to his Galatian readers, that he declare openly to them that he had stood opposed to, and had outright condemned in 2:13 as "cowardly," Peter. If Peter had been selected by Jesus as the sect's head, as Paul's later followers who wrote *Matthew* 16:18 and *John* 21:15-17 said, then Paul wouldn't have been able to get away with this; it would have been seen as blatantly insubordinate in the eyes of all members of the sect. In other words, what's striking is that, even though Paul was evidently prohibited from overtly standing opposed to James on this occasion, he had *no* such compunctions about publicly opposing Peter. Furthermore, as was previously noted, Paul would have had no reason to have even been mentioning to the Galatians the incident in 2:11-16 if he didn't have some reason to believe that they might possibly have heard about it already from his enemies. Clearly, Paul was here giving his side of a dispute that he had engaged in with his enemies, who are here clearly identified as (2:12) "agents from James." Peter had joined them by backing away from the table; but Paul didn't attack the agents from James – he attacked *only* Peter. Yet, Paul wasn't here DEFENDING himself against any charge of his having BEEN *insubordinate* then to Peter – this demonstrates that Peter was *likewise* subordinate to James. Obviously, Paul's enemies HAD NOT BEEN CHARGING PAUL AS HAVING BEEN *insubordinate* in treating Peter in this brazenly insulting manner. Clearly, that wasn't part of the charge Paul was now defending himself against. Equally obviously, Peter was Paul's predecessor and his senior in the sect; Paul has himself acknowledged this; but when Paul in 2:11 said "I opposed Peter in public," and in 2:13 called Peter an outright "coward," and proceeded to report how Paul had on this occasion been so arrogant as to have instructed Peter on the teachings of Jesus – a man whom Peter had known intimately and Paul had never even met – this could only have been seen within the sect as having been the rankest insubordination, IF Peter had, himself, actually BEEN the sect's leader. Yet, the charge of insubordination isn't what Paul was defending himself against here. Clearly, then, Peter *wasn't* the sect's leader, notwithstanding such later-written passages, from Paul's followers, as *Matthew* 16:18.

Moreover, the fact that the precipitator of this confrontation was the "agents from James" says everything, but only by implication (because Paul was struggling to avoid *admitting* to his readers even that the leaders *were* "leaders"). If they hadn't come, there wouldn't have *been* the event, that created Christianity, recounted in 2:11-21, because the spark which ignited this conflagration would have been absent.

Furthermore, Paul starts 2:14: "But when I saw that they did not walk uprightly about the truth of the gospel, I said to Peter in the presence of all, ..." In other words: Though Paul starts 2:14 by acknowledging that his argument is not only against Peter but also against the newly arrived "agents from James," Paul's attack and criticisms are directed *solely* against Peter. This differential treatment by Paul is absolutely stunning: Paul's text leaves a reader *no logical way to doubt* that Paul was deferring to James by excluding from Paul's attacks the men James had sent to check up on Peter's carrying out of his assignment from James.

Consequently, *Galatians* 2:11-16 provides *direct and irrefutable* evidence both that Peter WAS NOT the leader and that James *was*, which *Acts* 15:13-21 implicitly powerfully expands by its reporting that *James* made the final decisions within the sect.[52] This is why we can infer with *confidence* that Peter's role

---

[52]   Here is a good opportunity to explain more of legal/forensic methodology: This methodology started being applied after around 1950, which was the era when the first-ever trials of white-collar crimes took place.

These types of trials tend to depend largely upon interpreting documentary evidence and reconstructing a sequence of events based upon documents that refer to them. Nowadays this evidence can include e-mails, but originally it was more pedestrian and physical: letters, notes, memos, etc. Unlike a scholar of the New Testament or of ancient Greek classics, who may question whether such writers were accurate, but not whether they were intending to deceive, a court cannot afford to simply assume honesty, and has therefore developed ways of ferreting out deceptions and separating them from truths.

To cite just the main example here: *Galatians* 2:11-16 shows Paul condemning Peter in front of his men, and yet the "agents from James" weren't condemned even though they had precipitated the conflict, and Paul never condemned James by name to others in the group; moreover, *Acts* 15:13-21 shows

in *Galatians* 2:11 was AS AN AGENT FROM JAMES, who had arrived *earlier* than did the anonymous ones that Paul mentioned in the next line, 2:12. *Galatians* 2:11-16 makes crystal clear that on this occasion Paul had stood opposed to *both* Peter *and* the "agents from James"; and we can also tell, by logical inference from this passage, that Peter was, himself, on this occasion, ALSO an agent from James; albeit, an agent who (understandably) was loath to carry out this assignment, and who had arrived earlier.

Again, Paul has stated his most important facts IMPLICITLY, rather than explicitly. And, yet again, therefore, a scholarly reading of Paul's text, which – being scholarly – reads ONLY its explicit level, *misses* what's MOST *important* in it.

Thus, too, *Galatians* 2:11-14 proves that *Matthew* 16:18, and the other Gospel passages which explicitly place into Jesus's mouth the designation of Peter to run the group, are lies: not history, but calculated myth. Peter wouldn't have instantaneously buckled to James's emissaries, and wouldn't have been publicly humiliated by Paul, such as both happened here, if those later-written Gospel accounts about "Jesus" were true. *Galatians*, thus – the best evidence of all – under legal/forensic examination, exposes bare the Roman

---

James and not Peter making the ultimate decision concluding the council in Jerusalem; and thus both passages, in *Galatians* and in *Acts*, necessarily logically imply that James was the group's leader, and that Peter was not. By contrast, the Gospels, in *Matthew* 16:18 and *John* 21:15-17, explicitly assert that Peter was superior to James in authority within the group.

A key legal/forensic principle in interpreting documents is that what's logically necessarily implied by a document is generally better evidence than what's explicitly asserted, because the latter inevitably embodies the agenda of the writer, including any of his intended deceptions, whereas the former might even contradict the person's agenda. So, as opposed to scholarly method, legal/forensic method grants preference to what's logically necessarily implied, or what's demonstrated or shown by the described action, and normally rates this information higher than anything that's explicitly asserted which contradicts that. This principle, applied in conjunction with questioning not only the accuracy but the honesty-of-intent of assertions, and always employing only the best evidence, assists in "cross-examining" a given document, even when its author is, for whatever reason, not available for cross-examination.

Catholic Church (supposedly begun by *Matthew* 16:18) as a fraud, and consequently all of Christianity as nothing but a Roman Catholic hoax. (Of course, this excludes from "Christianity" the Ebionites and other Jewish Jesus-followers, who had nothing to do with writing and assembling the New Testament. By "Christianity" is meant the religion whose Scripture is the New Testament.) Paul's Roman Catholic Church retroactively made Peter, and not James, Jesus's successor, because Peter had been Paul's teacher, and because the Roman Church needed *someone* to connect it to Jesus, and they couldn't choose James, since he had been the enemy of Paul, who actually *started* the Roman Catholic Church.

Christianity a Double Hoax

There it is: Christianity is a hoax, not just as regards its beliefs, but also as regards its organizational authority. Paul *implicitly* confessed to both hoaxes (though he didn't himself perpetrate the hoax about Peter's heading the sect – his followers did).

When Paul, in 2:2, said that his entire career-success would be at stake in the upcoming conference in Jerusalem, there can be no reasonable doubt as to *who* called this conference or why: James called it, and he did so because the pressures upon James, as the leader, were now intense, both from the born Jews within the Jesus-sect, and from the born Jews outside it – these pressures being to get Paul's men circumcised, in accord with *Genesis* 17:14. Clearly, when Paul said in 2:2, "I went to the conference because God told me to go," he was blatantly lying, because James had ordered him to come to the conference: it was, by Paul's own implicit admission, *essential* for Paul to be there in order to present his case, which would be this conference's very focus. Moreover, inasmuch as James had, for 17 years, himself gone along with Paul's acceptance of uncircumcised "converts," James was

almost certainly extremely reluctant to reverse this
longstanding policy, and to thereby risk losing Paul's
congregations. One may thus reasonably assume that James
called this conference in the fervent hope that Paul would
offer there a persuasive case, which would somehow quell
these pressures that impinged upon James. Consequently, the
likelihood that James failed not only to tell Paul to come, but
to tell Paul that the conference's subject would be the non-
circumcision of his men, and so have avoided letting Paul
recognize to come well prepared to win a case that both he
and Paul fervently hoped Paul would win, is so remote as to
be virtually nil.[53] This means that the likelihood is virtually

---

[53]   James was, by all accounts, doing all he could to hold the sect together.
His own success was dependent upon retaining Paul's followers. If James had
wanted Paul to lose, then James would simply have publicly announced that no
one could be a member of the group who wasn't circumcised in accord with
Genesis 17:14. Paul's losing would have been essentially dictated by James's
deciding against Paul's position on this issue. The evidence is clear that James did
not publish any demand for the enforcement of *Genesis* 17:14 as a pre-condition of
membership in his organization.

   Legal/forensically, one cannot rely upon dubious documents that were
later written allegedly by or about "James" in order to understand James's position.
For example, the lone letter in the New Testament that alleges to be from "James"
cannot be relied upon. There are sound reasons why many scholars consider it to
be a forgery. However, perhaps the strongest reasons for ignoring *James* concern
the avoidance by this "letter" of all of the strong Torah-based arguments that were
available supporting the necessity for circumcision. This "letter" seems to have
been written instead with the intention to stand against Paul while using Paul's
underlying argument to do that (and thus leaving readers no real *alternative* to
Paul's viewpoint). For example, *James* 2:1-7 does precisely this, by the way it
argues against judging by "outward appearance," as opposed to judging by a
person's being "rich in faith." Using this, the fundamental Pauline argument,
"James" identifies people who do that as being prejudiced in favor of the rich
against the poor; and he condemns that prejudice. James would have condemned
that prejudice, but he wouldn't likely have used Paul's argument against the Law in
order to do it. There is no more of an actual reason to accept, as evidence, *James*,
than there is to accept, as "evidence," for example, *The Protocols of the Elders of
Zion*, or any other anti-Semitic forgeries which allege to be written by Jews but are
actually against Jews, and written by anti-Semites. Instead, such documents, which
use an enemy's actual arguments in order to allegedly present one's own case,
should be viewed with suspicion – certainly not with trust, and definitely not with
faith.

   James does not argue on any basis that James almost certainly *did*.
[continued]

100% that Paul was outright lying when he said in 2:2 "I went because God told me to." Paul, here as elsewhere, did everything that he possibly could, to diminish, in the view of his readers, James's stature as Jesus's heir. When Paul was writing this letter, perhaps three or four years after the event, he was trying to wean his men *away* from James's sect. The reason that Paul said that God had told him to come to the conference is that Paul refused to affirm explicitly to his men that James was Paul's boss. Paul didn't want to *remind* them of that. For Paul now to acknowledge James's supreme authority would be exactly opposite to Paul's primary goal of winning those congregations as his own, no *longer* James's. Also, Paul didn't want his Galatian readers to know how crucial this conference in Jerusalem really was; Paul especially didn't want them to know that their own membership in the Jesus-community was at stake here. Paul's goal was to keep these men with him, at the same time as he subtly removed them from Judaism altogether and made them his own without James's leadership, and without Judaism of any other sect, but rather in Paul's entirely new religion. Paul employed carefully calculated terminology, such as "*ekklesia*" (instead of "*sunagoge*") and "the gospel of Christ" (the then-Jewish-sounding phrase "the good news of the mashiach"), in order to achieve his deceptions. These lies from Paul not only tied him up in contradictions, but they exhibited – they displayed,

---

The only admissible evidence that survives regarding James consists of Paul's authentic letters, supplemented by the sole reference to him as Jesus's brother in Josephus's *Antiquities* 20:9:1, plus supplemented by whatever references there are to James the brother of Jesus in other documents that reasonably might have been written early enough to qualify (such as *Acts*, *Thomas*, and the canonical Gospels). However, nothing can reasonably be said about James that violates the theory of the case about him that's derived from *Galatians* – the most reliable evidence of all. The mere fact that Paul argues there against James doesn't diminish its legal/forensic reliability about James.

James, for 17 years, had been supporting what Paul was doing. For James to turn around, and finally recognize that he had made the wrong decision all that while, could only have been extremely painful for him. But he did it. What he didn't do is to follow through on that.

they proved by *logically necessary implication* – that James indeed *was* Jesus's heir. This testimony demonstrating that James was the group's leader is of even greater reliability because Paul did everything that he could to *hide* the fact, and to challenge it, on the *explicit* level (such as in 2:6). This is like a witness in court admitting something under cross-examination from the opposed attorney, acknowledging facts this witness had previously denied and had done everything possible to hide.

Further high quality confirmation of the hypothesis that's demonstrated in 2:11-14, of James having been the successor to Jesus rather than Peter having been, is provided by the testimony of Josephus. He wrote perhaps at about the same time as did Luke, the writer of *Acts*, whose testimony for confirmation we've previously mentioned. Josephus possesses even higher authority than does Luke and Luke's *Acts*: Josephus's testimony, unlike that of *Acts*, is entirely INDEPENDENT of Paul; he was *no* follower of Paul, and so his testimony cannot reasonably be suspected of having been accommodated to, and so *contaminated by*, Paul's still-earlier testimony. Josephus's *Antiquities of the Jews*, in its passage 20:9:1 (also sometimes cited by its line-numbers as 20:197-203), presents a fascinating, and evidentiarily extremely important, account of the murder of James, occurring in the year 62 CE, by a Jewish High Priest, Ananus. Josephus published this in approximately the year 94, and so it was a contemporary account. This Priest's action, according to Josephus, elicited such outrage from Jerusalem's Jews, that the then-reigning King, Herod Agrippa, was thereby induced to replace Ananus. Thus, James's personal renown, and his high regard amongst the Jewish public, receive Josephus's direct, explicit, and independent, confirmation, supporting the logical inferences that have been drawn here previously from the top evidentiary source, Paul, supplemented by an evidentiary source below both Paul and Josephus – Luke. Furthermore, Josephus wrote entirely as an uninvolved stranger to these people and events; he, unlike both Paul and Luke, had no personal involvement in these matters, and can, therefore, be presumed to have at least *tried* to present them as they, in fact, were.

This Josephan passage, also like Paul's testimony, refers to James as having been Jesus's brother. It furthermore independently confirms that Jesus "was called the Christ" (Josephus using here, like Paul, the Greek language and Messiah-term). Also very importantly (and importantly *un*like Christian sources), this passage asserts that the Jewish public typically held the High Priest in low esteem, which confirms the people's *opposition* to the "religious leader" who was imposed upon them by Roman authority.

Thus, Josephus's account confirms important things about BOTH James and Jesus.

Another very important thing it confirms about both of them concerns the respective ways in which Jewish and Roman laws *dealt with* the death penalty: James here was being put to death by a Jewish court (which was headed by a High Priest appointed by the Romans, but which was nonetheless executing Jewish and not Roman laws), and this court therefore applied the Jewish death penalty, which was by stoning, and not the Roman one, by crucifixion. This passage in Josephus provides, therefore, yet additional confirmation to the absurdity of the subsequently written Gospel accounts of Jesus's trial, in which Jesus was supposedly executed for his having violated Jewish, *not* Roman, laws, and yet was, incontestably, crucified (the Roman punishment for sedition), and NOT stoned to death (the Jewish punishment for blasphemy, specified in *Leviticus* 24:14-16).

Furthermore, unlike the infamous later anonymous Christian insertion into Josephus's *Antiquities of the Jews* (the passage often referred to as Josephus's TESTIMONIUM FLAVIANUM, which is *Antiquities* 18:3:3), the present Josephan passage (*Antiquities* 20:9:1) provides UNTAMPERED-WITH, authentic, independent, contemporary non-Christian mention of the historical Jesus. It's a far lengthier passage than the very brief TESTIMONIUM FLAVIANUM, and it provides a narrative that recounts many events, all in a credible cause-effect sequence. In stark contrast, the *TF* offers nothing more than a brief piece of rank (if not blatant) Christian evangelism that calls Jesus "a wise man, if it be proper to call him a man, because he performed miracles," and that claims Jesus "was resurrected on the third day after his crucifixion." The *TF* even goes so far as to assert that Jesus "was the Christ." Anyone who believed that Jesus was the Christ was, by definition, a Christian; and clearly the *TF* was written by a Christian. By contrast, the passage that we are here discussing calls Jesus nothing more than "the so-called Christ." In fact, since this passage contradicts in so many ways the Christian accounts, it's even ANTI-Christian; it clearly was *not* in any sense Christian propaganda, such as the New Testament is (and such as the *TF* is). It therefore constitutes *one of the best evidences (besides Paul's letters) to refute the Jesus-never-existed scholars,* such as Earl Doherty, Acharya S, Timothy Freke, George A. Wells, Robert M. Price, and others.[54] Consequently, this passage's historiographical importance is enormous with respect not only to James, but also to Jesus.

---

[54]   A certain Jesus-never-existed proponent refused to look at this book, and insisted that I provide him instead a *summary* of the evidence for rejecting his viewpoint; I responded:

"To start this summary: *Galatians* is universally considered the evidentiary gold standard for questions of earliest Christian history, irrespective of when or how one asserts Christianity to have started. The letter to the Galatians ranks as far superior-quality evidence as compared to the canonical Gospels, not only because it predates them, but also because it's written to an audience (the Galatians) who possessed or could obtain independent knowledge of some of the persons and events it refers to, whereas that's not at all the case regarding any of the Gospels.

"*Galatians* 1:19 refers to 'James the Lord's brother,' but doesn't refer to Peter or anyone else as a brother of Jesus, despite Paul's having been, on Paul's own testimony in *Galatians* 1:18-19, closer to Peter than to James, and having spent two weeks with Peter who was presumably teaching Paul how to preach to Gentiles. Consequently, this 'brother of Jesus' was evidently a biological brother, and not merely a 'brother'of Jesus in the metaphorical sense as simply a member of Jesus's community (like Peter, John, and some or all of the other disciples were). [continued]

"However, James couldn't have been a physical brother of Jesus unless Jesus actually existed, which you deny. Evidently, Paul's readers knew of this particular James as being the James who was a biological brother of Jesus, and Paul here was making clear to his readers which James he was referring to when he called him a brother of Jesus. But you deny that Jesus even existed.

"You're saying instead that, in or around the year 54 when *Galatians* was written, all of those people would be thinking of James as only metaphorically a brother of Jesus, and you're also saying that Jesus was a fictitious person. That's a bit much (to put it mildly) for Paul to have been able confidently to pull such wool over these Galatians's eyes without major fear of being subsequently exposed by any of them for his having perpetrated so stupid a fraud upon them. I describe and document highly sophisticated frauds by Paul, but nothing so dumb and incredibly unlikely as that: there's no evidence for it; to the contrary, such stupidity would contradict the brilliant cunning that's amply displayed in Paul's letters: it would be out-of-character for Paul. There's simply no reason to accept that interpretation.

"Furthermore, Josephus, in *Antiquities of the Jews* 20:9:1, also referred to this James as being Jesus's brother, and there's no reason to consider that reference to have been a later addition like the *Testimonium Flavianum*.

"This man James simply couldn't have been Jesus's brother unless Jesus himself existed, and so the hypothesis that Jesus didn't exist has to be considered to bear an immense burden of proof, far greater a burden than the assumption that Jesus *did* exist must bear.

"The burden of proof is thus upon you, Doherty, Freke, Gandy, Acharya S., etc., to explain exactly how and when and where and why and by whom Christianity started, without Jesus's ever having existed; and also to explain the entire New Testament, including Paul's letters, under that assumption; and none of you has ever met this burden, nor even attempted to do so. You might as well be fundamentalist Christians."

I received no answer.

George A. Wells, in his "Historicity of Jesus," in Gordon Stein (Ed., 1985), *Encyclopedia of Unbelief*, not only denies that Jesus existed, but asserts (p. 368): "This argument does not impute fraud to the Christians of the late 1st century, ... but simply honest reasoning from the data." Such denial of Jesus's historicity could then itself be a fraud which is motivated by a desire to protect or hide, as a mere "error," the fraud that Paul perpetrated, not in "late 1st century," but around the year 50 – and which was anything *but* "honest reasoning from the data." Such fraud protecting fraud is no more supportable by science, than is Christianity itself.

Nor is fraud that protects the frauds of scholars (concerning Paul's ancient fraud) scientifically supportable. It just piles fraud on top of fraud; it's just more scholarship. Robert M. Price, in his 2000 *Deconstructing Jesus*, also denies that Jesus existed, and he respectfully refers to scholars who disagree with him and who support the New Testament. He says of their numerous Christian-apologetic works (p. 13): "None violates historical method. All are the product of serious and

The entirety of this important passage will therefore be presented here.

In the way of an initial explanation of it (more extensive than the brief summary just given of it was): Josephus refers to the Emperor, or "Caesar," who is Nero, appointing Albinus to succeed the late-deceased Festus as the procurator, or governor, of Judaea, in 62 CE. The Judaean King, Herod Agrippa, took this occasion to instruct that new procurator, prior even to Albinus's arrival in Judaea, to appoint a new High Priest, Ananus, son of a retired High Priest, who had likewise been called Ananus. This Ananus Jr. was promptly appointed, and immediately exhibited the worst authoritarian traits of his elitist Sadducean sect. For reasons unstated by Josephus, this young Ananus hastily called together a "sanhedrin," or, it seems, essentially a kangaroo-court, of Sanhedrin judges, forthwith to convict James as a breaker of Jewish law and to have him instantaneously executed. The outrage against this amongst the Jewish public was brought to King Agrippa's attention, and the new High Priest was

---

deep scholarship. But what these learned labors have yielded may be called an embarrassment of riches. There are just too many that make too much sense." He asserts that this "vitiates the compelling force of any of them." Dr. Price might have been practicing excellent scholarship there, but it was lousy science, because a scientist knows that that sort of thing cannot be true: When thousands of works contradict each other right and left, they cannot all be true – and probably all of them are wrong, because such a field as that hasn't yet matured to become a real science; it's still just mere scholarship.

The Jesus-never-existed scholars are no better than the Jesus-is-God scholars. There are an infinitude of possible ways to falsify, but there is only one way *not* to. That's what science constantly aims to find, and no "embarrassment of riches" from scholars has any scientific standing. Trash is trash, whatever else it may be, *even if* it's an "embarrassment of riches," in the view of scholars.

For a person who is surrounded by Christians to reject Christianity, the most simple-minded way is to deny that Jesus even existed. After all, Zeus didn't exist; Jupiter didn't exist. So, Jesus didn't exist, either. Right? Wrong! Christianity is not being proven here to be just a myth; it's being proven here to be a hoax. Atheists who think it's a myth have too much faith, not just in their atheism, but even in Christianity – not to mention in scholarship itself. Atheists think that the basic issue is theism versus atheism, when it's really science versus faith.

promptly ousted. As described by Josephus, James's support on this occasion was LED by those Jews "who were the strictest in their observance of the laws," which is to say, by precisely the *same* group of Jews whom the mythological Christ, in *Mark* and the other Gospels (excepting only some parts of *Matthew*), had CONDEMNED with special fervor. Therefore, according to this Josephan passage, Jesus's brother and successor, James, was killed by a Roman-appointed High Priest; and James's STRONGEST SUPPORTERS – the strongest supporters, in other words, of Jesus's own appointed *successor* – were strict Jewish-Law-observant Jews, the very SAME group that the Gospel-writers claim to have been the strongest ENEMIES of *Jesus;* and this account therefore implicitly stands at *odds* against the Gospels' portrayal of Jesus-vs.-the-Pharisees. Josephus contradicts the New Testament, but affirms both Jesus and James. Here, then, is this historically very important passage, *Antiquities of the Jews* 20:9:1:

"Upon hearing of Festus's death [in 62 CE], Caesar sent Albinus to Judaea as procurator. The King removed Joseph from the High Priesthood, and bestowed the office on Ananus's son, who was called Ananus like his father. Although the elder Ananus had been well reputed, and had had five other sons who had likewise served long and well as High Priest, even despite the low esteem in which High Priests were customarily held by the Jewish people, this new High Priest Ananus showed himself immediately to be rash and arrogant. Furthermore, he was from the sect of the Sadducees, who are renowned among the Jews for being the most severely heartless in their judgments. Ananus, sensing an opportunity, since Festus had just died and Albinus was still en-route to his new post, immediately convened the judges of the Sanhedrin, to render judgment upon a man named James, and upon some of his companions. This James happened to be the brother of Jesus, the so-called Christ. Ananus accused these people of having broken the law, and then he delivered them up to be stoned to death. However, Jerusalem's inhabitants who were reputed to be the most fair-minded and the strictest in their observance of the law, were outraged at what had been done. These people secretly sent representatives to the King, urging that what Ananus had done was in blatant violation of the law, and that Ananus should therefore be prohibited from ever again doing so terrible a thing. Some even went to meet with Albinus, still en-route from Alexandria, and informed him that Ananus had broken [even Roman] law in doing this without his previously having acquired the procurator's explicit consent. Convinced that Ananus's action was indeed unacceptable, Albinus wrote an angry letter to him, threatening punishment. King Agrippa then fired and replaced Ananus. The new High Priest, likewise the son of a former High Priest, Damneus, went by the name of Jesus of Damneus."

The Australian scholar of early Christianity, Robert Crotty, in the seventh chapter of a book he's currently (as of my writing) producing about James, makes the perceptive comment on this passage, "Josephus had [here] revised his earlier estimation of Ananus in the *Jewish Wars* [4:5:2], where he spoke of him as 'most righteous, an able leader' who, if he had been followed by the people, would have averted the destruction of Jerusalem. Perhaps it was in the interval between the *Jewish Wars* and writing the *Antiquities of the Jews* that Josephus had been informed of the unlawful execution of James. It was sufficient cause for him to change his opinion of Ananus completely and forcibly."

There are also other documentary sources, later than
Josephus, which are discussed in Robert Eisenman's 1998
James the Brother of Jesus, and in other books about James,
indicating that James was so very important a figure, that his
execution was a precipitating event which led to the final
round of Jewish revolts that produced, within eight years of
James's death, the Roman attack upon and destruction of
Jerusalem. All of this late evidence suggests that the Jesus
movement was importantly involved in the Jewish resistance
to Roman authority. Consequently, it also supports the view
that Jesus was, indeed, a very real political threat to the
Roman occupation authorities, including to the Herodian
kings, and the High Priests. That, however, still remains
speculative, especially because of the lateness of these sources.
The majority of scholars, respecting the New Testament's
portrayal of Jesus as a "Prince of Peace" inauthentic to the
warlike sense of that phrase in the *Old* Testament (where the
successor to King David is supposed to become the "Prince of
Peace" by slaughtering the alien occupiers of Israel), continue
to see the group's founder, Jesus, as having carefully walked
the fence between cooperating with and resisting these
occupying authorities. This Josephan passage provides further
refutation of that view held by scholars and by other religious
teachers.

Providing yet further refutation of the New
Testament's portrayal is the following passage from Book XV,
Chapter 44, of *The Annals,* written by another Roman
historian, Tacitus, and published in or around the year 116,
likewise concerning the reign of Nero – here specifically the
fire that destroyed Rome:

"Neither the gifts which the Emperor granted to the survivors nor his offerings to the gods were able to quiet the public's suspicions that he had ordered the conflagration. Thus, he blamed the fire upon, and his agents exquisitely tortured, a widely despised group called 'Christians.' Their founder, Christus, had been executed by Pontius Pilate, the procurator of Judea during Tiberius's reign, and though that execution suppressed this group's rebellions for awhile, their resistance subsequently resumed not only in their original location, Judea, but even in Rome, the city towards which all horrible social movements ultimately gravitate and find their center. Consequently, arrests were made first of ones who pled guilty, and those confessions identified a vast multitude of other Christians who were convicted upon that testimony, which concerned not so much Christians having set fire to the city, as their hating all mankind. Public humiliations of every type were applied to these people's executions: first, they were covered with the skins of, and made to appear like, animals; then, some of them were ripped apart by ravenous dogs, while others were simply crucified, and still others were burnt alive to illuminate Rome through the night. Nero provided his gardens for these public entertainments, and mingled with the spectators dressed as a charioteer, standing in his chariot. Thus, even though those criminals deserved their punishments, a public feeling of compassion arose toward them, because it seemed that these convicts were being destroyed more for the Emperor's sadistic enjoyment than for the benefit of the public."

Without a doubt, the Emperor Nero was the very opposite of friendly toward Jesus's *authentic* followers. Paul referred to Nero in *Romans* 13:1-5 as being God's agent upon Earth to make and to enforce the laws as Nero saw fit, laws that one must obey "not only to avoid God's wrath and punishment, but as a matter of principle and conscience." Paul also said, with apparent pride, in *Philippians* 4:22, that some of *Paul's* followers were located "in the Emperor's palace." Nero burnt James's people, but Nero was being served in his palace by one or more of Paul's people. So, whom does the Pope, called in the Church's Latin tongue the "*Pontifex Maximus*," represent? In Nero's time, one of the Emperor's most prominent titles was "*Pontifex Maximus*." The Pope is his successor. That answers the question: The Pope is the successor not only to Nero who burned Jesus's followers, but also to Tiberius, the Emperor whose employee, Pontius Pilate, had earlier executed Jesus for sedition, which was threatening Tiberius's authority; the Pope is the successor to Jesus's ultimate executioner. He's not the successor to Peter, much less to Jesus. From the very start, Roman Catholicism – the Christian faith throughout its earliest centuries, and the largest Christian faith even today – represented Rome, not Jerusalem; the executioners of Jesus and his followers, not Jesus and his followers.

Where, one might ask, is Peter in this incident recounted by Josephus? Perhaps he was among the unnamed companions of James, who likewise were stoned to death by Ananus. But, in any case, Peter was historically too *inconsequential* a person to have been mentioned by name by Josephus or by anyone else than Paul and Paul's followers. Peter wasn't even mentioned anywhere in all of Josephus's voluminous writings, wherein can be found specific references to Jesus, James, Caiaphas, Pontius Pilate, numerous Herodian kings, as well as to other figures who were cited in the New Testament accounts. We know Peter's name today *only* because Paul's followers wrote not just the New Testament, but all other Christian works, such as the "histories" of

Christianity by Bishops Irenaeus, Eusebius, etc. Stripping away those apparent distortions of Peter as a "Christian," we are left, yet again, with a Peter who was NOT a Christian, but who instead remained, till the very end (whenever and wherever his anonymous end occurred, whether in Rome as the Vatican claims, or in Jerusalem, which is far more likely), a loyal follower first of Jesus, and then of James, as a proud Jew.

Far from Peter's having been the "First Pope" of the Roman Church, he was never a pope at all, nor even a Christian at all; and he was, in fact, so obscure a figure that, in his own time, the only person who mentioned him at all was his student, Christianity's creator, Paul. But the real key to understanding these matters is nonetheless the testimony of Paul, who personally knew Peter, James, John, and perhaps others of the disciples of Jesus. Paul is the only writer known to history who knew Jesus's disciples. Other writers are alleged to have, but there exists no evidence that any of them did; and no writer known to history (not even Paul) knew Jesus. Even Josephus wasn't writing of Jesus's disciples from his *personal witness* of them. Nor were Josephus's writings about these figures directed to, and being read immediately by, congregations of people who likewise possessed personal knowledge of those disciples, as was the case with Paul's letters. Paul's audience was of this unique kind, which constituted a powerful restraint against Paul's ability to lie in the most blatant and explicit of ways, for otherwise such frauds by him would have been immediately discredited by Paul's readers. That's one of the great legal/forensic advantages of Paul's authentic letters over the Gospels and other New Testament documents. Josephus's readers, in this regard, were such as to make Josephus's evidence regarding the disciples far lower quality than Paul's – and Luke's readers were likewise no such restraint against lies. Therefore, clearly, Paul's letters constitute legally/forensically the best evidence upon these matters, even though rabidly dishonest and biased and thus standing in need of stripping away their

Pauline agenda, as we're now doing, for the first time in history.

And, of all evidence concerning the event that created Christianity, nothing can compare with Paul's *eyewitness account* of that momentous occasion, which he provides in *Galatians* 2:11-21.

Christianity as the Solution to Paul's Problem

This is the explosive moment at which the Christian religion entered the world.[55] It can be understood only in the

---

[55]   "A religion" (as opposed to the generic concept of "religion" itself) is defined according to the pathway to heaven (or other desired afterlife) it asserts, the given faith's criterion for admission into heaven. Never before had this pathway to heaven (Christ-faith) been asserted. A secular religion, such as Marxism, modifies the basic criterion by positing not an afterlife/heaven, but instead an earthly heaven or paradise; and the given atheistic faith sets forth the criteria for achieving that paradise. However, most religions are theistic, not atheistic. The Jewish pathway to heaven is obedience to God's laws (and God's grace). Paul replaced that criterion with mere Christ-faith (and God's grace). What Paul was doing in *Galatians* 2:16 was to assert Christianity, and to negate Judaism. A given faith's pathway to heaven constitutes that religion's essence; and Paul was saying, in 2:16-21, that God's criterion was different after the Crucifixion, so that now the pathway to heaven is Christ-faith. Thus, Christianity was first conceived on this precise occasion, when it was forced upon him by the confluence of two factors: (1) the circumcision-issue (the combination of *Genesis* 17:14, and the absence of anesthesia and such during that era); (2) Paul's prioritizing his personal career-success higher than whatever loyalty (if any) he might have had to Jesus. When push came to shove, Paul's "God" turned out to be success itself – not Jesus, and not even the God of Judaism.

Paul was a traitor not *merely* to James, but even more to what James stood for, which was Jesus, and this *includes* Judaism, which Jesus had always taught and promoted, even at the risk and ultimate sacrifice of his life – the crucifixion. After Paul started out by persecuting and helping to kill Jesus's followers, he finally became a traitor to all of them, and *most* of all to the man whom he – in doing so – claimed to *worship*: Jesus. Paul was not ignorant. He knew what he was doing, and why.

context of understanding Paul's relevant personal background; and, fortunately, Paul provides this, too, within *Galatians*. *Galatians* is therefore the smoking gun of the hoax that is the Christian religion.

Unlike the scholars and other religious teachers who focus upon first the fictitious Christ and then the fictitious Peter in order to "understand" how Christianity started, a legal/forensic analyst takes the scientific approach, which is interested instead in reality.

Here's the little that we know of Peter, and the much that we know of the creation of Christianity, based upon *Galatians* and Paul's other authentic letters, and as supplemented by less-reliable Christian sources such as *Acts* (and the following will summarize the account provided in our first two chapters, and will conclude the present chapter):

Paul (according to *Galatians* 1:18) had first met Peter three years after joining Jesus's organization. Peter was his elder in the mission to convert Gentiles to this Jewish sect, and (according to *Acts* 11:2) had back then accepted uncircumcised members, the same as Paul was doing. Fourteen years later (*Galatians* 2:1), Paul returned to Jerusalem for a council at which he defended his gospel. At this council, Peter (*Acts* 15:7-12) defended Paul's practices. So, it's understandable why Paul (*Galatians* 2:13) would, immediately after the council, be surprised at Peter's change of position, and call Peter a "coward, … and even Barnabas was swept along by their hypocritical action." The "men who had been sent by James" were finally laying down the gauntlet to Paul, and demanding that his following of uncircumcised adult male Gentiles were either going to have to go under the knife, or else get out of the sect. If you try to place yourself in Paul's shoes, you'll probably feel them pinch so tightly as to break your feet. Paul thus removed those shoes. He was faced with either continuing a very "successful" mission, and enjoying the fellowship of followers – some of whom were of high social status – whom he had no doubt grown to love, and who had looked up to and come to love him; or else hewing to what

every indication is had been the Torah-based, standard
Jewish, teachings of Jesus himself, and losing those followers
and so failing in his life's work. Paul chose the former; Paul
chose "success."

Years earlier, when Paul was still trying to work within
the Jesus-sect, and before he was forced to make his choice
between Jesus and "success," Paul had put the matter this
way, in *1 Corinthians* 9:22-25: "I have become all things to all
men, so that by all possible means I might save some. I do this
for the sake of the gospel, that I may share in its blessings. Do
you not know that in a race all the runners run, but only one
gets the prize? So, run in such a way as to win the prize.
Everyone who competes in the game undergoes strict training.
They do it to win a crown that will not last. We, however,
compete to win a crown that will last forever."

Paul competed to win; he won. His prize has lasted for
2,000 years, and still counting.

But then, Paul had to find a "justification" for what he
had done. That's the rest of his mission, starting with *Galatians*
2:16, "A person is put right in God's view only through faith,
never by doing what the Law requires. ... For no one is put
right in God's view by obeying God's Law," and going on
through 3:10, and to *Romans* 2:25-29 & 3:20-4:13, as well as
elsewhere.

When Paul wrote, in *Galatians* 2:16, "For no one is put
right in God's view by obeying God's Law," he was saying
that no one can achieve salvation by adhering to the Jewish
religion. He was saying that any Jew who doesn't accept Jesus
as the foretold Jewish mashiach – and as even *more* than that;
namely, as an object of worship despite the first three of
Judaism's Ten Commandments prohibiting that – will spend
an eternity in hell, by the judgment of God. A more sweeping
condemnation of Jews and of Judaism would be impossible.
Paul's repudiation here of Judaism and of Jews (of *non*-
Christian ones, that is) is total. In this light, we can clearly
understand why Paul stated in *Philippians* 3:6-8, that, "As far
as keeping the Jewish Law is concerned, ... I have discarded it

entirely, for the sake of Christ, and I now consider it to be
nothing more than garbage." In essence, Paul had said the
same thing in *Galatians* 2:16, where he additionally explained
the reason *why* he viewed Judaism to be "garbage." God,
explained Paul in *Galatians* 2:16, treats Judaism as garbage.
Paul cited God as his own authority for considering Judaism
to be garbage. (Paul had already, in *Galatians* 1:5, prepped his
readers for this, by saying, "To God be the glory forever and
ever! Amen." Paul was there asserting that God possesses
high enough authority to trash Judaism, and Paul now
exploited this authority in 2:16 by saying that God *did* trash it.)

Unlike the Jewish dietary laws, which were also a
problem that was prominently mentioned as having been
raised with regard to the mission to the Gentiles (and which
Paul enforced), the circumcision of adult males was a mortal
threat in an age without antibiotics and antiseptics, and a
living terror in an age without anesthesia.[56] It was therefore
the kind of issue that could very well tear this Jewish sect
apart, and it did so. This is revealed unambiguously in the key
phrase in 2:2, "I did not want to be and to have been running

---

[56]   The first anesthesia was announced to the world by dentist William T.G.
Morton in 1846: ether.

Morton's invention of anesthesia, which was first successfully tested at
Massachusetts General Hospital on October 16th of that year, constituted perhaps
the greatest revolution in the entire history of medicine.

Maitland Edey and Donald Johanson's 1989 *Blueprints: Solving the
Mystery of Evolution* (pp. 41-42) gives the following explanation of why, only shortly
prior to that epochal event, the young Charles Darwin abandoned in 1825 his aim
to become a medical doctor: "While at Edinburgh he had witnessed two operations.
In the days before anesthetics, these were gruesome experiences even for
hardened stomachs. To Charles, whose stomach was queasy in the extreme and
who throughout life was unusually sensitive to pain or suffering, watching a patient
strapped to a table, writhing and shrieking as the knife went in and the blood
spread, was more than he could endure. He withdrew from Edinburgh." Thus, the
terror then of operations was enough to drive good men away from the medical
field. [continued]

The informative article "Surgery Before Anesthesia," by John T. Sullivan, in the September 1996 *Newsletter*, from the American Society of Anesthesiologists, says that, "Elective surgery was performed very infrequently prior to the advent of effective anesthesia. ... Surgery was a last and desperate resort. Reminiscing in 1897 about pre-anesthesia surgery, one elderly Boston physician could only compare it to the Spanish Inquisition. He recalled 'yells and screams, most horrible.'"

Furthermore, if anesthesia was not the most important advance in the history of medicine, then antibiotics were. And although the people in ancient times didn't know how and why some circumcisions were soon FOLLOWED by illness, and sometimes even by death – germs and infections were NOT at that time understood – the REALITY of diseases was recognized, even though the EXPLANATIONS of diseases were NOT.

This means that the men whom Paul was trying to convert recognized that they might die if they were to undergo a circumcision. Consequently, the basic assumption that the challenge that Paul faced was enormous, is not, from a legal/forensic standpoint, merely a hypothesis; it is nothing less than a crucial and scientifically established historical fact. Pauline scholars have simply been irresponsible in their avoidance of *dealing* with this key historical reality.

Today's obtuse scholars – living in today's society in which anesthetics are a part in all medical operations – falsely interpret the virtual universality of circumcision amongst Jews in the First Century as indicating that the issue of circumcision must have been minor amongst *non*-Jews in the First Century who were considering to convert to a Jewish sect. However, those born Jews had been circumcised when they were only eight days old. This decision was made by their parents. Infants in ancient times were property, not owners of property; but adult Gentiles who were *considering to convert* to Judaism were not infants.

This doesn't mean that infants who were being circumcised didn't mind it. On 23 December 1997 CNN headlined "Circumcision Study Halted Due to Trauma," and reported: "A new study found circumcision so traumatic that doctors ended the study early rather than subject any more babies to the operation without anesthesia." Moreover, here, "the researchers found that while topical anesthetics may help initially, they are woefully inadequate during foreskin separation and incision." During the First Century, not even topical anesthetics were available.

The first antibiotic was discovered/invented in 1942 by Drs. Howard Florey and Ernst Chain: a manufacturing process for penicillin, which was the first antibiotic. The first antiseptic was introduced in 1847 by Dr. Ignaz Semmelweis: he announced that washing his hands with "chlorinated lime solutions," prior to performing surgery, reduced patients' death-rate.

Only starting in the 1800's did scholars start to question the Bible as being history; prior to that, both the Old and the New Testaments were simply assumed to be historical works, not myths, much less possibly frauds. So: prior to the discovery of anesthesia, antibiotics, and antiseptics, scholars knew that circumcision had been torturous and life-threatening in the First Century, since all medical operations were torturous and life-threatening in their own time. So,

my race in vain." It's furthermore unambiguously and emphatically reiterated in 5:2-3, "Listen! I, Paul, tell you that if you allow yourselves to be circumcised, it means that Christ is of no use to you at all. Once more I warn any man who allows himself to be circumcised that he is therefore obligated to obey at all times the whole Law." With that, Paul explains why, in 2:2, the success or failure of his life's very mission is at stake in the circumcision-issue. Clearly, it was not the kosher laws that were behind the blowup in 2:12: Peter didn't want to be seen dining with Paul's *uncircumcised* "converts" in violation of *Exodus* 12:48-49, and thus *sharing* in those others' violations of *Genesis* 17:14. And Peter *especially* didn't want to, because he was being caught violating James's instructions to him.

In addition to circumcision's being by far the most dangerous law for these men to follow, it was also the signature-commandment, the one that *created* Judaism. The Jewish myth said that the covenant was to be signed in blood, and circumcision is how this was to be done. In *Genesis* 17:23-27, Abraham signed, and had all of his men do likewise.

Galatians 2:2 said that Paul was desperate to avoid subjecting his men to Judaism's signature-commandment, *Genesis* 17:14. It was too high a price for heaven. Paul knew that in an age lacking anesthesia, antibiotics, and antiseptics, demanding that his men go under the knife in order to remain his followers would mean losing almost all his followers and thus his life's work. His solution was inevitable, under the circumstances, given that he worshipped power and thus sought personal success above all else (*1 Corinthians* 9:22-25); so, he placed heaven on sale: *Galatians* 2:16.

---

scholars simply never even considered the implications of this reality; they were too much in the thrall of their churches to consider it. That's the only reason they ignored it. However, there are two reasons why *modern* scholars don't consider it: Not only are they still in the thrall of their churches; but anesthesia, antibiotics, and antiseptics now *do* exist, and so it's easier for scholars today to ignore the immense problem that circumcision presented during the First Century. So, they ignore it; they simply ignore the issue that sparked the creation of Christianity.

He was the supreme mass-marketer of all time, and he had to perpetrate the biggest hoax of all time in order to be able to achieve this distinction. The example he set for the future is not one that reflects favorably upon the economist Adam Smith's famous endorsement in 1776 of reliance upon the "invisible hand" of God. Paul's example shows that, sometimes, this hand turns out to be connected to the brain of a liar and deceiver – no real god at all. The recognition of frauds does not happen automatically; there is no natural law barring fraud, nor does any god's law. To protect people from frauds is not a bad thing, but is instead the right thing to do; and one of the many virtues of science is to *enable* such protection to occur. Without science, protection against fraud is impossible, and hoaxers then possess an enormous advantage against their victims: those victims' faith. But now, science reaches even into this field, where it's perhaps more necessary than in any other, since, in this field, science exposes (and thus makes less likely the *future* success of) frauds.

3. The Galatian Context: Analysis of the Rest

(NOTE: Presumably, by this time, the reader already has a Bible ready-at-hand, and so there would be little point in printing here the complete text of Galatians 3-6.*)*.

We can even go further now, to reconstruct the precise nature of the event that had precipitated Paul's writing this letter to the Galatians: this is revealed in 5:2-12, in which Paul warns the Galatian Christians of dire consequences "if you allow yourselves to be circumcised"; then reminds them, "You were doing so well!" when they had considered themselves to be pleasing God *without* circumcision; and Paul pointedly asks them, "Who made you stop obeying the truth?" and he concludes of those men who had induced them to do so – who were presumably "agents from James" (the issue here is the same, and so the proponents likely are as well) – "Let them go and castrate themselves!" This is one of Paul's strongest expressions of hate against the Jerusalem elders who were the disciples of Jesus. This passage reiterates Paul's earlier 1:8-9, in which he had repeatedly said, of these men, who "preach a different gospel," that they "should go to hell!" So, the men who should "go to hell!" should also "go and castrate themselves!" (In 1 *Thessalonians*2:16, he had said, "They even

tried to stop us from preaching to the Gentiles the message
that would bring them salvation.") He loathed them.

It's clear from 5:2-12 that the Galatian community had
presented Paul with the very real danger of the community's
blowing apart on account of one or more of its Gentile
members (and they probably were *all* Gentiles) having
accepted the Jerusalem elders' command to become
circumcised. Once one of the Galatians does that, the others
who haven't are thereby compelled to decide whether it's this
circumcised person, or rather they themselves, who are
following the *true* path to salvation. That's a prescription for
breakup of the Galatian community. Paul understood the
danger this threat posed, both to the Galatian congregation as
a congregation, and to himself, as the creator of that
congregation. He knew that, if the Galatians didn't unite
behind his stand on this, he would lose them, maybe even *all*
of them. And the same outcome would naturally follow for all
of Paul's other congregations. The principle that was involved
here threatened everything that Paul had built up during the
prior 17 years – all of his hard work, all of his achievements.

This was the emergency for him that had precipitated
his writing of this letter, which is the most important piece of
documentary evidence in all of human history – the
documentation of Western Civilization's conception-event.

What had precipitated this letter, in other words, was
Paul's outright war against the Jewish covenant, the Law,
Judaism itself. As he puts the matter in 5:4, "Those of you who
try to be put right in God's view by obeying the Law have cut
yourselves off from Christ. You are outside God's grace." He's
here telling these people that regardless of what they might
have heard about the Jewish God's mercifulness/forgiving-
ness, there is *one* sin that this God will never forgive, and that
this sin is Judaism itself. This message is the most intensely
anti-Judaic statement that ever could be or ever has been
made – even more anti-Judaic than Paul's later calling
Judaism "mere garbage" in *Philippians* 3:8. After all, garbage
isn't necessarily worse than murder and all other sins.

But here, Paul is saying that Judaism *is*.[57]

---

[57]   To call Judaism "garbage" or "waste matter," such as Paul did in *Philippians* 3:8, is entirely inconsistent with the "New Perspective" on Paul, which is the view that Paul was neither anti-Judaic nor anti-Semitic: this statement from Paul proves him to have been anti-Judaic, just as *1 Thessalonians* 2:14-15 proves him to have been anti-Semitic. New Perspective scholars assert that Paul wasn't disrespectful toward the covenant or the Law for Jews – the commandments from God – and they claim that Paul held that obedience to the Law for Jews would assure their salvation, just as that Paul held that faith in Jesus would assure Christians of their salvation. Prior to the event that Paul recounted in *Galatians* 2:11-21, Paul could indeed possibly have preached such a message, but certainly not afterwards, as the testimony of his letters written afterwards attests unambiguously. Although some of Paul's followers had been born Jews, they were *now* Christians – they accepted Paul's "gospel" – and that's the sole basis upon which Paul accepted them. He didn't accept anyone who lacked Christ-faith. To him, Christ-faith was the *prerequisite* to God's mercy or "grace."

Philippians* 3:6-8 is autobiographical about Paul, and asserts that "all these advantages" he had had as a "flawless" Jew – or as a Jew who followed all the laws – are now mere "garbage," because Christ-faith has replaced them. Paul made clear here his contempt for Judaism; that is, he made clear his holding it to be "garbage."

Moreover, *Philippians* 3:6-8 culminates 3:2-8, which starts by asserting that the proponents of circumcision – Judaism's signature-commandment – are "evil." Paul's argument here is all-out anti-Judaic, pulling out all the stops in condemning Judaism.

When we reject the New Perspective on Paul and assert it to be a lie about what Paul said (not an interpretation of it with which we disagree, but instead a direct and blatant contradiction of what Paul categorically stated, and an attribution *to Paul* of that position *opposite* to Paul's clearly stated position) we are not asserting any negative views of Jews as "legalistic," such as Martin Luther did; we're merely acknowledging the essence of Judaism, the Jewish criterion for salvation, which was also the Jewish criterion for inclusion within the Jewish faith-community or religion: adherence to the covenant – following the Law, not violating the Law of God.

Any scholar, such as E.P. Sanders, who asserts a distinction between, on the one hand, a given faith's criterion for salvation, and, on the other hand, that faith's criterion for membership, is asserting a fundamentally bogus distinction, because, for *any* religion, those two criteria are *necessarily* identical, *one and the same*. The essence of *any* religion is its criterion for personal salvation, and that's *also* its criterion for membership – *only* the faith's members can meet the given faith's condition for salvation: that's what *makes* these people *its* members. Other people might wish to become members, but they cannot actually *be* members if they fail to meet the given faith's salvation-criterion. A mere initiation-rite doesn't make a person a member; it simply provides public announcement of the person's intention to achieve salvation according to that given faith's criterion for salvation. Signing a contract doesn't fulfill its terms; it just makes fulfillment possible. [continued]

Moreover, right after the letter's climax in 2:11-21, Paul had picked up in this same vein regarding circumcision, but here addressing his readers directly (not Peter and the other representatives of James). In *Galatians* 3 & 4, Paul tells the Galatians that God accepted Abraham *not* because of Abraham's obedience – not because Abraham became circumcised and had all of his men circumcised – but instead because of Abraham's *faith*. Paul focuses here upon Abraham because Abraham was the person who, in the Jewish legend (believed then by Jews to be *history*), received from God the circumcision commandment. Abraham didn't receive from God the food laws – those were later (also according to the Jewish legend) received by Moses. The very fact that *Galatians* 3 & 4 discuss Abraham and *not* Moses is yet further *proof* that

---

Paul, in *Philippians* 3:8, was asserting that this essence of Judaism – Judaism's criterion for salvation, criterion for membership – was "garbage." Paul's asserting this proves that the New Perspective on Paul is itself, to use Paul's term (which those scholars don't consider to be pejorative towards Judaism), garbage.

In *Galatians* 5:4, Paul was telling his readers precisely *why* Judaism was, in his view, "garbage": It won't work, he said. His message was that *all* people are sinners, and that, since everyone sins, following the Law is impossible and God therefore no longer demands it. Paul was saying that there is only one successful way to heaven: Christ-faith.

The post-Holocaust Christian scholars who try to "re-interpret" Christianity as being neither anti-Judaic nor anti-Semitic are trying to make of Christianity something that it never was and never can possibly be: accepting of Jews and of Judaism. By means of no scientific reasoning, but only by means of faith, can any such scholars' self-deceptions deceive others. It's fine for Christians to want to be neither anti-Judaic nor anti-Semitic, but the only way they can actually achieve either aim would be for them not to be Christian. A Jew can accept Jesus (as a Jew, but not as the mashiach, and can't accept *anyone* as the Christ, since *worshipping* any man is *forbidden* in Judaism), but a Christian cannot accept Jews or Judaism – and therefore cannot accept Jesus, since Jesus was a Jew and tried to fulfill Judaism.

A Christian is a follower of Paul, and not of Jesus; and – unlike Jesus – Paul was not a Jew: Paul had *abandoned* Judaism. That's why Paul said, in 1:13, that he *used to be* a Jew. And that's also why he said, in *Philippians* 3:8, that he had given up that "garbage" for "Christ."

Galatians 5:4 presents Paul's *explanation* of why Judaism is, to him, "garbage": he sees Judaism as worse than any sin in Judaism – unforgivable.

the *subject* of this letter is *Genesis* 17:14, and *not* the food laws.

So, now we also know even why Paul strategically opened this letter the way he did: he was, from the very start, trying to convince his readers that he, Paul, knew Judaism as well as anyone, and that they could take his word for it that circumcision was *not* required, and that the Jerusalem elders were their enemies, and that this is why those elders were demanding the Galatians to circumcise themselves. When Paul said in 1:6, "I am surprised at you! In no time, you are already deserting the one who called you by the grace of Christ [namely, Paul himself], and are accepting another gospel," he was saying to them that they're about to abandon the very person who has brought them a chance of personal salvation, a chance to be forgiven for their sins and to go to heaven.

Anyone who might have doubted that the teachers of "a different gospel" that Paul was referring to in 1:8 were teachers of the necessity of circumcision, or have doubted that Paul's letter to the Galatians was directed specifically against those people, or have doubted that those were the individuals he was saying "should go to hell," or have doubted that circumcision and not the food laws were the issue at the council in Jerusalem and 2:11-21 immediately afterwards, cannot reasonably continue to doubt any of these things now, in the light of 5:2-7, which places all of these matters beyond any reasonable dispute. Yet nonetheless, scholars widely express befuddlement as to whom Paul was condemning in 1:6-9, and they assert that there is simply no way of determining whom those opponents of Paul were, nor what they were advocating; and scholars widely assert that violations of the food laws and not of the circumcision law were the issue in *Galatians* 2. Despite all such misdirections by scholars, it is now beyond any reasonable dispute whatsoever that Paul's enemies were agents from James, and were advocating the necessity of circumcision. Scholars may continue to debate these matters. But scientific historians – legal/forensic analysts of historical evidence – won't. All of these questions are clearly and definitively settled by the evidence, which isn't merely overwhelming – it's 100%, so that even Paul's vagaries and self-contradictions now make sense.

Paul has even opened *Galatians* 3 by 3:1, asking his readers "Who bewitched you [to think that circumcision remains demanded by God]," and by citing Jesus's crucifixion as the start of God's new covenant with mankind. Here, he is presaging *Galatians* 5:7-8, which says similarly, "You were doing so well! Who caused you to stop obeying the truth? That person certainly was not God, who instead calls you to heed the truth."

Just as Paul did throughout other parts of this letter, he veiled his meaning at the letter's opening, and for the same reason he did elsewhere: he didn't want to call attention to what the issue in this letter was, nor to whom he was attacking in it, unless a given reader already knew those things and needed Paul's argument against that. In other words, at the letter's opening, as throughout: Paul didn't want to do any of his enemies' work, but only his own. And, from start to finish in this letter, he knew how to pull that off; he was, indeed, the sharpest political operator in all of history.

Furthermore, 5:2-12 indicate that the Galatian community had only recently come under the influence of James's agents. Paul's 5:7, "You were running so well until now," means: these men hadn't lost anyone to circumcision until *just recently*. James's people got to one or more of them and convinced him to become circumcised (1:6 & 5:7). Again, Paul was using here the metaphor (used in *Galatians* 2:2, *1 Corinthians* 9:24-27, and elsewhere) of a race: he and his followers were engaged in a race for heaven, and nothing else mattered in life. James's men were trying to block them from reaching heaven, said Paul.

The entire context behind this amazing document is thus now clear.

Evidently, Paul's enemies were in a desperate situation, such that they couldn't afford to admit to the Galatians what was really at issue between Paul and their boss James. James's sect simply couldn't afford to admit that Paul had broken with their group – that Paul wasn't even accepted any longer as *being* a Jew, a follower of the Jewish faith. (Of course, no one denied that Paul had been *born* a Jew; the question here was whether he still remained one. Paul implied to his followers that he no longer was a Jew, but he couldn't very well say it *explicitly*, because then the game would be up, for both Paul and James.) Paul's enemies seem to have been under a constraint to avoid mentioning even that Paul was rejected in Jerusalem on account of his no longer being a Jew. The indication of this is provided in 5:11, where Paul says, "if I am still preaching [the necessity of] circumcision, then why do they persecute me?" This statement might have been referring to such events as were told in *Acts* 21:21 forward, in which Paul had been rejected and "persecuted" by Jerusalem's Jews. Paul doesn't want his readers to understand *why* those people were furious against him. But Paul nonetheless wants his readers to understand why they shouldn't become circumcised. He continues here by saying that if circumcision is still necessary, then "the cross ... is without meaning" – that Jesus then died for nothing (this reiterating 2:21). Paul, in other words, is here emphatic that those people from Jerusalem have been teaching "a different gospel" (see 1:7, 1:9, etc.), and *not* what Paul was teaching. Evidently, James's agents were telling this Galatian community that Paul didn't *really* repudiate the necessity of being circumcised. We don't know what reason James's men *did* give out to the Galatians to explain the riots in Jerusalem against Paul (*Acts* 21:21 forward), because no accounts survive from the community of followers of Jesus/James. All that we still possess are these records from those people's enemies: Paul and his followers. 5:11 is telling the Galatians, in effect: "Don't believe what they say – I certainly do *not* preach the necessity of adhering to *Genesis* 17:14, and that's the reason why I have been persecuted in Jerusalem." Yet, even while he is telling them this, he carefully avoids explaining to these people anything of his opponents' *reasons* for opposing him, and for supporting circumcision.

Paul wrote this letter, in other words, not only because one or more of the Galatians had recently become circumcised, but also because one or more of James's agents had told one or more members of the Galatian congregations, that Paul didn't *really* oppose a member's deciding to become circumcised. Word of this had now become widespread amongst the Jesus-followers in Galatia. Whatever else James's agents might have presented as parts of their argument that circumcision was still necessary, this part of their argument apparently caused Paul to respond on an *emergency* basis, by letter, rather than to wait until he might subsequently visit Galatia to reply to the challenge. This letter, *Galatians*, was sparked by that emergency, because Paul recognized that, no matter which of James's agents had said it, this allegation was calling Paul's "bluff" on the circumcision issue, and was forcing him to come out clearly against circumcision if he possessed the nerve to do so, or else to back down and get in line with James's order, and with the Torah. Paul possessed the nerve, and *Galatians* was the result. Paul wrote this incredibly revealing document in response to that do-or-die challenge from James's side.

The only thing additional that James could possibly do now to carry out his order (that Paul must get all of his men circumcised) was publicly expel Paul from the sect and so sever Paul's congregations from James's organization; but James didn't do that. Paul called James's bluff, and won.

Paul continued raising funds for the indigent followers of James in Jerusalem; Paul continued to keep James on a financial leash which prohibited James from informing Paul's followers that they were no longer really *in* James's organization. Paul successfully ended up taking his followers with him; and, for all future generations, Paul's followers had nothing more to do with James's organization, financially or otherwise, because James's organization died out – perhaps it was exterminated by the Roman forces. All that remained (other than the vast majority of individuals who followed neither James nor Paul) was, on the one side, Paul's organization – the nascent Roman Catholic Church – and, on the other, Jews who didn't accept Jesus as having been their mashiach: those Jews could see, very clearly, that the historical Jesus hadn't been what was foretold in the Old Testament as their mashiach. The split was, by that late a time, past history, and final.

Scholars cannot, and really don't even attempt to, explain what occasioned this letter of Paul, what shaped it, and what its message was intended by him to be on that momentous occasion. But all of these things are right there, right in the letter itself, for anyone who really wishes to understand the letter. However, in order to be able to read these things from it, one must be reading the letter as a document for scientific analysis, as an object of nature; not as a document for religious analysis, as an object of "the supernatural," such as scholars do when they take the letter on only its explicit level and fail to probe deeper without the prejudice that simply *assumes* this letter to be honest. The difference is like contrasting day and night.

The scholars have no basis (other than their desire to support faith) for believing that the conflict in 2:11-21 concerned the food laws, and that Paul's opponents were "Judaizers." Those widespread allegations by scholars are unquestionably false. All of the evidence decisively contradicts those completely unfounded scholarly beliefs.

The Tragedy Underlying Christianity

Why, then, does history not record that Paul's Jerusalem enemies ejected/excommunicated him from the Jesus-sect? The obvious reason is what was just stated: that Paul's followers succeeded in becoming the "Christianity" that we today know as such. And, as was furthermore

indicated, it's unlikely that Paul *was* ejected. To eject Paul
would have meant ejecting also his maybe thousands of
followers as not true followers, and members, of the Jesus-
sect. This could have meant ejecting a large portion of the
sect's *own* "success" – a large part of *James's* personal success.
Try to place yourself in James's shoes, and you'll understand
his tragic situation: he was trapped.

Success can become an addiction, and an addiction is a
trap. Any organization is reluctant to fire its "best"
salesperson and say, to his customers, "Here's your money
back; your salesman cheated you; he misrepresented our
product or service; it's not really what he said it is." And
although the real "currency" that measures success in any
membership organization is increase in the numbers, or
inventory, of members, not of money, money itself helps
crucially in building that; and Paul's mission (since it was
directed especially at converting those who possessed money
and power) was also valuable to the sect because it was
bringing in a much wealthier class of members. *Romans* 15:27
urges Paul's Roman followers that, "the Gentiles ought to use
their material blessings to help the Jews," right after
acknowledging in 15:26 the need "to help the poor among
God's people in Jerusalem"; and 2 *Corinthians* 8:13 says, "since
you have plenty at this time, it is only fair that you help those
in need."

Behind, not on, these amazing lines from Paul, stands a
tragedy which might surpass anything the ancient Greeks
ever imagined: Paul and James were the bitterest of enemies
who, nonetheless, *needed each other desperately*. Paul needed
James's tacit acceptance to continue for long enough a period
so that Paul's new religion would develop sufficient
respectability to be capable ultimately of breaking publicly
with Judaism; and James needed Paul's congregations to
continue as *being* James's, so as to permit Jesus's terribly poor
and powerless people to survive another day in their
incredibly hostile political and social environment.
Furthermore, Paul was James's best salesman or recruiter;

and, therefore, James depended largely, and increasingly, upon Paul for his, James's, *own* success.

Thus, from the leaders on *both* sides of this divide, there was silence about the deeper reality, whose prisoners they *both were*. In historical retrospect, we can see that Paul emerged the victor, but James's situation was hopeless in any event. James, as was noted, was trapped. For him to eject Paul and his many followers would have meant the virtual suicide of the organization he headed. James could send representatives to the Galatians – he could send the men whom Paul said should "go and castrate themselves!" (5:12) and "go to hell!" (1:8-9). But James couldn't afford to put his foot down and *eject* Paul's followers who disobeyed what he was thereby urging them to do.

However, a strong positive side would also have existed, from James's standpoint, in his actually making such a clean break: if James had publicly renounced Paul soon enough for Paul's charade to be exposed for what it was, then Christianity might possibly have collapsed aborning, in which case there would have been no Crusades, no Inquisition, no Holocaust, and none of the rest that Jews suffer from anti-Semitism that derives ultimately from *John* 8:44, etc., written by Paul's followers. But James probably had no idea of this future reality; indeed, he would almost certainly have been *shocked* to know of it.[58] And yet, Paul's charade would, also almost certainly, have collapsed if James had put his foot down.

---

[58] How could James possibly have known? Such fabrications about his brother as *John* 8:44, etc., hadn't yet been written. The precursors of those lies about what Jesus had said were in Paul's statements such as *1 Thessalonians* 2:14-16, which were within James's own time, and so James might possibly have known of these statements from Paul, but would James have even *imagined* that Paul's followers would expand these statements into lies about what *Jesus* had said – lies that Jesus had said anti-Judaic and anti-Semitic things, such as blaming upholders of the (Jewish) covenant for Jesus's crucifixion, or that Jews descended from Satan? Even to have imagined that Paul had such ends in mind could have appeared to be paranoia from James. It was much easier for James simply to slough off such outbursts from Paul as nothing more than expressions of Paul's frustrations with James and with all of the Jews who wanted Paul to demand his men to become circumcised.

Imagine Paul's situation if James had kicked Paul out: Paul would have continued to sell his discounted salvation, but there would have been few if any new takers. Jesus's appointed successor, James, would have, in this alternative scenario, publicly announced that Paul's people *weren't* followers of "Christ" or the mashiach. Paul's (few if any) Jewish followers would thus now be abandoning him, and only Gentiles would remain; Paul would be telling these Gentiles to worship the Jewish mashiach, and that the Jewish God will accept them in heaven for doing so. Such a fraud would be too obvious even for a master con-artist like Paul to pull off. Paul *needed* James's at-least-tacit acceptance; and he *received* it.

James wasn't as intelligent as Paul. James had no such understanding of the way the world works, which could compete with Paul's genius in that regard. Paul understood the workings of society deeply enough to be able to shape human history for thousands of years to come; James, quite evidently, did not. Thus, little could James have understood the historical stakes here (that's the sort of thing the present book is explaining, so that such mega-hoaxes won't be so likely to succeed in the future). Little could James understand that his (Jesus's) movement wouldn't shape history, but that Paul's movement – in opposition to it – would. Little could James understand that terminating Paul's movement was vastly more important to James's long-term ends (the security of the Jews) than was preserving his own movement. To put the matter bluntly: James was a failure both because he was up against immense odds, and also because he faced the most formidable individual opponent in all of human history; and Paul was a success because he was supremely brilliant, ruthless, and ambitious.

James felt himself to be hostage to his best salesman. But that's because James placed too high a priority upon retaining his members. He probably did the very best he could, on the basis of his limited understanding. Nonetheless, his ongoing decision not to call Paul's ultimate bluff was quite possibly the biggest executive blunder in all of human history (even though his doing that would have produced the quick failure of both himself and Paul). Or, at least, it seems to have turned out to *be* such a blunder for Jews, who, after all, were the people that James was tasked with representing as best he could.[59]

Additional evidence that James concluded that his success depended too much upon Paul to permit Paul's being overtly and publicly expelled from the sect, is provided in Paul's remarkable line, *Romans* 15:31, "Pray that I may be kept safe from the unbelievers in Judaea, and that my service in Jerusalem may be acceptable to God's people there." So, not only did Paul continue to solicit from his Gentile followers financial contributions for Jerusalem's poor, but he continued to represent himself to his followers as hoping to "be acceptable to God's people there": namely, to James, and to James's followers. Obviously, this presumes that the Roman congregation had *not* been informed from Jerusalem that Paul was excommunicated. (Paul knew that they hadn't, because if the congregations *had* heard, then Paul would immediately have received from them communications saying he was no longer a member of the sect.)

---

[59]   There are numerous similar examples in the business press concerning top executives whose organizations become corrupted by top salesmen. For instance, on 10 April 2011, the *Washington Post* bannered "The Trials of Kaplan Higher Ed and the Education of The Washington Post Co.," reporting how Donald Graham, the heir who controlled a large chain of for-profit colleges, became increasingly dependent for his success upon Sally Stroup, a top salesperson for chains (like his) of for-profit colleges. Stroup was even similar to Paul in being a citizen of the "Rome" of her time and culture. (She was, in fact, a member of George W. Bush's U.S. Department of Education, boosting there for-profit colleges.) And, like James, Graham did everything he could to support her work and the policy she pushed, even though this came at the expense of core objectives to which Graham was *nominally* committed: in his case, at the expense of his organization's exploiting (instead of serving) the poor. There are many different scenarios and cultures in which the sort of thing that happened to James and to Paul become repeated, in one form or another. However, none of them has had the vast impact of the instance involving James and Paul.

Another interesting feature of *Romans* 15:31 is its reference to "Judaea" instead of to "Israel." When Paul referred to Jews who didn't accept Jesus as the Messiah, or to Jews who did but who rejected his Christianity, he represented them as mere "Judaeans" instead of as "Israelites," because he wanted *not* to remind his readers that these rejectionists were themselves believing biblical Jews – i.e., heaven-bound *Israelites*. Thus, yet again, Paul's word-choice, this time in *Romans*, was cunningly and stunningly careful. He was nothing less than a PR genius.

As much as Paul hated James, and as much as James deplored Paul's "gospel of Christ," both men were locked into a mutual dependency that produced secrecy from both, and that has hidden till now how Paul's church, Christianity – specifically the Roman Catholic Church – actually started.

Paul was, in effect, challenging James to choose between James's own "success," versus authenticity to Jesus's cause, which was *simply Judaism*. Jesus had appointed James as the person to make such decisions as this; Jesus had entrusted this particular brother of his with that decision-making authority. Jesus had chosen James as the person who would, if need be, sacrifice even James's own "success," just as Jesus himself had sacrificed his own *life*. For around 20 years, James had been making the wrong decision. And now he was caught in the vise of its consequences. The longer James failed to extricate himself and Jesus's sect from this vise, the more dependent he became upon Paul and the sect's Gentile "members." The drug-addiction analogy fits well. By means of his actions, James didn't merely state, but he actually *demonstrated*, his top priority: his own "success" was more important to him than was his and his brother's religion (Judaism). That's why, when push finally came to shove, James reverted back to the very same passivity which had caused him, and Peter, during the prior twenty years, *not* to demand circumcision. James, it turned out, was like Paul in one important respect: he was addicted to "success"; he simply couldn't let it go.

Therefore, too, the events spoken of in *Acts* 21:21 forward (and which *Romans* 15:31 refers to in its opening prayer for Paul's safety against attacks by Jews), were probably viewed by the Jesus-sect elders in an essentially passive way; these men couldn't bring themselves publicly to repudiate Paul, even though he was so reviled by their followers and by virtually all other Jews. The Jesus-sect elders stood by and watched the disintegration of their organization. Further strong indication of this outcome is that *Acts* itself makes no reference at all to the event that Paul implicitly describes first-hand in *Galatians* 2:11-21: the very moment when Christianity was created, the moment when it broke away from being a sect of Judaism and became a new religion with its own new covenant or "gospel of Christ." *Acts* 21:25 even, in effect, denies that the event occurred: it presents Paul, upon his subsequent trip to Jerusalem, as still being subject to the same rule regarding Gentile converts that was imposed upon his mission by James's letter reproduced (accurately or not, we don't know) in *Acts* 15:23-29. This implicitly denies James's change-of-instructions that Paul implicitly and far more reliably reported in *Galatians* 2:11-14. If Paul had been *publicly* expelled from Jesus's religious organization, then that would have become known throughout all the congregations; and, even after Paul's death, when *Acts* was written, there would have been public knowledge that 21:25 was false, because Paul's instructions would have been *publicly* changed. Luke couldn't have gotten away with such a falsehood; but he probably didn't even know *himself* that it *was* false. Why would Paul have *told* him? Indeed, why would Paul have ever told *anyone*? Only the witnesses to the event recounted in *Galatians* 2:11-21 would have known, and perhaps they were all under instructions, from James and Paul respectively, *not* to discuss it publicly, unless and until the *other* side forced this issue by doing so – which, for very understandable reasons,

never happened. Paul, in *Galatians*, couched his description of
this event in such cautiously veiled terms that it took 2,000
years for anyone to be able to reconstruct what they refer to.
No doubt, Paul was hoping that every witness to that event,
and every participant in it, including James, would simply
keep silent about it until death, which, apparently, is *precisely*
what happened.

Furthermore, as was mentioned, James's people were
terribly poor; Paul's followers were much better-off and
included some who were well-to-do; James's community had
evidently developed a deep financial dependency upon Paul.
Paul wanted to make clear to his Galatian readers in 2:10 that,
"All they asked was that we contribute to the poor in their
group, which I insisted upon doing anyway." Paul was, in
effect, telling them that *all they have to do in order to win
salvation is contribute a few coins;* they don't need to go under
the knife in order to have an eternal afterlife in heaven. By
Paul's thus continuing the collections for the poor in
Jerusalem, encouraging his followers to contribute, he further
imprisoned James into silence. This made addiction-
withdrawal even harder for James, because not only would he
personally suffer – his people in Jerusalem would, too. He was
multiply trapped.

Therefore, it's tragically obvious why Paul was
probably *not* publicly expelled. In any case, however, the
Jesus-sect didn't survive to contest the "historical" accounts
provided by Paul's followers; the sect died out; perhaps it was
crushed by the Romans when they destroyed Jerusalem in 70
CE.[60] Christianity, in fact and not only in name as in *Acts*
11:26, actually started in Antioch (present-day Antakya in
Turkey, near the northeastern tip of the Mediterranean), at

---

[60]   Alternatively, the surviving Jesus sect could have been the dispersed
groups of Ebionites (Hebrew Ebionim or "poor ones"), also called Nazarenes,
whom Paul's Roman Church despised as heretics even as the sect faded into
obscurity and disappeared. See Robert Eisenman's 1998 *James the Brother of*

Paul's headquarters, in about 50 CE; not in and around Jerusalem during the lifetime of Jesus. It was Paul's followers, not Jesus's, who wrote the New Testament, and who built Christianity.

The Jesus sect of Jews shared the fate of Judaism in the Roman Empire, because it was part of Judaism; and it didn't survive, because it was left as a weak and small sect within a defeated religious community. Paul's new Gentile religion was both larger and stronger, within its predominantly Gentile world.

Scholars' Refusal to Face Reality

All aspects of this exegesis or interpretation of *Galatians* will naturally be challenged by scholars, mainly upon the basis of their taking as truthfully intended by Paul various statements that were actually intended by him to mislead and to deceive the reader – just as they have, indeed, misled everyone for two thousand years.

One such scholar, in a communication with this author, challenged my view that *Galatians* 2 refers to any *important*

Jesus, and his "Paul as Herodian" (at www.depts.drew.edu/jhc/eisenman.html); also see Hyam Maccoby's 1986 *The Mythmaker: Paul and the Invention of Christianity*. However, the written sources on the Ebionites were late and Christian; so, those sources provide only very corrupt access to the historical Jesus and even to Paul. And scholarly works based upon those sources cannot get closer to Jesus and to Paul than the sources themselves are.

Even though those works add considerably more "documentation" to our thesis (such as by asserting that Jesus's followers were poor people, and that Paul was their enemy), the best, most reliable, documentation is already supplied in Paul's authentic letters, and those scholarly works are essentially speculative, on account of the lateness of their main sources. Furthermore, to accept those late sources without accepting the Gospel accounts and other late NT documents, which generally predated them by more than a century, would be contrary to basic logic. Consequently, those scholarly works, just like other scholarly works on the origins of Christianity, are perhaps more novels than histories, and are not to be considered scientific, because they're not based upon the best evidence.

"council in Jerusalem," because Paul *said* in 2:2 that this was *merely* "a private meeting," and scholars generally prefer to think of all *important* meetings among early Christians (which scholars typically refer to as "councils" or else as "conferences") as having been *public*. Scholars don't assume the same regarding *non*-religious history, but that's the point: the same rules are followed regardless, and these rules are natural, *not* supernatural. Any leader can lie, and his lies can shape both history and our world. Many scholars also assume that an individual's actions cannot shape history in any major way, but are *only* "epiphenomenal" to history, or shaped *by* it. That, too, is wrong, as the present example shows.

TIME, 12 August 2002 (posted to the internet August 4th):

THEY HAD A PLAN:
Could 9/11 Have Been Prevented?

By MICHAEL ELLIOTT
        Sometimes history is made by the force of arms on battlefields, sometimes by the fall of an exhausted empire. But often when historians set about figuring why a nation took one course rather than another, they are most interested in who said what to whom at a meeting far from the public eye. ...
        One such meeting took place in the White House situation room during the first week of January 2001. ... Bill Clinton's National Security Adviser, Sandy Berger ... says ... he told [Bush's National Security Adviser Condoleezza] Rice, "I'm coming to this briefing ... to underscore how important I think this subject [al-Qaeda] is." Later, alone in his office with Rice, Berger says he told her, "I believe that the Bush Administration will spend more time on terrorism generally, and on al-Qaeda specifically, than any other subject." The terrorism briefing was delivered by Richard Clarke, a career bureaucrat. ... Senior officials from both the Clinton and Bush administrations ... say that Clarke had a set of proposals to "roll back" al-Qaeda. In fact, the heading on Slide 14 of the Powerpoint presentation reads, "Response to al Qaeda: Roll back." Clarke's proposals called for the "breakup" of al-Qaeda cells and the arrest of their personnel. ... In the words of a senior Bush Administration official, the proposals amounted to "everything we've done since 9/11." ...

Scholars don't like to think of there having been *any* secret or private event that was *important* in the founding of Christianity, because this would violate the scholarly assumption of supernaturalism, which is essential to a religious/scholarly "understanding" of religion and even of history itself; it would expose the magicians' tricks behind the amazing "history" that's told in the New Testament and similar frauds.

My reply to this scholar was the legal/forensian's rejection of the scholarly assumption that Scriptural documents such as Paul's letters are *necessarily* honest. The authors of Scripture can and do lie. In fact, since they're writing for an audience of faith, they know that lying will almost certainly work. An audience of faith virtually *invites* fraud. They *crave* to believe. This scholar was an example of that.

What Paul describes in *Galatians* 2:2 as "a private meeting with the alleged leaders" was, in fact, the precipitator of the creation-event of Christianity; it was a council in Jerusalem which was a closed meeting of only the top people, to deal with Paul, and no *mere* "private meeting," nor was it an open meeting of all of Jesus's followers, nor did Paul attend it due to "a revelation" as he asserts: he was *demanded* there by James, the group's leader.

Paul doesn't want to acknowledge these things to the group's followers in Galatia, because he doesn't want them to know that the way in which Paul had "converted" them into the group was a matter of hotly debated *legitimacy* amongst their group's leaders, and was finally ruled by the group's leader to be false. This fact had to be kept a secret from Paul's readers. We're extracting it by employing legal/forensic science, which didn't even exist in the time of *Galatians*. (In fact, the legal/forensic interpretation of documents didn't start until after WWII, when the first-ever white-collar criminal prosecutions took place.)

Why Paul Joined the Romans Against the Jews

Galatians cannot be truthfully understood without understanding this crucial historical background: The letter was occasioned by one or more of Paul's Galatian followers having declined Paul's new religion in favor of James's Jewish sect that Paul had originally brought this now-circumcised man (or group of men) into. This is why, near the end of *Galatians*, Paul says, in 5:1-2, that any of his followers who does what James is demanding, will be consigned by God to hell (just as 1:8-9 had said that the men who had *persuaded* one or more of them to become circumcised should). At the letter's beginning, in 1:6-9, Paul had said that anyone who tells others to become circumcised, as James was telling them to do, will be consigned by God to hell, and he reinforced this point yet again near the letter's very end, by implying, in 6:12, that James and the disciples were the actual guilty persons behind the Crucifixion of Christ. This dark and hazy smear was actually a more targeted version of an earlier-stated, broader, smear, in *1 Thessalonians* 2:15-16, against "the Jews," meaning against *all* supporters of the covenant. That passage had been the climax to one of Paul's autobiographical passages, *1 Thessalonians* 2:2-16; and it, too, cannot be properly understood unless one understands truthfully what *Galatians* was all about, which is circumcision. One cannot understand truthfully the other letters by Paul if one fails to understand truthfully *Galatians*, which is the key to understanding the New Testament.

6:12 is a statement like 2:11-14, intentionally vague in meaning; but among the things in it that are clear is that the people who are demanding the Galatian Jesus-followers to become circumcised are afraid of being persecuted for the cross of Christ, or persecuted for the Crucifixion. Paul wrote this approximately four years after the event that occurred in the year 49 or 50, which he describes in 2:11-21. Already at the time he wrote this, at around the year 54, he had written *1 Thessalonians* 2:14-16 approximately three years earlier; and so we know that he had already been alleging during the past few years that the Deicide was by Jews, and not by Romans. Paul is now saying that the Jews who were demanding circumcision are afraid of "being persecuted for the Crucifixion." Would Galatian readers in the year 54 have understood this reference as meaning that Roman authorities might "persecute" someone for having crucified Jesus? Even the Gospel accounts acknowledge that Roman authorities did it, so why would Roman authorities now be "persecuting" someone for having done it? However, if the "persecutors" here were themselves Jews (presumably Jews who were angry at the people who did it), then 6:12 could make sense. Paul's statement here could make sense *only* on that assumption, and so that assumption is logically necessarily implied in 6:12. Therefore, Paul was clearly suggesting here to his Galatian readers – who possessed no first-hand knowledge of who did it – that the people who did it were Jews who are now (in about the year 54) demanding circumcision. He is here saying, in effect, "We are the good Jews who became followers of Jesus, and they (the Jews who are demanding circumcision) are the bad Jews – they were behind the Crucifixion, and they are now trying to avoid being persecuted for that; they are hiding under a false claim to be the purest Jews of all." (Perhaps he was here explaining to his gulls why Rome was persecuting James's men. Paul's gulls were confused, and accepted being confused, because faith was to be their pathway to heaven.) In other words: The allegation, in all four of the canonical Gospel accounts of "Jesus," that law-obsessed Jews were behind the crucifixion of Jesus, was promulgated by Paul, even before it was ever written into *Matthew, Mark, Luke,* or *John.* However, when Paul was writing, such an allegation (that Jews were behind the Crucifixion) was still too blatantly false to be able to be expressed *explicitly*, so Paul was spreading it only *implicitly*: He was insinuating it, whereas his followers who wrote the canonical Gospels decades later,

created their "histories" explicitly around this lie – a lie Paul
had cooked up initially to increase the suspicions and fears his
congregations would hold against Paul's enemies in
Jerusalem. Paul was telling his readers, in effect: "I am the true
follower of Jesus; they are only *fake* followers." He was thus
here reinforcing what he had implied in 1:1: that, unlike the
disciples, who had known Jesus in-the-flesh, Paul's
authorization came purely from the Resurrected Christ: the
Holy Spirit untainted by corrupt flesh. Right at his letter's
start, Paul was already preparing the way for this con, that his
enemies (and not the Roman regime) were behind Jesus's
execution – an essential con, in order for Paul's new faith to
stand any chance of ultimately winning over the Emperors in
Rome.

This deflection of the source of the Crucifixion away
from the Emperor and his regime, who actually did it, and
onto Paul's enemies the Jews, would make possible future
Emperors worshipping a man whom one of their own
predecessors had actually executed. It would thereby make
possible future Emperors adopting and spreading Paul's
religion. Without the Deicide charge against "the Jews," Paul's
new religion would still have been a sale on heaven, but it
would never have been adopted and spread by Rome. It
would just have been Judaism at a discount, appealing *only* to
the masses.

Paul had cut himself off from the people of his birth,
the Jews, in order to bond himself, and his future heritage, to
Rome, the very power that he knew had actually crucified
Jesus.

However, apparently, his loyalty was *already* to Rome,
even before he announced himself for Christ. In *Acts* 22:27-28,
Luke quotes Paul as saying that he was a citizen of Rome *"by
birth,"* in other words, by descent from a father who had
become designated a Roman. Paul enjoyed the privileges of
Roman citizenship because his father did. This necessarily
predated Paul's Christianity; Jesus possibly hadn't even been
born yet, and Paul was already both a Roman and a Greek

Jew, and was therefore already set upon a path to emerge ultimately as Jesus's enemy – which he, of course, became.

How common was it for a Greek Jew, Paul's father, to win citizenship of Rome in that time? What did a Jew from Tarsus – Paul's hometown and presumably therefore also the residence of his father – need to do in order to become a Roman citizen? Tarsus was a distant outpost of Imperial Rome, near the southern tip of present-day Turkey, just 100 miles across the bay from Antioch (now called Antakya), and Antioch is the city where Paul ultimately set up his missionary headquarters. Tarsus was located about 500 miles straight north of Jerusalem; Jews were only a minority there. The rest of the population accepted the Roman gods, and before them the Greek gods. Jews were outsiders there. And yet, Paul's family were accepted as citizens of Rome – a status granting them special rights.

Acts 18:3 states that Paul was a tentmaker, and so his primary or sole customer was probably the Roman Army. In that era, almost all men followed in the same profession as their father. So, Paul's father was probably likewise a tentmaker, similarly in the service of the Roman Army.

This would have been during the reign of Tiberius's predecessor, Augustus.

The contemporary historian Suetonius wrote about how a non-Roman became a citizen of Rome during the reign of the Emperor Augustus. Augustus was the first Emperor to be called, during his reign, "*Pontifex Maximus*," the title that the Popes subsequently adopted for themselves. Suetonius, in his lives of *The Twelve Caesars*, in the 40th chapter of his biography of Augustus, said:

> "Augustus placed great importance upon not tainting Roman blood with that of the inferior races outside, and was consequently most sparing in his designations of new citizens of Rome. He likewise granted freedom to only very few slaves. On one occasion, [his successor] Tiberius requested that

Augustus grant citizenship to one of Tiberius's
Greek retainers, but Augustus answered that in
order to consider doing so, the applicant would
first have to submit himself to a personal interview
with the Emperor, in order to prove himself
deserving of such high honor. When [Augustus's
wife] Livia made a similar request regarding a
certain Frenchman, Augustus declined outright,
saying that he would do no more than to grant him
a holiday from the year's taxes, because, 'I would
rather that the Government suffer the loss of that
income than that the value of Roman citizenship be
cheapened.'"

So, according to Suetonius, the *only* way to become a
citizen of Rome, other than to be born a Roman, was to be
recommended by a friend of the Emperor, and to apply and
appear then in person directly to the Emperor. Furthermore,
during the time of this particular Emperor, Augustus (the
immediate predecessor of Tiberius who executed Jesus), only
people who performed especially high service to Rome were
granted this high honor.

Evidently, then, Paul's father had probably performed
some extraordinary favor to Rome, during the time of the
Emperor preceding the one who crucified Jesus.

In any case, Paul's father's status, once so designated,
would have been somewhat like that of a citizen during the
British Empire, from India or from some other colony in that
Empire, who, having performed services which the Crown
deemed to be of special value, became knighted by the King or
Queen, and thus a "Sir," and not merely a "Mister." Such a
person wouldn't thereby become a member of Britain's House
of Lords; Paul's father wouldn't have been a Roman Senator
under that assumption; but Paul's father would still have
been, by Imperial action, an aristocrat in his time; and Paul
would have inherited this designation of "Roman citizen," as

a *born aristocrat*, thanks to his father's loyalty to the Roman
Emperor.

This is the sort of thing that the Roman Emperor had
the power to do for a family of Jewish commoners who lived
at that time in Greece, and Paul's respect (if not his warm
regard) for the Caesars would be especially understandable in
this light.

Perhaps Paul's father might even have been the "Greek
retainer" of Tiberius – that is, of the Emperor who crucified
Jesus. Perhaps not. We don't even know whether that "Greek
retainer" won the Roman citizenship Tiberius sought for him
from Augustus. We know only that Paul's father very likely
did.

It's therefore almost inevitable that the reason Jesus's
followers were so suspicious of Paul when Paul first entered
this sect of Judaism was precisely because of Paul's family
background of being supporters of the regime that had
crucified Jesus.

In any case, when Paul cast aside his Jewish heritage,
he remained loyal to his Roman heritage, of which he might
understandably have been far more proud, given the power-
realities in the Roman Empire, and given Paul's worship of
Power (The Almighty).

And *this* heritage, it's also clear, Paul *never* betrayed.

In this sense, the Roman Catholic Church was Roman
before it was anything else.

The Centrality of Circumcision

Paul's situation was perilous, but he overcame it by
relying upon *non*-Jews: men who were *not* circumcised. They –
and *not* Jesus – were his real salvation. In order for Paul to be
able to retain his overwhelmingly Gentile following, and to
win yet more Gentiles, he had to do away with the
circumcision commandment, Judaism's signature-

commandment; and this meant his doing away with the covenant itself, which is what Paul did.

None of this can be understood unless one first understands the pain and danger of circumcision during that ancient time, when medicine was drastically different from what it is today.

This is the reason Paul said in *Galatians* 2:2 that his own success or failure was now at stake in the decision that James would be making here.

James's *initial* decision at this council in Jerusalem, according to both *Galatians* 2:10 and *Acts* 15:13-21, was favorable to Paul. Paul doesn't state what James's reason for his decision was. But according to *Acts* 15:19, his reason was "not to place too great a burden upon the Gentiles who are turning to God." James's alleged phrase there, saying that circumcision was "too great a burden," acknowledged a crucial reality that everyone in the First Century took for granted, even though all scholars ignore it: the terror and extreme danger of *any* medical operation – including circumcision – *in that era*.

And yet, Judaism, in *Genesis* 17:14, required that males – even adult males, Paul's target market – must, as a precondition to being approved of by God and so accepted by Him into heaven, have the medical operation of circumcision performed upon the penis. Surgical fatality rates, from either these operations themselves or the uncontrollable infections that (due to the lack of antibiotics and antiseptics) often followed, were undoubtedly high, even though untabulated in those pre-scientific times.

These fatality rates were made even worse because all medical operations in that era were also customarily preceded by *non*-standardized procedures to deal with the enormous problem of the patient's pain (which resulted from the lack of anesthesia). One reason these procedures were non-standardized is that in this pre-scientific era, there were no *purified* forms available of any drug, such as there are today from pharmaceutical companies; the only forms of drugs that were available at that time were in their natural, generally herbal, forms, with varying and unpredictable intensities of dosages, so that overdosages constituted an ever-present danger, which might sometimes kill. Therefore, physicians commonly underprescribed if an herb was toxic; an undermedicated patient was preferable to a dead one. In some instances, the pre-surgical patient simply drank wine until drunk, and was then strapped down so that his otherwise uncontrolled writhings wouldn't cause the surgeon's knife to catastrophically injure him amidst his howling, screaming, and struggling to evade that knife, which, of course, had to be very precisely controlled by the surgeon unless the operation was to be disastrously botched. But surgeons then needed to operate extremely fast, because of this writhing and howling – much faster than today. On other surgical occasions, the extremely toxic bark of the mandrake plant's root was infused in wine and this potion then swallowed by the patient, producing in him delirium, enabling him to endure the operation, but, in some cases, also producing in him madness, leading quickly to death for some patients. The great advantage of the mandrake was that, if it didn't kill the patient or else drive him insane, he was so delirious during the operation that he could simply ignore the pain, and thus not writhe so much as to botch the operation.

So, the dangers of death resulting from medical operations in that era were high not only because of the high infection-rates (from the lacks of antibiotics and antiseptics), and not only because of patients' writhings causing some operations to be botched, but *also* because of medication-overdosages – which were made yet more frequent by the non-standardization of doses – that were engendered to *prevent* those writhings. Circumcision was thus *far* more perilous than it is today.

Therefore, while a *non*-elective operation to amputate or else to save a person's life, was sometimes considered to be worth the huge risks, an *elective* medical procedure, which was *not* essential for the preservation of the patient's life, was virtually non-existent in that era, except in the case of male Jewish infants on their eighth day, to become circumcised in accord with *Genesis* 17:11-12. However, since those infants didn't know that it was going to be happening to them, they didn't fear it. Furthermore, they were small and weak. The adult male Gentiles whom Paul was aiming to convert were none of these things. They, of course, had their own agendas, which Paul necessarily had to cater to, in order for him to win them. These men can be expected to have found very appealing Paul's promises that their joining his religion would cause them to win God's approval, so that they'd enjoy an eternal life in heaven after their typically brief mortal life, during that pre-scientific era. However, for a great many of these men, the requirement to undergo this medical operation upon their penis, without anesthesia, antibiotics, or antiseptics, as a prerequisite to their being able to join the heaven-bound group, would have been far too high a price to pay, for the mere *possibility* that they'd be able to avoid the flames of hell resulting from their sins.

After all, even Paul acknowledged that faith would not *assure* these men of their being admitted into heaven; even Paul acknowledged, as Judaism itself had always done, that salvation required also the *grace* of a forgiving merciful God.

Paul, therefore, even if he was seen, by a prospective male Gentile convert, as having been unquestionably honest in the promises that he was making to him, was still offering, at best, only a *chance* of heaven. By contrast, for these men, circumcision entailed the short-term *certainty* of hell. No matter how drunk a person is from mandrake or wine, he'll still feel intense pain, and scream, and writhe, if his flesh is being cut into. And everyone in that era knew how *dangerous* medical operations were.

Furthermore, although the people in that era didn't know *why* it was that many individuals who had medical operations performed upon them developed infections shortly afterward, and became gravely ill and some even died – for they didn't understand that invisible tiny bacteria and viruses were what *caused* these infections – they still knew about these *results:* they knew of the high rates of sheer illness and of death that followed any medical procedures in their pre-scientific era. When circumcision was performed upon an eight-day-old infant, these dangers were, perhaps, not so noticeable, because so many infants died during their infancy regardless. The death of an infant wasn't perceived to be nearly so big a tragedy as it is today in our scientifically more advanced societies. (Perhaps the biggest perceived tragedies from infants' deaths in that pre-scientific era resulted when a male heir was thereby lost, not so much the baby's death *per se*. Intentional infanticides were also more common then, partly because of the unreliability and virtual absence of birth control.) But the men whom Paul was attempting to convert were far past their infancy; these were adults, who knew the deal that Jews were offering them, for an admission-ticket into heaven, and who recognized that, even at its best, the Jews' deal was extremely costly (in pain) and dangerous. Paul recognized that, if the new religion that he was designing were to stand any realistic chance of becoming a major world religion, then it would absolutely have to appeal to, and to convert, large numbers of *adult male Gentiles*, because they were the people who, in his era, possessed virtually all the property, and all the power. Women were merely men's property, and Jews themselves were just a small, poor, and weak, defeated people within Rome's vast Empire. Adult male Gentiles controlled the body-politic, the economy, and the entire culture, in those times. Paul needed to offer them a better deal than the Jews were offering. By bringing these men into his new faith, Paul wasn't only adding to his head-count, but he was also thereby obtaining the political and financial clout to be able to recruit still more.

Paul consequently understood the vital necessity of his reaching out to, and winning, large numbers of adult male Gentiles – uncircumcised men – if he was even *possibly* going to be able to "win the race" and avoid failure (in accord with *Galatians* 2:2 and *1 Corinthians* 9:24), and *succeed*.

Of course, the New Testament doesn't speak about any of these things, for the same reason that a sausage-maker doesn't write about or advertise the way that he slaughters animals and deals with the contents of their intestines, etc., or that a manufacturer doesn't publicize the working-conditions in his third-world sub-contractors. What sales-document (and the New Testament very skillfully is, collectively, precisely one such, for Paul's new religion) ever *volunteers* to *discuss* such unpleasant realities? As Paul said in *Romans* 3:4, "you must win your argument" at all costs, including, a few lines later (3:7), even lying, so long as it serves the glory of God; and certainly a tactful omission of details that might hinder this effort was considered acceptable to Paul and to his followers who wrote the New Testament. They displayed in their writings many things that they carefully avoided saying "out loud" or explicitly. Furthermore, just as the typical consumer of any service or commodity doesn't want to know the unpleasant details of its manufacture or production; so, too, it's unlikely that Paul's *customers* were particularly prying into this gear-grinding, which went on beneath the surface of the heavenly black box (Christ-faith) that Paul and his followers offered them; sometimes, the fantasy is *preferred* to what might turn out to be a depressing behind-the-scenes reality; and thus, people (especially people of faith, who strongly want to believe) don't wish to remove (so as to peer behind) the pleasing surface.

So, these unspoken realities simply *remained* unspoken.

However, the signs of these important omitted details are nonetheless pervasive throughout the New Testament, when it's viewed through a legal-forensic investigative lens, rather than through merely a scholar's lens. (For example, scholars even ignore the crucial fact that circumcision was, in the pre-scientific cultures of that era, a high price for one to have to pay in order to be able to join a sect; scholars don't themselves like to have to consider such unpleasant realities, unless they're absolutely required to do so, which they have not been in regards to this matter.) One such sign was given in *Philippians* 3:2, in which Paul referred to those who were demanding that circumcision be required as a prerequisite for admission into the Jesus-sect of Jews, by telling his Philippian readers, "Watch out for those who do evil things, those dogs, the men who insist upon cutting the body." Another: in *Galatians* 5:12, he said of these opponents, "I wish that the people who are upsetting you would go all the way, and castrate themselves!" Another: he had earlier, in 2:12, called them "the party of circumcision," meaning the men who were in favor of circumcising Paul's adult male Gentile "converts" in order to make these "converts" become *real* converts to Judaism. Paul's opponents argued this to be a *prerequisite* to their becoming converts to the Jewish Messiah. Another: in *1 Thessalonians* 2:16, Paul referred to proponents of circumcision as having "tried to stop us from preaching to the Gentiles the message that would bring them salvation." In confirmation from a lesser, later, hearsay, source, one might also consider *Acts* 15, discussing the council in Jerusalem that was finally called together by the sect's leader after Jesus's death, Jesus's own brother James, who had by then concluded that he was finally going to have to make a decision on this matter, after decades of his having postponed and postponed it. Were Paul's adult male uncircumcised "converts" *authentic* converts to this then Jewish sect, or not? James called Paul before him, to defend Paul's practice of admitting into the sect uncircumcised men. In James's ruling that's quoted there, in *Acts* 15:19, James said, "we should not impose too much difficulty upon the Gentiles who are turning to God." With these tactful words (if they are accurately reported there), he was referring specifically to his not imposing circumcision, which was the issue that had been presented just a few lines earlier, in 15:1-5, as having been the *central issue* that had *precipitated* this council in Jerusalem.

The Historical Background of Circumcision

Why would it have been so? Why would circumcision have been the issue that precipitated the crisis that led Paul ultimately to abandon Judaism? Consider the historical background, and the reason becomes obvious:

Jesus was believed by these people, Jesus's followers, to have been the mashiach, the Messiah, the Christ, a purely Jewish concept, which, in fact, possessed no meaning outside of Judaism. As was noted before, all followers of Jesus, during his life, had therefore unquestioningly been Jewish themselves, which means that they believed in Judaism, which is the covenant, the commandments or laws of God, "the Law," as being the *sole* pathway – *obedience* to the Law – by means of which one could win the approval of God and so be admitted by God, after death, into God's heaven. Regardless of whether a particular Jesus-follower had been born a Jew (and probably all who followed him during his lifetime had been), each Jesus-follower at that time had to view himself to be a Jew, inasmuch as his followership of Jesus necessarily *meant* his believing Jesus to be the Jewish Messiah. Even the earliest of Paul's own Christians had *entered* the group on the basis of this distinctively Jewish understanding; only subsequently was that to change, and gradually. So, at the beginning, all of the followers of Jesus considered themselves *necessarily to be* Jews, even regardless of whether they had been *born* as such.

In Judaism, the *only* pathway toward winning God's approval was a person's obedience to God's Law. There was none other, because obedience to God's Law was the *sole* requirement in Judaism, the sole condition that a person had to meet in order to *be* a Jew, and also the sole requirement which, to *fail*, meant that one was *not* a Jew. Judaism recognized that even people who tried their best to be obedient to God would *sometimes* fail to be obedient, and would occasionally "give in to sin," but Judaism said that God was merciful, up to a point, and forgiving, up to a point; but *only* up to a point. In Judaism, there were, and are, but two fundamental categories of people: Jews and non-Jews; people who obey God, and people who don't. Of course, it was believed that *everyone* who had not signed onto the covenant (via circumcision) and thereby not *agreed* to obey God, would "live in sin" and would disobey Him. These people were sinners because they were Gentiles; they didn't even *try* to obey; they didn't *sign* the agreement or "covenant" that God had offered. However, it was also believed that some people who *did* sign onto the covenant would fail to fulfill their commitments under it, would disobey God, and would thereby forfeit their membership in the covenant-people, the Jews; thus, essentially, reverting to the Gentile status of being *non*-members, just as if they had never signed in the first place. And, of course, as a man whom some Jews considered to be not only a Jew but the Jewish Messiah, Jesus himself had necessarily been circumcised, just the same as had any Jewish male, including Jesus's own great ancestor King David, especially because *Genesis* 17:14 said that *no* uncircumcised man could even *be* a Jew (or one of God's people).

Furthermore, not only was this circumcision-commandment a commandment, but it happened to be *the signatory commandment*, the one *by means of which* a male, through his obeying, effectively signed on the dotted line and "agreed" to be a Jew. This was true even if that "signing" was being done by a typical Jewish eight-day-old male baby, who thus would have been far below the age-of-consent in any of *today's* more scientific and democratic cultures. From a modern standpoint, a Jewish parent's having this operation performed upon his infant son in that era was equivalent to that parent's acting then as the son's legal agent, signing upon the dotted line on the child's behalf, by circumcising the baby. However, in that era, there wasn't even a question about a parent's *authority* to decide this for his child; the husband-father didn't own merely his wife; he also owned the couple's children. He likewise owned any slaves the family possessed.

He owned everything the family had, and therefore he possessed the authority to decide for his son, just as any owner has the authority to do what he likes with his property. So, performing this operation on the infant was taken to constitute that boy's own acceptance of the covenant that had required this operation, and therefore the boy's very *admittance into Judaism*. It wasn't just a ritual; it was also an extremely important act of obedience to God, the most important act in this person's entire life, because it announced his commitment to obeying God.

The covenant, which is to say, Judaism, had started, according to the Torah (the core Old Testament legend), when God, in *Genesis* 17:14, told Abraham, "No uncircumcised male will be one of my people, because he has not kept the covenant with me." According to 17:24-27, Abraham, even though he was then, according to the myth, 99 years old, promptly had himself circumcised, and proceeded immediately to circumcise all of his male human property, both his sons and his male slaves. Thus, according to the legend that is Judaism, Judaism itself started. Furthermore, in 17:10-14, God had *offered* His covenant, Judaism, to Abraham the father of the Jews, by saying to him, "You and your descendants must all agree to circumcise every male among you. From now on, you must circumcise every baby boy who is eight days old, including slaves born in your homes and slaves purchased from outsiders. This will show that there is a covenant between you and me. Each one must be circumcised, and this will be a physical sign to show that my covenant with you is everlasting. No uncircumcised man will be one of my people." When Abraham in 17:24-27 had this operation performed, the agreement, the covenant between God and His People the Jews, was *sealed*, and Judaism, according to its own mythological account, thus commenced.

In this sense, *Genesis* 17:14 was for Judaism the very same thing that *Matthew* 16:18 was later to be for Christianity: the religion's mythological start. It's an odd turn of fate that, were the mythological start of Judaism to have been written *differently* than it was written in *Genesis* 17 – i.e., with *no* circumcision-commandment – then the entire Christian myth, including its *own* mythological start, would never even have been written *at all*. There would be no Christianity, because the crisis that produced it wouldn't have occurred. (In other words: The New Testament wouldn't exist.)

Furthermore, when *Exodus* presents the important "historical" follow-up to this, after God subsequently laid out, to Moses and to the rest of God's people, the Ten Commandments, and numerous additional commandments (or "laws"), Moses and the other Jewish leaders are described as memorializing their people's re-affirmation of Abraham's circumcision-signature of the covenant, in *Exodus* 24:7-8, by collecting together the blood that had been saved from the circumcisions of 8-day-old Jewish boys, and sprinkling this blood over the assembled crowd, saying to them, "This is the blood that seals the covenant the Lord made with you when He presented all of these commands." Moses did this after having read aloud to the crowd all the laws in the book of the covenant (presumably a scroll that listed each law), and announcing, "We will obey the Lord and do everything He has commanded!"

So, to return to our immediate narrative here, the question now for James, Jesus's brother, concerning the imposition of the circumcision-commandment, related to the covenant itself, and moreover, it related to the very creation of the covenant, and thus, too, in the strongest possible sense, it related to his sect's *breaking* of the covenant. This is a question that had never come up during Jesus's lifetime, because, when Jesus was alive, there was no question about whether or not an uncircumcised man could be a follower of the mashiach; an uncircumcised man wouldn't be a Jew at all, much less a follower of the mashiach. (See *Genesis* 17:14.) According to *Acts* 11:2, the issue about circumcision had originally arisen after Jesus's death, when Peter was assigned (probably by James) the mission to convert Gentiles, and accepted uncircumcised males into the group. He was, of course,

challenged on this by other Jews, but he continued doing it
nonetheless, presumably until he was reassigned back again
to the main mission, which was, of course, to the Jews, since
this was, at that time, strictly a Jewish sect which was trying to
persuade *other* Jews that Jesus was the mashiach.[61]

Then, according to Paul's first-person account in
Galatians 1:16, Paul joined the mission to the Gentiles, and, in
2:7, he was preaching to the Gentiles while Peter was
preaching to the Jews. Paul had, according to his account
(1:18), been preaching for three years to the Gentiles, when he
"went to Jerusalem to learn from Peter," his predecessor and
senior in that mission; and (2:1) fourteen years later still, Paul
was called back to Jerusalem once again, now to attend the all-
important meeting James called of the council to decide what
was to be done with Paul's by-now perhaps thousands of
uncircumcised adult male "members." The issue here was, of
course: *are* they members?

That's the reason why placing this requirement upon
all of these men now, that they must all undergo this "cutting
of the body" (as Paul graphically called it in *Philippians* 3:2),
would cause many if not most of them to abandon the sect.
That's what Paul meant in *Galatians* 2:2, by saying that his
life's work was now at stake. And this is what James meant in

---

[61]   The commonly called "Great Commission," given at the end of *Matthew*, in
28:16-20, was, of course, actually written too late to qualify as best evidence and
would therefore be tossed by a scientific judge, not presented to a jury. However,
even that dubious passage in that dubious document doesn't assert that Jesus was
instructing his followers there to missionize anything other than a Jewish sect.
Baptism was a common first step toward the conversion of non-Jews into Judaism
during that era, and nothing from Jesus injunctioning his followers to baptize "all
peoples everywhere" to "make them my disciples" would have indicated converting
people into something *non*-Jewish. However, this passage's "Baptize them in the
name of the Father, the Son, and the Holy Spirit," was profoundly non-Jewish (even
violative of the Ten Commandments, which demand worship of only a unitary God),
and, as such, violates the best evidence and therefore disqualifies this passage as
"history." As was noted earlier, it even violates *Matthew* 5:17-20; the internal
inconsistency of *Matthew* is striking.

Acts 15:19 by saying "we should not place too great a burden on the Gentiles who are turning to God."

Paul's Only Other Choice Was Failure

Acts, having been written by a follower of Paul, and not by a follower of James and the Jesus-sect of Jews, doesn't provide even a *hint* that James subsequently changed his mind on this matter of circumcision. But far better evidence, Paul's *Galatians*, in 2:11-16, implicitly accepts the fact (because it was written so soon after this climactic occurrence, and to people who might have known independently of it) that he *had to do so in order for him to be reasonably confident that he would make his case successfully*. Paul there indicates – but by logically necessary implication, not explicit assertion – that James quickly changed his mind and sent a delegation to Paul in Antioch ordering Paul to circumcise all his men. The first member of this delegation to arrive was Peter, but he didn't possess enough nerve to put his foot down to his former student (according to 1:18). The group that came later that day did, and this is why James had sent them, to check up on Peter's work – understanding that Peter, as Paul's teacher and mentor, would be extremely uncomfortable carrying out such an assignment. (Probably, the reason Peter was chosen for this assignment was that, as Paul's predecessor and teacher in the mission to Gentiles, and as a supporter of Paul at the council, Peter seemed the likeliest person to be effective at it.)

This confrontation forced Paul to choose between Jesus and success. He chose success, and the result was the world's largest religion. Paul's (and the world's) first-ever statement of this "gospel of Christ" occurred at the event he recounts in *Galatians* 2:11-21, and this "gospel" is described in 2:14-21, the original form of his "Christianity," which *replaced* the Jesus-sect of Judaism, and replaced even Judaism itself.

Paul, in keeping with his becoming the world's supreme con-man, followed this replacement (both in *Galatians* and in his other letters) by his supplying fake "Jewish" arguments for his new faith. He warped what Jewish scriptures said, so as to turn them *against* Judaism.

THE FRAUDULENCE
OF PAUL'S
JEWISH ARGUMENTS

Since Paul had not originally converted these Gentiles into Christianity but into a *Jewish* sect that had been started by Jesus, Paul now faced the predicament of how he would argue his new position to them in a way that convincingly appeared, to such people who possessed little real knowledge of Judaism, to be a "Jewish" argument. If Paul had initially converted them into Christianity, he would have needed only to have said that Jesus had stated the same thing that Paul asserted in *Galatians* 2:16-21. But he hadn't converted them into Christianity; he had converted them to (Jesus's sect of) Judaism. Thus, Paul now needs to cook up Jewish-sounding arguments; that is, arguments which seem, to his Gentile gulls, to be based upon Jewish Scripture. That's what he does in *Galatians* 3:6-17, relying successively upon *Genesis* 15:6, *Genesis* 12:3, *Deuteronomy* 27:26, *Habakkuk* 2:4, *Leviticus* 18:5, *Deuteronomy* 21:23, *Genesis* 13:15&17:8, *Genesis* 17:9-13, and *Exodus* 12:40.

Before discussing the details of those citations by Paul, his bald lie in *Galatians* 3:16 about *Genesis* 17:9-13 must first be especially noted: Paul asserts in 3:16 that "God made his promises only to Abraham and his descendant. The Scripture [*Genesis* 17:9-13] doesn't use the plural 'descendants,' meaning many people, but the singular 'descendant,' meaning Christ." Paul blatantly lied on this; 17:9 referred explicitly to "generations," no mere singular "generation"; and, moreover, 17:13 said that this would be "everlasting." Paul's gulls were depending upon him to teach them Jesus's sect of Judaism, but he instead lied to them about Judaism there. The text of *Genesis* 17:9-13 couldn't possibly be more unambiguous, to the exact *opposite* of Paul's stunning misrepresentation of it: Paul's summary of it here is precisely the opposite of what *Genesis* 17:9-13 emphatically and unambiguously asserts and then reasserts. (In fact, Qumran 8Q1 – otherwise known as 8QGen – which is from a scroll written contemporaneous with Paul, presents just the fragment *Genesis* 17:12-19, but the "eternal" nature of this command is written even there.) This brazenness of Paul's lying is stunning. For 2,000 years, he's been able to get away with it, because we're still in the Religious Age; the Scientific Age hasn't yet arrived: Faith still reigns, especially in ethico-moral issues, but also – to a large extent – over history itself.

Paul's basic argument, founded supposedly upon *Genesis* 15:6, and given in *Galatians* 3:6-7, is itself a blatant fraud, because of *Genesis* 17:24. Abraham, according to the Scripture, in fact *did obey* God's command that all males be circumcised. Unlike the "converts" that Paul was determined to win to his new faith, the 99-year-old Abraham, the Scripture says, subjected himself to the knife, even in his era, thus nullifying Paul's sham of an argument here, which had been to the effect that God's acceptance of Abraham had *not* been conditional upon Abraham's carrying out the command – something that the Scriptural citations that Paul gave failed to support in any way whatsoever. Paul's argument that non-conditionality was proven by virtue of the fact that Abraham, according to the myth, circumcised himself after God's command rather than before it, is among the most ludicrous of Paul's fabrications – as if it were not *necessarily* the case that compliance with a command is judged after, *not* before, that command is issued.

Years later, Paul wrote *Romans*, and was there re-presenting his *Genesis* 15:6 argument in *Romans* 4, doing it this time to a congregation that had some born and circumcised Jews in it, so that such transparent falseness about Judaism would not pass. Paul thus added to his case (4:11) a reference to Abraham's having had himself circumcised after the command to do so was given to him. Paul's argument now was that "Abraham's circumcision was a sign from God that He accepted Abraham as righteous before he was circumcised." Paul was here saying that Abraham's decision to comply immediately with God's command showed nothing about Abraham, but instead something about God, even though this compliance-decision was Abraham's and *not* God's. At no point did Paul provide any reason for a rational reader to view *Genesis* 15:6 as being anything else than a *conditional* judgment on the part of God that Abraham was the kind of man who would *adhere to* the covenant.

Furthermore, Paul's entire argument about *Genesis* 15:6 is fatally flawed because that line refers to God's promise to Abraham that He will offer him a deal; the deal *itself*, the covenant that God will be offering to Abraham and to his descendants, has not, in the *Genesis* story, actually *yet been* offered to Abraham, but only *promised* by God to be offered to him. A few lines later, starting in 17:2, God actually prefaces his offer to Abraham, saying, "I will make my covenant with you," which obviously is not referring to an event that has already occurred in the past; then, in 17:4, He finally starts to deliver, by explicitly saying, "This will be my covenant with you." Then, in 17:9, He states what He will demand that Abraham and his people must do in return for His offer of victory during life and of heaven after death: "You will have to agree to keep the covenant with me, both yourself and your descendants in all future generations." This "all future generations" means: *it's eternal*. Then, in 17:10, God finally gets specific, as to the first condition that He will be placing upon each and every male Jew: "You and your descendants must all agree to circumcise every male among you." The culmination of God's presentation is the unyieldingly clear, totally uncompromising, 17:14, "No uncircumcised male will be one of my people, for he has not kept the covenant with me." In the immediately prior line, 17:13, God said that this covenant will *be eternal*. This eternality is repeated again in 17:19. Consequently, how much more clearly false could Paul's argument have possibly been? God said it there – and repeated it – *eternal*.

Later in *Romans* 10:6-10, Paul directly contradicts *Deuteronomy* 30:11-15, which quotes God saying, "The command I'm issuing here is doable. ... So, obey it, and I will approve of you and grant you life not death." Paul's version of this is: "What the Scripture says about winning God's approval is ... if you confess belief that Jesus is Lord and believe that God raised Him from death, then you will be saved. For it is by our faith that we win God's approval; it is by our faith-confession that we are saved." Paul here is citing *Deuteronomy* 30:11-15 to support his assertion that faith and not obedience wins salvation, even though *Deuteronomy* 30:11-14 *contradicted* that, in very clear and direct terms.

Prominently cited also by today's Christian apologists, *Galatians* 3:11 introduced into Paul's argument *Habakkuk* 2:4, "Those who are evil will not survive, but those who are righteous will live because they are faithful to God." However, this passage is at best ambiguous on the point that Paul is trying to make: there is simply no way of telling for certain whether "faithful to God" here means (1) obedient to God, or (2) believing in God's existence, or (3) accepting God as the one-and-only God. However, almost certainly it means precisely what Paul is here *rejecting*, which is the first of the three, the reason being that the opening, "those who are evil will not survive," has clearly set *opposite* to "faithful" "those who are evil," which throughout Judaism meant *only* those who *disobey* God. This fact annihilates Paul's *Habakkuk* argument. However, in any case, in Judaism, *Habakkuk*, being not a part of the Torah – the Jewish holy Scripture, the Pentateuch, which contained only the first five books of the Old Testament – Paul's argument from *Habakkuk* lacked reference to sufficiently high a Jewish authority to have been capable of threatening the continued validity of the covenant, even if that argument had been truthful. Likewise, too, another Pauline argument frequently cited by Christian apologists, the citation in *Romans* 4:7-8 of *Psalms* 32:1-2, also lacked such authority. However, even if that argument had possessed the requisite Jewish authority, the only thing that this passage affirmed was the standard Jewish concept of God's grace, which was His having the ultimate say-so regarding whether to admit a sinner into heaven. This was certainly not support for Paul's saying that the covenant that God had offered to the Jews, and that God had claimed in *Genesis* 17:13 and 17:19 would be everlasting, was henceforth simply past history. But above all, no argument for cancelling the 613 laws that constitute Judaism's covenant can be valid that is based upon any authority other than the Torah (the Pentateuch). The Torah is the source for all 613 laws. So, Paul's arguments from

Habakkuk and from *Psalms* – neither being in the Torah – were invalid on their face.

Paul restated many times the supersessionism that he introduced to the world at the incident he wrote about in *Galatians* 2:16. Perhaps his most extensive single expression of this replacement of Judaism by Christianity appears in *Romans* 3:20-26 & 4:5:

> *"No one is put right in the eyes of God by doing what God's Law requires; what the Law does is to make man know that he has sinned. But now God's way of putting people right with Himself has finally been revealed. It has nothing to do with the Law, even though Moses and the prophets gave witness to it. God puts people right through their Christ-faith. God does this to all who believe in Christ, because there is no distinction in the sight of God: everyone has sinned and is far away from the salvation that God offers. But by God's freely given gift of his grace that he provides to all who have faith in Jesus Christ, who set believers free from the Law, every believer is put right in the view of God. God offered Him so that by His death He should become the means by which people's sins are forgiven through their faith in Him. In the past, He was patient and overlooked people's sins so as to demonstrate His own righteousness. In this way, God shows that He Himself is righteous and that He puts right everyone who believes in Jesus. ... The person who depends on his faith, not on his deeds, and who holds that faith in the God who declares the sinner to be innocent, stands therefore as being a good person in the judgment of God."*

What Paul does here, at one breathtaking step, is to eliminate all of God's commandments save possibly the First of the famous Ten: faith itself (*Exodus* 20:3; *Deuteronomy* 5:7). Not only does he here eliminate the "eternal" circumcision-commandment, but he eliminates the entire covenant, except (as noted), perhaps, that First Commandment, to have faith in God (and we'll get to that one, the First Commandment, in just a moment). The Jewish admission price to heaven is obedience to all of God's commandments; Paul reduces that price to mere faith in Jesus as the Christ. He places heaven on sale, permanently, not just under-pricing his Jewish competition by removing the inordinately high Jewish cost of demanding a circumcision-operation, but under-pricing even beyond that, so as to, at one fell swoop, not only supersede Judaism, but effectively to remove it altogether from the religious marketplace. Paul, by his standing firm in his violation of the covenant, now proudly and defiantly hawks heaven no longer at the Jews' steep price of a circumcision-operation, but henceforth openly at the cost of a mere dunking in water, or "baptism," to mark his new believer's faith – a ritual that, by custom within this Jewish sect as similarly in some others, new Gentile members have been ritually subjected to in any case, as being a *non-obligatory* Jewish ritual ("mikvah"), which is now becoming obligatory for these Gentile "converts" *in lieu of* their becoming circumcised. Thus, Paul here was henceforth overtly *replacing* circumcision by this painless and safe existing Jewish baptismal ritual; and, recognizing that there is no way to toss out the signatory circumcision-commandment without tossing out likewise the entire covenant that it signs onto, he is now freed to cheapen his heaven's admission-price so as to make that cost essentially devoid of *any* of the covenant's requirements; and this is what he actually did. The Scriptural examples cited by Paul fail to make the point he draws from them, that God will accept any believer who disobeys Him; they actually show merely that God approves an obedient believer, and that at His discretion He *may* forgive a sinner (e.g., *Genesis* 15:6, *Psalms* 32:1-2).

In the long quote we cited from Paul, *Romans* 3:21, "But now God's way of putting people right with Himself has finally been revealed," and a few lines later there, 3:24, the other reference to the Law's having come to an end with "Jesus Christ, who set believers free from the Law ...," this supposed termination of the Law by God is simply a bald hoax from Paul, because (as was previously pointed out) immediately prior to God's explicit presentation of the covenant, He is quoted, in *Genesis* 17:13, as saying unequivocally, "My covenant with you is everlasting," which is sufficient *alone* to annihilate Paul's entire argument. Paul, of course, *never* referred to *Genesis* 17:13, nor to *Genesis* 17:19; he just hoped that nobody would notice this crystal clear statement of the Jewish God, whom they all looked up to for ultimate authority.

However, *Genesis* 17:9 & 17:13 & 17:19 are not the only places in the Torah where the covenant's eternality is indicated. Vigorous additional support for this annihilation of Paul's case for Christianity is given in the passages in *Deuteronomy* describing the presentation and re-presentation of the Ten Commandments (*Deut.* 6:17&25; 7:11-12; 8:1&11&20; 10:12-13&16-17; 11:1&8&13&18&22&27; and 12:1&32), and in the conclusion to the presentation of various other laws, *Deut.* 26:16. From all these, we shall quote now just 7:11, 8:11 & 12:32: "Obey what you have been taught; obey all the laws that I have given you today. ... Make certain that you do not forget the Lord your God; do not fail to obey any of His laws that I am giving you today. ... If you fail to obey the Lord, then you will be destroyed. ... Do everything that I have commanded you; do not add anything to it or take anything away from it." Obviously, Paul took *everything* away from it, except only the First Commandment itself.

Worse still, according to *Deut.* 11:28, which at least suggests that disobedience itself is equivalent to worshipping other gods, Paul's doctrine might have violated *even* the First Commandment. This interpretation of the First Commandment is further indicated by the fact that in both statements of the end-part of the Second Commandment, in *Ex.* 20:6 and *Deut.* 5:10, it says that only "those who love me *and obey my laws*" are in compliance with the First Commandment that was given three lines above it. Apparently, this phrase even defines what was actually referred to in the First Commandment by the concept there, "worship," in "Worship no God but me." But Paul nonetheless stripped out the "who obey my laws," and left only the "who love me," as his narcissistic God's explanation of the First

Commandment, given in *Ex.* 20:6 and *Deut.* 5:10, now remaining in that stripped-down form as his God's *only* commandment as this henceforth *Christian* God, which certainly is *not* the Jewish God. The Jewish God's "obey my laws" is *removed* from the Christian God's "love me," as the surviving Christian meaning of the First Commandment's injunction, "worship me." This God just wants to be loved.

Clearly, then, Paul's "interpretation" of Scripture was anything *but* that; it was instead a *gutting* of Scripture, editing out of it virtually its entire *core*.

Furthermore, the evidence indicates that this was consciously and even systematically done by him – no act of mere stupidity on his part – for he followed rigorously through with it, such as in *2 Corinthians* 3:5-9: "... The capacity we have comes from God; it is He who makes us capable of serving the new covenant, which consists not of a written Law but of the Spirit [faith]. The written Law brings death [in hell], but the Spirit gives life [eternal in heaven]. The Law was carved in letters on stone tablets, and God's glory appeared when it was given. ... If the Law, which brings death when it is imposed, came with glory, then how much greater is the glory that belongs to the activity of the Spirit [faith]. The system [Law] that brings condemnation was glorious; how much more glorious, then, is the activity [of the Spirit, faith] that brings salvation!" He then, in the very next two lines, 3:10-11, asserted the replacement of Judaism by Christianity, by saying, "Because of this new far brighter glory, the previous glory is terminated. If there was glory in what has now faded away, then how much more glory there is in what will last forever!" Having gutted the behavioral commandments that concern the activities of the person (e.g., lying, stealing, killing, etc.), he left only the one commandment, faith, "that belongs to the activity [of the Spirit] ... that brings salvation." This is a radical hollowing-out of Judaism, and one that is a total repudiation of Judaism, entirely at odds with it, and not merely superseding it. Then, shortly thereafter, in 4:2, Paul referred to this freeing of the individual to violate God's laws, as being *the exact opposite:* "We put aside all secret and shameful deeds; we do not act with deceit, nor do we falsify the word of God. In the full light of truth we live in God's sight and try to commend ourselves to everyone's good conscience," by not being held to obey God's laws against killing, lying, or anything else.

Paul was even so bold as to turn obedience to God into a sin *itself*, saying that God now hated His own laws; or, as *Romans* 4:15 put it, that, "the Law brings down God's anger, but where there is no law, there is no disobeying of the law." (Extending this principle into governmental affairs, the "good" way to deal with the problem of crime is to eliminate the laws against it; laws cause lawbreaking, so just eliminate laws and there will be no crimes.) A few chapters later, in 7:7-9, Paul explicitly, and shockingly, identified the *knowledge* of an act's evilness as being the very *same* thing as the act's evilness itself, when he said, "It was the Law that made me know what sin is. If the Law had not said 'Do not desire what belongs to someone else,' I would not have known such a desire. By means of that commandment, sin was able to stir all kinds of selfish desires in me. Sin cannot live unless the Law does." This latter assertion is alternatively translatable as, "Where there is no law, there are no violations." Paul's lie here is obvious, because the truth in this case is also obvious: it's NOT the law that causes the evil act; the law is what PUNISHES the evil act; it's not the law that causes a person to have the sinful desire; the law is what brings punishment against the sinful act, so as to RESTRAIN that sinful desire and so REDUCE sinful acts.

Paul has here resorted to outright and audacious lying in order to discredit Judaism – the Jewish covenant itself, the Jewish religion. (However, although he is here TRYING to trash ONLY Judaism, his reasoning would actually make impossible ANY effective legal system, because his underlying theory here, that law *causes* lawbreaking, is general, and is not limited ONLY to *Jewish* Law. Paul gives here no reason or argument that restricts his statements to Judaism alone. Instead, Paul's recommended approach to dealing with any crime in any society would produce gross injustice, and also mayhem; e.g., instead of punishing the murderer, it would eliminate the laws against murder.) This is also the viewpoint expressed in the equally shocking *Romans* 5:20, "Law was introduced in order to increase wrongdoing [translatable also as 'When Law was introduced, wrongdoing increased']; but where sin increased, God's grace in forgiving such wrongdoing increased even more." In other words, yet again, laws *cause* lawbreaking, and so God is relieved now that He has simply abolished the Law altogether. (Also worthy of note is that, a few lines earlier, in 3:25-26, Paul said that God's grace in forgiving such wrongdoing ended with the Crucifixion, so that the *only* path now toward salvation is faith in Christ.) Paul, however, once having made, and repeated, his core point that the law causes the lawbreaking, is expressing a view so scandalous that he's immediately impelled to qualify it with something that, though vague enough not to contradict this core point openly, would at least SEEM to put him on the side of the angels, and of respect for the Law. He does this just a few lines after his statement in 7:7-9 that knowledge makes an act evil, when he says, in 7:11-13, "Sin found its chance, and by means of the commandment it deceived me and killed me. Consequently, the Law itself is holy, and the individual commandment that I have violated is holy, right, and good. But does this mean that what is good caused my death? By no means! Sin did that, by using what is good; sin used what is good and so brought me death, in order that sin's true nature might be revealed. Thus, the commandment exposes sin as being even more terrible." Of course, since Paul's attack on the covenant is central to his case against (actually) circumcision, he still needs here, implicit even within the implicit, to affirm that sin "found its chance ... BY MEANS OF the commandment," and that "sin USED what is good," so that sin could not have succeeded (or perhaps even existed?) WITHOUT the commandment prohibiting it. In other words, even when Paul was desperately trying to reach out to the most committed believing Jews within the Roman congregation, he still needed to imply that, were it

NOT for the commandment, the sin itself wouldn't occur, because sin wouldn't have "found its chance." Paul, in other words, even when reaching out to Jews, insisted that, without laws *against* sinful acts, sinful acts would simply not be perpetrated.

Paul presented the same scandalously lying argument, in briefer form, in *Galatians*, where 3:19 says "What, then, was the purpose of the Law? It was added [to tribal descent from Abraham] in order to indicate what sin [violation of the Law] is." Paul denied that the Law was established in order to be followed; it was established, Paul said, *only* in order to make us know what is sinful. 3:23 asserts, "Before the time came for [Christ] faith, we were all prisoners of the Law," meaning that we all stood convicted by it (since no one can follow the Law, according to Paul). Then, 3:24 adds, "The Law was in charge of us [sinners] until Christ came, so that we could finally be accepted by God on account of our Christ-faith." Throughout Paul's argument here, the idea that the Law exists in order to be followed is firmly rejected.

What stands most fundamentally implicit behind Paul's sham argument is the obviously false assumption that, if an act is not CALLED evil, then the act is actually NOT evil. Paul thus found a way of blaming the Law as being a *prerequisite* to sin, while, at the same time, calling the Law itself "holy," so as to placate the Roman congregation's believing Jews. (He did the same sort of thing repeatedly in *Romans*, such as when he asserted in 3:28, "A person is put right with God only through faith, never by doing what the Law commands," and quickly followed this in 3:31 by insisting that "we uphold the Law" by negating the Law *equally* for BOTH Jews and Gentiles.) By such doubletalk, from which even the mythological Satan would have smiled and could have learned, Paul was cutting the salvational, or soteriological/eschatological, heart out of the Law's holiness to Jews, and so leaving this "holiness" an empty verbal shell. Paul was pretending to throw to the Roman congregation's Jews nutritious spiritual food, but actually delivered to them only an empty food-wrapper, with the brand "holy" stamped upon it. In *Philippians* 3:8, when addressing a congregation consisting, apparently, of ONLY Gentiles, Paul had no such need to mince his words; to these people, he called the covenant not "holy," but "mere garbage." It's as if the devil had taken on human form, and spoke and wrote as "Paul."

Back again to Paul's addressing the mixed congregation of the Romans, it wasn't enough that he was blaming sin on the Law; he went further: His boldness extended right into his own flock, insulting even themselves as fools, when in *Romans* 10:5-10 he dismissively quoted as coming from Moses, rather than from God Himself, the command in *Leviticus* 18:5 to "follow all the laws," which in fact *Leviticus* attributes instead *directly to God Himself*, and then Paul cited, incredibly, *against* that, *Deut.* 30:10-14, in which, this time, Moses is quoted as telling Jews about God by starting, "You will have to obey Him and keep all of His laws," and by ending, "Now, obey!" but which, in Paul's lying circumlocution in *Romans* 10:6-10, ends up miraculously scripting into

Moses's mouth, "If you confess that Jesus is Lord and believe that God raised Him from death, you will be saved." How interesting, that Moses (or was it instead perhaps the prophet Isaiah?) had taught, hundreds or thousand of years before Jesus of Nazareth, that a person would be saved only by believing that that very same Jesus of Nazareth, *yet to come*, is, in fact, "Christ!" Paul followed, in 10:11, by saying that this came from "the scripture," but this time, that "scripture" was *purely* his own fabrication.

A likely reason why Paul in *Romans* 10:5 would have attributed *Leviticus* 18:5 to Moses *instead of* to God is that this lie demoted the authority behind that statement ("Follow all the laws"), from God, down to Moses, who was merely a prophet. Then, promptly in *Romans* 10:6-10, Paul proceeds to contradict "Moses" – *instead of* to contradict God. In other words, the reason he had, in line 5, attributed this to Moses, instead of to God, was to enable him to contradict it in line 6, without spurring his readers to object. Cunning.

Paul was nothing if not thorough. However, the culmination was, of course, the replacement of circumcision itself, since it had been that law which had been the barrier that had precipitated all of this other verbal prestidigitation, and since the function of ritual induction into his new faith would now have to be met by some other means. This alternative means was fortunately ready at hand for him: the painless and safe baptism, or ritual dunking or "spiritual cleansing" in water, that had first been made prominent by Paul's fellow-Jew, John the Baptist, after centuries of Jewish non-covenantal (i.e., optional) ritual practice of it in the form of the Jewish ritual bath known as the "mikvah" (which had perhaps itself been inspired, or else institutionalized, by such passages as *Ex.* 19:10-11, *Lev.* 8:6 & 15:18, and *Num.* 19:13&20).

And that is how the religion we know today as Christianity was, in fact, cobbled together by Paul, not created by Jesus, who ended up being mythologized into serving posthumously as merely Paul's tool to rape Jesus's own Judaism. Paul's compromises with the Roman world around him – compromises that were originally driven by his need to attract into the Jesus-sect of Jews adult male Gentiles, since those men possessed all power and wealth in his society – ended up producing instead an entirely new religion, custom-tailored by Paul for success in the Gentile world. Not only had Paul eliminated the mythological Jewish God's circumcision-requirement, but he had, in *Galatians* 2:16, *Romans* 3:28, and elsewhere, eliminated all of this God's requirements other than mere belief in His Son – in fact, presenting this now-Christian God as even having given up on the hope of Man's obedience to Him, to the point that "The Law brings down God's anger," and no longer does disobedience to the Law cause Him anger. Paul's God is He who does not care any longer about what one person does to another, but whose only concern is whether He Himself – or, more properly speaking, that part of Himself that is His Son, Christ – is loved, regardless of what mayhem that given believer might happen to be practicing against others. (Of course, Paul denied this in such lines as *Romans* 3:31, when he was trying not to offend congregations that had some born Jews, but it's his core.) With his peculiarly narcissistic God, Paul now made it easy to become and to be a Christian, as it had never been to become or be a Jew. The admission-ticket into heaven could now be purchased merely by a ritual dunking in water, signifying the applicant's loving the Jesus that Paul and his followers had constructed carefully out of that mixture of fact and fiction, which goes by the name of religious myth.

Custom-tailored for success, this success is, in fact, the real God whom the religion has actually served, to such a point that this Paulianity, called "Christianity" by its believers, now has two billion of them worldwide, and remains rapidly growing. By contrast, little even survives reliably known today of Jesus's small Jewish sect, except that it believed Jesus to be King David's heir, and that, like virtually all Jerusalem Jews of its time, they were outraged at Paul's trashing of the covenant, as reported in *Acts* 21:21 forward. Thus, still more, in order for Paul to be able to succeed in his ultimate mission to convert the Romans, he needed to repudiate not only the followers of Jesus, but all of Judaism; and he did so.

Consequently, Paul's arguments that he gave for Christianity were all based upon bald lies, explicit and implicit, about Judaism, the covenant, the Law.

So, why were Paul's arguments accepted? The only reason these outrageous "arguments" worked is that his Gentile "converts" weren't really interested in Jesus's religion, Judaism, anyway: Paul hadn't *actually* sold them on that; he had sold them on just a ticket to heaven – and the cheaper the better.

And that's how it happened: heaven on sale.[62]

---

[62] People join a religion (if they really do, and aren't just "joining" in order to win friends and influence people so as to get ahead) because they've bought its ticket of admission into heaven for after they die. That's what preachers are selling, and what their gulls are buying. For example, the 9/11 terrorists did what they did because they had bought a fundamentalist Islamic admission ticket. Similarly, on 20 April 2007, the *Wall Street Journal* headlined "'Brotherhood' Blogs In Egypt Offer View Of Young Islamists," and Mariam Fam opened: "Like many young bloggers, Shaza Essam uses her personal Web site to list her favorite Hollywood movies," etc., "But some of the postings by the 21-year-old dentistry student in Cairo are far less typical. In an entry about her childhood ambitions, among becoming a doctor, a photographer or an actress, she adds, 'I dreamed that I was one of the mujahideen in Chechnya or Palestine, and that I was blowing myself up among as many enemies as possible so that I could be like the martyrs.'" (The martyrs, of course, are supposed to go to heaven.)

It's not much different from what the Medieval knights had in mind as they marched toward Jerusalem to slaughter the infidels and win it back for Christ – many of these religious fanatics knew, and were proud, that they might die in the effort; they sought only to slaughter as many heathens as possible, in order to win their place in heaven. [continued]

And it *worked* – and how! Paul knew, then, what marketers know now. (Scholars still don't know it; they'll be the last to learn it, because as creatures of the Religious Age, their function is to support faith, not to investigate it. To the extent they investigate it, they're no longer scholars, but become scientists instead.)

Paul the Master Salesman

When Paul sold his followers on his "gospel," he was selling them on a piece of "good news," because that's what the term "gospel" meant. (The later stories of Jesus's life and death became capital-G "Gospels" only because each of these stories constituted a different account of the supposed origin of this "good news," but "gospel" originally referred to the good news itself, and not to any supposed biography of Jesus.) And what was this good news, which Paul sold? It was that you don't have to go under the knife in order to win eternal life in heaven. In Paul's time, this was extremely good news indeed!

Paul's "good news" was/is: Heaven on Sale!

Instead of one's needing to obey all of God's laws, a person needed now only to possess faith in personal salvation via Christ's Crucifixion and Resurrection, and the pathway to an eternity in heaven was now clear. Instead of one's joining

---

And, of course, Judaism is also directed at salvation not only during life, but also after death. For example, *Isaiah* 28:18 promises that if one is righteous and meets the demands of "justice," the person may safely "trust" that "your covenant with death will be annulled; your agreement with the grave will be cancelled." Also, God is quoted in *Deuteronomy* 30:8-19 as assuring people that if "you obey all the commandments I am giving you today," then you "will go up to heaven" and "cross to the other side of the sea," so that "I have today offered you the choice between living and dying."

Paul was telling the people in his own time: God's commandments are past. The only price now is: Believe in Christ! What Sam Walton did with candy bars and detergents, Paul did with heaven, but he discounted it far more steeply.

God's people who were destined for heaven, via the medical operation of circumcision in an era that knew neither anesthesia nor antibiotics nor antiseptics, one now joined God's people via merely a dunk in water, or even via just a spritz of water – baptism.

Paul, in *Galatians* 2:16, eliminated the necessity for circumcision as the induction-ritual (or signature) into God's people. Soon, this induction-ritual was replaced by baptism. However, in Judaism, circumcision didn't assure a person of entrance into heaven after death; circumcision was instead merely a person's signature upon the Jews' contract or covenant with God. In order for a person to be able to enter heaven, in accord with the Jewish myth, more was needed than just this signature: a person needed also to adhere to the contract: to *follow* God's Law. And, similarly, in order for one of Paul's followers to be admitted into heaven according to the myth that Paul created, more is needed than just the initiation-ritual of baptism: the individual must also fulfill the promise of this form of signature, by keeping the faith that Christ's Resurrection cleanses of sin everyone who possesses such faith. Paul's follower who added *Mark*'s ending, lines 16:9-20, wrote there (placing these words into Jesus's mouth) in *Mark* 16:16, "Whosoever believes and is baptized will be saved; all nonbelievers will be damned." Paul himself wrote in *Romans* 6:3-4, "When we were baptized into union with Jesus Christ, we were baptized into union with his death. By our baptism, then, we died with him ... to have, like Him, a new life, granted by the glorious power of the Father."

The Jews had placed a very high price upon heaven. Paul and his followers lowered this price, drastically; they lowered not only the price to qualify for God's consideration, which now became only baptism, but also the price to win God's ultimate approval, which now became only Christ-faith.

Furthermore, as has also been noted, Paul and his followers additionally granted to the Emperor the lawmaking function that the Jews granted only to God, and thereby offered a far better deal to the elite, and not *just* to the masses.

This is how Paul became, for all time, the world's most successful deal-maker, who offered an overwhelmingly more attractive deal, both to the elite, and to the masses.

When Paul wrote *Galatians*, he didn't know that history would turn out exactly as he had planned and hoped. But we do. We know it now.

This is an account of Christianity's origins that – unlike the scholarly accounts[63] – is fully in accord with the most elementary realities of motivation and of psychology. All the other "historical" accounts, of Christianity's start, depend upon at least some of the miraclism of the Christian myth.

---

[63]   For example, Krister Stendahl's enormously respected 1963 *Paul Among Jews and Gentiles* asserts, in Part 6, that, "What Paul brands 'Judaizing' – circumcision and dietary laws for Gentiles – was not a barrier to Christianity but quite attractive to Gentiles, who were enamored of what was Oriental." In reality, however, circumcision was the very crux of the entire matter, and "dietary laws for Gentiles" were simply irrelevant to the split. And, in reality, circumcision wasn't "attractive to Gentiles," but was, instead, as Paul called it in *Philippians* 3:2, the aim of "those who do evil things, those dogs, those who insist upon cutting the body," and, as he said in just the line before that, the proponents of circumcision constituted a threat to the very "safety" of his readers. And, as he said in *Galatians* 5:12, such dogs or proponents of circumcision should "just go and castrate themselves!" And, as he said earlier in that same letter, in 1:8-9, they "should go to hell!" And, as he said there in 2:2, his very own success or failure in life depended upon the outcome of this issue; and, in the next line, his companion was even almost *compelled* to be circumcised. Furthermore, Stendahl's reference here to Paul's converts being "enamored of what was Oriental" was similarly a pure concoction of that narrow-minded scholar, who transposed onto the earliest Christians the prejudices that he, a 20th-Century devout Lutheran and ultimately the Lutheran Bishop of Stockholm, felt to be exotic, or (from Stendahl's perhaps ethnic perspective) "Oriental." None of Stendahl's bizarre assertions here were required, by other scholars, to be *documented*, not even to be *poorly* documented; it was enough for them that Stendahl presented Christianity in a favorable light.

You will not find, in the works of any of the scholars of early Christianity a discussion of the horrific and dangerous *reality* of circumcision during an era that knew no anesthesia, and no antibiotics, and no antiseptics. Essentially, what you'll find instead is merely sophistical defense and perpetuation of that elaborate hoax. Just like Stendahl himself, it makes no difference whether these people were teaching in Harvard or preaching in Stockholm, because a hoax is a hoax regardless, and these scholars/preachers are just as fake "experts," either way.

The rest of this letter to the Galatians consists of reinforcements of the agenda that we've discussed. For examples:

After his account of 2:11-21 – the event that actually created Christianity – Paul introduces the third element of the Trinity. The Holy Spirit (the Holy Ghost) enters in 3:14, 4:6, 5:16-18, 5:22, 5:25, and 6:8. This reinforces, yet again, Paul's superiority over Paul's enemies, in Jerusalem, who knew Jesus "from man or by means of man." It also reinforces the superiority of faith (the Spirit) over Law (mere works). Brilliant.[64]

In 3:10, Paul says "Whoever depends upon obeying the Law lives under a curse." Paul is saying, yet again, that such a person is condemned to hell. Yet again: Only via Christ-faith will anyone find a way to heaven.

3:23 asserts: "Before the time for faith came, we were all prisoners of the Law." Paul frees his followers from the Jewish Law, so as to enslave them to his lies and thus to himself.

4:4 says: "But when the proper time arrived, God sent his Son." What the Jewish God in *Genesis* 17:13 had said must be "eternal" was said by Paul to be now *ended*.

4:5 continues by explaining why Christ came: "to redeem those who were under the Law," and not to re-establish Israel's independence and sovereignty.

4:21 challenges his readers: "Those of you who want to be subject to the Law must heed what the Law says." Paul's point is, yet again, that they're *free* of the Law.

---

[64]   Theologians have no interest in understanding the origin of the Trinity. Their view, as one scholar put it to me, in declining my offer to him to consider this work in manuscript, is that, "The doctrine of the Trinity is not invented but revealed by God himself in Jesus Christ." Of course, this person didn't offer evidence for his belief; perhaps he felt that, as a recognized "authority" on the subject, he had no need to do so. Or perhaps, as a Christian, he felt not only that the reality of the Resurrection mustn't be questioned, but that even its meaning mustn't be questioned – that the Resurrection was exactly what Paul and his followers said it was, and that even to question this is wrong.

5:1 asserts directly: "Christ has set us free!" In other
words, yet again: because of Christ, one can now go to heaven
without first having gone under the knife.

5:4 asserts that "Anyone who tries to achieve salvation
by following God's commandments will be rejected by God."
It's pure anti-Judaism.

6:11 (which was cited at our start) is remarkable
because it asserts, "See what big letters I make as I write to
you now with my own hand!"

What an artifact the original letter would have been if it
had survived – the most important physical historical object
ever. Sadly, it doesn't exist. But instead, we fortunately do
possess copies, which were made of it. Very few written
originals from 2000 years ago exist, and few documents
survive even as copies; but, by an extraordinary stroke of luck,
Galatians is among the latter.

We're simply blessed – scientifically, and certainly *not*
religiously – that this document, *Galatians*, exists; because
now, with the advent of science, this document exposes
history, whereas, before, there was only the Christian *myth* that
Paul had intended, and that scholars have since promulgated.

The biggest blunder of the Roman Catholic Church was
that they didn't only preserve this letter – they canonized it.
They performed this blunder prior to the existence of science –
at the peak of the Religious Age – and so they had no way to
know then that this would become their *un*doing, in some
later Age, the emerging Age of Science.

Finally, the "DNA" in this letter, and in the other
authentic Paulines, and in Christianity itself, is exposed.

We can thus now more fully understand why Paul had
started this letter with 1:1: "From Paul, whose call to be an
apostle did not come from man or by means of man, but from
Jesus Christ and God the Father, who raised Him from death."
Paul said, in 2 *Corinthians* 3:6, "The written law brings death,
but the Spirit [Christ-faith] gives life." And here, in his very
first line of *Galatians*, Paul has emphasized not just Jesus's
godhood, but His death and Resurrection, and so has pre-

encapsulated the coming climax: that the works of man, obedience to the Law, lead only to eternal death, which can be replaced by eternal life only via one's faith in the Resurrection. It's right there, in embryonic form, in 1:1. As Paul said in the climax, *Galatians* 2:16, "No one wins God's approval by obeying the Law." Five lines later, in 2:21, Paul asserted, "For if God approves of a person on account of the person's following His Law, then Christ died for nothing!" Paul thus started this letter, in 1:1 and 1:8-9, by denigrating the authority of, and by attacking, Jesus's disciples, Jews, *who preached the exact opposite* – they preached that *only* by *following* the Law could one win eternal life. Paul was waging this war right at the letter's start.

The rhetorical coherence of this letter is more than stunning; this letter is the supreme masterpiece of sales/PR writing, the proven model towards which today's most highly skilled in the crafts of persuasion/manipulation[65] can aspire. As an object of legal/forensic analysis, this letter displays its tactics, which are beyond brilliant. As an object of scholarly speculation, this letter asserts whatever any given scholar wants to believe, which has been little more than pedantic and deceptive, serving Paul and not the public. That's to continue in the ancient tradition of the academy, as an extension of and preparation for the priesthood. To understand this letter is to know its tactics, and not merely its claims, because its claims are tools toward Paul's persuasive goals, and those objectives aren't merely to inform, but are also to deceive whenever deception advances his persuasive ends. To the extent that this letter is understood as to its strategy and tactics, it opens the Pandora's box of Christian history, and reveals inside the brain that actually shaped Western Civilization.

---

[65]   A scientific audience is persuaded by diametrically opposite appeals, *not* by manipulation. Paul was directing his arguments to a specifically *religious* audience. Manipulation is the most effective way to persuade those people. Scientists, to the extent that they *are* scientists, don't respond at all to manipulative pitches, but only to evidence and logic, such as is being employed in the present work. Advertising and marketing during the Religious Age adhere to the strategy of which Paul was the master: manipulation. [continued]

Maybe? No – Is!

Christianity's being a hoax isn't just maybe so; it is definitely so – proven far beyond any reasonable doubt.

For example, the documents which aver that Jesus appointed Peter and not James as his successor, or as the "Pope" (as the Roman Church subsequently called it), would be excluded from presentation to a jury as constituting "evidence" under the best-evidence principle, which requires that when best evidence contradicts lower quality evidence regarding any particular allegation or inference, *only* the best evidence can be admitted *as* "evidence," when a prosecutor

---

On the cusp of entering the Scientific Age, a strictly scientific presentation of the origins of Christianity becomes publishable. In previous times, it simply wouldn't have been: there wouldn't have been a sufficient market for it, and scholars would thus have succeeded in suppressing it – they would have had success because, in the Religious Age, the public is authoritarian and consequently relies upon authority more than it relies upon science, in which the tests are applied by the individual himself on the basis of his own experience analyzed as a scientist does, and not by means of authority at all. (Expertise, yes; authority, no. An expert reduces his arguments to purely authentic evidence and logic; an authority does not. In the Religious Age, no distinction is drawn between expertise and authority. But the difference is real: An expert empowers his audience to judge for itself, whereas an authority intellectually cripples his audience and does the judging for them by presenting to them other pre-selected authorities who "just happen to" agree with his own opinion.)

The present work is directed at a scientific audience. Obviously, a religious audience will be more persuaded by the presentation that the New Testament supplies regarding the "history" of Christianity's start. The present work covers this same ground from a scientific perspective, and might be placed next to the Bible, as a scientific companion to that Scripture. Placing the two together would provide both a Religious Age, and a Scientific Age, approach to the question: How did Christianity begin?

Even though the present work relies upon the Bible for evidence, a scientist uses that evidence fundamentally differently than does a religionist. Any presentation that uses evidence so as to manipulate people is unscientific, even though, as in Paul's case, the presentation can still be enormously skillful.

presents a case to be considered by a jury.[66] Such textual lines as *Matthew* 16:18 and *John* 21:15-17 are inadmissible as "evidence" during the Scientific Age, because such lines contradicting them as *Galatians* 2:11-12 constitute legally-forensically far superior evidence, since they come from a far more reliable source. A judge following the best-evidence principle would be required to throw out the inferior evidence, given this contradiction. (Furthermore, *Matthew* and *John* constitute, at best, only hearsay "evidence," and some courts would throw them out even if the far superior evidence – the authentic Pauline letters – didn't exist. By contrast, the authentic Paulines present first-person witness testimony;

---

[66]   Some nations apply the best-evidence principle as a means of "weighting" evidence, so as to grant higher consideration to evidence that is rated higher as to its credibility. The alternative approach is simply to prohibit presentation of inferior evidence regarding a particular question, whenever higher-quality evidence is available: the inferior evidence is excluded in much the same way that the exclusionary rule prohibits presenting, to a jury, evidence that has been illegally obtained. Both methods are, however, the same whenever the best-evidence principle is being rigorously applied: Weighting evidence and granting higher credence to the best evidence is effectively to discount lower quality evidence. However, the two methods can differ in result when a case entails lots of poor-quality evidence pointing in one direction, versus only one item of high-quality evidence, which points the opposite way. Cases in which a single item of DNA evidence overrode lots of dubious witness evidence, have been, in effect, applications of the best-evidence rule in its either-or sense of entirely excluding consideration of inferior evidence.

Some countries, during our still-primitive era, are so sloppy about rules of evidence, virtually anything qualifies as "evidence"; and even some nations that purport to be democratic are like this. For example, Germany has no rules of evidence – even hearsay qualifies to such an extent that a lawyer has no legal ground to object if it's used against his client. That's more characteristic of a dictatorship than of a democracy. However, in some other respects, the German legal system is superior (more scientific, more democratic) as compared to, for example, the American, where "expert" testimony is hired by a litigant and so is clearly motivated to testify for the paying side. By contrast, in Germany, the court (judge) hires experts; though the German judge *might* be prejudiced for one side, the American lawyer *certainly* is. Legal/forensic methodology, like any scientific methodology, tends to improve over time, and it has experienced rapid advancement since WWII. It's not static, but – because it *is* science, rather than faith – it *is* good, and it's getting better.

and, for example, in American courts, documents that are twenty or more years old are accepted into evidence if and when the authenticity of the given document is established, such as is the case with these letters; and, moreover, even in hearsay which would otherwise be inadmissible, statements that are against the interests of the alleged declarant are accepted into evidence if the declarant is unavailable to testify. Rules of evidence are more accepting of self-incriminating than of self-exculpatory evidence. As we have shown, the Paulines are *full* of self-incriminating evidence – such as evidence that outright proves false some of the things that Paul himself asserts.)

The earliest and by far the most reliable evidence regarding the creation of Christianity is *entirely consistent*. It proves, beyond any reasonable doubt whatsoever, that Jesus lived and died a Jew and was never a Christian, and that all of his followers were likewise devout Jews. And it proves – it even exhibits or displays; it is itself the result of the fact – that, after the incident recounted in *Galatians* 2:11-16, Paul was no longer one of them, and started his own religion, Christianity. Furthermore, it *explains* all of the other, inferior, "evidence," which has served for two thousand years as the "history" of how Christianity started, but which was instead merely the Christian myth.

Paul's "Christ" was the essential tool for Paul's success, and Paul used this tool to overwhelming effect.

Paul took a far-from-basic concept in Judaism, the concept of the mashiach (which was unimportant in Judaism),[67] and transformed it into the basic concept in his entirely new religion, "Christianity." He did this on account of a basic concept in Judaism, circumcision, which he couldn't afford even to discuss openly with his gulls.

---

[67]   Details of how unimportant the mashiach was to Judaism were presented at fn. 21, in Chapter 1, the second footnote to the exegesis of *Galatians* 1:5. It starts on page 74.

Paul's Confession

As we've mentioned, Paul didn't *want* to include a description of the event that created Christianity, 2:11-21, but he *had* to do it. This was his *hidden confession*. He was, here, in exquisitely veiled but stunningly complete terms, confessing, to the Galatians, and ultimately to a Scientific Age posterity (us), that what he was now teaching (what we today know as "Christianity") – what he was teaching to the Galatians and to all of his other followers – was his own invention, and wasn't actually Jesus's and God's, as he claimed (in 1:1, 1:11, and elsewhere). The rest of his letter confesses *why* he committed this fraud against them.

Like most confessions, this confession was a result of circumstances, not strictly a voluntary act. However, no prosecutor has forced it from him. This is an eminently admissible confession. And Paul hid the confession as effectively as he could. (Scholars, even today, refuse to see it.) Unearthing this – revealing Paul's implicit confession – is like finding well-preserved DNA evidence after 2,000 years.

Furthermore, it's an especially trustworthy confession, because, like one extracted during cross-examination of a witness in court, it has been extracted (in this case, from a document) despite the witness's (Paul's) clear desire *not* to reveal what actually happened – as was mentioned, Paul *did* hide it as well as he possibly could, and it has worked for a full 2,000 years.

The care he devoted to hiding it is, in fact, directly proportionate to his confession's credibility. For example, if a letter from Paul were to be found in which he had bragged "I created Christianity," that wouldn't be nearly so credible as the confession we actually possess in *Galatians*. If he had written "I invented the idea that salvation can be achieved just via Christ-faith," then that wouldn't nearly match the credibility of Paul's confession that we possess in *Galatians*. Here, despite his desire not to admit what he did, he tells us not just *that* he did it, but *how* and *why* and *when* and *where* he did it; and every bit of this confession makes sense, and accords with everything else that we know, such as the scariness of medical operations in an era that possessed neither anesthesia nor antibiotics nor antiseptics. Moreover, all of Paul's other authentic letters support his confession in *Galatians*.

Legal convictions are commonly obtained upon the basis of cases that are far less consistent, far less comprehensive, far less complete, and far less conclusive, than we are offered in the present instance; and, for this documentation of history, all future generations of mankind can quite reasonably feel extremely fortunate, that such important history (which may be considered to be the most important event in all *of* history) is, after so long a period of time, finally able to be reconstructed from the existing evidence, with such a stunningly high degree of both confidence and detail, in the understanding of those events.

The highest standard of proof that a court demands, for the most serious of crimes, is "beyond a reasonable doubt," and what we possess in the present case is indeed that, and then some.

Why Scholars Talk About 'Table Fellowship' Instead of About Circumcision, in 2:12

What difference would have resulted if the event that is recounted in *Galatians* 2:11-21 had – as scholars simply assume – been concerning the food laws instead of circumcision? A huge difference. In such a case, the cause of the blowup here would have been Peter's disobedience of James's instruction to impose the kosher laws upon Paul's congregations), instead of whether or not Paul's perhaps thousands of adult male congregants were members of the Jesus sect of Jews – whether they were, indeed, Jews at all. The issue here would then have concerned only Peter – not the faith-community or religion itself, and thus not the creation of a new faith.

If the issue here were what scholars assume, that Paul's men were dining at an un-kosher table, then Paul could easily have corrected the deficiency, simply by ordering in kosher food. However, there's no indication that he did that. Nor is there any indication, anywhere in Paul's authentic letters, that Paul wasn't enforcing the kosher laws anyway. To the contrary, in *1 Corinthians* 8, Paul admonishes his followers who still believe in their old Gentile or "pagan" religious customs, telling them (*1 Corinthians* 8:4) that "an idol represents a false god, and all of us must recognize only the one true God"; in other words, he indicates that the violations his men were practicing were their pre-existing "pagan" rituals concerning food belonging to the gods (8:7). He tells his men that they shouldn't continue heeding traditional Gentile ("pagan") rituals pertaining to ancient polytheistic gods. He *isn't* telling these people that they can now relax their newly acquired adherence to Judaism's kosher laws. In 8:10, he advises his men to discontinue serving as models, to others, of traditional pagan food customs, and he specifically condemns any eating practices "for the purposes of idol-worship." Implicitly accepting Judaism's food laws in this regard, Paul equates the practitioners of those traditional pagan food rituals to (8:12) "sinning against the Messiah."[68] Then, in 10:20, he asserts, "What is sacrificed on pagan altars is offered to

---

[68]   The concept of "sinning against the Messiah" wasn't Jewish, but purely *post*-split; this passage was clearly written after the split, because Judaism recognizes as sins nothing except violations against God's laws, which is to say violations against God, not against the mashiach or any other person; this statement from Paul was already an implicit violation of the strictly monotheistic opening laws within the Ten Commandments. Consequently, this passage, which respected the Law even while citing for doing so a reason that violated Judaism, can reasonably be considered as having likely been written during the transition period, early enough after the split so that Paul was still trying to avoid provoking James into going public about Paul's ostracism from the sect, and yet Christian nonetheless.

demons, not to God. And I do not want you to be partners with demons." Paul is here telling his men to heed Jewish morality – the Third of the Ten Commandments, in fact – *not* to heed pagan morality. In 10:32, he says, "Live in such a way as to cause no trouble either to Jews or Gentiles." This means for them to adhere to all the kosher laws when in the presence of Jews. However, in 10:25-26, he asserts: "You may eat any meat, because Scripture says, 'Everything on Earth belongs to the Lord.'" Paul wasn't concerned about all of the kosher laws when there was no practicing Jew present, but he was concerned about the Third of the Ten Commandments (banning idols) when any issue of food came up. He was self-acknowledgedly inconsistent (saying in 10:33, "Just do as I do. I try to please everyone"), but as regards the food laws, he unquestionably favored compliance with Jewish practices, *especially in Jewish company*.

Clearly, the Corinthians he was writing to were Gentiles, and the laws that they were violating were kosher laws in Judaism; Paul was teaching these men to adhere to Jewish food-laws – not to adhere to their former food-practices, from their prior pagan faith. And so, since Paul was *already* compliant with the kosher laws, *that couldn't possibly have been* the point at issue in *Galatians* 2:11-21.

Similarly, in *Romans* 14:1-12, Paul (in 14:3) admonishes omnivores, on the one hand, and vegetarians, on the other, to ignore all food laws, except (14:10-12) the commandments of "the Lord ... God," for, "We shall all stand before God, to be judged by Him" (14:10). Paul was there asserting the Jewish position, unambiguously.

Paul was always faithful to Judaism's food laws. In this respect, he was doing his job as a salesman for James's sect, bringing Gentile men into this Jewish sect.

James could take no exception to that, and he didn't.[69]

---

[69]   Why, then, do scholars widely misinterpret *Galatians* 2:11-21 so that the Jewish food laws, instead of *Genesis* 17:14, were at stake here? As was said before, scholars don't wish to say things that violate their culture's deepest prejudices. [continued]

Even in *Galatians*, Paul didn't tell his followers not to obey the food laws, and he actually had no objection to any of

If the food laws were at stake here, then this incident would have concerned only the obedience of Peter to James's instructions, and *not* the identity of Paul's perhaps thousands of followers as being followers of Jesus via James, and would thus have been consistent with the myth that Paul's group wanted to promote (that Paul's "gospel of Christ" *hadn't* changed). Probably, Paul was hoping that his immediate readers would misinterpret the passage in this way, but he had to allow that they would not, because James's men might have previously gotten to them and said otherwise about this incident. Thus, Paul had to write this passage vaguely, and he skillfully wrote it so as to mislead gulls to think that Peter, and not the very faith itself, was the focus of this passage. Scholars eagerly pick up on and promote that deception.

For scholars instead to have acknowledged that the Christian faith was created by a seemingly trivial incident ("trivial," that is, in the view of scholars, whose analyses grossly misunderstand what's important, because they're not scientists), would be for them to deny what their lives are dedicated to, in an overwhelmingly religious culture, where faith itself is respected instead of (as a scientist has it) repudiated. Only if circumcision and not food was the subject here, is Christianity a hoax; otherwise, Paul really *did* reject whatever was involved here (presumably then the Jewish food laws), because he rejected the (Jewish) covenant; and he did not reject the covenant on account of his having been forced by tragic circumstances to repudiate circumcision – which was actually the case.

If what was at stake in this incident was only the correctness of Peter's obedience to James, then the incident recounted in *Galatians* 2:11-21 concerned not the momentous matter of whether or not Paul's followers were members of the Jesus sect of Jews, but instead only a personal dispute between Paul and Peter – *just as Paul hoped his dupes would believe to be the case.*

One ought to keep in mind here that Paul recounted this incident only with terrific reluctance, to protect himself against what might have been told to his readers by James's representatives in Galatia. Paul couldn't have been certain what James's men had told his readers about this; Paul had to write defensively. He succeeded in fooling scholars for thousands of years.

That's why this incident – and its context, and its background, and its results – weren't known until now, and why Christianity was viewed as a holy thing, or else as a mere happening, and not as what it now clearly is: a hoax, which resulted from Paul's personal career-crisis, and which produced Western culture, in the ways that it did and that are described here.

Though this Scriptural passage was always there, modern legal/forensic methods were not. It's like the application of DNA evidence to an old murder case from the pre-DNA era. Except that this case concerns the very creation of Western Culture.

the laws *except* circumcision. 5:19-21 tells his parishioners that if they engage in "immoral, filthy, and indecent actions, in worship of idols, ... " then "I warn you, as I have before, that anyone who does such things will be excluded from the Kingdom of God." Here, he was telling them to adhere to the covenant, but was carefully avoiding to *mention* the covenant ("the Law"), which he elsewhere had been saying had been superseded by the Resurrection. And yet, only a few lines earlier, in 5:3-4, he had *reasserted* this very supersession: "Once again, I am warning that anyone who allows himself to be circumcised is obliged to obey the whole law. Anyone who tries to win God's approval by obeying the Law has cut himself off from Christ – you are outside God's grace." So, the *only* law that Paul *really* was condemning is actually the *circumcision*-law. However, Paul couldn't very well *admit* this to his parishioners, because, if he were to have admitted to them that he rejected the covenant because he rejected its circumcision-law, instead of rejected the circumcision-law because he rejected the covenant, then he would have been admitting to them his scam, and he would have lost these followers altogether. Paul apparently expected that they'd be too stupid to recognize his scam, so long as he didn't state it directly (as I've just done here); and the evidence, that subsequent history provides, of Paul's (i.e., of Christianity's) stunning success, suggests he gauged their intelligence (or rather lack of it) correctly.

Many scholars refer to the split between Judaism and Christianity as "the parting of the ways" between the two religions. The view that the blowup in 2:12 concerned the kosher laws reflects this mild reading of a "parting of the ways" between the two faiths, but such a phrase misrepresents profoundly what actually happened. What occurred here wasn't nearly so peaceful and frictionless as such a phrase suggests; it was more like a very nasty, ugly, and even violent, divorce. *Acts* 21:21 forward describes some of the public expressions of this blowup; but, when Paul, in

Galatians, 1:8-9, writing to his followers, said, and repeated, that Jesus's disciples, who were Jews, "should be condemned to Hell!" for not joining him in abandoning the covenant in favor of Paul's own gospel of Christ, this was a private expression of his passionate hatred, as was Paul's venting in 6:12 that those people were behind the crucifixion. And he showed it yet again in *1 Thessalonians* 2:15-16; and yet again in *Philippians* 3:2-8. To call this type of separation a "parting of the ways" is simply grotesque.

In *1 Corinthians* 13:11, Paul said, "When I was a child, I said what a child says, and thought like a child does, but now that I have matured, I am finished with childishness." Paul was here justifying to his now-Christian followers his repudiation of the Judaism that he had previously taught to them. Contrary to Paul's repeated assertions that his "gospel of Christ" had never changed, he needed to rationalize to his followers the profound changes that his teachings had actually undergone. Belief in salvation via adherence to the Law was "garbage"; it was "childish," and Paul had "matured." Paul was now insulting all Jews who did not worship Jesus. But no Jew *could* worship Jesus – or any other human – because that would have violated the first three of the Ten Commandments; it would have been his abandonment of Judaism, like Paul did.

Indeed, if any Jew says to his rabbi, "I worship you," then the rabbi is obliged by the very faith he teaches, to respond, in effect, "Then you are no follower of mine, because I teach Judaism, whose First Commandment is to worship no one but God." Thirteen times in the canonical Gospels (as previously noted here to have been *Matthew* 26:25&49; *Mark* 9:5, 11:21, 14:45; and *John* 1:38&49, 3:2, 4:31, 6:25, 9:2, 11:8, and 20:16), the followers of "Jesus" addressed him *specifically* as "rabbi." If any of the authentic Jesus's followers had ever told him, "I worship you," he would similarly have been obliged, by the very faith he taught, to respond by saying, "Then you are no follower of mine." That didn't happen, because none of the real Jesus's real followers ever said they worshipped him –

they were all Jews and remained as Jews. Jesus's name and identity were purloined and abused by Paul, whose followers were – like Paul – enemies of the actual Jesus's authentic followers.

The exegesis presented here differs from all others in its applying legal/forensic – not scholarly – methods of interpreting a document. Unlike any other exegesis of *Galatians*, it relies not upon the opinions that other people – scholars – have expressed as representing what Paul meant, but rather *upon what Paul himself said*. This exegesis is therefore a repudiation of scholarship itself for interpreting documents, and an affirmation and embodiment of (legal/forensic) science[70] as a *replacement* of scholarship for interpreting documents, so historians will view documents as do courts of law in a democracy.

A typical example of the scholars' view of the "parting of the ways" is Michael F. Bird's "Jesus and the 'Partings of the Ways'," in the 2011 *Handbook for the Study of the Historical Jesus, v. II*. His "Conclusion" there (p. 1215) is that "constituent elements of the Jewish-Christian rift find their germinal roots in the historical Jesus," and that these "roots" were supposed "points of contention between Jesus and his contemporaries."

---

[70]   The phrase "the scientific method," which some writers employ in such contexts as this, is internally redundant, because science *is* a method (or actually a *meta*-methodology), and *isn't* a subject-area or group of subject-areas, to which "the scientific method" (whatever *that* would be) is supposedly applied (as scholars prefer to believe). Science has nothing to do with any given subject-area, but only with how it is being treated. And there is actually no *one* scientific method; *all* methods that fulfill the epistemology science are scientific. Thus, what's being applied here is simply "science," and not "the scientific method." Legal/forensic methodology is the application of science to a certain subject-area – the field of reconstructing a sequence of events upon the basis of evidence, by a court in a democracy. The sub-field here is documentary (or document-based) legal/forensic methodology, or the field of scientific application in which the evidence being scientifically analyzed happens to be document(s). What's important here isn't the subject-area, but the epistemology or "method" – the criteria for determining truth. To the extent that the method is faith, an interpretation is scholarly; to the extent that the method is science, an interpretation is scientific – and that's legal/forensic in the present case. Courts in a democracy require science and reject faith; that's basic, and it's *why* legal/forensic methodology is employed.

By "contemporaries," he doesn't refer to the Romans who actually executed Jesus for sedition, but instead to supposed "violent opposition from other Jews." Dr. Bird takes the Gospel accounts as being historical narratives from followers of Jesus, and his entire article is based upon that false assumption. All of the numerous scholars he cites in supposedly arguing for this conclusion are likewise unquestioning acceptors of the historical veracity of the New Testament. Some of these scholars he cites are Jews, such as the ubiquitous Jacob Neusner (perhaps the world's most-published scholar, with nearly a thousand works published), who likewise accept unquestioningly the veracity of the New Testament accounts of "Jesus." Further distancing their accounts from Jesus, some of the primary sources upon which these scholars base their accounts were written centuries after the Gospels, such as the Babylonian Talmud (which was anti-Jesus because it argued against the Gospels and *assumed* that Jesus was accurately portrayed there). On the basis of these bogus accounts of "Jesus," by Jesus's actual enemies, both Christian and Jewish scholars formulate their "historical" accounts of Christianity's start.

Paul's Key to Success

Paul was the most gifted manipulator in all of human history; his skill at the conning crafts was awesome; nobody else comes close. But dissecting *Galatians* is ultimately a close analysis of a merely mechanical act. What Paul did was purely mechanical; he was no artist. What we have done here in legal/forensically analyzing *Galatians* is like getting under the hood of a car in order to find out how it's put together. This is reverse engineering of the evidence, and the evidence here is documents. Billions of Christians happen to think that these documents are holy, and that the Bible is the Word of God. By getting under the hood, our reverse engineering shows that this vehicle isn't holy; it's a hoax.

Nothing but ruthless scheming and deceit were necessary in order for Paul to succeed and shape our world more than any other person ever has. He had what it took to do the job. And he did it; he won. During the Religious Age, he took advantage of the religiosity, the faith, of his followers, to fill them with his deceits, and so to enslave them to his goals, for thousands of years.

Our discussion of 1:1 started: "Paul has here, implicitly, CORRECTLY identified his target market ... as consisting of RELIGIOUS people: people for whom the most persuasive forms of alleged evidence are *not* natural ... but rather *supernatural*." A corollary of this is that a religious person tends to accept assertions to the extent that they're false, and tends to be skeptical of assertions to the extent that they're true. It's not just that religious persons tend to weight evidence from religious authorities over evidence from secular authorities, but rather that scientists weight evidence from their own systematic investigatory researches above any "authority," and to repudiate the very concept of "authority," while acknowledging (where unavoidable) reliance upon expertise and findings which have been demonstrated by other scientists. During the Religious Age, hoaxers enjoy this enormous advantage against scientists, because a scientist's naturalistic arguments encounter, from the audience, more skepticism than do the religionist's supernaturalistic arguments: hocus-pocus generates credibility, not disbelief, during the Religious Age. Each religion has its supposed "miracles," which supposedly "prove" the given faith's truth. Religion is, for the buyer, a way to deal with his fear of death.[71] But for the seller of religion, it's a way of enslaving buyers to his personal ends (which can likewise be a craving for salvation).

---

[71] For example, on 30 March 2011, a scientific research article, "Death and Science: The Existential Underpinnings of Belief in Intelligent Design and Discomfort with Evolution," was posted online, and rawstory.com summarized and linked to it that day headlining, "Death Anxiety Linked to Acceptance of Intelligent Design." This study, by three scientific psychologists (Tracy, Hart, and Martens),

found that fear of death correlated with belief in the faith-based, anti-scientific, "Intelligent Design" theory of human origins, and did so (as the paper said) "regardless of participants' religion, religiosity, educational background, or preexisting attitude toward evolution."

Only "natural-science students" did *not* react on the basis of fear-of-death. Everyone else (and there were a diverse range of 1,674 participants total) did move toward Intelligent Design Theory and away from Evolutionary Theory when reminded of their own mortality.

The researchers found that: "Reminders of one's mortality ... promote relative support for IDT [Intelligent Design Theory], and skepticism toward ET [Evolutionary Theory]. Individuals respond to existential threat by becoming more accepting of a theory that offers a greater sense of meaning by depicting human life as having ultimate purpose [beyond itself and beyond its effects on the lives of others]." By contrast, natural-science students actually exhibited "the opposite responses," perhaps because they "view naturalism as a source of meaning," and thus (in a sense), worship nature *instead of* "the supernatural."

Many studies have shown that religiosity, belief in the supernatural, and specifically belief in a supernatural God, are far less prevalent amongst professional scientists than amongst the general population; and even that this tendency is more extreme amongst leading scientists than it is amongst the general scientific population. In other words: Religiosity (or faith, in any of its forms) clearly is based upon fear of death. The spirituality of a person like Albert Einstein or Charles Darwin is based on the universe as it is, not on the universe as they wish it to be. They feel no need to lie to themselves. This is partly because, rejecting faith, they reject authority, and therefore rely only upon themselves, for what they believe. They may trust certain people to report honestly to them, but they have faith in nothing and in no one, because they do rely ultimately only upon themselves, for what they believe. They are thus the ideal objective jurors, evaluating the evidence set before them.

Moreover, when the fear of death is low, there might be a tendency for a person to be less social. The part of the brain that deals with fear, the amygdala, also seems to make a person more social, or at least this might be indicated by a study in *Nature Neuroscience*, 26 December 2010, "Amygdala Volume and Social Network Size in Humans," which found that "Amygdala volume correlates with the size and complexity of social networks in adult humans." Two days later, *TIME* summarized these findings headlining "How to Win Friends: Have a Big Amygdala?" Consequently, an ideal juror – a scientist – would generally *not* be a very social person. This makes sense because a very social person would tend to be influenced by what other jurors think and therefore not be as likely to evaluate independently the information that's presented during trial, as a scientist would.

Three days later, on December 29th, London's *Daily Mail* headlined "Tory Voters Found to Have Larger 'Primitive' Lobe in Brain," and reported that Colin Firth (who was soon to win the Best Actor Oscar for *The King's Speech*) had commissioned a study which found that in "an MRI scan of the brain, the right amygdala – an ancient part of the brain – was larger in those people who described themselves as conservative." [continued]

People join a religion for many different reasons, but Paul recognized that the basic reason is fear of death (and similarly the phrase "deathbed conversion" is known everywhere). Paul wanted to scare the living daylights out of his members – he said these people would be beyond salvation if they didn't join and stay. In Judaism, this is done in order to get members to obey the law, so that God will favor them with heaven rather than with hell after death, and with support and defense of their lives prior to death. In Christianity, it's done in order to get members to have faith in Christ, so that God will favor them with heaven rather than with hell after death, and with God's approval (and thus

---

Then, *Current Biology* published the finished Firth-financed study, on 7 April 2011, "Political Orientations Are Correlated with Brain Structure in Young Adults," which "found that greater liberalism was associated with increased gray matter volume in the anterior cingulate cortex [which evolved about 15 million years ago in humans' evolutionary line], whereas greater conservatism was associated with increased volume in the right amygdala [which evolved about 150 million years ago]." Ryota Kanai and the other researchers reported that with about 75% accuracy a person's political orientation could be identified from MRI's showing the relative sizes of the anterior cingulate cortex (which produces decision-making ability in the face of contradictory information) predicting liberalism, versus the right amygdala (which produces fear and also sociability) predicting conservatism. So, yet again, an ideal juror (in this case, someone with the ability to make decisions in the face of inputs that contradict each other) would generally *not* be highly social.

Numerous studies over many decades (such as the many by Bob Altemeyer) had already established a solid positive correlation between religiosity and conservatism; and, therefore, if conservatives are more fear-motivated and more social, then it would be reasonable to expect that religious people also are. (Richard Traunmüller's 2008 study, "Religion als Resource Sozialen Zusammenhalts?" strongly confirms this expectation.) And if conservatives have less ability to function intelligently in the face of contradictory information (as the Firth-financed study would suggest), then religious people are likewise probably weak at this.

Consequently, both the social sciences and the biological sciences are developing information that will enable improved jury-selection. On the basis of current data, scientific and liberal individuals probably produce more-accurate (or "fairer") juries than do religious and conservative individuals. The numerous studies showing higher prejudices amongst both religious and conservative individuals are especially strong indicators that this is so.

protection) during life. In every religion, fundraising for the clergy is likewise done with this death-focused motivation by the members, so that joiners will belong to God's people (heading for heaven rather than hell, and enjoying God's protection throughout life). Eschatological (or death-focused) motivation is the foundation of any religion. Each faith has its tricks to spike this motivation. Paul knew the pattern; he merely applied it to the circumstances of the time (a time that was especially tumultuous, which made his end-times talk especially effective, like saying, "Buy heaven now, while you still can").

Some religions have variants of heaven and hell. For example, Buddhism has reincarnation and karma, but the basic concept is the same: Be a good person as the given religion defines "good," and you will go to a better situation after death; be a bad person, and you will go to a worse situation. Fear of death spikes faith in any religion.[72] This motivation metastasizes in some people – like in the 9/11 bombers, and in the Crusaders – within whom eagerness for heaven exceeds even the fear of death.

We remain in the Religious Age. The Scientific Age is only gestating and hasn't yet been born; and so, in our era, almost as much as in Paul's, the most effective way to sell things is still through skillful use of deceits; and thus Paul remains, even today, the model for success.

---

[72] J. Edward Wright's 2000 masterpiece, *The Early History of Heaven*, traces the development of the concept of heaven, and finds that it went back prior to Judaism. In particular (p. 25), "The Egyptians can be credited with having one of the earliest, if not the earliest concept of humans having a blessed afterlife in the heavenly realms." Virtually all religions believed that a heavenly place existed in which gods lived, but (p. 51), "Heaven as a place for humans to join the gods after death was, it seems, an Egyptian invention." That concept gradually found its way into later Scriptures of Judaism, and was then adopted (from both Jewish and non-Jewish sources) by Paul and his followers in their writings of the Christian Scriptures.

Removing the Sugar-Coating

To speak of a mere "parting of the ways" between Judaism and Christianity is to avoid coming to terms with Paul's actual legacy. For scholars not to acknowledge what Paul did, is for them not to recognize the scale of his actual achievement. He created Western Civilization: Christianity is Western Civilization's basis. He worshipped power (its *personification* in The Almighty), and he became as he hoped: the most powerful person in history.

This deception by Paul was allegedly in worship of the "Prince of Peace"; but the real aim was the peace of the graveyard, the peace that a conqueror brings, after his enemies have all been killed or otherwise subdued by force, which may include (as with Paul) deception – force that's applied against the mind (fraud), instead of against the body (violence). (There is also a *third* form of force, which is applied against one's property: theft.) According to the Jewish legend, which defined the mashiach, the peace that the "Prince of Peace" was supposed to bring was to arrive via his defeating the enemy upon the battlefield in war; it was to be peace via the sword, *not* via peaceful means. Jesus was no mashiach.

And so it has been; and Paul is his realm's true King, Christ's ventriloquist – reigning almost unnoticed from the side, but pleased nonetheless to be the *real* dictator, over an entire kingdom: his kingdom of mental slaves who have followed after him, such slaves they don't know the truth even about their master's identity. It's Paul, and not Jesus, whom they've *really* been serving.

Christians are, and have been, in fact, mental slaves to an enemy of the very person they *thought* they had worshipped.

This is how the moral base of our culture was created: by deceit. By fraud. By controlling people through controlling their thoughts. This is how our culture was created.

Paul's deceit started small, but it became enormous. His deceit began as a means to preserve his phenomenally successful career, but it metastasized naturally into a means for him to continue this success into the future, and for that success to become as big as possible, to continue growing even long after he died. Initially, Paul refused to circumcise his followers, because he knew that he'd lose them if he did, and because he knew that he'd get few if any new followers if he did. But his supreme focus on success became ultimately a cancer within his character, and consumed any decency he might possibly have had. (An obsession with success can be just as dangerous as an obsession with salvation.)

Despite scholars' myths about "the parting of the ways," Paul's separation from Judaism was actually extreme. For example, when he said in *2 Corinthians* 3:6, "The written law brings death, but the Spirit [Christ-faith] gives life," he was condemning the very thing – God's Law in the Torah – that was the most sacred thing *of all* to Jews, and he was saying that it's the exact opposite: the bringer of damnation. Paul couldn't be more extreme than that, because no one even possibly *could* be. Paul's hatred of Judaism, and of Jews (the believers in Judaism), was laser-like, focused *only* upon them, and unlike anything else in his entire universe of concern.

A prosecutor is handed the evidence by the police, and tries to construct from this evidence a case that serves as a juggernaut against the defense attorney's arguments. Scholars have amply presented Paul's defense; I am now presenting the prosecution case against Paul. The jurors make the ultimate judgment. The evidence about Paul has been presented, and is suitable now to be finally judged.

The myths can thus end here. This hoax, which worked for thousands of years during the Religious Age, is herewith exposed, and its exposure provides a suitable marker for the start of the Scientific Age – a marker indicating that, henceforth, science will, at last, dominate over faith.

Legal/Forensic Analysis a Logical Microscope

There have been many repeated references made here to certain lines in *Galatians* (e.g., 2:16) and to some of the other items of evidence (e.g, *Genesis* 17:14), and this work has therefore been "repetitious" in that sense. A legal/forensic reconstruction of events, or "theory of the case," often tends to be this way, because the objective of legal/forensic investigators is to extract, from a given (and sometimes small) "body of evidence," a historical narrative (or reconstruction of "the crime") which is as complete as possible, and this necessarily means that sometimes a single item of evidence will be cited in many different contexts, so as to extract from it – or to cite it in proving – a number of *different* facts about what had occurred. For this reason, the ratio of the information that's drawn from the items of evidence (or, in scholarly parlance, from the "sources") tends to be extremely high in legal/forensic analyses. A court may keep out of evidence many unreliable "hearsay" or other "sources," which a scholarly analysis would admit into evidence, but it will nonetheless seek to provide the most complete reconstruction of events that is possible, from the more-reliable sources. Consequently, a court seeks to extract the maximum of information from the minimum items of evidence, which are precisely those sources that are of the very highest reliability (or "trustworthiness"). And, similarly, the reconstruction you've just read here of the start of Christianity has aimed to cite only the best evidence, but to extract from that high-quality evidence the most complete description possible of the start of Christianity.

This exegesis or interpretation of *Galatians* has contained 41 times as many words (131,119) as does *Galatians* itself (3,231). (That 131,119 count *doesn't* include the word-count from the footnotes.) This 41 multiple doesn't reflect polluting Paul's letter by the opinions numerous selected scholars have expressed interpreting the letter, and by asserting that those selected scholars were correct in their interpretations of those particular lines, and that the scholars who disagreed (and who usually aren't even so much as mentioned by the given scholarly writer) were wrong in their interpretations. This interpretation hasn't at all been built upon the interpretations by others, but instead upon what Paul himself *said*, in *Galatians*, and in his six other authentic letters. Secondary reliance has been placed here upon less-reliable evidence, such as *Acts*, the Gospels, writings by Josephus and other historians, and so forth. In addition, there has been considerable citation here of passages in the Old Testament, whenever Paul was himself drawing from those particular passages in order to argue for his points, to his audience. In other words, the evidence here has been *only the evidence*, not opinions that selected other people have expressed regarding the evidence. Instead of amplifying Paul's words via polluting them by interpretations from numerous selected scholars, we've taken, in a metaphorical sense, a real 41x logical microscope to them, in order to be able to observe details, in his letter, which no one was able to see before (because they lacked this methodology). Furthermore, by drawing logically so close to this subject, we've been able to identify not only the explicit level of meanings, but also the deeper, logically implicit, level of meanings in them, which Paul's writing didn't assert, but instead actually displayed or exhibited.

For a simplified example of this method: it's like interpreting the assertion "This sentence is 100 words long," by discussing *not only* what it *asserts*, but *also* what it *displays* – which in this case is that that sentence is, in fact, *false*, because that sentence is actually only *six* words long. When an assertion displays one thing, and claims something that contradicts this, the thing it displays is generally true, and the speaker is generally a liar. When this pattern occurs time after time in a particular work, the author of that work *is* a liar, to an almost mathematical certainty. This analysis has been, not a *physical* microscope, such as Zacharias Jansen invented in

1595, but rather a *logical* microscope, which exposes the logical details and interrelationships (instead of the physical details and interrelationships) within the letter; and this logical magnification enables the reader *truthfully* to understand *Galatians*, at last, after 2,000 years of Paul's success in his hoax. These additional details are not the "deeper layer of meanings" such as scholars derive via piling opinions on top of opinions, but instead are an authentically deeper *level* of meanings, which only an authentic logical analysis of the best evidence can and does display. Instead of preserving interpretive problems via piling opinions on top of opinions, as scholars do, the aim of *any* science is to *solve* interpretive problems, so as to achieve understanding, not just needless confusions which help prop up mere faith. Whereas scholarship maximizes confusion, science minimizes confusion, and this is done via solving problems (instead of via *preserving* problems, as scholars do). The purpose here has been to solve problems concerning the start of Christianity.

Moreover, the strength of our logical microscope was even higher on the climax, *Galatians* 2:11-21, where Paul's mere 365 words describing this event that created Christianity were magnified by means of 18,751 words of text here analyzing it, a 51x logical magnification, which likewise didn't entail citing opinions, only facts. By 51x logical amplification of Paul's sparse description of this event, we described with reliable accuracy much important detail in human history's most important single event.

What's especially astounding in this case is the massive amount of evidence, all of it consistent, that Paul left to us – from his own (and/or scribe's) pen, no less. He actually convicted himself, far beyond any reasonable doubt; but only modern legal/forensic methodology is able to penetrate below the surface-level of his letters and thus expose his guilt, in what is and has been, in historical retrospect, by far the most successful and longest-lasting fraud in all of human history. To science, it's an open-and-shut case; but to faith, it's simply non-existent, because a person of faith believes whatever he wants to believe (in accord with psychologists' findings regarding "confirmation bias" or "motivated reasoning"), and because (as a religious person) what he *wants* to believe has nothing at all to do with what *is*. The gulf between science and faith is epistemological, a gulf separating opposite epistemologies.[73] Faith will always protect Paul and perpetuate his hoax; but, finally, a scientific approach is possible and is now available, and its findings display Paul's guilt via cascades of evidence, whose quality is of the highest.

Buried in *Galatians* is Paul's confession, and even more than that (because not *all* confessions are true), is actually Paul's *proof* of all significant details of his hoax. What *Galatians* displays is vastly more – and vastly more credible – than what *Galatians* asserts. But the assertions in inferior evidence (such as the Gospels, *Acts*, etc.) are even less credible than what *Galatians* asserts, and the next scientific challenge is to probe here into those other documents, likewise in a scientific way, by exposing what they display, not merely what they assert.

NOTE

A certain scholar wrote me after reading up through this point (the end of Chapter 3), and said that he disagreed with my view that "Paul refused to circumcise his followers, because he knew that he'd lose them if he did, and because he knew that he'd get few if any new followers if he did." His view was instead that "Paul refused to circumcise his followers, because he believed that God wanted to save as many Gentiles as possible in the end time that was at hand." I responded:

"Your interpretation (which is consistent with standard Christian views, which have been shaped by Paul's intentions) fails to explain the things that my text explains, including the internal contradictions within Paul's writings, and also the internal contradictions within (as well as the contradictions between) the Gospels (which will be discussed in the

---

[73]   Though trust might be appropriate, faith never is – it's never acceptable to a scientist. One shouldn't even have faith in a source that one trusts. Trust is merely a presumption of rightness when there is no overriding reason to doubt that presumed rightness. Trust is not faith: it's never a closed-minded assumption of a source's rightness. Trust is consistent with an open mind; faith is not. Faith is never acceptable to a scientist – not faith in anything nor anyone. Trust is appropriate in some circumstances, but faith never is.

following chapters). In other words: your interpretation fails the legal/forensic standard of offering a theory of the case which explains (or is consistent with) all of the evidence, even including any contradictions that exist or may exist within the evidence, both internally, and also between the various exhibits.

"In other words: your theory of the case fails.

"Furthermore: your theory presumes (or takes as an assumption) the viewpoint Paul is asserting; your theory doesn't even deal with the *possibility* that Paul was lying.

"Rather than analyzing Paul's views, you are simply taking on those views as your own, as Christians do because their views were actually shaped by Paul's deceits and inventions. You've paraphrased Paul, rather than analyzed him. This is no way to legal/forensically analyze evidence: The mere assumption, that people are speaking and writing with the intention to inform instead of with the intention to manipulate, has to be dropped, because such an assumption turns an 'investigation' into a really low-order sales-contest between attorneys who win or lose only on the basis of their skill as deceivers and totally disregarding (if not distorting) what the evidence shows, rather than into a real search to find the truth of what actually went on (such as legal/forensic rules are intended to enforce). The assumption that a person is telling the truth is like the assumption that a person is lying: it's unacceptable, because whether or not a person is telling the truth or lying has to be determined as a conclusion from the evidence, not asserted as an assumption. Taking it as an assumption discredits one's conclusions.

"Unsupported assumptions are not acceptable, and your interpretation is an unsupported assumption, which, on top of that, is proven false because Paul contradicted himself whenever convenient for him to do so. Without a doubt, Paul, when provided with a choice either to inform, or else to persuade by manipulating (outright lying, or else evasion), chose manipulation, and he even virtually admitted doing so when he said *1 Corinthians* 9:20-27. Paul tried to defend himself against that same charge when he said *Romans* 3:4-8. However, his statement there doesn't indicate that he wasn't a liar; only that he was considered to be a liar to such a pronounced extent that he was driven to deny it. Whether or not he was a manipulator is to be determined from the evidence, but this cannot be done simply by assuming either the truthfulness or else the deceptiveness of a given writer. Whether or not Paul was a liar is to be determined not by his confession (*1 Corinthians* 9:20-27) but by his numerous internal contradictions, all of which served his purposes as I have described, but not as in your theory. Your theory doesn't even *attempt* to explain his numerous self-contradictions; it's not a theory of the case, much less a good or likely-true theory of the case.

"Or, at least, that's what I think, unless you provide me with reasons for your view, not just state the view with the unspoken assumption that it explains all of the evidence including the internal contradictions within the evidence.

"I remain to be persuaded by you that your interpretation is a theory of the case, and that it is moreover the likeliest-true theory of the case. What you have presented here is simply a paraphrase of Paul. If there were no internal contradictions within Paul, and also no contradictions between Paul and what he was referring to (such as between *Galatians* 2:16 and *Genesis* 17:14), then it would be possible for a mere paraphrase of Paul to constitute a theory of the case (an interpretation of Paul that's worthy of being considered by jurors). But that's obviously not the situation here.

"So, please tell me what your argument is."

He responded: "I do not deny the deceitful elements in Paul's argumentation. ... You are right in claiming that a theory should explain all of the evidence. The problem is what a scholar decides to put in the center. In the case of Paul taken up in your work the problem is whether he was cheating his converts or not. ... [My question of you is:] What kind of liar is Paul? Is he like a man selling used cars, knowing that they are in bad condition, or is he more like a man courting a woman, trying always to show his best side and hide his weaknesses? In other words, is he himself involved in his lie, part of the lie itself, or is he just trying to make profit out of his lie?"

I replied: "He was like most liars: He lied in order to succeed.

"Up until Peter and the other 'agents from James' visited him in the event recounted in *Galatians* 2:11-21, he might not have had to lie in any fundamental way in order to succeed. (As I said, 'Paul's deceit started small, but it became very big.') Three years before that incident, he wrote *2 Corinthians* 12:1-7, and admitted that he didn't know whether the Holy Ghost's appearance to him on the Damascus road in about the year 33 had been real or only imaginary. But after the event Paul recounted in *Galatians* 2:11-21, he could no longer admit this doubt, and instead he said in *1 Corinthians* 15:14, 'If Christ was not resurrected, then we have nothing to preach.' None of Paul's accounts of his experience of the Resurrection except *2 Corinthians* 12:1-7 was written prior to the event he recounted in *Galatians* 2:11-21, and this is why only *2 Corinthians* 12:1-7 admits that maybe he hadn't really encountered Jesus, not even Jesus's ghost. I think that *1 Corinthians* 9:20-27 accurately admits what kind of liar Paul was. However, he covers it over, there, with phrases about how it was just different ways of living, depending on circumstances – but this device, vagueness, was employed merely to present himself or his case in a less clear and less unattractive light, because he knew that followers are *not* attracted if you tell them *outright* 'Say whatever you need to say in order to win.'

"I look at the most successful politicians today, and at the most successful financiers and other top businesspeople of today – certainly this is so in the United States, where the sales people at mortgage brokerages were told to say whatever they needed to say in order to win the sale – and those top people seem to me to be basically like Paul was, except that Paul (after the year 49) worked for far higher stakes: not just his career, but the religious future of the world. Paul, then, was more ambitious, and also more successful, than anyone else in history. And he had to be extraordinarily cunning in order to be able to win. But otherwise, he was quite normal.

"In *Galatians* 2:2, Paul said that he refused to lose life's race; he was determined to be a winner. In *1 Corinthians* 9:24-27, he said that he was determined to win at all costs, and he made clear that he was proud of this and recommended that his followers be like himself in this regard.

"Do you think that you now understand what kind of liar he was?"

His response merely paraphrased Paul: He said that Paul's objective was to save souls. "Paul's rejection of the Torah in his Gentile mission was due to his apocalypticism and his Christ mysticism. ... I think that his yearning for success was subordinated to these motifs. I think you have a point here, but I would not set aside everything else that we have in Paul's letters in order to make him a liar." To support this view, he denied that *2 Corinthians* 12:1-7 was about Paul's conversion-experience of Jesus's ghost. He said that there was no way to know what it referred to, other than that "It is one of his visions and revelations of the Lord (Jesus)."

Part One Appendix:
Galatians Text through 2:21

for reference[74]

1:1 [From] Paul, whose call to be an apostle came not via man or by means of man, but via Jesus Christ and God the Father, who raised him from the dead.

1:2 And [this letter comes also from] all brethren who are with me, [and it is addressed] to the churches ["*ekklesiais*"] in Galatia:

1:3 May you all be granted grace and peace by God our Father, and by the Lord Jesus Christ,

1:4 Who sacrificed himself to free us from our sins during the present evil age, in accord with the plan of God the Father.

1:5 To God alone belongs all glory, forever and ever! Amen.

---

[74] For the lines after 2:21, see the parenthetical note at the end of this Appendix.

1:6 I am shocked that you are so quickly abandoning the one who called you by the grace of Christ and that you are turning instead to another gospel.

1:7 But of course, there isn't really any other gospel, and it's only a perversion of the gospel of Christ, and has been offered by some others, so as to mislead you.

1:8 However, even if we or an angel from heaven were to proclaim a gospel contrary to the one which we have taught you, then such a person should be condemned to hell!

1:9 I shall repeat what I've said before: If anyone preaches to you a different gospel, he should go to hell!

1:10 Do you think I'm just trying to please people? It's only God I'm trying to please. If I were pleasing people, I wouldn't be serving Christ.

1:11 For I want you to know, my brethren, that the gospel I teach isn't of human origin.

1:12 For I didn't receive this gospel from a human source; I received it from a revelation by Jesus Christ.

1:13 You've probably heard how I behaved in my earlier life, as a Jew, how I persecuted mercilessly the church of God, and tried to destroy it.

1:14 I was more advanced than many Jews of my age in the practice of Judaism, and was much more devoted to Jewish traditions, the traditions of my ancestors.

1:15 But when God, who had cast his grace upon me before I was born,

1:16 Saw fit and was so pleased with me as to reveal His Son to me, in order that I might proclaim Him among the Gentiles as the gospel [the good news of personal salvation], I didn't then seek counsel from any human being,

1:17 Nor did I go to Jerusalem to those who were apostles before me, but I immediately travelled to Arabia, and then returned to Damascus.

1:18 Three years after returning, I finally went to Jerusalem, to make the acquaintance of Peter, and to stay with him for fifteen days.

1:19 But I didn't see any other apostle, except for the Lord's brother James.

1:20 In writing this to you, I swear to God I'm not lying!

1:21 Then I went into the regions of Syria and Cilicia.

1:22 And throughout this time, I remained unseen by the churches of Christ that are located in Judea.

1:23 They only heard people say, "The man who formerly persecuted us is now proclaiming the very faith he had tried to destroy."

1:24 And so, because of me, they glorified God.

2:1 Then, after fourteen years [away from Jerusalem], I went again to Jerusalem, this time with Barnabas and Titus.

2:2 I went because of a revelation, and I presented the gospel that I preach among the Gentiles. I presented this privately, to the reputed leaders. I didn't want to have been running, and to be running, in vain.

2:3 Moreover, even Titus, who was with me, wasn't required to be circumcised, though he's a Greek [who isn't circumcised].

2:4 False brethren had been secretly smuggled in to spy on the freedom [from Judaism's commandments] that we enjoy in Jesus Christ, and they wanted to enslave us [to those commandments].

2:5 But we stood our ground, so that the truth of the gospel would be protected for you.

2:6 The supposed leaders – and what they actually were makes no difference to me, because God doesn't judge by such outward appearances – made no new suggestions to me.

2:7 On the contrary, they recognized that God had assigned me to carry the gospel to the uncircumcised, just as Peter had been entrusted with spreading the gospel to the circumcised.

2:8 For God had given each of us our assignments.

2:9 James, Peter, and John, the reputed leaders, recognized my divine assignment, and offered, to me and Barnabas, the right hand of fellowship, and agreed that we should work among the Gentiles, while they worked among the circumcised.

2:10 They requested only one thing: that we ought to keep in mind the poor in their group, and this was something I was actually eager to do.

2:11 But when Peter came to Antioch, I opposed him in public, because he was clearly wrong.

2:12 Before some men who had been sent by James came, Peter was dining with the Gentile brothers, but when these men arrived, he withdrew from the table and refused to dine with the Gentiles, because he feared the circumcision party.

2:13 The other Jewish brothers joined Peter in this cowardice, so that even Barnabas joined their hypocrisy.

2:14 When I saw that they weren't honest [in expressing their support for the gospel of Christ], I said to Peter, in front of them all:

"You are a Jew [i.e., circumcised], yet you have been living like a Gentile [i.e., as if you weren't a Jew]. So, how can you try to force Gentiles to imitate [born] Jews?

2:15 "Although you and I are Jews by birth and not Gentile sinners [i.e., not *non*-signers to the Jewish covenant, under the signatory law *Genesis* 17:11&14],

2:16 "We know that a person is viewed favorably by God only via Christ-faith, never by following God's Law. Even we [you and I] have believed in Jesus Christ in order to be viewed favorably by God via that Christ-faith, instead of by adhering to God's Law. For we cannot please God by following God's Law.

2:17 "However, if our effort to please God by our union with Christ causes us to sin as the Gentiles do [since they didn't even *sign* the covenant], does this mean that Christ is assisting us to sin? Of course not!

The Event that Created Christianity

291

2:18 "For, if I were to rebuild the system [the Law] that I have torn down, then I would violate the [purpose of the] Law [which is personal salvation].

2:19 "I am dead to the Law, killed by the Law itself, in order that I might live for God. I have joined Christ's death on the cross,

2:20 "So that it is no longer I who live, but Christ, who lives in me. I live this life by faith in the Son of God, who loved me and gave his life for me.

2:21 "I don't nullify God's grace; for, if God views a person favorably upon the basis of a man's following God's Law, then Christ died for nothing!"

(After 2:21: Everything else in *Galatians* is post-climax, and therefore readers are referred to their Bibles for that. Up through 2:21, Paul has completed his description of the event that created Christianity, and of what led up to it. Only a summary of 3-6 is offered here, as a quick review of our own Chapter 3: *Galatians* 3 through 6 consists of Paul's shoddy arguments from Jewish Scripture and from other Jewish sources, *pro-forma* in order for him to seem authentic to his followers, who thought he had converted them to Judaism. Also, 3-6 refers to some of the context that caused Paul to write this letter, such as 5:2-12, which recapitulates his rage in 1:6-9, but now explicitly mentions, in 5:2, circumcision as the issue concerning this letter; and, in 5:7, an anonymous proponent of circumcision, who had been the spur to Paul's writing this letter, and who was, in 1:8-9, the object of Paul's condemnation who "should be condemned to hell!")

The Evidence, Part Two:
Christianity in Light of
Galatians

4. The Gospels as Pauline Propaganda: How They Carried Out Paul's Agenda

If the people who wrote the four canonical Gospel accounts of Jesus as the Christ were followers of Paul rather than of Jesus, then their agenda was also Paul's rather than Jesus's, and so all or virtually all of the New Testament can be truthfully understood *only* as extensions of Paul's agenda, and *not* of Jesus's. This would mean that the New Testament would be an extension or embellishment of Paul's sale on heaven (*Galatians* 2:11-16), the event that created Christianity. And thus, Paul would have become Christ's ventriloquist, *through these men*. The purpose here will be to document that this was, in fact, the case. Not only was it so in respect to Paul's core purpose of promoting the supremacy of faith over Law, but it also was so with respect to the transference of the guilt for the Crucifixion from the Romans (including subsequently the Emperors' adopted religious arm, the Roman Catholic Church) onto the Jews, and with respect to all other key aspects of Paul's theological and "historical" program, as we now intend to show: the Gospel writers continued and promoted this sale.

Robert M. Grant's 1963 *A Historical Introduction to the New Testament* said (in Chapter 6): "The most important question of all" regarding the New Testament documents, and

their authors, is "why they wrote, and this is the ultimate
question of New Testament study. ... What impelled their
authors to write" these works? Most of the scholarly
speculation on the authorship of these documents concerns
the identity, the name, of the given author; but what's actually
far more important is the author's *motive*: What was his
agenda, which guided the "historical" account he presented?
That's the question addressed here; and its answer is: His
agenda was Paul's, but his *execution* of that objective was
shaped by the given writer's *particular circumstances*. The four
different Gospel-writers wrote in different times from each
other, and faced different challenges of persuasion, which
depended upon their respective surroundings.

Paul's followers, who wrote the Gospels decades after
Paul's letters and probably after his death, went far beyond
Paul in providing detail to the myth of Paul's *1 Thessalonians*
2:14-15 and *Galatians* 6:12, that "the Jews" crucified Christ; this
crucifixion was just a single event, and the public had no way
to know its details, and so virtually anything that the Gospel-
writers said about it would have been believable in their
relatively late era, if they included – as they did – such basics
as the "King of the Jews" charge against Jesus and his
crucifixion – things that were, evidently, so well known even
long afterwards, so that these facts couldn't be explicitly
denied without the writers thereby exposing themselves as
self-evidently fraudulent. Likewise, what Jesus preached, and
especially his core message, were, in that era, still too well
known for the Gospel writers to be able to place *explicitly* into
Jesus's mouth Paul's core supersessionist message (replacing
Judaism); and the Gospel-writers judiciously avoided doing
so. Paul himself had always given, instead, only contorted
Jewish Scriptural "reasons" for his overthrowing of the
covenant, and he never cited Jesus's sayings to "justify" that
position; and it seems that, even long after Jesus's death, it
was really not practicable to place supersessionist words
directly into Jesus's mouth. The *only* effective constraint at that
time upon the mythologizers was that such lies in the Gospel-

writers' works would have immediately discredited their accounts. This is the reason why Paul's small-"g" gospel of salvation by faith alone (and God's grace), as the core message of this actually Roman "Christ" he was creating, didn't end up being placed by the Gospel writers directly into the mouth of the Jewish "Messiah." These hoaxers went as far as they could in Paulifying their "Christ" – but, even in their era, there still remained some limits.

By the time when the Gospel accounts were being written, Paul's personal enemies – especially James, but also the other authentic disciples of Jesus – were no longer around to constitute a threat; only the Jews were. They were saying that Jesus wasn't the Messiah. *No bigger threat to the beliefs of Paul's followers could possibly have existed.* Thus, just for Jews to *remain* Jews constituted a danger to Paul's new faith. Who were the "experts" on the Messiah, if *not* the Jews? And *they* were saying that Jesus *wasn't* him! They thus needed to be marginalized, if not killed: They had to be eliminated *somehow.* Consequently, Paul's anti-Judaism and anti-Semitism figured far more powerfully as influences shaping the Gospel accounts about Christ and His supposed words than was the case in *Paul's* writings, but there was no *similar* need for the Gospel writers to make equally overt, in *their* "histories," Paul's implicit *personal* attacks against James and the other disciples. This is why the Gospels omit details that would flesh-out the implicit attacks Paul had leveled against James and the other leaders in *Galatians* 6:12, and 2 *Corinthians* 11:3-5&12-15, and 1 *Thessalonians* 2:15-16, which blamed the Deicide upon those particular individuals and called them deceivers who had been sent by Satan. (Paul condemned them directly to hell in *Galatians* 1:8-9.) Instead, the Gospel writers' aim regarding those people was chiefly just to *ignore* (or deny) their leadership roles as much as possible, especially James's leading role and succession after Jesus's death, and retrospectively to re-assign James's top leadership role to Peter, since he had been Paul's *own* predecessor and mentor in the mission to the Gentiles, and was therefore the sole possible legitimator of Paul. Thus, James, the brother and chief disciple of Jesus, was simply written *entirely out* of these "historical" accounts of the living Jesus, so that scholars, even today, still debate whether or not this James was among Jesus's disciples while Jesus was alive. (Paul's followers created a second "James" whom they said was one of the twelve, so that the James who was referred to in Paul's writing would *lack* such authority.) And Peter, the predecessor of Paul, was denominated by these Gospel writers as having been Jesus's *favorite* disciple and first Pope.

Mark was the earliest-written Gospel, and it established the general pattern for the other three; many of its lines even became copied in *Matthew* and in *Luke*. And all four of these "biographies" of Christ picked up on Paul's anti-Semitism, from 1 *Thessalonians* 2:14-16 and elsewhere, and built that into an important part of their stories about Jesus's life, and especially about Jesus's death.

The four Gospel accounts placed into the fictitious Christ's mouth the real Paul's agenda. Thus, Paul became Christ's ventriloquist, and Paul's followers performed crucial roles in making that happen: They wrote what "Jesus" "spoke." This is how it came to be that, when Christ spoke, it was Paul's voice and words that came out. And so, unlike the religionist, the scientist sees and hears the *puppeteer* – the ventriloquist, *not* the puppet.

That guy selling all of us Christianity – Paul's "gospel of Christ," the "Good News" about salvation-on-the-cheap, or heaven on sale – wasn't really Jesus of Nazareth, but *only* Paul of Tarsus.

5. Pauline Signs in *Mark*

The *chief* Pauline purpose was the replacement of circumcision by baptism as the religion's entrance-ritual, so as to free Paul and his followers from having to expel most of their "converts," and to enable them to win substantial numbers of future converts.

For this reason, Mark starts right out with the story of Jesus's baptism by John the Baptist. Jesus's own circumcision as a Jewish infant can be taken for granted, and was by Mark's readers during his own time, but it is irrelevant to Mark's story, and furthermore it emphasizes Jesus's being a Jew, and is thus suppressed – not mentioned. Mark's Jesus is the mythological Christian one, whose assumed Christianity started with his baptism, in accord with Paul's own central purpose of changing the initiation-ritual. Consequently, the fact that Mark OPENS with the CHRISTIANIZATION-RITUAL[75] is itself extremely significant in displaying the propagandist's agenda. Subsequently, in 10:38-9, "Jesus" asserts that his disciples will be baptized like himself. This further cements baptism as the faith's initiation-ritual.

---

[75]   The source of this Christian ritual is the Jewish ritual bath known as the "mikveh" (which had perhaps itself been inspired, or else institutionalized, by such passages as *Ex.* 19:10-11, *Lev.* 8:6 & 15:18, and *Num.* 19:13&20). [continued]

Another Pauline purpose – though actually a LESSER one (despite scholars presuming otherwise) – was the affirmation of Paul's rationalization for this abolition of circumcision as the faith's initiation-ritual: Paul's rationalization, of course, was the cancellation of the Jewish covenant or "the Law," and the covenant's replacement by Paul's own manufactured "gospel of Christ," salvation by pure faith-and-grace instead of by obedience to God's laws or commandments. This affirmation by "Jesus" is found in *Mark* 8:35, 9:23, 9:47 and 10:17-21. 16:16 was added by a later writer, and repeats the affirmation. Passage 2:6-7 presents as Jesus's first enemies "some teachers of the Law," so as to suggest that Paul's enemies had also been Jesus's own foes. The second appearance of Jesus's enemies occurs in 2:24; this time, his opponents are identified as "Pharisees" who assert that what Jesus is doing is "against our Law." The incident ends in 3:6, in which verse these same Pharisees go to Herod's people to plot Jesus's death. Then, in 3:22, "some teachers of the Law" declare Jesus to "have the devil in him!" This charge is repeated by them in 3:30. Again in 7:1-15, "some Pharisees and teachers of the Law" condemn him and he reciprocates. 7:21-23 directly implies Paul's own point that the cause of evil is lack of faith, lack of what's "inside a person," or else the wrong faith inside a person, rather than any lack of obedience to the Law. 9:19 presents "Jesus" explicitly asserting the importance of faith by accusing the Jewish crowd, "How unbelieving you people are! How long must I put up with you?" 11:18 has "the chief priests and the teachers of the Law

---

Paul's followers selected as their replacement of circumcision (since an initiation-ritual was still felt to be constructive, to enhance members' feeling that they *were* members of something, to tie these gulls emotionally to their organization), a safe and painless Jewish ritual, which had already been widely employed in Paul's congregations in lieu of circumcision. The born Jews who were objecting to Paul's men's not being circumcised were probably somewhat mollified by Paul's "cleansing" of these non-signers via the mikveh bath (due to its being a Jewish ceremony), and so it's highly likely that Paul's men had been "baptized" anyway, even prior to Paul's removing these men from Judaism and bringing them into his new faith.

... looking for some way to kill Jesus." 14:1 repeats the charge. These verses could very possibly have been concocted on the basis of Paul's own earlier-written *Galatians* 6:12, if not *1 Thessalonians* 2:15-16.

As part of this second purpose, Mark even presents his "Jesus" as asserting, in 7:14-19, that Judaism's food laws, the kosher laws, are invalid: that *no* food is sinful to eat, because only what comes out of a person can be sinful, what goes into a person cannot even possibly be sinful. This extends from Paul's repeated injunction that what's important is what's inside a person, not what's outside. Especially interesting here is that this "Jesus" isn't saying that the *circumcision law* is invalid: such words weren't placed into his mouth, for two reasons: First: Everyone in Mark's time knew that Jesus would never have said that Judaism's signature law was invalid. Anyone whom any Jews considered might possibly be the mashiach would never have said such a thing, because that would have stopped the aspiring mashiach's chances cold. Second, Paul's followers had already been instructed, by Paul (*1 Corinthians* 8-10), that the kosher laws should be followed whenever dining with a law-observant Jew. This "Jesus" was simply reiterating that God didn't demand such observance – that it was only a practical matter, just as Paul had said (though by using a different argument). Mark was fully consistent with Paul's supersessionism.

Similarly, 10:9 asserts that God's command in *Deuteronomy* 24:1, permitting a man to divorce his wife, is nullified by a command from "Jesus" saying "What God has joined together cannot be broken apart by mankind." This alleged statement from Jesus is exceptional in its being essentially duplicated by something Paul alleged Jesus to have said: *1 Corinthians* 7:10-11 asserts, similarly, that Jesus had commanded prohibition of all divorces. Consequently, since Paul's is the most authoritative evidence that exists upon the subject of earliest Christianity and of the people who had known the living Jesus, this alleged statement from Jesus is more likely authentic than are Jesus-statements that were alleged only in the Gospels by Paul's followers. Still, however, the confidence-level here is low, because this statement that Paul attributes to Jesus is consistent with Paul's agenda against James, of separating Jesus from Judaism. If this alleged Jesus-statement is authentic, it would provide additional depth to James's predicament: James's brother Jesus, in that case, wasn't unambiguously clear in strictly supporting Judaism. To this tiny extent, we cannot know whether Paul's *coup d'état* against James was 100% traitorous against Jesus. It's possible that Jesus was a less than fully strict Jew, even though a respected rabbi. What's certain is that Jesus was never anything but a Jew. In any event, *Mark* 10:9 reinforces Paul here.

However, if Jesus actually did assert that the same restriction against a wife's divorcing her husband applied also in the opposite direction, and restricted a man from divorcing his wife, then Jesus wasn't actually subtracting from Jewish Law, but adding to it – applying it to men, and not *only* to women. So, he still wouldn't have been inclined in Paul's direction, but, in fact, in the *opposite* direction: stricter even than the Torah.

A third Pauline purpose was the Deification of Jesus as Christ – the extension of the Jewish messiah-concept beyond its authentically Jewish, purely political, base as the Scripturally foretold Davidic restorer of Israeli independence, so that Jesus became instead a supernatural Godly being, worshipped in direct violation of the first three of the Ten Commandments. This Pauline agenda is promoted in the following: 13:26 states that Jesus "will appear in the clouds with great power and glory, and will send the angels to the four corners of the earth." 13:31 has "Jesus" saying, "heaven and earth will pass away, but my words won't." 14:61-2 has "Jesus" affirming that he is Messiah, Son of God, and Son of Man, who will soon be "seated at the right side of the Almighty and coming with the clouds of heaven," thereby transposing an allegorical non-

Torah (i.e., non-Pentateuch), and therefore non-authoritative, Jewish scriptural verse, *Psalms* 110, into being a literal and core authoritative Scriptural commitment of this entirely new, Christian, faith. Furthermore, Jesus is variously called "Son of God" (1:1, 3:11, 5:7, 9:7, 14:61, 15:39); "Son of Man" (14:62) synonymously with that "Son of Man" as a god who possesses the power to deliver a general forgiveness for an individual's sins (2:5-12), "Son of Man" who is "Lord even of the Sabbath (2:28), "Son of Man" who will come in "the glory of his Father with the holy angels"; and, in 9:4-9, simultaneously, both the God-anointed "Son of God" and "Son of Man," in a sense that EVEN the Jewish prophets Moses and Elijah failed to attain. It's important to reiterate, in this context, that Jews did not WORSHIP their prophets such as Moses; the first three of the Ten Commandments forbade that. In 4:38-41, "Jesus" commands the wind and the waves to become still, and they immediately comply. Also, in 5:19, "Jesus" performs a miracle and then says to the beneficiary, "tell your family how much the Lord has done for you." In 6:52 and 8:21, Jesus's disciples fail to grasp the true significance of Jesus's miracles, the implication being that they fail to recognize his Godly powers.

A fourth Pauline purpose was the fraudulent portrayal of the Deicide-charge against "the Jews," instead of against "the Romans" whose favor, for his new religion, Paul and his followers hoped ultimately to win. This goal was embodied in 10:33-4, 11:18, 14:55, and 15:13. The original for it was Paul's own *1 Thessalonians* 2:14-16 (which will be our subject in Chapter 7). Paul also promoted this smear in *Galatians* 6:12, and (as was discussed in fn. 25, the last of the three footnotes to our discussion of *Galatians* 1:14) in *1 Corinthians* 11:23.

A fifth Pauline purpose was the denigration of Jesus's authentic apostles, since those people were Paul's own enemies after the circa-50 CE split. Even Peter was rebuked as "Satan" in 8:33. In 7:17-19, Jesus rebukes his disciples as being just as overly respectful of the Law, and as insufficiently respecting of faith, as are other Jews. 10:41-45 presents Jesus rebuking his disciples for seeking to have rank and status

among themselves, perhaps the intended implication being
that a later "follower," perhaps EVEN one such as Paul who
never MET the living Jesus, might, in fact, become their
SUPERIOR in the eyes of God. (Also, this recapitulates such
Pauline passages as *Galatians* 2:6&9, which played down the
importance of the group's leaders.) 14:27-31 presents Jesus
predicting that all of his actual disciples will "run away and
leave me." Paul had already vaguely alleged in *Galatians* 6:12
that the disciples of Jesus in Jerusalem were the individuals
guilty of the Crucifixion, and this was as far as Paul was able
safely to go, during his early era, to identify the specific
"Jews" in *1 Thessalonians* 2:15 he alleged to have killed Jesus.
Mark picked up on this by claiming, in 14:27-31&66-72, that
"all of the disciples" refused to speak up for Jesus at trial, and
that Peter particularly refused. (James wasn't mentioned there,
because Paul's followers wrote him entirely out of their
"histories" of the disciples' group.) Mark, in his later era, went
yet further, in 14:10-11, picking up on Paul's insinuation in *1
Corinthians* 11:23 that some unnamed person had "betrayed"
(= "handed over") Jesus, by Mark's adding specifically that
Judas had "betrayed" (= "handed over") Jesus to the chief
priests. And (as the footnote to our discussion of *Galatians*
1:14, which was just referred to, had mentioned) Paul used
there – and Mark then *copied* from him – the term that in their
time had two meanings ("handed over" and "betrayed") and
which scholars *subsequently* translated predominantly as
"betrayed" (thus transforming Judas into the now-legendary
archetypal traitor). This was another of Paul's tricks, similar to
his using "ekklesia" instead of "sunagoge" or "threskeia"; and
it was similarly copied by all of the Gospel-writers, and then
spread about by scholars. (However, the evidence is
overwhelming that Paul *himself* actually *was* traitorous to
Jesus. Though there is no evidence that Judas was traitorous to
Jesus, Paul *certainly* was: not merely "*a*" traitor to Jesus, but
the *ultimate* traitor, in all of history, for his turning the very
name and identity of "Jesus" into a mighty weapon against
Jesus's religion – against both Jesus's fundamental belief *as* a

Jew, and also against Jesus's Jewish *people* for whom Jesus had courageously sacrificed his life.)

A sixth Pauline purpose was the condemnation of Jesus's birth-family, since they actually led the apostles, and since Jesus appointed his brother James (Paul's chief enemy) to be his successor. This objective was directly advanced by 3:31-5 and 6:4. Furthermore, both 10:29-30 and 13:12-13 suggest that the disowning of one's birth-family can be justifiable in the service of Jesus. 12:35-7 has Jesus actually denying that biological descent from King David is a prerequisite to becoming the Jewish mashiach. This implication separates Jesus from even the prophetic ancestral foundations of his own asserted mission, and was evidently so extreme that both *Matthew* and *Luke* explicitly denied what Mark had here merely implied, and instead they directly asserted that Jesus had biologically descended from King David.

A seventh Pauline purpose was the implication that Peter, not James, was designated by Jesus to be the leading disciple. This implication was embodied in 8:29 and 14:29-31. It was reinforced by placing Peter first in the sequence of three – Peter, James, and John – each time that the three were mentioned together, in 5:37, 9:2, 13:3, and 14:33. (In Jewish scriptures, the Old Testament, the routine was to mention the highest-status person first in any list.) On this basis, the writer of *Matthew* subsequently made Peter's primacy explicit in *Matthew* 16:18. However, *Mark* was written too early for any such *explicit* statement of that to be credible; when *Mark* was written, explicit assertion that Peter instead of James led the group would have been too widely recognized as fraudulent.

An eighth Pauline purpose, in line with Paul's own *Romans* 13:1-7, though less blatant than that, was the affirmation of Roman Imperial authority that's indicated in Mark's verse 12:17, alleging that Jesus instructed Jews to pay their taxes to Rome, and, less directly, granting the Emperor the authority to make the laws generally for Jews. This line in

Mark, 12:17, "Render to Caesar what is Caesar's, and to God what is God's," wasn't merely copied in *Matthew* 22:21 and in *Luke* 20:25, but it was also one of the most important of all the concessions to the Roman Emperor which Paul's followers made in their "historical" accounts of their mythological "Christ." Although Paul's followers, in this line, didn't include all of the concessions to the Emperor that Paul had made in *Romans* 13:1-7 (especially, Paul's followers didn't assert here that the Emperor was God's *appointed agent* to make and to enforce the laws), those followers did make the central concession that Rome demanded, and that Judaism was constitutionally opposed to accepting – these men granted Rome the authority to determine what was the constitution or basic Law which was binding upon Jews.

This laid the foundation for constitutional democracies ultimately to emerge (the American Revolution, etc.), because it separated the moral realm from the legal realm, and made whatever the ruler dictated to be law, into an *automatic surrogate* for God's will, without reference to any Scriptural commandments (or laws) whatsoever. Jews couldn't do that. On 4 September 1931, the Council of the League of Nations, and later the United Nations, required that Jews accept equal rights for religious and other minorities in order to control Israel, and so this demand was accepted, but Jews avoided explicit institutionalization of it: they avoided violation of the Torah, by avoiding to write an Israeli constitution, which either would have complied with the Torah as the *ultimate* constitution of Israel, and been discriminatory, or else civil war among Jews would have resulted, with conservatives demanding a constitution subordinate to the Torah as the *real* and sectarian constitution, and with liberals demanding a *non-*Jewish and secular constitution. Since Jews had been a persecuted religious minority everywhere, they embraced minority rights in modern Israel's early phase, though the Torah might prohibit such equality. But in the years after independence, Israel increasingly came into conflict with the

UN for violations of its commitments to equality. Muslims in
the occupied territories of Israel are especially violated in their
rights guaranteed under international law. And Muslim-
majority nations similarly run into huge democratic-
constitutional problems, because the Islamic faith – like the
Jewish faith – claims that any law which violates Scripture is
morally invalid. Paul's breaking the law-God bond didn't
create democracy, but it created the *possibility* for democracy
to emerge in a religious culture. This was Paul's only positive
contribution, and it resulted not from good intention, but from
his need to accommodate future Emperors. It's the basis for
constitutional democracies anywhere in the world – even in
majority-non-Christian countries – because majority-Christian
countries created the League of Nations, the UN, and all of
modernity. Furthermore, theocratic faiths, such as Judaism
and Islam, are intrinsically hostile toward democracy. Paul
freed his followers from that dictatorial-theocratic
commitment.

A ninth Pauline purpose was to assert the Resurrection,
because otherwise Paul's sole connection to Jesus wouldn't
even exist. Apparently, Paul's assertion that he had met the
risen Jesus was such an extraordinary claim, in its own time,
so that others of Jesus's followers at the same time weren't
making similar allegations, inasmuch as the earliest
manuscripts of the first-written Gospel, *Mark*, didn't include
it. The ending, 16:9-20, wasn't included until later manuscripts
of *Mark*, when none of the founders were still alive to be able
to contradict it. If the people who had known Jesus during his
life had been saying that they'd seen Jesus after his death, then
presumably this ending to the earliest-written Gospel would
have been included in the original version; but it wasn't. And,
therefore, the *addition* of that passage served an important
Pauline purpose. (Since the other Gospels were written later
than the original *Mark*, at a time when all of the founders were
already long-since dead, they included the Resurrection. The
addition of the Resurrection to *Mark* occurred much later than

the other Gospels, to which the Resurrection was an intrinsic part.)

A tenth Pauline purpose (based upon such passages as *1 Thessalonians* 4:15-5:3), was to quote Jesus as predicting imminent end times, as in *Mark* 13:7-37. Paul was trying to scare people to convert to his new religion; if they didn't convert quickly enough to Paul's Christianity, Jesus might return and consign them to hell even before they die. *Mark* even borrowed some of Paul's imagery: Whereas *1 Thessalonians* 5:3 says that the end "will come as suddenly as the pains that a woman experiences in child-birth, and no one will escape" being judged when it comes, *Mark* 13:8 quotes "Jesus" as saying, "These things are like the first pains in childbirth." This "Jesus" closes (13:36-37): "If he comes suddenly, you mustn't be caught sleeping. So, I say to you what I say to all: Watch out!" *Mark* merely amplified upon Paul's "Jesus," by writing the words of Paul's "Christ."

For these ten reasons, *Mark* cannot be seen as a Jewish document, but only as a Christian – that is to say, Pauline – one. Even though *Mark* is probably the first-written of the canonical Gospels (and I would place *Luke* as probably second, and *Matthew* as third), it must have been written after the destruction of the Jewish Temple that occurred in 70 CE, inasmuch as 13:1-2 refers to this event. Many scholars, unaccountably, don't consider this to be evidence of a post-70 compositional date, but, apparently, prefer, instead, to believe in the existence of supernatural powers of prophecy, and to attribute here such supernatural powers to Jesus as Christ. Even more oddly, some of the very same scholars who implicitly reason this way, nonetheless attribute the similar passages in *Luke* (21:5-6), and/or in *Matthew* (24:1-2) to their authors HAVING written AFTER the destruction of Jerusalem. Importantly, Jesus in this passage is quoted as speaking of that destruction of Jerusalem and massacre of Jews in a FAVORABLE light, as being God's retribution, even though it was ACTUALLY Rome's retribution against the Jewish revolt; and this passage, which pits Jesus against the Jews, thus reinforces yet again, and very strongly, Paul's own *Romans* 13:1-7. By implication, scholars who accept the supernatural interpretation of *Mark* 13:1-2 are thereby historicizing Jesus's there-alleged RESPECT for Rome's Emperor as being an agent of God, and Jesus's there-alleged HATRED of the multitude of Jews whom that Emperor's forces slaughtered on that occasion.

 Mark embodies RICHLY the Pauline agenda.

6. Pauline Signs in *Matthew, Luke* and *John*

Of course, *Matthew,* being largely COPIED from *Mark,*[76] absorbed much of Mark's Pauline agenda. However, many scholars deny *Matthew*'s Paulinism specifically on account of *Matthew* 5:17-20 & 19:17, explicit affirmation of "the Law" despite Paul's having strongly condemned salvation-through-obedience-to-the-Law. That common scholarly view ignores the critical fact, which is that Paul's denial of the Law was MERELY a *pretext* to replace circumcision with baptism as his faith's initiation-ritual.

---

[76]   Even if, as Delbert Burkett's 2004 & 2009 *Rethinking the Gospel Sources* hypothesizes, *Matthew* and *Luke* were not based on *Mark*, but were instead drawing from common prior sources, those prior sources would have been taken into each of these three Gospels, and the result is much the same: A Pauline agenda in *Mark* would be expected to show up also in *Matthew* and *Luke*. The present work is neutral as regards possible "Q" or other putative earlier sources about Jesus and his alleged statements. The most reasonable assumption on those issues is that earlier sources did exist and were selectively adapted – and, where need be, changed – by each Gospel-writer to suit his purposes, so that, if those purposes were Pauline, then the "Jesus" that was transmitted via the given Gospel account would also have been, even if those sources had been 100% accurate. Even if the sources were accurate, the Gospels could still lie; sources can be distorted and falsified.

Speculation about the possibility that "Q" or other earlier sources on Jesus existed – sources that didn't survive – is, in any case, irrelevant to a legal/forensic reconstruction of events. This reconstruction can be based only upon the evidence that *does* exist, not at all upon evidence which might possibly have once existed and is gone (if it ever *did* exist).

Matthew 28:19 replaces circumcision with baptism, and therefore affirms Paul's necessary point in this matter. And, of course, Jesus, according to Matthew's account, just as in Mark's, became baptized at the very start of his mission, and one might say that in that earlier portion of Matthew's account, 3:13-5, baptism is implicitly being introduced as superseding circumcision – which Jesus must have undergone as an infant, but *Matthew,* again like *Mark,* suppresses that fact. 3:15 even goes so far as to present Jesus as saying that baptism is required by God – a purely Paulist Christian notion, not Jewish at all, and therefore emphatically at odds with the scholarly opinion that *Matthew* is non-Pauline. Even though some Jewish sects had come to require baptism of Gentile converts or "proselytes" as an additional entrance-requirement beyond circumcision, even those sects didn't accept baptism as a SUBSTITUTE for circumcision; and the very idea that a born Jew such as Jesus *needed* to be baptized is a gross violation of Judaism. *Matthew* in 3:15 is clearly Pauline, not Jewish at all.

What scholars fail to acknowledge about *Matthew* largely embellishing upon *Mark,* is that by its doing so, *Matthew* was embellishing upon the Pauline religion, rather than building upon the Jewish one. Scholars seem to be the only people not to have noticed this obvious – and obviously important – fact. The historically concerned lay public acknowledges it readily: *Matthew* is clearly Christian and NOT Jewish.

As I noted, the first thing that should be recognized about the affirmation of the Law in *Matthew* 5:17-20 & 19:17 is that the only reason Paul had renounced the Law was to enable replacement of circumcision by baptism, which, as I've mentioned, *Matthew* – following *Mark* – does, in fact, do. However, I shall now add, also, a second, subsidiary, factor to both Paul's and Matthew's motivation here, which might help explain Matthew's ENDORSEMENT of the Law in this passage:

Matthew, recognizing *Mark*'s earlier virtual writing-off of Judaism, was clearly trying to RECTIFY *Mark*'s story-line so as to keep the Christian door open at least a crack to the admission of Christian-believing Jews. Evidently, unlike Mark, Matthew thought that it might still be possible to get the best of BOTH worlds – superseding Judaism, and yet inviting believing Jews to become Christians – and this was in keeping with Paul's own admonition in *1 Corinthians* 9:22-5 and 10:33: "I become all things to all men. ... Just do as I do; I try to please everyone." Paul also reflected this tactic extensively in *Romans*, such as in 3:31 and in 9-11, straining to avoid repelling the few Jews in the Roman congregation. In this sense, *Matthew* is Pauline not only in strategy, but also in his tactics or concept of how to go about achieving it. The reason why Matthew felt FREE in 5:17-20 to accept explicitly *Jesus's* being Law-respecting, which Paul didn't, is that, when Paul was writing, Paul needed to establish a RATIONALIZATION for throwing out the circumcision-commandment, *Genesis* 17:14, and this rationalization had to avoid *explicit* mention of Jesus's respect for the Law (including *Genesis* 17:14). However, by the time that Matthew was writing, circumcision may already have been, to a large extent, effectively discarded amongst Christians, and so Matthew didn't face the same demand that Paul did; there were no longer – perhaps after the Roman massacre of Jews in 70 CE – so many Jesus-followers who had been *born* Jews and who thus even *cared* about circumcision. It also should be emphasized, in this context, that Paul never *explicitly* said that Jesus had *not* been a respecter of the Law. Paul wrote too early for such an *explicit* statement about Jesus to have been credible to his readers. Consequently, Paul had to *imply* this without *explicitly* stating it; and so that's exactly what he did. But the Gospelists wrote later. *Matthew's* inclusion of 5:17-20 reflected, therefore, merely a *tactical choice* by its writer, a choice to *attract* Jews if at all possible. This choice was in accord with Paul's strategic goals; it didn't contradict those goals. Matthew wrote in a different time and environment, and he applied Paul's strategy to that changed situation; therefore, his tactics were different.

Furthermore, it's critically important to recognize that all other Pauline purposes, within *Mark,* were, indeed, imported into *Matthew.* Take, for example, very importantly, the Deification of Jesus:

Matthew 28:17-19 says, "When they saw him they worshipped him [which violates the first three of the Ten Commandments], ... and Jesus said to them, 'All authority in heaven and on earth has been given to me [placing within Jesus's own mouth an endorsement of this violation of the first three of the Ten Commandments]. Go, therefore, and convert all nations, baptizing them."

It couldn't possibly have been more blatant than that. *Matthew* here actually ties the core baptismal replacement of circumcision, right into the divineness of Jesus, and thus implicitly into the denial of the first three of the Ten Commandments; and so, too, into the denial of Judaism itself.

This emphasizes the key fact that when *Matthew* 28:19 replaces circumcision with baptism, this one passage, alone, actually *settles* the case of Matthew's being Pauline.

And that confirms what I had said earlier: it is only Matthew's *tactics* that were different from Mark's. Unlike Mark, Matthew thought that it might still be possible to get the best of both worlds, in keeping with Paul's admonition in *1 Corinthians* 9:22-5 and 10:33. Even though Matthew, in 23:31-8 and 27:25, was shifting the "guilt," for the "Deicide," from the Romans onto the Jews, he nonetheless still hoped to convert at least *some* Jews to his new faith, and it's this conflict of goals that has confused scholars – just as it has historically confused numerous popes who, like Matthew, alternately wanted BOTH to condemn Jews, and to "save" them.

The writer of *Matthew* was strategically 100% Christian, but he didn't accept Paul's and Mark's tactics 100%, because of the different *situation* in which he wrote.

As regards the so-called "Great Commission," *Matthew* 28:20, Jesus is there quoted as commanding obedience ONLY to himself, NOT to the Jewish covenant. So, this passage isn't really an affirmation of the Jewish covenant, not even in the

compromised sense in which 5:17-20 was. Moreover, in
Judaism, according to the First of the Ten Commandments, it's
impermissible for any man to command as God. Judaism was
strictly monotheistic. 28:20 therefore contradicts Judaism by
saying "I" command, *instead of* "God" or "The Lord," or some
other reference that's *not* first person, commanding. For
example, in the Torah, Moses said that the commandments
were coming from God, *not* from Moses himself. The "Great
Commission" is clearly alien to Judaism, by violating its First
Commandment. And Christians bow down to likenesses of
Jesus and to the Cross, which violates the Second
Commandment. And they refer to Jesus as if he were God,
which violates the Third. Jesus would have been appalled.

Furthermore, even with respect to Matthew's attempt
to welcome any remaining Jews who might possibly still be
open to conversion, *Matthew* 10:34-37 has "Jesus" say: "Do not
think that I have come to bring peace to the world. No, I did
not come to bring peace, but a sword. I came to set sons
against their fathers, daughters against their mothers,
daughters-in-law against their mothers-in-law; a man's worst
enemies will be the members of his own family. Whoever
loves his father or mother more than he loves me is not fit to
be my disciple; whoever loves his son or daughter more than
he loves me is not fit to be my disciple." One of the Jewish Ten
Commandments is "Honor thy father and thy mother."
Consequently, Matthew had "Jesus" speak out of both sides of
his mouth about the Law, not very differently than Paul
himself did.

Concerning the Gospels *Luke* and *John,* there is virtually
no scholar who seriously questions their Paulinism – not even
scholars who lack the foggiest idea of what Paul was actually
saying. Therefore, the Paulinism of those two Gospels won't
be much discussed here, other than to observe simply that,
like *Matthew*, both *Luke* and *John* imported *Mark's* Paulinism
into themselves. *John* went far beyond *Mark* in extending some
aspects of that Paulinism, such as Paul's eschatology, and
Paul's concept of "faith" being grounded by John in "the

Word,"[77] but those extensions of Paulinism don't make *John* any the LESS Pauline – in fact, to the contrary. Furthermore, *John* 19:11 places into Jesus's mouth the gist of Paul's *Romans* 13:1. And *John* 14:6 places into Jesus's mouth the gist of Paul's *Galatians* 2:16.

Moreover, Luke went perhaps the farthest of all Paul's propagandists in placing Paul's supersessionism into the mouth of "Jesus." Jesus is quoted in *Luke* 16:16, as saying, "The Law which God gave to Moses, and the writings of the prophets, were in effect until John the Baptist, but now and forever there is the good news about the Kingdom of God, and everyone wants it so badly as to force his way into the Kingdom." The writer here, Paul's follower Luke, then puts words into Jesus's mouth to contradict this, so as to appease any Jews who are still in the group: "However, it would be easier to destroy heaven and earth than to destroy the Law." But is this "Jesus" really saying here that the Law continues as before? Or is he instead saying that arriving at the Kingdom of God (where, supposedly, the Law won't apply) will be immensely difficult to achieve? Paul's follower Luke had learned his arts of deception from the master, and so he left his readers guessing which belief "Jesus" held. But then, in line 18, this "Jesus" goes on to say that, "Any man who divorces his wife and marries another commits adultery, and any man who marries a divorcee likewise commits adultery." This revisits *Mark* 10:9 reversing *Deut.* 24:1. Moreover, the Torah condemns a woman's adultery, but never a man's.

---

[77]   *John* opens: "Before the world was created, the Word already existed, and He was God, and He was with God." That Pauline God was multi-part, both Word and God. Perhaps the writer of *John* held this "Word" to be synonymous with the Holy Ghost; but, in any case, John intended to convey that to reject the Word of God was to reject God. This view actually went all the way back to at least Judaism's legendary start, in *Genesis* 2:16-17: "God told Adam, 'You may eat the fruit of any tree in the Garden of Eden, except the tree that gives knowledge of right and wrong. You must not eat the fruit of that tree, for, if you do, you will die on that very day.'" Like any religion, Judaism and Christianity start with faith: the belief that to question its teachings will bar one from salvation. That's what any religion is about – fear of death, and a resulting mental enslavement to its Scripture.

Leviticus 20:1 commands killing both a man's wife and her paramour when the two have been caught, but this passage, too, criminalizes *only* a woman's adultery, not a man's. The paramour is to be killed only because he used the other man's property without that man's permission. That's a very different situation than what "Jesus" here commands. And so, Luke seems to present a thoroughly supersessionist "Jesus," in keeping with Paul's supersessionist agenda. But is that really the case? As was noted in the prior chapter, this "Jesus" is saying that the strict law that pertains to women pertains *also to men*. The Torah never went so far: this is actually nothing more than adding a law to the covenant – definitely not *ending the covenant*. This is not Pauline *at all*.[78] Evidently, even at the time when Luke wrote, any placement of Paul's supersessionist agenda into the mouth of "Jesus" would have exposed Luke's writing to be a fraudulent misrepresentation of Jesus.

---

[78] Paul says in *1 Corinthians* 7:10-11 that neither a man nor a woman may divorce, and that if a husband does, he may remarry, but that if a woman does, she's prohibited from remarrying. This was Paul's interpretation of *Malachi* 2:16: "'I hate divorce,' says the Lord God." However, *Malachi* was far from being binding or Torah; it was instead one of the last books in the Old Testament, and was written at around 460 BC. So, Paul was citing here a relatively recent contradiction of the Torah's *Deuteronomy* 24:1. The writer of *Malachi* was supposed to be amplifying upon the Torah, but instead contradicted it, and Paul picked up from his sloppiness. *1 Corinthians* 7:10-11 happens to be part of a passage in which Paul asserts (in line 7:19) "What matters is to obey God's commandments," and so this passage pre-dated Paul's creation of Christianity in the year 49 or 50. The passage is therefore not Pauline (i.e., not Christian). It's pre-Christian. Whether or not it is Jesuine (i.e., accurately reflective of what Jesus's views had been) is unknowable.

David Instone-Brewer, in his October 2007 *Christianity Today* article "What God Has Joined: What Does the Bible Really Teach About Divorce?" and in his 2006 *Divorce and Remarriage in the Church* and his 2004 *Divorce and Remarriage in the Bible*, reported that at the time when Jesus was living, rabbis were hotly debating the acceptability of divorce. (It's not hard to understand why this was such a contentious issue, since the Torah and other parts of the Old Testament were, at best, sketchy on this subject.)

In any event, nobody has ever presented a sane reason why the Bible should be consulted for guidance on whether or under what conditions to divorce.

Luke slipped up yet again when he wrote, in *Acts* 1:6, "The apostles asked Jesus, 'Lord, is this the moment when you will restore the independent nationhood of Israel?'" And this "Jesus" played coy and didn't answer. He didn't outright say no, that he wasn't going to overturn Rome's reign over Judaea. *He didn't deny* that he was soon going to fulfill his followers' hope in sedition against Rome, by his restoring Israeli sovereignty – the *core meaning* of "mashiach." This line in *Acts* implicitly acknowledges that "Jesus" was accepted by his followers as being seditious, and that Jesus didn't deny his being seditious, against Rome. Evidently, even as late as Luke wrote, everyone knew that Jesus had been considered seditious, by his followers, and that he had accepted that he was. However, this recognition was implicit, rather than stated explicitly, because the writer of *Acts* wanted to avoid telling future generations that Jesus had been executed for violating Roman law, rather than for violating Jewish law. Like the other writers of the four Gospels, Luke wanted future generations to be deceived into believing that "the Jews" and not "the Romans" had "killed Jesus." This lie fulfilled a Pauline agenda, which was necessary in order for future Roman Emperors to be able to accept Christianity.

Even the Gospel that was written the latest, and that is generally considered to be the most anti-Semitic, *John*, had to acknowledge, in the late period in which it was written, that Jesus was passionately a Jew: *John* 4:22 quotes its "Jesus" as asserting "[only] we [Jews] know whom we worship, because salvation comes from the Jews." And, of course, *Matthew* quoted Jesus as asserting to his disciples (*Mat.* 10:5-6), "Go nowhere among the Gentiles, ... but go instead to the lost sheep of the house of Israel." Again: Paul's followers could go far in their lies; but, even for them, limits existed on just how far they could *afford* to go.

It's interesting to track the different ways in which *Mark*, *Matthew*, *Luke*, and *John*, adapt to their respective situations their water-carrying for Paul. For example, whereas

Matthew 16:18 is explicit about Jesus's appointing Peter as his
successor, *John* 21:17 and *Luke* 22:32 are close to that, but, by
contrast, nothing in the earliest-written, *Mark* is. Mark could
only imply that Jesus preferred Peter above all other disciples,
not go beyond that to suggest, in any way, that Jesus had
appointed Peter as his successor. Each writer went as far as he
could, and relied upon the faith of followers to carry the hoax
to the next stage.

        Another example of this evolution of the hoax, over
time, is the way in which the four canonical Gospels change or
modify the respective statements of their "Jesus," over time,
so as to amplify Paul's theology to the fullest extent that could
still be believable to the audiences of each respective time. For
example, the *earliest*-written Gospel, *Mark*, quotes Jesus, in
Mark 12:28-3, as saying that, of *all* the laws, "The most
important one is this: Listen, Israel – the Lord our God is the
one and only God. Love the Lord your God with all your
heart, with all your soul, with all your mind, and with all your
strength." The phrase there, "The Lord our God is the one and
only God," is actually the First of the Ten Commandments,
and Mark's "Jesus" was stating it here as being *part* of the
"most important commandment." This "Jesus," however,
mixed into it an *additional* command, to "love" this God; and
this was actually similar if not identical to the Second of the
Ten Commandments, which is "Worship no god but me." If
the "love" within the lexicon of this Markan "Jesus" was
supposed to be interpreted as being synonymous with the
"worship" within the Second Commandment, then the answer
of this "Jesus" was that the "most important commandment"
is the *combination* of the First and the Second of the Ten
Commandments. However, when *Matthew* (in 22:36-38) and
Luke (in 10:25-28) copied this statement from *Mark*'s "Jesus,"
they notably *left out of it* the First of the Ten commandments.
It's not included at all in "the greatest commandment" from
either "Jesus." Apparently, whereas the "Jesus" that was
recollected in Mark's time was widely known to have believed

that the First of the Ten Commandments is *at least part* of "the most important commandment," the memory and recollection of Jesus had become sufficiently vague decades later when Matthew and Luke were writing, so that those men could drop it *entirely* from *their* "Jesus." The reason for their dropping it is obvious: Attributing the First of the Ten Commandments to Jesus was a cardinal violation of Paul's Trinitarian agenda, since Paul had said (in such places as *Galatians* 2:16-21) that *all* of the commandments became invalid following the Resurrection, and that the unitarian Jewish God was now replaced by the Trinitarian Father-Son-Ghost God. The way that Matthew dealt with the then-undeniable reality of the actual Jewish Jesus was via the "Great Commission" (as theologians call it), which is the last three lines of *Matthew* (28:18-20), alleged to have been spoken by the Resurrected "Jesus," or the Holy Ghost. Hundreds of years later, the churchman who added to *Mark* its soon-to-be-canonized ending (16:9-20) included, copied from *Matthew*, an expanded "Great Commission," in *Mark* 16:15-18. This is how a Jesus whom virtually everyone when Mark wrote knew to have been a committed Jew, transmogrified during the coming decades and even centuries into the Christian (i.e., Pauline) Christ. It was a hoax that took centuries to complete.

What's critically important to a legal/forensic analysis of text, or to a legal/forensic hermeneutics, is always to understand the purposes for which the writer *actually* wrote. Scholarship seeks to interpret only what a given writer meant to say. If a writer meant to hide something, rather than to say it, scholars go along with that. Scholars don't want to get involved with issues of intent (especially if that intent is to deceive) – it's "too controversial," especially with classical texts, and most especially with religious Scriptures. However, legal/forensic hermeneutics is based upon an understanding that to explicate a text's meaning without a simultaneous explication of its writer's purposes (its objectives), will fail, unless the writer's purposes happen to be 100% HONEST.

Scholarship is tolerable if it studies ONLY honest texts. It assumes the honesty of all classical texts (especially of religious ones, such as the NT), even if it sometimes questions the truthfulness and authenticity of those texts. But, just as not all classical texts are necessarily truthful, they also aren't necessarily honest. And that's where scholarly hermeneutics falls flat onto its face. And that's why many scholars wrongly view *Matthew* as non-Pauline.

Consequently, all of the canonical Gospel accounts of "Jesus" reflect Paul and not Jesus. Any "historical" account of the start of Christianity that asserts, or even suggests, Jesus started Christianity, is false. It's not really history at all; it's just a myth about a myth – a piling of misrepresentations onto the existing Christian myth. This doesn't mean, however, that scholars who assert that Jesus never existed are correct, because their accounts are *also* false (as has likewise been demonstrated in this work). Jesus did exist, and Christianity is the religion that was created by enemies of the Jewish sect he started, enemies who never met him: Paul and his followers. Christianity is the religion that was created by these enemies of Jesus. Today's Christians are followers of Paul, not of Jesus. They are people who are fooled by Paul, and who teach each other a religion that they mistakenly think was created by Jesus, who would actually be furious against Paul if Jesus were to come back today and see what has happened. Instead of such a "Jesus" (as Christians have been taught to expect, based upon the Pauline-derived lie called "The Great Commission") being delighted to see that billions of people worship him in violation of the first three of the Ten Commandments, the *real* Jesus would be shocked and enraged to find that it is so. And he would especially be beside himself with a raging fury when discovering that the anti-Judaic and anti-Semitic religion that Paul created has thereby become the world's largest and most successful religion.

7. Paul's Own Anti-Semitic Blurt

As was stated concerning *Mark*, the fourth Pauline purpose in that earliest Gospel was to blame the Jews instead of the Romans for killing Jesus. This Deicidal charge became the basis for anti-Semitism. The most direct Pauline expression of it – and of hatred against Jews in the broadest sense – is *1 Thessalonians* 2:14-16; and defenders of Paul don't like this passage, because the Christian Holocaust against Jews made anti-Semitism no longer fashionable among Christians. (*Prior* to the Holocaust, the authenticity of *1 Thessalonians* 2:14-16 was challenged little if at all.[79]) Thus, in the wake of the Holocaust, the authenticity of this Pauline passage is widely challenged by scholars.

Predominant scholarly opinion holds that even the canonical Gospels are not THEMSELVES anti-Semitic, despite passages such as *John* 8:44 and *Matthew* 23:31-38, which assert Jews to be descended from Satan. But, more strongly still,

---

[79]   The chief pre-Holocaust scholar to question the passage's authenticity was F.C. Baur, who said in his 1845 *Paul*, that 2:14-16 is "quite out of place for him to speak of these persecutions in Judaea; for he himself was the person principally concerned in the only persecution to which our passage can refer." However, Baur's view of this passage was not influential until after the Holocaust. In order to make less blatant the anti-anti-Semitic motivation for challenging the passage's authenticity, scholars now said that 2:13-16 is the interpolation or editorially added passage, not just 2:14-16.

scholars hold virtually UNIVERSALLY that the writings by PAUL
are NOT anti-Semitic, because acknowledging that *1
Thessalonians* 2:14-15 is authentic places anti-Semitism in the
earliest-written of all Christian documents. This mainstream
post-Holocaust "New Perspective" on Paul goes so far as to
maintain that Paul wasn't even anti-Jewish. However, *1
Thessalonians* 2:14-16 says "the Jews ... killed the Lord Jesus, ...
displease God and are enemies of all men," and exults in their
misfortune; and this is so blatantly anti-Semitic that the only
way scholars have found to prop up such a lie as that Paul
wasn't anti-Semitic, has been for them to assert this passage to
have been an interpolation or later addition by some
anonymous editor. Unfortunately, there is no reason to
consider that to be true.

The letter itself, *1 Thessalonians,* it should be noted here,
is generally regarded as the earliest-written authentic
Christian document, dated at around 49-50 CE, probably
within about a year after the council in Jerusalem and that
meeting's immediately following event, as recounted in
Galatians 2. Indeed, some scholars even date *Galatians* itself as
early as 50, but still after *1 Thessalonians.*

If *1 Thessalonians* was, in fact, written in the immediate
AFTERMATH of Paul's passionate encounter retold in *Galatians*
2:11-16, then *1 Thessalonians* should be expected to reflect
Paul's most uninhibited anti-Judaic, perhaps even anti-
Semitic, sentiments; and this would especially be the case if
the Thessalonian congregations, who were his immediate
intended audience, contained few or no born Jews, since there
would then have been a substantially reduced (if any)
incentive for Paul to have written to these congregations in
language moderated so as to AVOID offending Jews. In that
case, the sole restraining influence upon Paul's expression of
his hatred of Judaism would have been that, until just a short
while PRIOR to his writing this letter, Paul would have been
speaking of Judaism in ONLY a FAVORABLE light, inasmuch as
he had, until that time, been converting people to, or selling

people on, the Jesus-SECT OF JUDAISM. In other words, when Paul was writing this letter, he knew that its recipients, until this time, had always thought of him as being PRO-Jewish, and, indeed, as still being himself a Jew. After all, Paul had only just NOW become a FORMER Jew; the event retold in *Galatians* 2:11-16 had happened not long before Paul wrote *1 Thessalonians*. This letter would have been, perhaps, even Paul's "coming out" as a FORMER Jew, if he had been sufficiently honest to have done such a thing. But yet, at the same time, the recipients of this letter, as all Gentiles, might nonetheless have had little, if anything, emotionally invested of themselves, personally, in a specifically JEWISH identity, especially if these "converts" were relatively new, as would most likely have been the case if there were no born Jews in the Thessalonian congregations.

And, to judge by the letter itself, all of this seems to have been the case. The letter does, indeed, condemn Jews (in lines 2:15-16) but NOT Judaism. For example, it instructs its readers, in 4:1-12, to OBEY the Law, so that (4:12) "you will win the respect of those who are not believers." It even says – referring presumably to Paul's own immediately prior teachings to these people – (4:1) "you have learned from us how you should live in order to please God," right before it paraphrases some of the covenant-commandments. That statement, viewed within the broader context of the subsequent Pauline epistles, is simply stunning; it is Paul's virtual admission, at this crucial time in his life, that, PRIOR to the event which created Christianity, Paul had himself been teaching thorough respect for the Jewish covenant, EVEN soteriologically/eschatologically; i.e., even as being a valid path to achieve salvation in heaven, rather than damnation in hell. Paul couldn't very well now DENY to these people, at so early a time, that he had indeed been teaching this. He always had done so. Only SUBSEQUENTLY was that to change.

Therefore, this was NOT really an anti-Judaic letter at all; it was not against Judaism PER SE. Paul's hatred had to take a DIFFERENT form here – specifically, an ANTI-SEMITIC form, in

2:15-16. The problem for Paul in this passage was NOT Judaism
– not, at least, when he was addressing this particular
audience at this particular time. The problem here was, in fact,
not at all "the Law," meaning the covenant, Judaism itself.
Instead, the problem in this instance was "the Jews" (2:14), as
(2:15) Deicidists, enemies of all mankind, and the people who
are condemned by God. The passage was, indeed, ANTI-
SEMITIC, not MERELY anti-Judaic. Scholars who are (especially
after the Holocaust) personally invested in the denial that
there is anything INHERENTLY anti-Semitic in Christianity
ITSELF, have therefore wanted to NEGATE this passage's
authenticity, and so, as was mentioned, they have asserted
that Paul didn't write it; that it "must" have been added later,
by some editor.

Elsewhere in the present work is discussed the
scholars' chief "reason" for this (actually) unsupported
assumption: namely, that the punishment of the Jews that
Paul relishes in 2:16 "must" have been referring to Rome's
sacking of Jerusalem in 70 CE, which, of course, occurred
approximately two decades LATER than the letter itself. It has
been previously pointed out here that these scholars have
ignored the expulsion that took place of all Jews from Rome
by the Emperor Claudius in probably 49 CE (though some
historians place it in probably 41 CE), which might have
occurred only shortly prior to this very letter, and therefore
been most timely to have been referred to in it in that context.
Some scholars have replied against this incident, as being
Paul's referent in 2:16, by introducing the culturally crude
observation that such an expulsion, of every Jew from the
Imperial capital – which we should note occurred, in any case,
during the great war between Rome and the Jews, a war
Josephus called the biggest war that ever was – was too
"inconsequential" an event to have been seen, in its own time,
as so mortal a threat to Jews everywhere, such as to have
warranted reference by so ominous a phrase as appears at the
end of 2:16. As is usual for such scholarly "arguments," no
support has ever been proffered by its proponents, nor have

scholars deemed it necessary to provide any, since this fiction props up a myth they find culturally convenient to sustain.

It's also highly relevant here to note that the *Romans* 13:1-7 endorsement of the Roman Emperor as being God's appointed agent on earth punishing evildoers, would support EITHER inference, the 49 CE event or the 70 CE one, as presenting the Emperor's action as executing God's will, and so it's supportive but indeterminate as between the two.

Further deserving of note here is that even IF Paul was NOT referring here to the expulsion of all Jews from the Imperial center that pre-dated, and so presaged, by about twenty years, Rome's sacking/burning of the Jewish capital city of Jerusalem, this STILL would NOT mean that Paul's reference here was NECESSARILY to the LATER, 70 CE, event. This passage might THEN have INSTEAD been a reference to some event that went UNRECORDED in all of the few SURVIVING historical documents from and about that era. In other words, scholars' *mere* ASSUMPTION that the 70 CE event is what this passage in *1 Thessalonians* was referring to, is, *in any case,* UNFOUNDED.

Another historically recorded event that Paul might possibly have been referring to here was a famine in Judea, which might have occurred in the year 48, and which Josephus referred to in book 20, chapter 2, of *Antiquities of the Jews.*

Some scholars have asserted that 2:14-16 breaks from and is different from what immediately preceded and immediately followed it, because a prior passage (2:7-12) and the following passage (2:17) both assert Paul's familial fondness for the Thessalonians, whereas 2:14-16 concerns instead the Jews trying to stop him "from preaching to the Gentiles [who include those Thessalonians] the message that would bring them salvation." These scholars believe that all of 2:13-16, not just 2:14-16, was a later interpolation. But they simply ignore the structure of the entirety of 2. Chapter 2 opens with 2:1-2, describing Paul's previous success in holding the congregation together despite the mistreatment,

insults, and opposition, he had received from Jews who tried
to prevent him from preaching to Gentiles that they didn't
need to be circumcised. This theme is picked up again in 2:14-
16. Other portions of 2 present Paul's personal bonding with
the Thessalonians, including the two specifically familial
passages. Taken all together, 2 is actually a brilliant unity,
presenting Paul's expressions of gratefulness to God, both for
his own success with the Thessalonians, and also for God's
hatred of the Jews who had tried to stop him from that
success.

Moreover, both 2:1-2 and 2:14-16 allege persecution of
Paul's followers, and this is a theme that Paul asserts
elsewhere, in *Galatians* 1:8-9, 4:17-20, 5:7, and 6:12-13, as well
as in *Philippians* 3:2. The very same passage, 1 *Thessalonians*
2:14-16, that is in question here, by the scholars who allege
Paul didn't write it, is actually *typical* of Paul in its alleging
persecution by the proponents of circumcision.

The only other "argument" for the INAUTHENTICITY of
2:14-16 has been that this passage employs a number of Greek
words that aren't used (or that aren't *often* used) elsewhere
amongst the seven generally-regarded-as-authentic letters
(including this letter) by Paul. However, this argument, of the
occurrence of such "hapaxes" in this particular passage, has
been based upon statistically faulty grounds. Every writing,
by every writer, naturally tends to contain a few new or
unusual words, especially if the subject-matter is new or
unusual for that given writer. This passage is the only one in
which Paul deals with this specific subject-matter, of Jews'
alleged evilness; consequently, it contains some terms not
found, or not frequently found, elsewhere in his writings. And
that fact has NOTHING to do with the passage's authenticity or
lack thereof.

Furthermore, by sheer RANDOMNESS, such "hapaxes"
will sometimes naturally occur more, within certain clumps or
"passages," than they do in the "average" passage from the
same writer. Every letter, and other writing, contains such
clumps that have unusually many new words. Yet it's not

normal to conclude from this that EACH such clump must NECESSARILY indicate the passage itself to be a later addition, by a different writer. Indeed, that's only very RARELY assumed.

Furthermore, it's entirely FALSE to treat, as "a passage," for such a hapax-analysis, what is actually, and obviously, only an *essential* PART of what is, in fact, a much LONGER PASSAGE. Yet this is precisely what such scholars are doing here: they're treating 2:14-16 as if it were a later addition, which should therefore be expunged from the text, even though 2:14-16 is, as we've noted earlier, merely the CLIMAX of 2:2-16, an obviously longer passage. To expunge 2:14-16 would decapitate that entire longer passage. Consequently, a fair hapax-analysis of 2:14-16 would have to compare the hapax-ratio of the ACTUAL entire passage, 2:2-16, as against the Pauline norm, and this kind of hapax-analysis indicates no hapax-abnormality, even DESPITE the anomalous subject-matter encountered in its 2:14-16 segment.

Given the shoddiness of all arguments for 2:14-16 being inauthentic, a few scholars have proposed instead that Paul meant here to condemn not *all* Jews, but *only* "all Jews *who killed the Lord Jesus and the prophets, and who persecuted us.*" However, if Paul wasn't intending here to promote the collective condemnation of Jews, then why did he end this passage by exulting, about the expulsion of *all* Jews from Rome: "And now God's wrath has at last come down on them!"? That's clearly a damnation of *all* Jews, and not *only* of "all Jews *who killed the Lord Jesus.*" Paul there introduced, for the first time in any surviving writing, *the collective damnation and Deicide-guilt of all Jews* – anti-Semitism. Consequently, scholars stress their arguments that 2:14-16 is inauthentic; since this argument is more complicated, it's better for befuddling gulls.

Scholars who have argued against the authenticity of this passage, 2:14-16, have had only one REAL reason for doing so: they simply don't LIKE this passage. It's full of obvious hatred against Jews. But, when one really understands Paul's epistles, one recognizes that, so too was he. If scholars weren't

clergymen wearing a different hat, and clergymen weren't
scholars wearing a different hat, then the *authenticity* of 2:14-16
wouldn't even be a scholarly issue at all, but would be
accepted just as is the authenticity of *1 Thessalonians* itself.

Indeed, the real irony of this whole matter is that, after
the split, Paul evidently felt free to express to Gentile
audiences his anti-Semitism even BEFORE he felt free to express
to them his anti-Judaism. This makes sense within our context:
He had converted his gulls to Judaism, and so wasn't free to
condemn it, but he could – and did – condemn his enemies,
who were born-Jews: the circumcised. That's why he
promulgated anti-Semitism *before* he promulgated (as in
Philippians 3:8) anti-Judaism. The reality, then, is that, instead
of anti-Judaism leading to anti-Semitism in Christianity – such
as scholars commonly but falsely suppose – anti-Semitism
actually PRECEDED anti-Judaism, at least in the writings of Paul,
who invented anti-Semitism, as part of his invention of
Christianity. Paul's writings reflected his goal of catering to
power, and, consequently, his broad socio-political
calculations. The fact that Paul had previously been selling (a
sect of) Judaism, represented, for him, a bind/predicament,
which temporarily restrained his expressions of anti-Judaism.
But, by the time of *Philippians,* later in his career, Paul had no
compunctions in calling Judaism ITSELF (3:8) even "mere
garbage." The original Greek term, ZEMIA, is also variously
translatable as trash, or as damaged goods, or EVEN as
"excrement" – the term that, oddly, one scholarly FAN of
Paul's (Lloyd Gaston) chose in his exegesis of that passage,
arguing that Paul was *pro*-Judaic. But, however translated,
Paul's reference here reflected clearly (except to scholars) his
utter CONTEMPT for Judaism.

Also late in his career, in *Romans,* which was addressed
to a congregation that contained some Jews, Paul had a
difficult balancing-act to perform, which caused that letter to
stand out for Paul's sophistical distinction between Israelites
(whom he favored, since he considered himself to be one: one

of God's people) and Jews (whom he, of course, now hated: proponents or preachers of Judaism). In *Romans* 3:28, and also in 3:20, he clearly expressed his supersessionist, anti-Judaic message; yet in 3:31 and 2:6 he directly denied it, while giving no argument for the contradiction. Indeed, in 3:30, he had already just previously denied this denial, when he said that for both Jew and Gentile there is only *one* path toward personal salvation, which is the Christian path, of pure faith, that's stated in 3:28 and in 3:20. He had even explained *why* the Jewish pathway, of total obedience to the Law, is, in his view, inevitably doomed to failure: in 3:23, he said that *everyone* violates the Law, and so to try to please God in that way (the Jewish way) can *never* succeed. Yet elsewhere in *Romans*, likewise in order to placate the Jews in the Roman congregation, Paul stated, in its chapters 9-11, that God retains his love for all Israelites. So, for Paul, God loves Israelites, the nationality of the Kingdom of God; but yet in *Philippians* 3:2-8, Judaism itself, the religion or belief-system, is called trash; and, in *1 Thessalonians* 2:15-16, Jews themselves, the people, are asserted to be damned by God. Paul clearly hated both Judaism and Jews; but in order to placate Jewish believers in Jesus as the Messiah (and he needed *those* Jews desperately, for providing credibility to his con), Paul nominally paid honor to their nation of Israel. He wouldn't explicitly tell Jews, however, that the new *people* of Israel were Paul's own Christians, no longer Jews, since Jews (as in *Romans* 3:23-26 & 28, and *Galatians* 2:16) were doomed to perdition so long as they failed to *convert* to his own, new, Christian faith. But, it seems, from *Acts* 21:21 forward, that Jews in Paul's era knew anyway; they weren't so dumb; they understood Paul quite well, even if scholars today choose not to.

Paul invented anti-Semitism, and he did it systematically. His followers, who wrote the Gospel accounts of "Christ" and of his allegedly Jewish Deicide, merely PERFECTED it, by placing this sentiment, PAUL'S sentiment, into the mouth of "Christ." This was perhaps their most barbaric violation of the historical Jesus. However, their having been followers of Paul – the enemy of Jesus/James – made this barbarism inevitable. The original deception was by Paul.

8. Why Scholars Don't Know This

One might reasonably ask: Why don't scholars know that the four canonical Gospel accounts of "Jesus" reinforce Paul's agenda? This question's answer, however, is ridiculously simple: In order to know that the Gospels embody Paul's agenda, one must first know what Paul's agenda *was*. Scholars haven't known what Paul's agenda was, because they didn't want to. All their interpretive (or "hermeneutical") verbiage thus ignored this key issue – these people were *determined* to believe Paul's honesty; *not* Paul's creation of Christianity. (Scholarship is "motivated reasoning"; for scholars, the findings are more important than the methodology – *not* the converse, as for a scientist.) Scholars have even employed extreme measures in order to *avoid* making sense of Paul's writings: they've used measures such as assuming that the issue in *Galatians* 2:11-21 was the food laws instead of the circumcision law, and such as assuming that Paul was there accusing his opponents of "Judaizing" – even though no evidence exists for these assumptions, and the evidence is consistently contrary to them. Scholars haven't been merely passive in misinterpreting Paul; they've been active and imaginative at the task, whenever they needed to be, in order for them to be able to present Paul as an honest person. They've served as Paul's legal-defense team. And *that's* why no scholar has pointed out that the Gospel accounts of "Jesus" reflect *Paul's* agenda: scholars didn't want to know *what* Paul's agenda *actually* was.

This is how scholars enabled themselves to perpetuate the myth (actually the fraud) that the canonical Gospels reflect Jesus's agenda. To know that the Gospels reflect Paul's agenda – *instead* of Jesus's – is to know that Christianity is a hoax; and that's the last thing scholars want to understand.

After all, it's not as if scholars were unaware that Paul wrote first. So, why didn't they explore the *possibility* that the authors of the Gospels, etc., were *his* followers?

As was noted, scholars – wittingly or not – have served as Paul's defense attorneys; but a court of law in a democracy needs a judge, and jurors, and a prosecutor, as well. That's the difference between what scholars do, and what courts in democratic nations do: taking testimony at face-value, as scholars do; versus cross-examining it (etc.), as courts do. These differences in methodology *produce* the differences in findings.

The present book sets forth the prosecution case against Paul, and – unlike the defense team's case – the prosecution case doesn't require faith, because all of the evidence supports it: an entirely scientific theory of the case, one that's constructed from the best evidence on each and every matter, convicts Paul conclusively, even beyond the strictest legal standard, of "beyond a reasonable doubt." You, the reader, are the juror, and only you can make the decision for yourself: No judge, prosecutor, or defense attorney, can make it. It is entirely up to you, whether you are a person of science, or a person of faith.

Scholarship has been an extension of the church. But (just as happened with Galileo in physics, and then with Darwin in biology) history and the other social "sciences" require something better than that, in order to become authentic *sciences*.

Perhaps if professors of earliest Christian history at accredited colleges and universities were barred from ever serving in a church's pay, and preachers in church-run institutions were barred from ever teaching earliest Christian history outside of a church-financed setting, there would be a difference between preachers and teachers, but that's not the case now: These two fields are essentially one, and calling its practitioners "historians" is to insult the historical profession. Any historian who accepts such people as being historians has a very low opinion of his field, and accepts its being corrupt, not an authentic science.

The "revolving door," between government regulatory agencies and the companies they regulate, is widely recognized to be corrupting, and this is the reason legislation exists in democracies to minimize that "revolving door," laws to require (for example) that no one who regulates a firm may be hired by that firm for some set period of time after government employment. No such restrictions exist in academia. They should.

Corruption doesn't just distort science; it blocks science. It doesn't block technology (even dictatorships can promote technology), but it prevents the prerequisite for science, which is unbiased (or "fair") interpretation of evidence.

For example, the U.S. Food and Drug Administration's monitoring of the safety of America's drugs was so unreliable, and so poor, that on 22 November 2004, the editors of *JAMA*, the Journal of the American Medical Association, publicly gave up on the FDA; and, *The New York Times* headlined the following day, "A Medical Journal Calls for a New Watchdog on Drugs." Denise Grady reported: "Arguing that it was unreasonable to expect the same agency that approves drugs to 'also be committed to actively seek evidence to prove itself wrong,' the editors … recommended that the nation consider establishing an 'independent drug safety board' to track the safety of drugs." This was a tactful way of saying that the FDA operated as an arm of the pharmaceutical manufacturers, not of the public. The field was corrupt.

Scientists do not accept corruption of their field.

Scholars necessarily do, because they'd otherwise jeopardize their careers. Thus, for example, the Summer 2010 *Wilson Quarterly* headlined "Atheists Anonymous" (playing on the Alcoholics Anonymous theme), and summarized and linked to "Preachers Who Are Not Believers," by Daniel C. Dennett and Linda LaScola, in the March 2010 *Evolutionary Psychology*. This study interviewed, in depth, five clergy who anonymously admitted they didn't believe in what they preached. One said that he "and his wife are raising their son to recognize that Bible stories are not factual. 'And so when we talk to him about Bible stories, we remind him constantly that these are just stories; ... think about them in no different way than you would any other stories.'" Another minister said that his son had asked, "'Dad, do you really believe?' Before I could think, I said, 'Son, I don't.'" But still he wouldn't tell his wife this, because "It's going to turn her life upside-down. ... She's a very dedicated Christian, very devout." All of the interviewees were afraid to let their congregation know their beliefs. For example, one of them, "When asked his opinion of why ministers do not pass on their knowledge of Christian history to parishioners, ... said: '... They don't want to lose donations. ... They don't want to lose members.'" For a minister to say that his religion's Scripture is false would be for him to jeopardize his career. Another said, "I see it as play acting. ... I know how to pray publicly. I can lead singing. I love singing. ... But I see it as taking on the role and performing." The financial motive to deceive was clear. This man admitted bluntly: "I need the job. ... I do feel kind of hypocritical. It used to be the word 'hypocritical' was like a sin. I don't hold that view anymore, ... that there's absolute truths." He seemed basically a post-modernist, someone for whom the lack of "absolute truths" (whatever that is supposed to mean) justified a contempt for truth itself, or at least an unconcern for truthfulness, an unconcern for honesty. In some cases, there was a contempt for the parishioners, who need to believe the Bible. One minister said, "As long as ... you're talking about God and

Jesus and the Bible, that's what they want to hear." Another said, "The whole heaven thing makes no sense, either. Why would I want to walk on streets of gold?" Yet another minister explained his situation as purely a matter of personal necessity: "Financially, I don't have a choice, [because leaving the ministry] ... would cause a huge financial burden on me. I mean, how would I continue to make my house payment and support my family?" He also noted, "Secondly, ... I have zero friends outside the church."

Some preachers are also professors, who teach future preachers. As has been noted here, the same people often go back and forth between these "two" professions. The same basic demands, for them to endorse orthodoxy, are working on them, in "both" capacities. No field of science, especially not an advanced field such as physics, can have such orthodoxy, or else it's not really a field of science but is instead functioning more as a field of faith.

Faith is a "virtue" in religion, because every religion is based on faith. Faith is what the salespeople of religion are selling. But it's the supreme epistemological vice in science.

And this is how it comes to be that scholars – just like the billions of Paul's fooled people – cite the words and actions of the "Jesus" that were written by Paul's followers, Jesus's enemies. Scholars cite this, even when they don't believe it themselves. These people cite, as the words and actions of "Jesus," the words and actions those enemies of Jesus concocted, and lied, nearly two thousand years ago, attributing to Jesus.

What would Jesus (the *real* one) think of that?

And what would a committed scientist (someone who applies science instead of faith as the basis for beliefs) think of it?

The only way to understand faith is by means of science. The only way to understand *anything* is by means of science.

Conclusion:
How Scientists Think About History

Methodology is more important than findings: this is the basic attitude that makes a person a scientist. It's an attitude that doesn't yet exist in the academic professions outside the subject-areas identified as the physical and biological sciences. Practitioners of the social "sciences" don't customarily have this attitude, and are therefore usually not scientists. The fundamental field of social science is history or the production of entirely true narratives, since history is the social science that supplies the *data* from which all the other social sciences theorize and test their theories. (Economics, sociology, political science, and cultural anthropology, are based upon the data from – and generalize from – history.) The product of the scientific investigation of history is history, as opposed to myths. The present work has modeled how history is produced from evidence. The moral base of Western Civilization has been taken as the case-example, investigated here.

Science is an epistemology, or a meta-methodology, which determines the methodology that scientists within a given subject-area use. The scientific methodology for reconstructing history from a body of evidence is legal/forensic methodology. It's the methodology that courts in democratic nations use. It's also the methodology that scientific historians use, in order to reconstruct history (or historical narratives) from evidence. Historians who don't use this methodology aren't scientists; they are scholars.

Basic to science is using only the most-reliable evidence, and making as little use as possible of lesser evidence. In legal/forensic methodology, this guiding principle from science is known as the best-evidence principle. Although best-evidence "rules" may vary from one jurisdiction to another, the best-evidence *principle* does not, because it actually comes from science itself.

In order to reconstruct the history of earliest Christianity, from the available body of evidence, the first thing that needed to be done here was to rank the evidence, as to its reliability. The best-evidence principle is to avoid ever granting more reliance to inferior evidence than is granted to superior evidence. Thus, the first task of any scientific historian is to rank the evidence, concerning any given question that's being investigated.

Since the subject here has been the event that created Christianity, this is the question that directs the identification and reliability-ranking for our investigation. The first question, therefore, is: upon what evidence will the theory of the case here (the *basic* historical narrative) be constructed? Scholars have blindly assumed that documents that explicitly say "Jesus" asserted and did various things should be the basis for their "historical" (often mythological) accounts of Christianity's start. Most scholars even especially privilege the canonized four Gospel accounts, which the Roman Catholic Church produced. The only basis for that common scholarly practice is faith, not science.

What follows here will be a systematic description of the methodology that has produced the first authentically *historical* account of the start of Christianity. This will bring together into a single and sequential discussion the methodology that has been sporadically described throughout the preceding chapters (mainly in our footnotes). This discussion concludes the work, because this methodology has produced this work:

As is well known, the canonical Gospel accounts of Jesus – *Matthew, Mark, Luke* and *John* – are, at *best*, witness testimony about him. As is also well known, there are problems with witness testimony as evidence. In some court cases, people have been wrongly convicted because witnesses falsely remembered things, or else lied. And even the best-intentioned of witnesses have sometimes provided false testimony, because the defendant physically resembled the actual perpetrator of the crime, or for other reasons. Moreover, witness testimony recounts what a person saw or heard, and a professional magician is routinely able to deceive people into thinking that they see things that don't actually happen.

Thus, the canonical four Gospel accounts of Jesus (which, at best, described what people actually saw and heard) would be highly questionable as to the accuracy of their accounts, even if they had been written by personal witnesses to the events they recount – which almost all scholars say they were *not*.

Furthermore, those accounts of Jesus were written to be works of persuasion, evangelical documents, both to win and to retain converts to their new religion, instead of to be objective and carefully researched historical records.

So, on many major grounds, no reasonable person would assume the Gospels to be *historical* accounts of how Christianity started.[80]

---

[80] Individuals who started with an assumption that the Gospels are the divinely inspired Word of God had two options at the outset: Either they could change that assumption into a hypothesis and read further to investigate the evidence on this hypothesis, or else they could simply abandon reading any further. [continued]

How, then, is it possible to penetrate *closer* to an
authentic history of the creation of Christianity than the
normal method, which falsely treats these canonized New
Testament documents as if they *were* objective historical
accounts of Christianity's start? (After all, nearly everything
that's written about "Jesus" is based upon those four
documents. Moreover, what's not, isn't based upon sources
that are necessarily more reliable. Some alternative "sources"
have even been exposed as rank frauds.)

In order to achieve an authentically *historical* account of
Christianity's start, we here relied upon a field of
legal/forensic methodology which developed after World
War II in courtrooms in democratic countries throughout the
world, during trials of white-collar crimes, where the evidence
has (like the evidence about Christianity's start) consisted
largely of documents – which in these cases were memos, e-
mails, etc. – and where the motives of the authors of those
documents have been as much the focus of investigation as

In deciding whether to abandon reading further, the basic question is
whether one's primary commitment is to Jesus, or is instead to the Roman Catholic
Church that wrote and assembled the New Testament during the four centuries
after his death. In other words: Is one's basic commitment to Jesus, or to those
Gospels? If the reader's primary commitment is to the Roman Catholic Church,
then such a reader is committed to the texts which that Church canonized, and this
means that such a reader should not read this book, because this book questions
those texts. However, if the reader's primary commitment is to Jesus, then that
reader is obliged to read it: Jesus would obviously not want anyone to be
vulnerable to believing misrepresentations about him from anyone who was his
enemy or who was a follower of an enemy of his. This is why Jesus would wish any
of his followers to consider very carefully the possibility that any writing about him
might have been written or shaped by a follower not really of Jesus, but of an
enemy of Jesus. Thus, the opening of this book, "Why Read This," warned that this
work will disturb anyone whose primary loyalty is to the Scriptures that the Roman
Catholic Church produced, instead of to Jesus.

Of course, if an individual's primary commitment is to finding the truth
(regardless of where the truth leads), then there is no problem with recognizing that
the Gospel accounts might misrepresent how Christianity started. Only people of
faith encounter a problem here.

were the allegations which those people made in those documents. For example, sometimes, in order to reconstruct, from evidence, a sequence of events – or a "history" – that can explain how a given contract came to be written the way it is, misrepresentations are crucial to identify in the prior communications between the two negotiants, and the *intentions* (and not *merely* the words) of the writers are crucial for the court to interpret accurately. Sometimes, it's necessary to get *beyond* merely what the words *say*, and to reach the mental state and *intentions* of people, in order to become enabled to reconstruct a history accurately, from a given body of evidence, and so to explain the contract or other outcome.

This has been done here, concerning the start of Christianity. The documentary evidence, in this case, has been explored, identifying not only what it says, but also what the agendas of the individual writers were. However, instead of explaining a contract or other such object, this work has explained the New Testament itself.

Furthermore, higher quality, more-reliable evidence, than the four Gospel accounts, has been the basis upon which this investigation especially focused, because an important feature of this new methodology is that it places greater weight upon the most reliable evidence than it places on less-reliable evidence. Though much of this more-reliable evidence is itself within the New Testament, some of it comes from other sources; but all of this evidence is necessary to consider with the proper weighting, in order to reconstruct the actual history of the start of Christianity.

As has been suggested, the most rigorous methodology for reconstructing, from a given body of evidence, a sequence of events (or "history") is the methodology that's used in courtrooms in democratic nations, when they attempt to reconstruct from a given body of evidence not only how a particular crime was committed, but by whom, and when, and

where, and why. Of course, courts can make errors, just as
scholars can, but courts are routinely far more rigorous than
scholars are, and the reason for this is that the stakes are far
higher in courts. People's lives, their personal fortunes, their
social relationships, and their very fates, are routinely
determined in courtrooms, but the stakes when a scholar
makes an error are typically far less (and the few scholarly
exceptions tend to *end up* in court, such as the famous 2000
case of David Irving versus Deborah Lipstadt, the "Holocaust-
denial trial"). Moreover, because the stakes are so high in
court, a courtroom in a democracy is an intellectual
battleground in which lawyers, representing contending sides,
research the case and fight each other to persuade jurors[81]

---

[81]   One of the first things the French Revolutionists did in 1789 was to
terminate the ancient aristocratic custom of verdicts being made by a judge, and to
transfer that function (the *interpretation* of evidence) over to a jury of one's peers.
Russia and Spain in recent decades ended their dictatorial regimes; and, in both
cases, they, too, terminated judicial verdicts in favor of jury trials (1978 in Spain,
and 1993 in Russia). The U.S. has had jury trials since even before the U.S.
existed, because the Magna Carta had institutionalized it in England in 1215. Jury
trials are not encountered in any dictatorship, and were not encountered anywhere
in the West prior to 1215 (other than in ancient Athens), but are a clear mark that a
nation is a democracy, anywhere that they're employed.

    Many of the nations that provide the right to a jury trial restrict this right to
only the most serious of offenses, the reason being that these are the sorts of
cases where it's *the most important for truth to reign*. This is yet another reason
why verdicts (*interpretations* of evidence) should come from a *different* source than
the one that perforce rules over the trial – the judge (who determines what the
evidence *is*). Separating those two essential functions (defining the evidence, and
interpreting the evidence) is characteristic of democracies.

    The right to a jury trial is provided in Austria, Australia, Belgium, Brazil,
Canada, Denmark, France, Georgia, Ireland, Japan, New Zealand, Norway,
Sweden, Switzerland, Russia, U.K., and U.S. It was cancelled in India in 1959 as a
result of the sensational botched murder trial of K.M. Nanavati – a case in which
the trial judge had grossly misinformed the jury as to the applicable laws. Though
the judge and not the jury had erred, the jury received the blame, and juries were
thus abolished. [continued]

who are screened, as much as they can be, for their impartiality. And, also because the stakes are so high, each lawyer, representing one side in a case, is maximally motivated to expose any falsehood in the opposite side's case, so that misrepresentations are the least likely to go unchallenged, and are the most likely to be exposed to that jury.

Simply put, the procedures that courts employ, at each and every step of the way, in order to separate fact from fiction, are far more careful, and far more bound by rules to exclude forged or otherwise bogus "evidence" from being considered and from misinforming and thus misleading

---

Overwhelmingly, the right of a defendant to a jury trial is considered to be characteristic of democracy itself, and the reasons for denying this right to defendants have nothing to do with the search for truth, but rather with reducing the costs of trials. The only other rationalization (such as in India) for denying this right has to do with an alleged *need* for professionals (judges) to *interpret* the evidence, and not merely for judges to determine what the evidence in a case *is*, or which evidence to *exclude* as being immaterial or prejudicial – the *identification* of "evidence," which is one of the two *core functions* of any trial judge, in any country. (The other is that a judge interprets the law; the reason he doesn't *also* interpret the evidence, in a democratic system, is that doing this would provide the judge with a totalitarian power over the cases in his court: he'd not only say what the evidence is, and what the law means, but what the evidence means.)

The world is, over the centuries, moving more and more toward jury trials. Some democratic nations (e.g., Germany, India) have cancelled this right, so as to cement the authority of the government, but this can be viewed as an anti-democratic feature in those societies which have achieved democracy in some other respects – temporary backsliding – and not at all as an advancement in the procedures for determining truth in the reconstruction of events; not at all as scientific historiography, in court or out.

Separation of these two functions (authenticating evidence, versus interpreting evidence) is intrinsic to any scientific reconstruction of events. Although there are a few exceptions, democratic nations carry out this epistemological principle by allowing jury trials, especially in high-stakes cases. Inasmuch as the case in the present work is reconstructing the event that started Christianity, it's a high stakes case, if not the highest-stakes case ever (because this event started Western Civilization).

jurors, so that to prove a case in court is vastly more challenging, and far more bound by the rules of science, than merely a scholar's routine, regardless of how sophisticated the latter might be.

Some professional scientists explicitly recognize that this is so. For example, the physicists Alan Sokal and Jean Bricmont wrote in their 1999 critique, *Fashionable Nonsense: Postmodern Intellectuals' Abuse of Science*, pp. 58-59, "In our view, the 'scientific method' [that's employed by physicists] is not radically different" from the methodology that courtrooms in a democracy use, except that the latter "deals with criminal investigations," which are "intermediate between scientific and ordinary knowledge" (as any historical investigation necessarily must be, even at its best). The reader of this history thus experiences here the first-ever scientific analysis of the evidence concerning Christianity's start: a scientific reconstruction of history.

Of course, this is not to say that scholars violate science on *all* methodological matters. Wherever scholars routinely respect the rules of science, that has been noted, and, on such an issue, this work does not vary from the existing predominant scholarly opinion. But, on all other issues, legal/forensic methodology has here been independently applied to the evidence, so as to advance scientific knowledge on the given subject, and to produce a more *accurate* account of Christianity's start.

Any work of scientific research is guided by the questions it seeks to answer. The primary objective of this work has been to identify the event that created Christianity, and to describe who did it, and why, and how, and when, and where. Finally, this work has aimed to describe how that event affected, or even shaped, important aspects of the Christian faith, and so to produce, for the first time ever, an accurate understanding of Christianity.

In order to examine these questions scientifically, some common preconceptions about them were first dispensed with, so that those preconceptions could become topics that are investigated, rather than assumptions that heedlessly guided and shaped the answers.

For example, we have all been told, and have read, that Jesus started Christianity (such as was described in *Matthew* 16:18 or other Gospel passages). As was noted, most of what we've been told about Jesus derives from the four canonical Gospel accounts of his life, which are routinely treated as historical accounts. But what if the Gospels aren't actually historical accounts? And what if Jesus didn't actually start Christianity? Scientists can't start with assumptions about such things; and we did not.

Christianity isn't Jesus. Christianity is the New Testament, just as Judaism is the Torah, and Islam is the Quran. The basis of any religion is its Scripture. Everything else builds upon that. Therefore, to ask how a religion started, is to ask how the religion's Scripture came to be; this question doesn't directly concern the faith's founder, real or otherwise.

Moreover, the Jesus known to Christianity is the Jesus described in the New Testament. A faith's alleged founder is known through the faith's Scripture, and this is what defines the given faith, regardless of whether the alleged founder is the actual founder.

So, how did the New Testament come to be; how did Christianity come to be? We have been trying here to understand the New Testament truthfully, *regardless* of whether it's history or myth, and even if understanding it might show it to be mythological. Even *if* it's mythological, identifying how it started produces *a truthful understanding of Christianity*.

Scholars widely recognize that the authentic letters (or "epistles") of Paul in the New Testament were the earliest-written parts of the New Testament, and were written before the Gospels – the parts in the New Testament that describe Jesus. This consensus has been accepted here. However, scholars have ignored a crucial possibility presented by this consensus: that the people who wrote the Gospels were all followers of Paul, and that Paul might *not* have been actually a follower of Jesus.

Paul's assertions alleging himself to be a follower of Jesus (such as his repeated statements that he was an "apostle" of Jesus), are taken at face-value by virtually all scholars,[82] but the present work assumes neither that he was, nor that he wasn't, and concludes, from the best evidence of all, which is Paul's authentic letters, that, during the period of his life (late in his career) when he was writing these letters, he *definitely wasn't* a follower of Jesus, but that he was instead an enemy of the sect of Jews that Jesus had established – an enemy who had departed from this sect in the year 49 or 50, with the intention to replace it by an entirely new religion, which Paul designed specifically to satisfy the Roman Imperial regime that had executed Jesus.

---

[82]   The two exceptions are Hyam Maccoby's 1986 *The Mythmaker: Paul and the Invention of Christianity*, and Robert Eisenman's 1998 *James the Brother of Jesus*. Both works are rejected by scholars, because both works rely primarily upon sources which were written hundreds of years after Jesus's death, and hundreds of years after Paul's authentic letters (which are dated c. 20-30 years after Jesus's death). Eisenman's work also relies upon unsubstantiated dating of Dead Sea Scrolls as having been written in the First Century – dating repeatedly proven false, via carbon-dating to the prior century at the latest. (E.g.: Plicht, 2007, "Radiocarbon Dating and the Dead Sea Scrolls: A Comment on the Dating"; Doudna, 2001, "The Effects of Possible Contamination on the Radiocarbon Dating of the Dead Sea Scrolls"; and Jull, 1995, "Radiocarbon Dating of Scrolls and Linen Fragments from the Judean Desert.")

The precursor to those two works was Cardinal Jean Daniélou's 1967 "Une vision nouvelle des origins chrétiennes: le judéo-christianisme," in his *Études* 327: 595-608, which was likewise based upon late sources. Daniélou's article remains cited today primarily second-hand through its influence upon the French Muslim, Maurice Bucaille, who quoted it extensively in the 9th chapter of his 1976 *La Bible, le Coran, et la Science*, arguing that the Quran is superior to the Bible.

The precursor to those works was F.C. Baur's 1845 *Paul*. Baur's view became popularized at the beginning of the 20th Century by William Wrede, who famously called Paul "the second founder of Christianity." However, this isn't quite the view that Maccoby and Eisenman propound: both of those writers hold that Paul was the actual founder of Christianity, and that Jesus was not a founder of Christianity at all. [continued]

This work has found that the four canonical accounts of Jesus provided in the Gospels (*Matthew, Mark, Luke,* and *John*) were written by followers of this enemy of Jesus's sect: Paul. The New Testament is shown here to have been written by these enemies of Jesus – by Paul and his followers – instead of by *authentic* followers of Jesus.

Of course, the contrary, standard (Jesus-centric) "history," of how Christianity started, is (and has always been) all around us; it's in the Bible, in the churches and traditions that are based upon the Bible, and in academic courses concerning the start of Christianity. Believing in such a "history" of Christianity's start is easy, if one doesn't look critically at it.

By contrast, legal/forensic methodology, which is employed in the exploration here, developed only during the past century, and starts from careful methodological (as opposed to historical) assumptions, rather than from stories we learned as children. There's no other way possible to look at such a work than critically.

Similarly, when a court of law in a democracy attempts to reconstruct from documentary evidence the sequence of events that occurred in an alleged crime, no other way exists to do that, except a critical way, and that's the way a jury is instructed to do.

Matti Myllykoski, in his "James the Just in History and Tradition ... (Part I)," (in *Currents in Biblical Research*, 2006) traced the start of this line of research further back, all the way to what he described as the "masterpiece" *Nazarenus*, by John Toland, in 1718.

Neither Maccoby nor Eisenman present any documentation or explanation of precisely when Paul started Christianity, or of why he did it, or of the circumstances that led Paul to formulate it in precisely the way that he did. Numerous writers have identified Paul's borrowings from prior religions; but that, too, fails to explain Christianity.

The purpose of the present work is to identify and describe the event that created Christianity, and who did it, and what led up to this event, and how this event shaped the religion; and *no* prior work has attempted to document such things.

Here, in detail, is how that's done, and how the event
that started Christianity has been investigated in these pages:

A court presents to the jury not (as scholars are
accustomed to doing via huge bibliographies and numerous
footnotes) the largest *quantity* of evidence regarding a
particular matter, but instead the highest *quality* of evidence
regarding any specific question. For example, DNA evidence
trumps witness testimony, and that's why many convicts have
been released from death rows after the advent of DNA
testing. (DNA tests proved those prisoners to have been
innocent.) Similarly, the best-evidence rule is employed so as
to winnow out evidentiary gold from evidentiary chaff, to
avoid contaminating jurors' judgment by less reliable
"evidence" which prejudices rather than informs judgments.

The difference between legal/forensic methods and
other methods is, in fact, always the difference between
history and myth. When innocent convicts have been released
from prisons after DNA analysis, the mythological accounts of
the crimes for which they were convicted became publicly
revealed to have been myth and not history. (Typically, those
convictions were based upon perjured testimony from plea-
bargained witnesses – bogus "evidence" that ought never to
have been allowed by the judge to be presented to the jurors.)
In cases where DNA evidence identified whom the true
perpetrator of the crime was, that myth was replaced by a new
account of the crime – an account which offered, for the first
time, a *history* and not a *myth* about the crime.

This is how important legal/forensic methods are: for
the sake of history as opposed to myth, it's simply essential to
employ only the best evidence,[83] to do the utmost to exclude

---

[83]   For another example of the application of the best-evidence principle, this
time in white-collar-crime prosecutions (which are usually the cases in which this
principle is the most applied in interpreting *documentary* evidence), consider the

anything prejudicial, and to adhere strictly to all other aspects of legal/forensic methodology.

Paul's letter to the Galatians is widely considered by scholars to be the best evidence regarding early Christianity. That consensus has been accepted here. Not only is *Galatians* accepted as direct witness testimony to the events it describes (which, for example, the Gospels were formerly widely thought to be, but no longer are: they're second- or third-hand accounts at most, just hearsay), but, as *The Oxford Companion to the Bible* stated in 1993, "None of the letters bearing Paul's name is so indubitably his as *Galatians*. *Galatians* is, indeed, the criterion by which the authenticity of other letters ascribed to him is gauged."[84]

2009 case of Madoff Securities International Limited Default, which stemmed from the largest-ever Ponzi scheme, a fraud which had been perpetrated by the American Bernard Madoff, and which was being prosecuted around the world. The London Stock Exchange issued rules to be "used by member firms to answer their queries in relation to the default." The Exchange said: "In accordance with Rule D121, this net amount will be certified by the Exchange and may be proved as a debt by the defaulter or counterparty as applicable." The problem here was to determine who owed what to whom and how much. Form N32/09 for "Data Reconciliation and Net Amount Certification Process for Relevant Principal Contracts" informed member firms that, "In essence, the 'best evidence' principle means that, where the evidence in relation to the status of a particular trade is inconsistent – or, at least, not entirely consistent – the Exchange will make a judgment as to its status which involves choosing to prefer the evidence having the greatest weight." Whereas opposing attorneys might contest amounts due, courts would be the most likely to *affirm* legal obligations that were calculated *on a best-evidence basis.*

---

[84]   Virtually no scholar challenges its authenticity: *Galatians* is the most solid rock upon which a history, as opposed to a mythology, of earliest Christianity can be built. F.F. Bruce (1982, *The Epistle to the Galatians*, p.1) asserts that, "the standard of assessment is this fourfold group [*Galatians, Romans, and 1&2 Corinthians*], and pre-eminently *Galatians.*" Richard N. Longenecker (1990, *Word Biblical Commentary, v. 41: Galatians*, pp. lvii-lviii) says that, "The most uncontroverted matter in the study of *Galatians* is that the letter was written by Paul ... If *Galatians* is not by Paul, no NT letter is by him, for none have any better claim." [continued]

If any of the evidence (either inside or outside the New Testament) that concerns earliest Christianity is authentic, it's Paul's letter to the Galatians. This is thus the strongest foundation upon which to build an authentic history of Christianity.

A legal/forensic analysis of Christianity's origin is therefore based upon that document, the best evidence.[85] And under its first-ever legal/forensic analysis, *Galatians* does, indeed, reveal how, when, where, why, and by whom, Christianity started.

This essentially unanimous opinion of scholars about *Galatians* contrasts markedly with the widespread view by scholars that none of the NT's four Gospels was written by an actual witness to the events it describes. Consequently, from a legal/forensic standpoint, there is a vast difference between constructing the history of Christianity's start by using *Galatians* and the other six widely-agreed-authentic Paulines, versus the traditional approach which uses the four Gospels and *Acts*.

[85]   A certain scholar, in private communications with the author, objected to this. Nothing is unanimous among scholars. Since they don't adhere to science, they have difficulty achieving anything close to unanimity on what their epistemology ought to be; and, like many scholars, this one distrusted courtrooms, even in democracies. (Perhaps he preferred dictatorships.)

He asserted that historical research should be based on "basic facts" instead of on "best evidence." He quoted an earlier statement he had made in defense of this position:

"In the case of the basic facts there is no question as to the possibility of their nonexistence. They are there and cannot cease to exist. The Battle of Waterloo in 1815 is a basic fact that can never cease to exist. But secondary facts derived from that basic fact, such as the precise course of the battle, or the actions of particular individuals in that battle, may only be able to be indirectly inferred. Such secondary 'facts' are often disputable and may not always survive. Secondary facts are derived from some 'cooking process', but [Geoffrey] Elton is clear that these are not the foundation of historical enquiry. Historical enquiry begins with raw, uncooked, existential facts. (Epistemology, the question of whether these facts are 'knowledge' or 'belief on the basis of very good reasons' is another question.)" [continued]

Like any document that's considered in a court, *Galatians* must be interpreted. In interpreting it, the best evidence, the data cited in order to perform this legal/forensic interpretation of *Galatians*, are the assertions by Paul himself, not opinions by scholars (who can be cited selectively so as to support any given interpretation the presenter might happen to prefer) about Paul's assertions. Consequently, the present analysis, by excluding opinions and citing only Paul, cites far fewer sources than is customary in scholarly practice. However, these are vastly higher quality sources – Paul himself – so that the reader (namely, you) derives opinions, as much as is possible, *directly* from Paul's testimony, and not third-hand from what some pre-selected group of "experts" (regardless whether New Perspective on Paul, Old Perspective

---

I replied: "I object to your starting with 'basic facts' and to your saying 'there is no question as to the possibility of their nonexistence.' I object to your saying 'Historical enquiry begins with raw, uncooked, existential facts.' It does not; or, at least, from a modern legal/forensic standpoint it must not; because such 'basic facts' may be nothing better than raw prejudice, uncooked assumptions, falsehoods which are introduced at the level of assumptions instead of being reached by means of faulty logic from truthful assumptions. Root out the falsehoods; do not let them rot your 'historical' account."

I noted that, "Even under George W. Bush, the FBI's 'wanted' poster on Osama bin Laden did not list, among the specific charges, the 9/11 attacks; and the reason it still does not is that the FBI says it lacks sufficient evidence to prosecute him for that. (They are still hoping to obtain such evidence; they just don't have it as yet.) [This was written when Barack Obama was U.S. President, but prior to bin Laden's location and killing.] Is bin Laden's role in causing those attacks a 'basic fact'? Your epistemology is false."

My core point was that, "Legal/forensic methodology starts with evidence, not with 'facts,' and the reason for this is that all 'facts' must be determined on the basis of evidence, and of interpreting evidence. There are *no* 'basic facts.' Your 'basic facts' are unsupported assumptions, or else are assumptions which are supported on the basis of evidence, and of interpreting that evidence – so name the evidence and not the 'facts'; and I ask you, yet again: What is the best evidence (not 'what is the basic fact') regarding the event that started Christianity; and what is the best evidence for interpreting it?"

He did not answer.

on Paul, or any other) say that he meant. No "perspective on Paul" has been assumed here. The result has been that instead of building the interpretation upon other people's interpretations of Paul's statements (as scholars routinely do), the reader has built it upon Paul's statements – a source that *isn't* arbitrary.

The authentic Paulines, from which his assertions have been cited as the data for the legal/forensic interpretation of *Galatians*, have been taken to be, besides *Galatians* itself: *Romans, Philippians, Philemon, 1 Thessalonians,* and *1&2 Corinthians.*[86] Nothing has been cited from the others, which scholars widely consider to be questionable as to their Pauline authenticity. (This exclusion of the "pseudo-Paulines" is simply the exclusionary principle at work.)

Those seven letters from Paul are considered by scholars to be the earliest-written of all Christian documents, and the ones written closest to Jesus. Unlike all other documents in the New Testament, only these seven were written to an audience of people who were living during the

---

[86]   This group's constituting the authentic Pauline letters has been the predominant scholarly conclusion for a long time. For example, Shirley Jackson Case opened the sixth chapter of his 1912 *The Historicity of Jesus* by saying: "The genuineness of the principal Pauline epistles is among the most generally accepted conclusions of what may be called modern critical opinion. The evidence for this acceptance is usually regarded as exceptionally good." He went on to observe: "The results of the Tübingen criticism, reworked to meet the requirements of later investigation, leave not only Galatians, I and II Corinthians, and Romans as unquestionably Pauline, but also Philippians and I Thessalonians." He didn't list *Philemon*, and a few scholars today also don't, but *Philemon* is usually included. The present work cites *Philemon* only once as evidence, in Chapter 7.

A good historical description of the earliest physical manuscripts is available online at www.religion-online.org/showarticle.asp?title=91, "The Oldest Extant Editions of the Letters of Paul," by David Trobisch, 1999. Originals of ancient documents, such as of Thucydides' *The Peloponnesian War*, or of Plato's *Republic*, do not exist. The oldest fragments that survive are almost invariably from hundreds, or in some cases, thousands, of years later. So, ancient classics are known only by late copies. The earliest complete manuscript currently known to exist of any of Paul's letters (including *Galatians*) is "Papyrus 46," dated around a hundred years after Paul's writing, and that's remarkably early for any classical document.

time when Jesus's disciples – the people who had known Jesus personally, and who had heard him speak – were still around to comment about Jesus, and about the veracity of what these seven documents were saying about him and about his authentic disciples. All other documents in the New Testament were written for readers who had *no way to verify them* – no one to consult who could say, with any credibility, whether they were true or false, or what in them was true, and what was not.

Another important reason why these letters from Paul are of higher evidentiary quality than the four canonical Gospel accounts, *Acts*, non-canonical gospels, etc., is that, whereas the Gospels, *Acts*, etc., were written for a mixed audience, which included some people who were only considering to become Christians, Paul's letters were written to an audience containing only committed Christians. Therefore, the writer of Paul's letters knew that anything he said that was blatantly false about Jesus and about what Jesus's religion was, would be exposed as false by representatives sent from Jesus's followers in Jerusalem, people who had known Jesus while Jesus was alive. By contrast, the Gospels were not written to, but instead written for, an audience; and this was largely an audience of people who were prospective possible converts to join the Jesus-following group. That audience didn't necessarily have ready access to Jesus's original apostles.

Thus, these letters from Paul are in a class by themselves, far more reliable than any other New Testament documents or than any other evidence regarding Christianity's start.

Evidence from the canonical Gospels, *Acts*, and other primary sources, is inferior to the 7 authentic Paulines and thus suitable only for use to expand upon a reading *which is derived from or based upon these seven*. And, since scholars' interpretations of what Paul meant are opinions and not facts, they don't qualify *at all* as "evidence" about what Paul meant;

only what Paul *said* is evidence about *that*. Nonetheless, a consensus of scholars' opinions regarding the authenticity and dating of documents is employed here, solely in order to identify, for example, that those seven Paulines *constitute* the best evidence, and that other alleged Paulines do not; and so to determine the sequence and approximate dates of these seven. Scholars are never cited here to interpret Paul; only Paul is; but scholars' opinions are the basis for identifying *Galatians* as the best evidence, and for identifying (for example) *Colossians* (etc.) as not legal/forensic evidence at all.

Consequently, this work started with a legal/forensic analysis of *Galatians*, and used in this analysis quotations from the other six authentic letters from Paul. In other words, all of Paul's letters have been applied to explain the meaning of each and every line that we analyze from *Galatians*, so that we draw from *everything* that Paul said, in order to understand *each* line in *Galatians*. The inferior evidence, such as *Acts*, the canonical Gospels, Josephus, Tacitus, Suetonius, etc., is not used at all, *except* to fill in *more details* of the historical account that is drawn *only* from the best evidence: Paul. The pseudo-Pauline epistles, such as *Colossians*, aren't cited at all, because – if they are bogus, as they are widely suspected of being – they are fraudulent and would therefore pollute the evidence-stream with fraud if they were to be admitted into evidence in even a subordinate capacity. In addition, wherever Paul in *Galatians* is drawing upon the authority of, or paraphrasing from, specific lines of Jewish Scripture, such as from *Genesis*, those lines in the Old Testament are necessarily drawn into evidence, because no true understanding of any such line from Paul could even possibly result from doing otherwise: Paul's sources, wherever those sources are clear, are included into evidence whenever interpreting a line from Paul that is based upon them.

We start with the first line of *Galatians* and proceed forward, line-by-line, until we reach the climax, toward which each of those earlier lines has been building. This climax, fortunately, consists of Paul's description of the actual event that created Christianity. After this climax is reached and has been fully described by Paul (drawing, wherever necessary, from Paul's other authentic letters, to provide a more complete understanding of the event), all of the lines following the climax are analyzed no longer one-by-one, as was the case with the prior lines, but instead selectively, on a topic-by-topic basis, as topics each of which is reinforcing Paul's climax. Especially prominent here (in these post-climactic lines) have been Paul's citations from Jewish Scripture, providing us an understanding of what Paul was using as "authority," and of how he was using it.

By starting with *Galatians* 1:1 and going forward line-by-line until the climax is reached (2:11-21), the reader here sees and experiences how Paul was attempting to persuade his audience. By means of applying to each line legal/forensic methodology, the reader is entering the mind of the writer (Paul), even thoughts the writer didn't want the reader to know, even matters Paul was struggling to hide and did successfully hide for 2,000 years. This cannot be achieved without adhering to a sequential, line-by-line, analysis, because persuasion is inevitably a process, and the laying-out of that process is necessarily step-by-step: the specific order of presentation in a document is a crucial aspect of the evidence when legal/forensically analyzing any document, especially a letter. Furthermore, Paul structures *Galatians*, from its start all the way up through its climax, in a predominantly chronological way, so understanding the climax would be impossible without understanding everything that had built toward it in the letter.

A line-by-line analysis of a document is called by scholars an "exegesis" of that document; and there have been many exegeses published of *Galatians*. What is new in the present instance is not that an exegesis of *Galatians* (up though 2:21) is being provided, but that the first-ever legal/forensic exegesis of *Galatians* is being provided – the methodology

makes all the difference, not just in what is found, but in how
reliable the findings are.

After the legal/forensic analysis of *Galatians* 1-2:21 has
been presented, and is followed by a topical analysis of the
remainder of *Galatians*, we know Paul in ways and in depth
that are unlike anything previously known about him; and all
of this is Paul revealing Paul, Paul revealing his meanings
(even sometimes exposing things he doesn't want us to
know), not writers about Paul saying what they think he
meant (and failing even to investigate whether a given
statement from him might have been intentionally false).
Consequently, you, the reader, derive your understanding of
Paul from Paul himself, without speculative interpretations
from a selected group of scholars of Paul, who "just happen"
to support the view of the given writer – in this case, being
myself, who serves you, the juror, as an attorney presenting
this evidence in a court in a democracy. You have been
making your judgment solely upon the basis of the very best
evidence that concerns each and every statement that Paul
makes – never on the basis of any inferior evidence about the
given matter. You are thus enabled to make your judgments
with the confidence that each is on a best-evidence basis.

Following the exegesis of *Galatians*, has been an
analysis of each of the canonical Gospel accounts of "Jesus,"
and you now (after having entered so fully into the mind of
Paul) are able to compare what they are saying, with the
agenda of Paul that has been laid out and exposed by Paul's
own writing in *Galatians*. You are now in a position to
determine whether or not each of these Gospel accounts of
"Jesus" – each one of which was (it's important to note)
written later than *Galatians* – was actually written by a *follower*
of Paul; i.e., by someone who was writing with the same
agenda as Paul, even to the extent of joining Paul's side
against Paul's argumentative opponents. The legal/forensic
exegesis of *Galatians* provides so complete a laying-out of
Paul's argument, you now know what Paul in *Galatians* was

arguing against, not only what he was arguing for. Paul, the earliest of all writers in the Christian tradition, was facing passionate opposition among some other members of the Jesus-following group, and in *Galatians* he is passionately opposing them. The legal/forensic analysis of *Galatians* even informs you as to which side, in these disputes, actually had the better evidence, and had been the closer to, and possessed the superior knowledge of, Jesus: Paul, or his opponents. So, you are now in a position to evaluate both sides of this dispute; and, on that basis, to evaluate on which side of it each one of the Gospel accounts of "Jesus" was actually standing: with Jesus, or against him.

Historical research concerning controversial matters – issues such as the start of a major world faith – typically exhibits substantial scholarly disagreements about what happened, and what did not. As has been noted, legal/forensic methodology hasn't previously been applied to such questions. And here are the *consequences* of that lack:

Without applying legal/forensic methodology, such interpretive disagreements become virtually inevitable, because nothing then is convincing on controversial issues; no way is yet established to persuade people who disagree. Individuals thus have no choice but to rely upon "authority" – whatever opinion-leaders a given person is told to believe, or otherwise happens to be inclined to prefer. Contending schools of thought arise, and remain entrenched, because no mutually agreed way exists for settling these differences of opinion. In other words, people believe essentially whatever they want; faith inevitably reigns over such "historical" matters. Whereas, in scientific fields, clear methods for resolving disputes are known, that's not so in these fields; legal/forensic methods are, as of yet, unknown regarding these subjects, and that's *why* disagreement reigns here. Thus, legal/forensic methodology will now be introduced to these issues, in the hope of providing the basis for a scientific consensus to emerge on interpretive matters.

Concerning questions of when and how Christianity began, scholars' opinions vary *especially* widely. The feature that most importantly separates one "history" of Christian origins from another, isn't that one historian has possessed access to different "evidence" than another (since we all work from the very same base of evidence), but is instead each given historian's response to the problem: "Which of these items of 'evidence' shall I use to *formulate my thesis (or theory)* of how Christianity started, and which of them shall I use *only to fill in details* of that theory?" The choice of inferior evidence upon which to base the "history" of the start of Christianity has generated widespread scholarly disagreements, because dubious evidence inevitably produces only dubious "history."

In fact, on account of the lack of legal/forensic methodology in this field, virtually every "historian" until now has chosen to use the four canonical Gospels, plus *Acts*, in order to *formulate their theory* of "The Birth of Christianity" (a common phrase for these, essentially, retellings of myths; they're not *actual* histories of Christianity's start), and then has used the seven authentic Pauline epistles (if at all) *only* to fill in details of their thesis which has been formulated upon the basis of the Gospels and *Acts*. They formulate their theory of the case upon the basis of the later documents (such as *Acts*), and then add to that dubious "historical" reconstruction some details from the earlier evidence (such as *Galatians*). So, they have chosen to *start* with the Christian myth. They then merely add onto that myth a bit of real history, from the superior evidence. But they also disagree often with each other *about* this myth. That's because this myth, in many places, actually disagrees with itself. Those later documents, after all, are only low quality evidence. Each of the Gospels, and *Acts*, contains numerous contradictions *internally* (such as *John* first quoting Jesus in 8:15 as telling an assembled crowd of Jews "I don't judge anyone," and then promptly quoting him as informing *this very same crowd*: 8:21, "You'll die in your sin"; 8:23, "You're from below, I'm from above"; 8:26, "I've got much to say in judgment of you," and finally, condemning all of them outright to hell in 8:44). Furthermore, those sources also contain many contradictions *between* each other (such as *Matthew* 1:1-17 and *Luke* 3:23-38 providing mutually contradictory "historical" accounts of Jesus's paternal genealogy). Thus, the fake "histories" that are derived from these contradictory, and sometimes even *self*-contradictory, documents, contradict each other. When scholars, on top of this failure, then refer to, and rely upon, supposed "expert" opinions of selected *other* scholars, with whom they just happen to agree – while they ignore or slight scholars' interpretations that *dis*agree with their own – then even this base in poor evidence can be essentially lost. All of these scholars' "histories" are consequently, at best, merely myths that are grounded upon myths.

That's the *current state* of the "history" of Christianity's start.[87]

---

[87]   The source of this problem lies in the method by which scholars are professionally evaluated.

Scholars maximize their employability by being cited frequently by other scholars as "authority," irrespective of whether their opinions are well founded, or even relevant, on independent scientific grounds. The larger the number of citations there are of a given scholar's publications, the higher an "authority" this scholar is regarded to be by others in his field, and thus the higher he scores on "research," which (along with teaching) is one of the two main criteria determining whether the scholar will receive tenure at a prestigious, high-paying, college or university. It's also the basis for determining whether the scholar will be hired by another such academic institution. A scholar's income is thus raised if he's frequently cited. Consequently, any proposed alternative methodology, which would systematically minimize the number of citations that scholars receive, might pose a threat to scholars' careers, under the prevailing academic system.

In scientific fields – that is, fields where science has already become the dominant methodological approach – other criteria than mere frequency of citation exist for determining the quality of a given scientist's research. For example, experiments are replicable, and therefore the reader of a research report on an experiment can repeat this experiment and discover by his own experience whether its results match what was described in the report. Such restraints against fraud don't exist in the scholarly professions, and thus frequency of citation doesn't necessarily correlate with quality there. [continued]

By contrast (as has just been explained), the thesis in
the present work is formulated from *only* the seven widely-
viewed-by-scholars-as being the highest-quality items of
evidence, which are the generally-agreed-as-authentic letters
from Paul; and the canonical Gospels and *Acts* are employed
here solely to fill in *more details of that thesis*. This procedure
does the most that can possibly be done to avoid using
tampered-with or otherwise unreliable "evidence" as the basis

---

The reason that the present work accepts scholars' consensus opinions
regarding the authenticity and approximate dates of documents, even while barring
use of scholars' opinions about the meaning of those documents, is that these are
two very different subjects, from a legal/forensic standpoint, and that a court of law
in a democracy makes a clear distinction between these two competencies and
admits into evidence the opinions of experts regarding authentication and dating of
documents, but not regarding the meaning of documents – which is left for the jury
to determine.

Furthermore, no reason exists to reject the consensus opinions of
scholars regarding the authenticity and dating of these documents. If an
acceptance of this evidentiary consensus failed to produce a legal/forensically
sound solution to the problem of how Christianity started, then the necessity would
exist to repudiate that scholarly consensus and to explain why, and to provide and
document an alternative theory to explain when and by whom these documents
were created, before formulating and presenting in court a theory of the case.
Fortunately, that did not happen here. A consensus of scholars can therefore be
accepted as authoritative regarding the authentication and approximate dating of
these documents.

As a general rule, the aim of science is to solve problems, whereas the
aim of scholarship is to preserve problems. When a problem is solved, this solution
becomes, in turn, a tool to solve the next frontier of problems, and so science
makes progress. If, however, the solution is found to be deficient, then more
research is done on the original problem, and so a better (more accurate) solution
is found, which, in turn, becomes a better tool to solve the problems at the new
frontier. However, *only* science can solve problems. Thus, if a problem in a
scholarly field is ever solved, it's solved by means of introducing science to that
field, and the scholarly field is gradually abandoning scholarship, and adopting
science instead. This is what has been happening when scholars more accurately
date documents in the New Testament. No longer is the scholarly prejudice that
favors the priority of the canonical Gospels being accepted. Instead, scientific
means of authenticating and dating documents are applied. Until the present
instance, scientific means of *interpreting* documents have not been applied within
the traditional fields of scholarship. The chief epistemological purpose of this work
is to introduce science to the *interpretation* of these documents.

for reconstructing history from the available body of evidence.

As has been noted, the reliability-ranking of evidence, *prior to* the interpretation of evidence, is crucial in this process. Thus, for example: One can reasonably ask whether an allegation in *Galatians* supports *Acts*, but one cannot reasonably ask whether an allegation in *Acts* supports *Galatians*. Weaker evidence can never support stronger evidence, but can only add *likely additional details* to the account provided by stronger evidence. The stronger evidence is then supporting that detail within the weaker evidence. (E.g.: One may validly argue that Paul's direct witness testimony presented in *Galatians* 2:10 supports the anonymous hearsay "testimony" that is presented in *Acts* 15:19-21, but one cannot validly argue – as many scholars assert – the converse: that the latter supports the former. And wherever these two accounts conflict, the weaker evidence is nullified. The principle involved here is the best-evidence principle applied to interpreting those two documents.) Scholars routinely try to interpret Paul's authentic letters by applying to them the "evidence" from *Acts*, instead of to interpret the evidence from *Acts* by applying to it the evidence from Paul's authentic letters. They thus botch their interpretations of Paul, because no such interpretation can be trustworthy. Though scholars routinely violate legal/forensic methodology, in this way and others, it is not violated *anywhere* in the present work. Thus, for the first time ever, legal/forensic methodology here reconstructs, directly from the available evidence, what can reasonably be considered to be the *actual* start of Christianity – the history, rather than the myth (or even scholars' myths about the myth) of Christianity's start.

I take no side among other writers' interpretations/theories of how Christianity began, because they're all derived from inferior evidence. And they're also derived from *non*-evidence, which is just *claimed* to be evidence: other scholars' opinions. A given scholar's interpretive opinion may be false, and it may be true; but, even if it's true, it's *not evidence*. Opinions aren't evidence, not even if they're true. If they're truthful interpretations of evidence (such as one would hope that the present work is), they're still not evidence. Such an interpretation is instead a truthful theory. It's not a fact (a true representation *of* the evidence), it's a truthful theory (a true representation *about* the evidence); and so, for a scholar to cite any theory *as if it were* evidence, is for him to nullify his own work, because he's then confusing evidence with opinions about evidence; he's confusing facts with theories. Each theory is supposed to be based only on evidence, *never* on a theory. In courts of law in a democracy, and in any other scientific forum, that's prohibited; it's recognized as prejudicial, rather than scientific. (That violation of science is unfortunately so widespread in scholarship as to constitute virtually a defining characteristic of scholarship.)[88]

---

[88]   For example, all referees of the present work at scholarly presses attacked it with the same criticism: e.g., that "This book does not appear to engage in lengthy detail with the massive amount of (regularly controversial) secondary literature on Paul," or that it displays "no obvious awareness of the sheer breadth of contemporary discussion," or other phrases to similar effect. (They said that, even though this work makes clear right up front, as you've already seen, that that's no objective in it – that this work *won't* include a survey of the prior literature interpreting *Galatians*.) One referee even told me *directly* (rather than the publisher), "Before I can recommend your book, you're going to have to put in a few ... footnotes to me, ... as such 'shout outs' and 'due respect' seem to be severely lacking. Otherwise, fine." (Of course, I refused to do that.) In other words, the sole reason for their rejecting this work was their refusal to consider, much less to accept, the methodology that has just been described here. No scholar defended scholarship against this work's criticism of the scholarly practice of employing, as "evidence" (that's supposedly supporting a given scholar's interpretive opinion), the interpretive opinions from *other* scholars. Scholars have, to the contrary, blindly *insisted* that this work *adhere to* that scholarly norm (of pumping each others' works via citations of them), even though no scholar has *defended* that interpretive norm. In other words, scholars seem to feel no need to defend their blatant and systematic violation of science. Perhaps the reason they refuse to defend it is that they've never before been publicly challenged on it. However, the purpose of the present work is not to challenge scholarship's failures, nor even its systematic corruption, but to identify and describe the event that started Christianity. Since no *purely* scholarly way exists to do this, the present work *necessarily* violates, as stated here, the meta-methodology which defines scholarship. Wherever this occurs in the present work, the two meta-methodologies of science and scholarship are standing in mutual conflict, and this work adheres *always and only* to science. To interpret evidence requires that inferences will be drawn from that evidence; the only methodological issue is whether that's done as scientists do it, or as scholars

Thus, what's different here is the methodology, not *merely* an interpretation that's based upon applying it; what's improved here is the methodology *itself*. The only thing that makes *findings* legal/forensic, is that the *methodology* is; and here, that's the case.

Though almost everyone knows that evidence is critically important, methodology is unfortunately often ignored, even though methodology is at least as important as evidence (and is *always* more important than findings). For example, the freeing of innocent convicts from death rows, which resulted from DNA evidence, usually didn't occur upon the basis of discovering any new evidence about those crimes. Instead, what was really crucial in reconstructing the actual history of these crimes was the application of a far higher quality (i.e., more reliable) method of "reading," or interpreting, the evidence that already existed: the evidence in these crimes had simply never been analyzed this way before.

---

do. Scholars were demanding that I cite, as evidence supporting my interpretation of *Galatians*, the interpretive opinions by previous writers on *Galatians*. However, in a legal/forensic analysis of *Galatians*, those previously published interpretations are prohibited from being cited as evidence: they're *not evidence for this*.

Although scholars are not cited in this work to interpret Paul, scholars are (as you've *also* already seen) cited here to authenticate and date Paul's letters. That's because the systematic violation of science by scholars lies within the realm of interpretation of evidence, not within the realm of authentication and dating of evidence; and those are two fundamentally different epistemological tasks. Up until around the year 1800, scholarship was an abject failure on both tasks, but now it abjectly fails on only the interpretive task. Many scholars have told me that science *cannot* interpret; but every scientist knows that interpretation is essential to science, where it's called "theory." Many scholars have told me that any theory is necessarily speculative; but that too is false: that assumption confuses "theory" with "hypothesis" in science. The misunderstandings of science by scholars could fill millions of volumes, and they unfortunately already do.

On rare occasions, scholars even admit their profession's methodological cluelessness. For example, John Dominic Crossan's 1998 *The Birth of Christianity* asserts (p. 139): "There still is no serious discussion of methodology in historical Jesus research, and the same applies to the birth of Christianity. That does not make me very proud of myself and my scholarly colleagues."

A similar methodological improvement now occurs regarding the reconstruction of an important historical event: the creation of the Christian faith – the creation, indeed, of the very value-base of Western Civilization. (However, in this case, the methodology of reading DNA evidence isn't what is applied; the methodology of reading documentary evidence is, and this methodology developed almost entirely after World War II, but has never before been applied to this particular subject. So it's new to this field of research.)

As has been previously acknowledged here, none of this assumes that courts are infallible, not even in democracies.[89] So, we recognize that legal/forensic methodology is sometimes violated in courts; the methodological ideals are not always adhered to in actual practice; and judges, lawyers, and jurors, are fallible just as everyone is. Unlike faith-based beliefs, science *acknowledges* fallibility, and recognizes that no one is infallible and that no scripture is Scripture (infallibly true). (This recognition of fallibility is, in fact, the very reason why appeals courts even exist.) Courts of law in a democracy, and any other forum for scientific investigation and interpretation, have the procedures and rules that they do, precisely so as to minimize erroneous judgments, but minimization of errors can be achieved only if the possible falsehood of each allegation is acknowledged; to do the contrary and merely assume an allegation's

---

[89]   This was discussed in a news report by Agence France Presse, on 4 January 2011, headlined "'Bad' Science Still Rampant in US Justice System." For example: "'Changing the way photo lineups are done is key, because memory is flawed and witnesses are prone to subtle suggestion by police who want to catch a criminal,' according to University of Virginia School of Law professor Brandon Garrett. 'There have now been thousands of studies with incredibly consistent results all showing that suggestion has this outsized powerful effect on eyewitness memory,' Garrett said. 'Even if police are trying their best not to signal anything, the eyewitness ... may be looking to the police officer for reassurance and for cues.' ... Garrett estimated that hundreds of police departments have begun to change the way they conduct lineups." Science is the ideal, and progress consists in more closely approximating this ideal. A dictatorship has no such ideal, because whoever holds authority wants "findings" to be whatever he wants, which might be entirely regardless of the truth. Only a democracy can have legal/forensic methodology whose goal is finding the truth. Democracy is the basis for progress.

truthfulness is virtually to *invite* falsehoods into judgments. The best that any investigation can achieve is to adhere rigorously (100%) to science, never to violate it for any reason. Instances of poor legal/forensic practice – or of any other failure or fraudulence in any other type of allegedly scientific investigation – reflect negatively upon violators; not upon democracy, not upon legal/forensics, and not upon science itself.

On matters where this work diverges from common scholarly opinion, there is a clash between the way that courts in democratic nations customarily deal with evidence, and the way that scholars do. For example, a preliminary draft of this work was sent to a certain scholar whose writings on early Christianity agreed with this work on some conclusions. He replied by expressing disappointment that this work didn't cite him on those matters. I told him that his opinions, like mine, are only opinions, and that I don't cite opinions, but only evidence, so I cannot cite his works, since they're not evidence, regardless whether I agree with them or not. He responded: "You seem to reject anyone else's efforts to do the same thing" that I had done. I answered him: "The 'thing' I'm doing is methodological: it is to approach the entire question of reconstructing the sequence of events that led up to and produced Christianity's creation, by means of employing the type of analysis of evidence that courts in democratic nations apply when they reconstruct a sequence of events ('the crime') from the given body of evidence. I don't 'reject anyone's efforts to do the same thing.' Instead, I reject all *alternative methods* of reconstructing history from evidence. If the methodology violates the methodology that produces a fair trial, then I cannot accept the 'findings' that the 'historian' presents, even if I happen to agree with him on those particulars. (For example, if I were a juror in such a trial, I could not vote to convict, because the rational basis for 'conviction' would then be lacking.) But if the methodology adheres fully to the methodology that produces a fair trial, then I will not 'reject anyone else's efforts to do the same thing.' In other words, we don't actually 'do the same thing,' even where our 'findings' happen to agree. Your work is no more evidence than mine is, and so I cannot cite it. However, if I were a juror and heard your prosecution argument, then I would not vote for your side, even if my opinion inclined in your direction. And the reason is that, even where our 'findings' agree, we simply *don't* 'do the same thing.'"

This means that the important thing is the methodology, not the findings. (Though that's a point made before, this example provides a different application of it.) Regardless of whether some previous writers have "found" things that are found here, the value of this work depends upon its methodology, and nothing else. A corollary is that whether any given writer says something "new" is unimportant; what's important is whether or not what that writer says is 100% acceptable to a scientific reader. Convincing a fool is no achievement; convincing a person who analyzes evidence by applying to it the systematic skepticism that constitutes science – *that's* the goal. Like all legal/forensic analyses, and like all other forms of scientific writing, the only objective that merits primary respect (in *non*-fiction writing) is scientific truth. As a result, whatever is new in the findings here is incidental, and is of value only because of the methodology by which it has *been* found, not because of what it is.

In our Introduction, three basic principles of modern legal/forensic methodology were mentioned: (1) Assume as little as possible; (2) Always rely on the best (most reliable) evidence; and (3) Explain (instead of ignore) any contradictions within the evidence. The key technique for (3), when the evidence is of a verbal and especially documentary type, is (3-a) to rank, what a witness's evidence *shows*, as being higher than, what that witness's evidence *says*. For instance, if a witness says "This sentence has 100 words," then this sentence shows that it has five words, and so it *has* five words (since showing is superior to mere saying), which means that the witness asserted there a falsehood, which is either intentional (a lie, perjury) or unintentional (an error). If the witness does this sort of thing repeatedly, then perjury appears increasingly likely as the explanation. Paul repeatedly perjured himself, such as when he stated, by logically-necessarily implication in *Galatians* 1, that his gospel of Christ had never changed, versus when he showed, in especially the *Corinthians* letters and *1 Thessalonians*, that Paul previously had, in fact, taught *different* gospels of Christ. Another prime example of Paul's perjury was his logically-necessarily implying, in *Galatians* 1 and 2, that there was doubt as to whether anyone was the leader of Jesus's disciples, versus Paul's showing, in *Galatians* 2:12 and the ruckus that was initiated there by James's agents (and especially by Peter's immediately lining up there behind James's agents), that, in fact, James *was* their leader.

To assert that a statement "shows" something is to assert that the statement logically necessarily implies that thing, and this is the most powerful evidence that a statement can possibly provide. This is why, even if a witness says "This sentence has 100 words," that witness's explicit assertion is vastly less powerful than the evidence *by logically necessary implication*, that the sentence is false: it actually has five words. (Footnote 52, the footnote to "The Fictitiousness of *Matthew* 16:18, Etc.," discussed further the priority that evidence by logically necessary implication has over evidence by explicit assertion.) Thus, when a scholar accepts what a witness explicitly asserts and ignores what that witness logically necessarily implies, that scholar invalidates his own work.

This methodology does not, like scholarly works do, seek directly to explain historical *events*. It instead seeks directly to explain historical *evidence*. In a courtroom in a democracy, each of the two opposing lawyers has a different theory of the case, to explain the evidence. That's all a jury has to go on. If the jury fulfills its obligation to the broader society, then it will choose the theory of the case (or the explanation of the evidence) that explains the most (or ideally, *all*) evidence. There may be contradictions within the testimony and/or

other evidence, but each theory of the case seeks to explain all
of the evidence, and not merely some of it; and, as far as the
two theories of the case are concerned, this is the contest that's
presented to the jury for verdicts.

Historians, especially when the subject is (as here)
ancient history, tend to be at such a remove from the events
they seek to explain, so that it should not be difficult for them
to recognize that their function is to explain evidence, not to
explain events directly, if for no other reason than that for
events in ancient history, the body of evidence is so obviously
distinct and different from the events themselves.
Nonetheless, at least as regards the history of earliest
Christianity, scholarly "historians" continue, even down to the
present day, to try to explain events directly – such as to find
rationalizations (rather than authentic explanations) for the
contradictions within the alleged "Jesus" statements in the
canonical Gospels, or within the statements by Paul in the
authentic letters he wrote. Whereas rationalizations are
acceptable in scholarship, no scientist in any field of
investigation, legal/forensic or otherwise, is satisfied with or
persuaded by a rationalization. Every scientist considers *only*
explanations. When the subject-area that a given scientist
investigates is history, the methodology that's applied is
legal/forensic methodology, not mere scholarship. That
methodological difference is between mere rationalizations of
the events (such as scholars produce), versus authentic
explanations of the evidence (such as scientists produce).

Finally, one other important difference between
scientists and scholars should be noted here: Only scientists
recognize the supreme importance of beginnings, and thus
scholars haven't even cared to find the event that created
Christianity.

A fact which scientists especially acknowledge – and
which scholars (and others) commonly ignore – is the
enormous effect a conception-event has upon the future
structure and attributes of the thing that's thereby being
created. For example, scientific biologists know that when an

organism is conceived, at the moment when a sperm meets an egg, the organism's entire DNA is thereby established; and that this unseen DNA structure, which is established in this single act, will largely determine not only how the future organism will appear, but how it will behave, and even what diseases it will experience, and how long it will live. Similarly, scientific engineers know that when a Macintosh computer leaves the factory of Apple Computer Inc., this computer will forever after possess very different attributes than will a computer leaving a factory that produces PC-based computers, even though software might minimize some of the more obvious of these differences. And also, when the idea for a business first occurs in the mind of an entrepreneur, the most essential feature in that future business is thereby established. The embodiment of this conception-idea in a business plan will even play a role in deciding whether or not the business ever becomes more than a mere chimera in the entrepreneur's mind. Thus, in a wide range of different settings, scientists understand the gargantuan importance of conception-events.

By contrast, conception-events are generally ignored by scholars, who are unfortunately unaware of their crucial, determinative, importance. Though scientists routinely know that the knottiest and most significant questions generally concern a thing's beginning, other people do not. For example, humans commonly celebrate births, which are visible events, but generally ignore or are even unaware of conception-events, which typically occur nine months earlier and are unseen and even unknown. This unknown and unseen conception-event will shape the life of the person who is created by it. However, the far less consequential birth-date will be celebrated, as if it *were* the important event. Thus, scholars commonly confuse birth-events and conception-events, as if the two were one, and mistakenly believe that "the birth of Christianity" (whatever *that* was) *constituted* Christianity's start. These two things not only are not the same, but their difference is enormous – and it's the conception, and *not* the birth, that's actually key.

In such a light, one can more clearly appreciate the *importance* of knowing the event that created Christianity. A scientist recognizes immediately that to know the event that created Christianity is to understand Christianity in the deepest sense possible. By contrast, many scholars of Christianity are uninterested in this event, and – in fact – no scholar of Christianity has ever published any research to identify and describe it.

Further exploring this analogy with the biological sciences, one might wonder whether an example can be cited of an important analogue in history to the biological reality that a DNA structure (precisely the zygote that's established when a sperm meets an egg at the moment of conception) may produce a tendency toward a specific *disease*. My previous book (2000), *WHY the Holocaust Happened: Its Religious Cause & Scholarly Cover-Up*, argued that Paul's creation of the cultural gene (or "meme") for anti-Semitism produced the long history of Christianity's disease of anti-Semitism, culminating in Hitler's decision, in the Fall of 1919, to enter politics, so as to become enabled to organize Germany to exterminate all of the world's Jews in the Holocaust. Hitler's private notes in 1919 outlined his theory behind the Holocaust-to-come. That theory of "History" was motivated by his reading of, as he put it, "The Bible – Monumental History of Mankind." His misunderstanding the Bible to be a work of "History," instead of a mythology, provided him his interpretation not just of the past, but of the present and future (since he, as a believing Christian, believed in biblical prophecy and even planned his "Thousand-Year Reich" upon the basis of his reading of *Revelation* 20:1-7), and thus it guided him and his subsequent leadership of Germany, for the rest of his life. The writings by Paul and his followers in the New Testament permeated also the wider Christian culture to such an extent that Germans were thereby enabled to accept Hitler as their leader and to carry out his plan, almost to its very completion. Thus, the gene for anti-Semitism, which was created by Paul in 49 or 50, produced the cancer of pogroms, climaxing in the 1940's, with the Holocaust, bringing death to many millions. As is documented there, Hitler had entered politics not actually in order to perpetrate World War II (such as is commonly assumed), but rather in order to "cleanse" the world of Jews; and WWII was, for him, the essential means toward that grisly end – the Holocaust. As he told a group of supporters on 18 December 1926, "The teachings of Christ [*John* 8:44, etc.] have for thousands of years laid the foundation for the battle against Jews as the enemy of Mankind; the work that Christ began, but was not able to complete, I shall finish."

Jesus, for his part, would have been outraged at what Paul did, and have called Paul's sale on heaven a cheap trick to win converts, who were decidedly *not* converts to Jesus's religion (Judaism), which Jesus had always preached (after all, as was noted earlier, Jesus wasn't *merely* a Jew but a rabbi: even the Gospel-writers referred to him as *specifically* a "rabbi" in *Matthew* 26:25&49; *Mark* 9:5, 11:21, 14:45; and *John* 1:38&49, 3:2, 4:31, 6:25, 9:2, 11:8, and 20:16). After Paul's *coup*, Paul's men were converts not to Judaism but to a new religion built upon *rejection and replacement* of Jesus's religion, and upon the fateful *lie* that the adherents to Jesus's religion had murdered God. Furthermore, rabbi Jesus would have been wrathful at Paul for preaching a replacement of the unitary Jewish God by a tripartite Christian God in which that Jewish God was part of a family and so had a Son who also is worshipped. As to whether the rabbi would have been angrier at Paul than at the Roman soldiers who nailed this rabbi to the cross, any answer would be speculative, but Jesus knew that those troops were only doing their jobs for the Emperor and that other men would have done this job if they did not, whereas what Paul did was his own choice and no one else would have done it if Paul had not. Furthermore, whereas those troops did no harm to Jesus's religion of Judaism, Paul did vast and permanent harms both to Judaism and to Jews, throughout thousands of years into the future. Thus, if Jesus were a juror deciding Paul's guilt, there can hardly be reasonable doubt as to what *his* verdict would be.

Paul created a cultural disease by being a traitor to the very man he claimed to worship. And finally, jurors can now make the determination on his case, though this case has already shaped their own lives. Jurors can now decide whether or not Paul perpetrated a hoax, a violation of Jesus by knowingly and for personal reasons misusing Jesus's name, and abusing and misrepresenting Jesus's faith.

Consequently, the application of legal/forensic methodology to the understanding of history can ultimately help to *avoid* cultural diseases, and to understand and control such diseases as have already started, just as – in medicine – controlling a disease *requires* understanding its origin. (Since medicine became a scientific field, the importance that proper diagnosis has for proper treatment has become generally recognized; but the social "sciences" remain scholarly fields even today, so there's little demand yet for history to become a scientific field. This is the reason, for example, why Hitler's theory behind the Holocaust has been ignored by "historians," political "scientists," and other social "scientists," who, as people of faith themselves, would rather blame the Holocaust on "the spirit of science" than on *any* form of faith, regardless of the facts in the case. In a pre-Scientific-Age culture, such witch doctors are unfortunately the "experts" upon whom the public relies to understand cultural ailments.)

What we have been describing here is the difference between two epistemologies, two meta-methodologies: faith, which scholars rely upon; and science, which scientists rely upon. Faith produces whatever "findings" a person wants, and therefore the only honest description of that epistemology refers to the given faith-believer's desires, not to any actual findings at all. For a person of faith, there aren't any real findings; there are, in fact, only desires. Desires produce the "findings." Insofar as faith is operative, findings are inoperative. Only science can produce real findings.

The findings in the present book concern a particular faith, but this does not mean that they were produced by faith. These findings concern the particular faith, Christianity, but were produced by science, not by any faith at all.

Further details about legal/forensic methodology have been presented, where appropriate, in this work's footnotes.

Since the methodology that has been described here is adhered to in this work, but is violated by all[90] prior works that purport to set forth the "history" of earliest Christianity, it's clear that the reason this work provides a very different history of the start of Christianity than has ever before been offered is the methodology – nothing else.

---

[90]   This includes works that have applied legal/forensic methodology from previous eras, such as Simon Greenleaf's 1846 *The Testimony of the Evangelists*, and Frank Morison's 1930 *Who Moved the Stone?* Only after sociologist Edwin Sutherland, on 27 December 1939, introduced to the world the (then) entirely new concept of white-collar crime, has any serious legal attention been paid to these *types* of crimes, which happen to be the types in which documentary evidence is often of *central* importance. Historical research often relies heavily on documentary evidence, and so some of the principles that have been stated here weren't even present then.

More recently, Lee Strobel's best-selling 1998 *The Case for Christ* applied only pre-1939 legal/forensic methodologies, and thus came to the same conclusions as those earlier writers did: that the canonical Gospel accounts of Jesus are true.

Unfortunately, law schools, even today, largely ignore teaching the principles for interpreting documentary evidence. Some textbooks on evidence go so far as to assert that there are only three categories of evidence – circumstantial evidence, witness evidence, and physical evidence – and thus ignore altogether the principles for interpreting documentary evidence (which have been set forth here).

Furthermore, like any area of science, legal/forensic methodology is itself an evolving field, and so there are details in it that are constantly being improved and filled in. One example of this is the Ancient Documents Rule, which admits into evidence (though without assuming the honesty or accuracy of) a copied document (such as ancient works generally are), if it (1) is at least 20 years old (and thus an "ancient document"), and if it (2) is expertly determined to be authentic (instead of

That's it: the thing that causes this account of the start of Christianity to be different from the others is its methodology. Any disagreement between this work and any other is *due to* that *methodological* difference. All writers on earliest Christianity have access to the same body of evidence. Prioritizing the evidence on the basis of reliability, and using all the other features of modern legal/forensic methodology, has made all the difference, not just in the findings, but in the reliability of those findings. Choosing between this work, and any other work about the start of Christianity, is choosing between the respective methodologies.

So, the basic choice doesn't really concern findings at all, but rather methodology; and, most basically *of all*, it concerns epistemology: either science, or else faith.

---

forged). That second requirement is itself usually evaluated by reference to 2(a) the document's provenance, and to 2(b) internal indications within the document showing it to be what it purports to be. However, until modern times, the criteria for authenticity were almost nonexistent; the case law on authenticity has been advancing especially rapidly since the 1939 introduction of the concept "white collar crime." Some documents that were considered to be "authentic" before 1939 are now no longer considered to be so. This exemplifies the advancement of a science (here of legal/forensic methodolgy), rather than the advancement of the appication of a science to its subject-area.

The bottom line is that no other historical account of earliest Christianity is similar to this one, because no other account adheres to the methodology that has been described here. They all violate it rampantly, not just on a few details; and all of them build their "historical" reconstructions primarily upon the Gospels and *Acts*, documents which are falsely alleged to be witness testimony, rather than upon the seven authentic letters by Paul, which are far higher quality evidence.

Acknowledgements

I wish to express my appreciation to Larry Rowe, Abe van Luik, Paul Burghardt, James Robinson, Tim Piatek, and Valerie Tarico, all of whom provided constructive feedback on the manuscript.

References/Sources

A different system has been used here than other works use, for citing sources, and for references. In each instance, the goal here has been to make things easier for the reader, and to eliminate unnecessary ambiguity – in other words, to facilitate the reader's accurate understanding of this work.

First to be noted (and as was briefly pointed out in the "Note on Style" at the front of this book) is that this work rejects the scholarly norm of not italicizing the titles of the books that comprise the Bible. The scholarly norm is to italicize the titles of all books, except for the books that comprise religious scriptures; scholars choose instead not to italicize the title of such a book. However, unfortunately, when a writer prints something like "Mark says that Jesus's followers ..." and not "*Mark* says that Jesus's followers ...," the reader is being encouraged subliminally to think that some person Mark said this, rather than that some document *Mark* said it. As scholars themselves recognize, no one actually knows the name of the person who wrote *Mark*. So: the common custom, of not italicizing the titles of the books in the Bible, misleads readers toward a fundamentalist viewpoint that's false, by encouraging them to think the *disciple* Mark wrote this document. This is encouraging deception, as even scholars recognize. Therefore, the titles of the books in the

Bible are italicized here, in order not to encourage readers' being deceived (such as other works do).

Furthermore, the author of *Mark* is referred to herein as Mark (never italicized, because the reference is to whomever wrote *Mark*). This "Mark" is simply a stand-in for that person's actual name, whatever it was.

Second to be noted here is that the Sources have already been cited and identified in this work, within its text and footnotes, where those Sources are being used. Consequently, a bibliography would be superfluous.

Two widely accessible sources of Sources are employed here especially frequently: the Bible, and the internet. This work cites predominantly sources that are widely available *on* the internet, because most readers have ready access to the internet. The aim is to cite not just credible Sources, but credible Sources that are available on the web, and that the individual reader can thus readily access without needing to visit a first-rate university library (which might be some distance away, or otherwise inaccessible).

The characteristic manner of citation of internet sources that's used in our text and footnotes is via a quotation (which may be a headline, or the title of a given work), and its date (either byline- or publication-date), and the name of the news-medium or other publisher from which the report first appeared, and the author. One or more of those four items, if employed in a web-search, will normally bring up the cited Source.

My aim in citing Sources this way has been to facilitate the reader's ability to verify and to learn more about anything that interests him in this book.

The Author: A Personal Note

This work pursues a line of research I started in my teen years – an effort to find the source of people's values.

My own values were science, an epistemology – a systematic set of criteria for distinguishing truth from falsehood. My god was truth, and my path was science.

It's not what I was surrounded with at home, as a child. I went briefly to a Unitarian Sunday school, and the family celebrated both Christmas and Hanukkah, but religion held little real interest for me. Unitarians reject the Trinity, but accept Christianity, and this contradiction made no sense to me. During one of my college years, I headed the Unitarian society (the campus Channing Murray Club), but my path as a scientist took me elsewhere, and my graduation thesis ended up being a survey of the values held by the residents of a nearby neighborhood.

The irrationality of people's values struck me constantly and forcefully. I became an investigative journalist and won a national award, but kept coming back to this question of people's values. One book, *QUALITY: How to Know It & Get It*, dealt with the values that would guide a rational consumer. Another, *WHY the Holocaust Happened*, dealt with Adolf Hitler's values that had led him to the goal of a Jew-free world. Another, *IRAQ WAR: The Truth*, dealt with

George W. Bush's values that had caused him to become obsessed with bringing about "regime-change in Iraq." I found that genocides and invasions were based upon values that, in turn, were based upon falsehoods.

CHRIST'S VENTRILOQUISTS is my first book dealing with the source of the values of the culture in which I live. A sequel to it will be titled JESUS & HIS ENEMIES, and will deal not just with Jesus's relationship to Paul, but with Jesus's relationship to the entire Roman Catholic Church, which Paul merely started. These books apply, to the problem of scientifically reconstructing history from the available evidence, the particular scientific methodology that has evolved for this specific purpose – legal/forensic methodology.

31228031R00227

Made in the USA
Lexington, KY
03 April 2014